INTRODUCTION TO THEORETICAL ECOLOGY

PETER YODZIS

University of Guelph

1817

HARPER & ROW, PUBLISHERS, New York
Cambridge, Philadelphia, St. Louis, San Francisco,
London, Singapore, Sydney, Tokyo

This book is dedicated,
With thanks,
To my parents.

Sponsoring Editor: Sally Cheney
Project Editor: Ellen MacElree
Cover Design: Wanda Lubelska Design
Text Art: RDL Artset Ltd.
Production Manager: Kewal Sharma
Compositor: TAPSCO, Inc.
Printer and Binder: R. R. Donnelley & Sons Company

INTRODUCTION TO THEORETICAL ECOLOGY

Library of Congress Cataloging-in-Publication Data

Yodzis, Peter, 1943–
  Introduction to theoretical ecology.

  Bibliography: p.
  Includes index.
  1. Ecology. I. Title.
QH541.Y63 1989   574.5'01   88-31050
ISBN 0-06-047369-X

89 90 91 92 9 8 7 6 5 4 3 2 1

The leaves dropping from the trees in the autumn, the interior of an airplane engine, the entrails of a dissected rabbit, the city desk of a newspaper, all appear to be chaos if they are seen without comprehension. Once they are understood as systems of order, they actually *look* different.

Jane Jacobs

Contents

Preface

I have been lecturing on theoretical ecology regularly for the past ten years, first at the University of Zürich, Switzerland, then at the University of Guelph. When I began lecturing in Zürich, it was suggested that I provide a "*Scriptum*" to go with the lectures, in keeping with European academic custom. When I moved to Canada I continued updating and refining these "prepared lecture notes," as there was no book I could use as a "textbook" in the North American sense.

Over the years many people suggested that it would be useful to publish the notes for a wider public, but I resisted this notion, mindful that it would entail an order of magnitude more work on my part. But as the lecture notes evolved, on the one hand, and I became increasingly aware, on the other hand, of widespread misunderstanding among ecologists as to the nature and functioning of theory, my resistance weakened. The result is the present volume.

The writing retains something of the informal, "conversational" character of its lecture note forebears. The audience I have in mind is mainly students of ecology with empirical interests, though I would hope that a budding theorist could find inspiration here as well. A very strong attempt is made to communicate mathematical thinking to people who may not by nature find this way of thinking very natural—the reader is "taken by the hand" far more than is customary in mathematical writing.

The book contains the basics (and somewhat more) of population, community, and life-history theory. It does not attempt a comprehensive survey of theoretical ecology. Relatively few topics are covered, but those that are covered are treated in considerable depth. A text with comprehensive coverage would have to be either impracticably immense or impenetrably condensed. My aim, instead, is to give students a deep enough understanding of the topics that are discussed to enable them to pick up other areas of interest (including new developments) from the primary literature.

I have not discussed data analytic techniques such as mark-recapture and so on, but the book of Krebs (1989) is dedicated to this topic. I have also not treated the ecology of infectious diseases, except for one example, as this topic has been cogently reviewed by Anderson (1981) and Anderson and May (1985). Similarly, Clark (1976) is a superb introduction to management problems. The volume edited by May (1981c) covers a number of other topics that I have not touched upon, and May's volume will be accessible to the student of this book.

I have written for advanced undergraduates or graduate students. In particular, I presuppose one or two years of ecology and a year of calculus. Thus, for example, I start out by simply writing down the logistic equation, assuming it is familiar to the student. There is an appendix that discusses certain mathematical topics beyond first-year calculus, which are used in isolated places in the main text. These places are all flagged, and the book is written so that the reader who does not wish to go quite so deeply into mathematics can skip over them (and the appendix) and still follow the gist of the argument.

As well, quite a lot of mathematical material—indispensable, to my mind—is developed within the main text. While this does to some extent interrupt the flow of biological ideas, I did not want to segregate the mathematics so much that the student would fall prey to the temptation to just "take my word for it." I believe students will find they can view ecology from a theoretical perspective much more tellingly if they really understand the theory for themselves and don't have to view theoretical results as Pronouncements. The basic spirit of the book is that advocated by Albert Einstein: "Everything should be made as simple as possible—but not simpler."

I think it is vital that we develop a common understanding in ecology as to what constitutes a scientific explanation (within the particular science of ecology), and what are valid protocols for research that aims at such explanation. To get the student thinking along these lines, I have explicated some methodological basics, especially pertaining to pluralistic (introductory paragraphs to Chapter 6, and Section 6.4) and probabilistic (Section 8.1.2) explanations.

Because the variability from one institution to another in the students' preparation for this kind of course is greater than in the more standard biological fare, it is impossible to estimate how much of the book can be covered in a given time. The book probably contains enough material for a one-year course at most universities. Parts One and Two form an integrated unit that must be taken in the order given. Part Three is essentially independent. Thus a one-semester (or, with supplementation, possibly a year) course in theoretical population and community ecology could be based on Parts One and Two, or a one-semester course in life-history theory could use Part Three. The minimum that should be covered in Parts One and Two is Chapters 1 through 6. Chapters 7 and 8 could be included if time permits, or left for students to read on their own. (Or, one might want to cover Chapter 9 instead.) The minimum that would constitute a reasonable treatment of life-history theory is Chapters 9, 10, and 13.

To mention one further element of flexibility: some instructors might find that their students are happier to start with Part Three (which is mathematically simpler), then go on to Parts One and Two. I have put Part Three at the end because I feel that this topic is less well founded than the others, because of the pervasive use in it of problematical optimization arguments. The difficulties in the optimization program are discussed at the very beginning of Part Three.

Pictorial material is dealt with here in a somewhat unusual way, which I should perhaps explain. The book contains figures that are placed on the page and labeled in the usual way, and "sketches" that are integrated directly into the text. The hope is that treating the sketches in this way will aid in the flow of the argument. Basically, the sketches are things that would be drawn on the blackboard in a lecture; they are virtually an integral part of the text, and are so presented here.

The book includes exercises. These are almost entirely mathematical calculations. Most of them fill in gaps in the text and are included in the text at the appropriate places. Additional exercises, which extend the text, are given at the ends of chapters.

Some students complain that a lot of the exercises, especially among those that fill in gaps, are boring and routine. In some cases this is because the exercises in question really are too easy for the student. Sometimes, though, the student just does not want to plod through the preliminaries. The painful truth is that you must learn to walk before you can dance; you have to master scales and arpeggios before you are ready to attempt sonatas.

The student who wants real mastery of this material should do all the exercises; the instructor has, of course, the option of setting a mandatory standard short of this, or indeed of adding more exercises. I have even taught the course with *no* assigned exercises. These students wrote nonmathematical term papers that applied the ideas developed in the course to systems that they were familiar with or particularly interested in.

Some of the exercises are computer projects, and here, again, there will be a lot of variability from one institution to another in the appropriateness of such exercises.

I should make one more point about the exercises that fill in gaps in the text. In mathematical writing, it is quite common to sketch how a calculation or proof is done, without giving all the details. Serious readers will often fill in these details as they go along (at least, on second or third reading), and this is certainly to be recommended to students. By calling attention to these gaps in the form of exercises at the places where gaps occur, I hope to train the student to spot places where an argument needs to be rounded out.

Ultimately, the idea of writing this book originated with Hans Burla, who invited me to lecture on theoretical ecology in Zürich and suggested writing a *Scriptum* for the course of lectures. As well, I have spent many happy hours discussing biology with Hans. Several generations of students, both in Zürich and in Guelph, forced me to think clearly with their questions, kept me honest with their skepticism, and encouraged me with their interest. I wish I could name them all, but I do need to mention two excellent students, Dominique Anfossi and Susan Glenn, who provided detailed criticisms of late versions of the lecture notes.

I am very grateful to Ted Case, Joel Cohen, Jim Drake, Mike Gilpin, Robert Holt, Dave Lavigne, Sandy Middleton, Bob May, Craig Pease, Georg Ribi, John Roff, and David Tilman for their comments on the manuscript or parts thereof. Special thanks to Don DeAngelis for his very thorough criticisms. And my very special thanks to family, friends, and colleagues for their patience and encouragement.

Peter Yodzis

Chapter 1

Introduction

Science is an attempt to understand the world around us. In part, it proceeds by very carefully, very precisely, very thoroughly describing what we observe. But, while description is the ultimate foundation of science, it is not enough. For our world—indeed, almost any given small part of it—is very, very (some would say boundlessly) complex and diverse. Eventually description, in itself, overwhelms.

So scientists seek patterns in the data. One way of doing this is to scrutinize the data themselves, sometimes utilizing sophisticated statistical methods. This kind of analysis, too, is an important part of science, but it is still not enough. How do we know what kind of pattern to look for? Could it be that some patterns in the data are too subtle for ad hoc scrutiny to detect?

Moreover, even when we do see pattern, we may wonder what *causes* it, whether we can explain it in terms of some underlying principles or processes. The contemplation of underlying causes, by accounting for discerned patterns in the data, may please our desire to understand. Furthermore, it may suggest to us new kinds of pattern to look for in the data (and new kinds of data to gather in the first place). This is the scientific activity that we call *theory.*

Theory proceeds by making assumptions about how things work, assumptions that simplify the vast complexity of nature by abstracting out certain features that the theorist regards as essential. It then deduces the consequences of these assumptions—and comparing these consequences with observed data is a way of looking for pattern in the data.

Ecological theory has over the past few decades made very extensive use of mathematical models, and since this sort of approach is perhaps a bit unfamiliar to many biologists, I am going to start out with a few general remarks about mathematical models.

1.1 MODELS

First, what is a model? *Webster's* defines it as "a hypothetical or stylized representation," and I think this is an excellent characterization of the sense in which the word is used in science. The purpose of a model is not to provide a literal *description* of some system, but to provide a *conceptualization* (representation) of the system and its workings, in terms of which one can think about the system and understand something of its behavior. Any model will inevitably be incomplete and even false in some respects, but in discovering these defects we often learn new things about the system—and come up with new and better models.

A common misconception about mathematical models is that it is characteristic of them to very much simplify the actuality being investigated. It is true that mathematical models simplify very much. But this is not characteristic of mathematical models—it is characteristic of *any* attempt to comprehend the world. For instance, even decades of intensive empirical study of an ecosystem leave us with a simplified view of the system. The real issue is: How much simplification, and what kind of simplification, is it sensible for us to make? Right now, we in ecology are still very far from being able to address this issue conclusively.

Models can be expressed in several different ways: verbally, in graphs or diagrams, or mathematically. In current theoretical ecology, while verbal, graphical, and diagrammatic models are often used in preliminary formulations of ideas, it is seldom long before the train of thought finds expression as a mathematical model.

There are two reasons for this prevalence of mathematical models in ecology. First, the systems being studied in ecology tend to be very complex, and mathematics is ideally suited to the expression of complex relationships in a form that makes it relatively easy to work out the consequences of these relationships. In principle, one could attempt to do all the same reasonings verbally, or in some extraordinarily complicated diagram, but in practice this would be far too mind-bogglingly confusing.

Second, mathematics is very exact. It forces one to (try to) say *exactly* what one's ideas are, and it enables one to find out *exactly* what their consequences are. Mathematics is not the only form of clear thinking, but it is the most powerful, and it imposes a certain discipline which helps to keep one from sliding into fuzzy thinking.

It is not inconceivable that the phenomena of ecology are just not amenable to such a rigorous approach. Theoretical ecology, while enjoying a measure of success, has yet fully to prove itself. But the promise is too great to be ignored. The scientific spirit—to say nothing of the urgency of the environmental crisis—demands that we explore this promise to the fullest.

One should be aware that two quite different kinds of models are commonly used in ecology (and elsewhere). C. S. Holling (1966) uses the terminology "tactical" and "strategic" to distinguish the two kinds of models.

A tactical model in Holling's sense is a very detailed model of a very specific system. Such a model is often referred to as a "simulation" because its aim is to mimic as closely as possible the detailed actual behavior of some particular system. Because it attempts a highly detailed and realistic representation, such a model is immensely complicated and can be handled only on a substantial computer.

The tactical approach probably seems the more natural to many biologists, and yet it is, I think, fair to say that this approach has contributed little to ecological theory, in comparison with the strategic approach. This is because tactical models are so terribly specific that it is difficult to extract general insights from them; and they are so complicated that calculations with them are cumbersome and not at all transparent. Nevertheless, these models can be vital tools when one's goals are sufficiently concrete and specific, and one has at one's disposal the extensive resources that are required to build a reliable tactical model. A number of excellent books with a tactical orientation are available (for instance, Watt 1968, Patten 1971, Hall and Day 1977).

The strategic approach is a little harder to describe. It will be my approach throughout this book, so you will become familiar with it anyhow if you just read on. The basic idea of this viewpoint is to sacrifice detail for generality. One tries to build relatively simple models that, while not taking into account every detail of any one system, do capture the *essence* of *many* systems. Such an approach lends itself very well to the perception and formulation of general insights, largely because it is predicated on the assumption that such insights can be had!

It is, however (as Holling himself is at pains to emphasize), far too crude to draw an absolute binary distinction: tactical or strategic. It makes more sense to think of each model as lying somewhere in a continuum of approaches, with "tactical" and "strategic" as the two extremes (or, more precisely, as the two "directions" in this one-dimensional continuum). One can, as we shall see, add or subtract bits of detail to or from a model in order to strike the right balance between detail and generality, between thoroughness and workability.

1.2 ON THE RELATION BETWEEN THEORY AND OBSERVATION

I am not going to discuss much data in this book. I am just going to discuss theory for the most part, and will leave it to each reader to fill in examples from his or her other studies in biology and ecology, and experience of particular organisms.

When I do discuss data, it will be to illustrate the relation between theory and observation. This is a very important relationship; indeed it is crucial to the scientific enterprise. I would like to suggest to you at this point a couple of vague generalities to keep in mind as we go along.

Most observers develop hypotheses about their systems and try to test these hypotheses. Often they start work on a system with some hypothesis already in mind. Now, one function of theory is to *sharpen hypotheses*. This process of sharpening hypotheses can take two forms: it can involve making the hypotheses themselves more precise, or it can involve pinpointing just exactly which measurements need to be made in order to test the hypotheses (perhaps most efficiently in some sense). Or it can involve both these aspects.

But there is another, more subtle and marvelous, function of theory. As I hope you will see in the rest of this book, a theory has a sort of life of its own, a course of development that flows from its inner logic. And in the course of this process the theory will often *generate new hypotheses,* which, often enough, can be tested in the field or lab.

PART ONE

THE GROWTH OF SINGLE POPULATIONS

The growth of a population depends upon many factors. Some of these are abiotic characteristics of the environment, some are characteristics of the population itself, and some arise from interactions with other populations. We begin our study of ecological theory by considering the growth of a population for which interactions with other populations are negligible.

There are, to be sure, precious few, if any, populations in nature for which interactions with other populations are *completely* and *utterly* absent. But it is often enough a reasonable first approximation to neglect interspecific interactions. Moreover, we shall make the acquaintance in this relatively simple setting of a host of important concepts whose usefulness extends far beyond the single-species situation.

I will make some additional simplifying assumptions in this part. I will assume unless otherwise stated that all abiotic factors remain constant (no seasonal or random environmental fluctuations). Environmental fluctuations are discussed in Sections 2.4 and 3.6. I will also neglect age structure within our populations (until Part Three, where I discuss age structure), as well as all phenotypic variation. I will assume further that we are dealing with populations that lack any spatial structure (until Section 5.4). In short, at first we consider populations that are homogeneous in every respect: the state of such a population will be specified by a single function of time: the density (number or biomass per unit area or volume) N.

These are a lot of simplifying assumptions, but they will enable us to get started. As indicated in the preceding paragraph, we later drop some of these simplifications. But even at our present level of simplicity, we will gain some fascinating insights from these models.

Under certain circumstances (explicated in Section 2.5) it is appropriate to view population growth as a continuous process in continuous time (Chapter

2), and under other circumstances it is appropriate to view it as a discrete process in discrete time (Chapter 3). We begin our study of continuous-time models with some general remarks about the qualitative behavior of these models (Section 2.1). A major feature here is the existence of multiple domains of attraction, which is explored in several examples in Section 2.2. In Section 2.3 we continue the general discussion of qualitative behavior and indicate why certain pathological models ("structurally unstable" ones) need not be considered. The role of environmental fluctuations is explored in Section 2.4. In Section 2.5 we look in some detail at the question of just what are the circumstances in which continuous-time vs. discrete-time models are appropriate, addressing the seeming paradox of using a continuous description of processes (birth and death) that are by their very nature discrete. Section 2.6 elaborates a little on the link between mathematical abstractions and biological "reality."

Sections 3.1 to 3.3 explore the qualitative behavior of discrete-time models, finding a new and rather amazing phenomenon called "chaos." Chaos is discussed from a biological standpoint in Sections 3.4 and 3.5, and Section 3.6 returns to the issue of environmental fluctuations.

Chapter 2

Continuous Time

Under certain circumstances, it is a reasonable approximation to think of population density as changing continuously with time. In this case the appropriate mathematical description of population growth is a *differential equation*. You will have seen differential equations applied in this way in earlier ecology courses. For the time being let us say that this way of doing things is appropriate when there is a lot of overlap among generations—I will be a lot less glib about this issue in Section 2.5. The most familiar example is the logistic equation

$$dN/dt = rN(1 - N/K) \tag{2.1}$$

which I am sure you have encountered in earlier ecology courses. Here N, which is a function of time, is the number or biomass density, r is the intrinsic growth rate, and K is the carrying capacity of the population.

Now, as a *quantitative* model of population growth the logistic equation is far too simple to be of much use. There are examples of isolated laboratory populations, or of domesticated populations, whose growth in time—the function $N(t)$—can be fitted quite well by solutions of the logistic equation, but it would be silly to expect, and is not in fact the case, that many natural populations can be said to obey the logistic equation in a strict quantitative sense.

The real utility of this equation is, rather, as a simple embodiment of a *qualitative* behavior which is not so uncommon: if the density N starts out with a value that is bigger than zero but smaller than the carrying capacity K, it will gradually increase and approach the carrying capacity asymptotically, and if N starts out with a value that is bigger than K it will gradually decrease and approach K asymptotically.

This behavior follows immediately from the qualitative shape of the logistic growth rate [right-hand side of equation (2.1)] as a function of N:

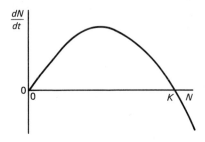

It isn't so terribly essential that this curve has the exact shape it does (which happens to be a parabola); the essential thing is just that the growth rate is positive for densities N such that $0 < N < K$, and it is negative for $N > K$.

But there are other interesting qualitative possibilities, even within the context of simple continuous single-species models.

2.1 THE QUALITATIVE THEORY OF CONTINUOUS SINGLE-POPULATION GROWTH

Under the assumptions discussed in the opening paragraphs of this part, and assuming that population growth can appropriately be thought of as continuous, the growth rate dN/dt will be some function of density N:

$$dN/dt = f(N) \qquad (2.2)$$

Before discussing the associated biology, let us undertake the purely mathematical task of developing a general qualitative theory for models of the form (2.2).

This may sound a little daunting at first, but in fact such a theory is easily delineated. For each value N of the density, the growth of the population in the immediate future is determined simply by the value of $f(N)$. In particular:

1. In those regions of the N-axis where $f(N)$ is positive, the dynamics (2.2) will cause the density to increase:

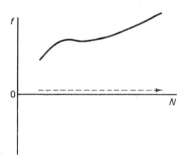

The dashed arrow in this picture indicates the direction of population growth (toward larger values) in the immediate future, in case the initial value of N falls in the region occupied by the arrow.

2. In those regions of the N-axis where $f(N)$ is negative, the dynamics (2.2) will cause the density to decrease:

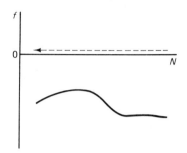

3. If $f(N_e) = 0$ for some density N_e, then the value N_e of density is called an *equilibrium value*. If N has initially the value N_e, then it will remain at this value [since $dN/dt = f(N_e) = 0$] until it is displaced away from this value by some external influence. An equilibrium is almost[1] always a point at which the curve $f(N)$ crosses the N-axis.

4. Suppose the slope of the curve $f(N)$ is negative at some equilibrium N_e:

$$\left.\frac{df}{dN}\right|_{N_e} < 0 \qquad (2.3)$$

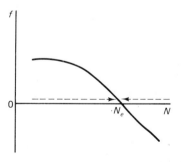

and consider what happens if the density is moved away from its equilibrium value N_e by some small amount. If the density is moved a little bit below N_e, it will be in a region of positive growth and will therefore increase back to N_e. If it is moved a little bit above N_e, it will be in a region of negative growth and will therefore decrease back to N_e. The tendency of the population's intrinsic dynamics is to push the density toward N_e once it gets somewhere near it (as suggested by the dashed arrows in the previous sketch). In such a case N_e is called a *stable* equilibrium.

---

[1] See Section 2.3.

Now, "stable" is one of those words about which ecologists have been arguing among themselves for many years, and they continue to do so.

Basically, the reason for all the controversy is that this word "stable" can be used in many different ways, and different stability concepts may be appropriate in different biological contexts. For instance, we might use the word "stable" to mean constancy of species composition (that the same species are present each year), or we might use it to mean that the *density* of each species remains constant. Perhaps we have in mind the "structural stability" of Section 2.3. Or, instead of using "stable" to mean a property that is either possessed or not in a given instance, we may use it in a relative sense, for instance, calling a population whose density has a smaller coefficient of variation over time a "more stable" population.

Unfortunately, it is not always obvious which stability concept is appropriate; and the situation is not made any less confusing by the circumstance that some ecologists are not always careful in their writing to specify just which notion of stability they are using.

So in order to avoid confusing our present notion of stability with any other one, we had better have a special name for it. The term favored by mathematicians is: asymptotically stable in the sense of Liapunov. This sort of stability is often called *neighborhood stability* in the ecological literature; another term (which I prefer) is *local stability.*

To call it simply "stability" is an inexcusable crime unless it is absolutely clear from the context (as, for instance, when I first used the word above) what kind of stability is meant.

The property of a locally stable equilibrium that we discovered six paragraphs ago is best regarded as the *defining* property of local stability: an equilibrium is locally stable if the system returns to the equilibrium after being displaced away from the equilibrium by a sufficiently small but otherwise arbitrary amount. This is by far the most commonly used stability concept in theoretical ecology. Its biological significance should become apparent if you think about the equilibrium at $N = K$ in the logistic model (2.1), which is locally stable. We will see plenty more examples in what follows.

Please notice carefully the proviso "sufficiently small" in the above definition of local stability. It is extremely important. In the following example

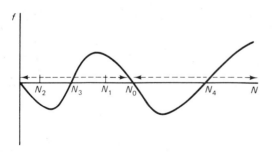

the equilibrium at N_0 is locally stable. For instance, if N is displaced to the value N_1, it will thereafter return to the equilibrium N_0 (so this is a "sufficiently small" displacement). But if the density is displaced to N_2, it will *not* subsequently return to N_0; instead it will decrease still further.

Local stability in itself does not tell us *how* small is "sufficiently small." So of any locally stable equilibrium we must go on to ask: What is the largest set of values of N such that, if the density is initially somewhere in that set, it will subsequently move toward the equilibrium in question? This set is called the *domain of attraction* of the equilibrium, at least in the ecological literature (mathematicians prefer the term "basin of attraction"). In the previous example the domain of attraction of the equilibrium at N_0 is the set of densities N such that $N_3 < N < N_4$.

5. Suppose again that for some N_e we have $f(N_e) = 0$. [In case you've forgotten in all this long aside about local stability, we're talking about $f(N)$ in the right-hand side of equation (2.2).] But suppose now that the curve $f(N)$ has *positive* slope at N_e:

$$\left. \frac{df}{dN} \right|_{N_e} > 0$$

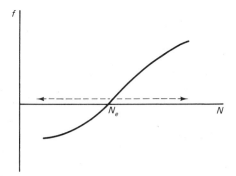

In such a case, the density will move farther *away* from its equilibrium value after the *slightest* initial displacement away from equilibrium (you should convince yourself of this), and the equilibrium is called *locally unstable*.

That completes our qualitative theory for systems of the form (2.2).

With these concepts in mind, let's look a little bit at the biology of single-species growth. If there is no immigration or emigration, we can write the growth equation (2.2) in the form

$$dN/dt = N[b(N) - d(N)]$$

where b is the per capita birth rate and d the per capita death rate.

One possible form for these curves, and the corresponding form for the growth rate $f = N(b - d)$, is the following:

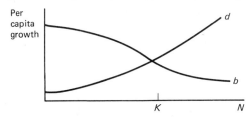

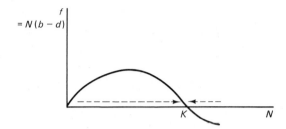

In this example the per capita birth rate declines with increasing density, perhaps due to lack of food or of nesting sites. The per capita death rate increases with density, possibly because of lack of food or of refuges from predation. Under these circumstances population growth is qualitatively the same as logistic (or of "logistic type"), where "qualitatively the same as" means: having the same configuration of dashed arrows along the N-axis, if one draws them in as I have been doing.

This form of the per capita birth and death rates implies logistic-type population growth, but of course it is not true that logistic-type growth implies these forms for the per capita birth and death rates. This is just one example of a biological basis for logistic-type growth. (For instance, if the per capita birth rate were just a constant—the same for all densities—together with the above form for the per capita death rate, we would still have logistic-type population growth.)

It can easily happen that the per capita birth rate declines also at low densities because, for example, of the increased difficulty of finding a mate. This is known as *Allee-type behavior* (of the per capita birth rate), and its effect on the growth rate f, shown below, is called an *Allee effect* (Allee 1931).

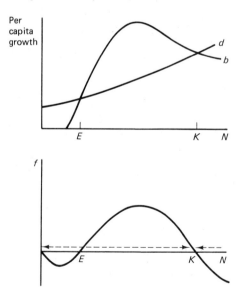

We now have *three* equilibria (counting the one at $N = 0$). Notice that, while $N = 0$ is an unstable equilibrium for logistic-type growth, it is *stable* when we have an Allee effect. The domain of attraction of this equilibrium consists of those N such that $0 \le N < E$, where E (labeled in the prior graph) plays the role of an *extinction threshold:* if for some reason (bad weather, overharvesting, whatever) the density falls below E, then the population will go locally extinct. Allee effects are especially likely for highly social animals such as whales, and for this reason special care is needed in managing such populations.

It could be in addition that the per capita death rate declines at high densities. This could happen, for instance, if there is group defense against predation. Then we may see something like this:

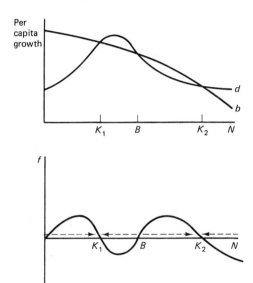

Now we have two different locally stable equilibria, with positive densities K_1 and K_2, and a so-called *breakpoint B* (which is also an unstable equilibrium) separating them. For positive initial values of the density that are smaller than B, the system will tend toward the equilibrium at K_1, and for initial values of N that are larger than B, the system will tend toward the equilibrium at K_2.

So even in the simple context of the growth of a single species, we can have *multiple domains of attraction.* One might very well expect multiple domains of attraction to be all the more likely when several species interact. This seems indeed to be the case (Gilpin and Case 1976).

2.2 BREAKPOINTS AND THRESHOLDS

The existence of multiple domains of attraction has some very interesting and important biological consequences. There are many examples in nature of sudden jumps (often associated with human intervention) from one apparent equilibrium to another. We are not going to be able to understand ecosystems (much less manage them) if we cannot explain such jumps.

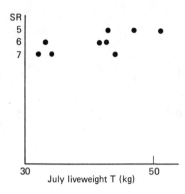

Figure 2.1 Mean biomass (July live-weight, kg) in each of three replicate pastures, for three stocking rates (SR, ewes per acre). (From Morley 1966.)

The curious thing about these jumps is that they are often associated with a continuous change in some system parameter. A *continuous* change in a system parameter can cause a *discontinuous*—sometimes quite large—change in the system. Most of us have a deeply ingrained feeling that small causes ought to have small effects, but this intuition doesn't necessarily apply in ecology.

This can be seen, for instance, in the history of exploitation of Lake Huron whitefish (as well as in numerous other fisheries). After a prolonged period of high yields early in this century, there was a sudden "crash" of the population to a quite low level. More puzzling still, even when the harvesting pressure was greatly relaxed, the population failed to return to its previous level. Similar phenomena have been seen in terrestrial grazing systems. For original sources documenting these and other examples, consult the review articles of Holling (1973) and May (1977a; 1981c, pp. 100–101).

The simplest example is Morley's (1966) controlled experiment with grazing sheep. He stocked three replicate pastures with five ewes per acre, three replicates with six ewes per acre, and three pastures with seven ewes per acre, and measured the sheep biomass after a year. Figure 2.1 is Morley's plot of the results. In this depiction, the mean sheep biomass in each of the three replicates is given for each stocking rate (SR, ewes per acre). Rather than the continuous variation in mean biomass that one would expect to see, the system seems to have two rather distinct "states" (one with a biomass around 33 kg, the other with a biomass around 45 kg), with each pasture occupying one state or the other.

2.2.1 A Vertebrate Grazer

As a simple example of a mathematical model that behaves in just this way, consider a "resource" population with density R which when left to itself has logistic growth, but which is harvested by a fixed number N of consumers, following May (1977a). The consumption rate of an individual consumer will depend on the density R of the resource population through a functional response $F(R)$ = consumption per unit area per unit time per consumer. You have probably seen this concept already in earlier ecology courses, but let me just briefly refresh your memory.

At relatively low resource densities R, we expect that consumption F will be an increasing function of R, since it will be easier to find and obtain resource items if there are more of them around:

But as the resource becomes more common, we expect that the consumer will eventually be unable to process resource items at a fast enough rate to keep up with further increases in resource density, so the consumption curve will level off.

Holling (1959) has distinguished three shapes for the functional response:

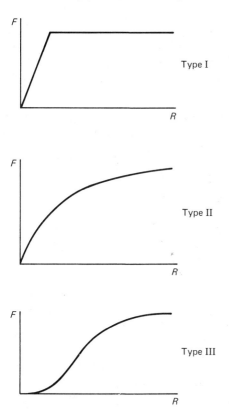

The Type I functional response might occur for a filter feeder, which simply traps a constant proportion of the individuals passing through the filter, and saturates rather abruptly. The Type II functional response corresponds to a more gradual approach to saturation. Type III also has this gradual saturation, but as well, a Type III consumer is particularly inefficient at low resource densities. One possible reason for this might be the loss of a "search image," and Type III is sometimes, rather loosely, called a "vertebrate" functional response. For more discussion on this, consult the old introductory ecology textbook.

We are going to use a Holling Type III functional response, of the form

$$F(R) = ER^2/(R_0^2 + R^2) \qquad (2.4)$$

Here E is the consumer's saturation level of consumption (which can be thought of as a measure of harvesting efficiency) and R_0 is the *half-saturation density* of resource individuals—the resource density at which consumption attains half its saturation level (the consumption rate increases only rather slowly with increasing R when $R > R_0$).

Exercise 2.1. Consider the functional response (2.4). We want to analyze its form to verify that it really is Type III. We can simplify the analysis by recasting (2.4) in "dimensionless" form. First, what are the dimensions of the quantities that appear in (2.4)? Clearly R and R_0 both have the dimensions of density: number or biomass (whichever we are using) per unit area or volume (whichever we are using). Therefore, the combination $R^2/(R_0^2 + R^2)$ has no dimensions at all—it is dimensionless—since its numerator and denominator have the same dimensions (density)^2. Hence E must have the same dimensions as F, namely, from the definition of F: (number or biomass) per unit (area or volume) per unit time per consumer.

Since R and R_0 have the same units and F and E have the same units, the quantities

$$x = R/R_0 \qquad y = F/E$$

are dimensionless. Moreover, if we rewrite (2.4) in terms of these dimensionless variables,

$$y = x^2/(1 + x^2)$$

it looks simpler. We can often simplify equations by rewriting them in terms of dimensionless variables. Of course, at the end of any analysis using dimensionless variables, it is easy to transform the answer back to the old dimensional variables if you wish: it just involves multiplying the appropriate variables by the appropriate constants everywhere they appear. Now: to the exercise.

First, show that

$$dy/dx = 2x/(1 + x^2)^2 \qquad \text{and} \qquad d^2y/dx^2 = 2(1 - 3x^2)/(1 + x^2)^3$$

Plot y as a function of x. Notice that there is a point of inflection at $x = x_i = 1/\sqrt{3}$: y "bends up" in the region $x < x_i$, where d^2y/dx^2 is positive; and it "bends down" in the region $x > x_i$, where d^2y/dx^2 is negative. This is the defining characteristic of a Type III functional response.

If $F(R)$ is the consumption per unit area per unit time per consumer, and there are N consumers, then the *total* consumption per unit area per unit time is $NF(R)$. From the standpoint of the resource population, this is a loss from the population density per unit time, so we have to subtract it from the growth rate dR/dt of the resource population:

$$dR/dt = rR(1 - R/K) - NF(R) \qquad (2.5)$$

Putting equation (2.4) into (2.5), we get

$$dR/dt = rR(1 - R/K) - ENR^2/(R_0^2 + R^2) \qquad (2.6)$$

for the dynamics of the resource population.

Of course, if the consumers were uncontrolled natural predators, the consumer density N would be a function of time, with a dynamical equation of its own. (We will get to this later.) By treating N instead as an adjustable parameter, that is, a constant whose value we can fix at will, we are assuming that the density of consumers is under our direct control, as in Morley's grazing experiment. Then N would be the number of sheep per unit area (stocking rate) and R the biomass density of vegetation. Let us think in these concrete terms for the remainder of this section.

If the half-saturation density R_0 is small enough, the differential equation (2.6) can have three different qualitative structures, depending upon the value taken on by the sheep density N. This is apparent from the following sketch:

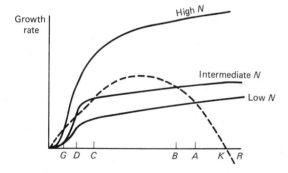

The dashed curve is the logistic growth curve, which is the growth rate of the vegetation biomass when no sheep are present. The solid curves are three possible versions of the harvesting term, $ENR^2/(R_0^2 + R^2)$, in equation (2.6), corresponding to three different densities N of sheep.

For each value of sheep density N the growth rate dR/dt is obtained by subtracting, for each R, the corresponding solid curve from the dashed curve. Let us look at the resulting growth rates.

For low N, the growth rate is positive for R less than A and negative for R greater than A (in the previous sketch), so we get

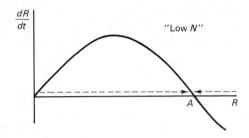

The equilibrium at $R = A$ is locally stable; in fact, this is just logistic-type growth.
For intermediate values of N there is a stable equilibrium at $R = B$, another stable equilibrium at $R = D$, and a breakpoint at $R = C$:

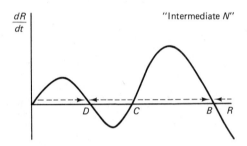

You should verify for yourself, using the sketch before the last one, that this is the correct qualitative form.
When N has a high enough value, we again have logistic-type growth, but now with a very small equilibrium density G:

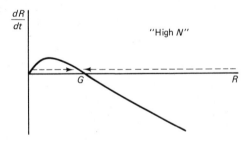

Again, please verify that this is indeed what one gets, reasoning from the third sketch before this one.
May (1977a) points out that a good way to appreciate the significance of all this is to plot the equilibrium values of vegetation biomass versus the sheep density N:

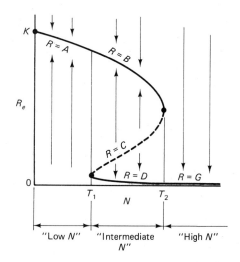

The arrows in this diagram show the direction of vegetation biomass growth at nonequilibrium values of vegetation biomass R, for selected densities N of sheep.

I have indicated on the N-axis the ranges of N that are "low," "intermediate," and "high" in the sense of our previous discussion. The *threshold value* T_1 that marks the transition from "low N" to "intermediate N" is also indicated, as is the threshold T_2 for the transition from "intermediate N" to "high N."

The solid curves give the stable equilibrium values of R for each N, and the dashed curve gives the breakpoint density $R = C$ for each N (only, of course, in the region of intermediate N, for it is only there that we have a breakpoint).

It should be clear to you how the qualitative form of this last sketch follows from that of the three sketches leading up to it. In case it is not clear, you should go back and study the last couple of pages again. If we wanted to work out the *quantitative* solution, we would have to set $dR/dt = 0$ in (2.6):

$$0 = rR_e(1 - R_e/K) - ENR_e^2/(R_0^2 + R_e^2) \qquad (2.7)$$

put in numbers for all the parameters, and solve this equation for the equilibrium density R_e as a function of N. But the qualitative form of the last sketch will suffice for our present purposes.

From this rather pretty picture we can immediately read off the consequences of any change in stocking policy, *given* the biological assumptions underlying the model.

If, to start, there are no sheep in the field, the vegetation will eventually reach the value K of biomass density. Suppose we then stock the field with sheep, at a low or intermediate density (that is: with $N < T_2$). If we keep the flock constant for a while, the system will eventually settle into an equilibrium with the vegetation biomass somewhere on the upper solid curve, since we are starting out from a value of R (namely, K) that lies above this curve. And we can increase the density of sheep with no drastic effects, so long as we stay below $N = T_2$: each slight increase in N will just result in a slight decrease in equilibrium vegetation biomass.

However, if we push the sheep density above T_2, even if by only one sheep, a catastrophe will occur.

Beyond T_2, there is in the previous sketch no longer any "upper" stable equilibrium, and the vegetation biomass must plummet to the "lower" stable equilibrium curve! We no longer have a very healthy pasture: our new "high N" flock can subsist, but only rather precariously; the pasture, and our flock of sheep, may suffer severely from some relatively small misfortune such as a sparsity of rain.

Worse still, we cannot easily get back to the "upper" stable equilibrium curve. If we remove a few sheep from the pasture to get back into the "intermediate N" region, the system will remain on the "lower" stable equilibrium curve, because the vegetation density is below the breakpoint value $R = C$. The only way to get back to the "upper" stable equilibrium curve is by removing enough sheep to get below the threshold $N = T_1$, into the region of "low N."

Perhaps you are thinking: isn't it still worth the risk inherent in a high N flock, because you do after all, in case there are no little disasters such as a sparsity of rain, have a big flock of sheep. The problem with this is, you've got a big flock of very scrawny sheep, for the level of vegetation biomass density associated with a high N flock is very low relative to the saturation density R_0 of the sheep. Therefore, the sheep have only enough food to barely survive: when the vegetation biomass crashes down to the "lower" stable equilibrium curve in the previous sketch, the sheep biomass will crash along with it. This seems to be what Morley (1966) has observed.

Notice one more thing about this system. In reality it will be subject to all kinds of unpredictable influences (weather, disease, other grazers, etc.) which will make it fluctuate around any equilibrium. Even if we are below the threshold T_2, if we are too close to T_2 these random fluctuations may bring the vegetation biomass R below the breakpoint value C, resulting in a "crash" just as if we had overstocked. If you take another look at the previous graph, you will see that the domain of attraction of the upper stable equilibrium $R = B$ is smaller the closer N is to T_2, making the system more susceptible to the kind of crash just described. To be on the safe side, we should not stock too close to T_2.

This kind of possibility makes Hardin's (1968) "tragedy of the commons" all the more poignant.

2.2.2 The Spruce Budworm

These considerations are of obvious importance to the range or fisheries manager. But if the human "super predator" has to worry about these matters, then so must other grazers and predators. And it would hardly be surprising to find species that have not "solved" these problems in a way that we would consider satisfactory for our own species.

A prime candidate for such a species would seem to be the spruce budworm, *Choristoneura fumiferana,* which occurs in the mixed spruce-fir forests of eastern Canada and the northeastern United States.

The budworm is usually quite rare in these forests, but every 40 years or so there is a sudden eruption of the budworm population, causing serious damage to the forests. After a year or two the forest is so decimated that it can no longer support such a large budworm population, and the budworm numbers crash back to their "normal" levels.

There is a strong suggestion here of a breakpoint phenomenon, and indeed it seems likely that this is the correct viewpoint. Ludwig et al. (1978) have produced a relatively simple model that appears to fit the data well. The following simplified version of their model (May 1977a) expresses the essentials of their three-species model in a single-species model.

The budworms are, in this model, normally limited by avian predation, and we can represent the growth of the budworm population by an equation with the same form as (2.6):

$$dN/dt = rN(1 - N/K) - EPN^2/(N_0^2 + N^2) \qquad (2.8)$$

where now N is the number of budworm larvae per unit area of forest and P is the number of budworm predators per unit area of forest.

The budworms preferentially attack balsam fir trees. Therefore, if we denote the average fir leaf area per unit area of forest by R, then the budworm carrying capacity will be proportional to R:

$$K = kR \qquad (2.9)$$

with k a constant.

If the predator attack rate saturates at some fixed number n of budworm larvae per unit area of leaf, then the corresponding density N_0 of larvae per unit area of forest is

$$N_0 = nR \qquad (2.10)$$

If we were to fix the leaf area R and plot budworm equilibrium density versus predator density P, we would get exactly the graph of the last section for grass equilibrium density versus sheep density. But it would not make sense to do this now, because the birds have alternate prey and are not limited by budworm density, so P remains more or less constant. The quantity that varies here is R, the leaf area per unit area of forest.

The meaningful thing to do, then, is to hold P fixed and vary R. But there is a problem here. In our discussion of grazing sheep, we treated the harvester density N as an adjustable parameter, under our direct control. This made sense because we can stock as many sheep as we wish in our pasture. But the leaf area R is governed by the intrinsic dynamics of tree growth and budworm attack. What we really ought to do is to write down equations for these processes, which is what Ludwig et al. (1978) have done.

However, May (1977a) has shown how to get at the essentials of the model of Ludwig et al. through the "one-dimensional" model [(2.8), (2.9), (2.10)] by means of the following observation. The growth of the budworm population is much faster than the growth of the trees. So for each value of R the budworm population will generally be near equilibrium. Therefore, we can use intuition to get at the (slow) dynamics of leaf area R, and use equations (2.8), (2.9), and (2.10) to fill in the budworm density for each R. (As mentioned above, in this process the predator density P is to be treated as a constant.)

If the budworm density N is at equilibrium, the relationship between N and R is as follows:

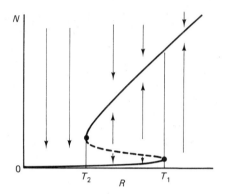

This is similar to the diagram on page 19: the two solid curves give the stable equilibrium values of N for each value of R, and the dashed curve is a breakpoint value for N. Again the curves show the direction of budworm population growth away from equilibrium for each R.

Exercise 2.2. Verify that the above diagram is qualitatively correct by putting equations (2.9) and (2.10) into (2.8), setting $dN/dt = 0$, and proceeding as we did in Section 2.2.1.

Let us see how the system behaves, starting out with a normal (low) equilibrium budworm density N.

At first the system is located somewhere on the lower solid curve in the above diagram. The budworms are kept under control by their predators, and the trees are able to grow. Since the trees are growing, the system will slowly move along the lower solid curve, as R increases. But eventually the threshold T_1 will be reached, and then the budworm population can no longer remain in equilibrium: it will erupt (at the much faster growth rate of the budworm dynamics) to the upper solid curve.

However, the trees cannot support such a large budworm population, so the system will move quite rapidly down and to the left along the upper solid curve as the budworms defoliate the trees. When the threshold T_2 is reached, the budworm population will experience a final crash back down to the lower solid curve, and the same cycle will begin anew.

This cycle of budworm population eruptions and crashes will repeat itself over and over.

The full model of Ludwig et al. uses two more differential equations to express the dynamics of forest growth (hence of R). Not only does the model yield the above qualitative behavior, but when the various parameters in it are estimated from field data, the correct period of approximately 40 years emerges from the model.

Since the model seems to "work" in the sense of having solutions that behave pretty much the way the real system does, we are entitled to entertain the possibility that the biological assumptions used in constructing the model are not too far from the biology of the actual system. This does not necessarily mean that we have "the right explanation" of the budworm cycles, since other biological assumptions may also yield as much of the correct system behavior as ours have thus far. But we do at least have one viable explanation for the budworm cycles.

Having a model that works, the temptation is unbearable to "tinker" with it, to see what happens if we change some of the parameters or if we interfere with the system in some way. There are all kinds of *predictions* implicit in the model, just waiting to be discovered. In this way we might very well gain new insights into the system (which, of course, we would want to test observationally if at all possible), or we might find that the model makes nonsensical predictions of some sort, which would indicate the need for changes in the model. (When this happens, it is usually pretty clear from the particular kind of nonsense what kind of changes in the model are needed.) The more successful the model proves under such "tinkering," the more confident we are entitled to be that the complex of biological hypotheses about the system embodied in the model is in fact the correct way to conceive of the system.

We can, for instance, study the possible effects of employing insecticides to control a budworm outbreak. I cannot show you the full details of how this works until we have done a little mathematics on two-species systems, in Chapter 4. Then we will tinker with the spruce budworm system.

2.2.3 Transmission Dynamics of Schistosomiasis

Schistosomiasis (also known as bilharzia) is a family of human diseases caused primarily by three species of *Schistosoma* flatworms. The adult worms inhabit the blood vessels lining the bladder, intestine, or liver, inflicting considerable damage. It is estimated that approximately 1 out of every 20 people on earth suffers from the disease (that is, about 200,000,000 people). Actually, 1 out of *every* 20 is misleading, for the disease is virtually unknown in the rich countries of the world.

The life cycle of the schistosomes is sketched in Fig. 2.2. The transmission to humans takes place via certain species of snails, which serve as intermediate hosts and release free-swimming cercariae, which can penetrate the skin.

A fair bit of theoretical work has been done on schistosomiasis, but we still lack a model that represents the entire cycle of the organism. Cohen (1976, 1977) has written a couple of excellent reviews of theoretical work on this system. Thus far, theories have concentrated on one aspect or another of the cycle. I

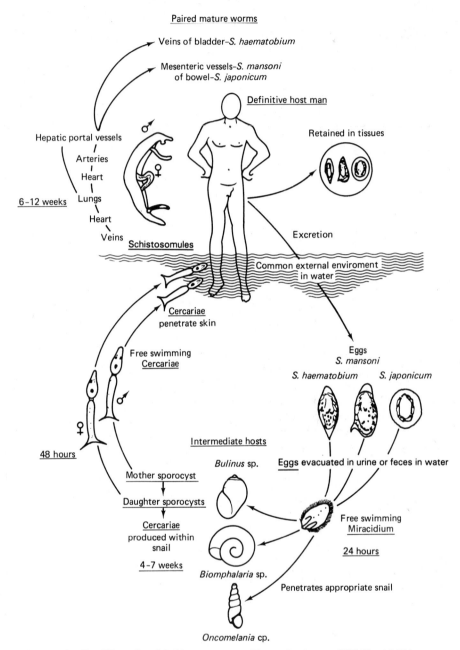

Figure 2.2 The life cycle of *Schistosoma* spp. (From Jordan and Webbe 1969.)

will briefly discuss here some work of Macdonald (1965), Nasell and Hirsch (1973), and Bradley and May (1978) on the transmission from snails to humans, as an example of breakpoint and threshold behavior in an (essentially) single-population system.

The single population to be modeled is the population of worms carried in human hosts. We will assume that the host population size is essentially constant over time periods relevant to the worm dynamics; then it makes sense to simply ignore the human population dynamics.

Let m be the mean worm load in the human population (m = mean number of worms per human). The worms reproduce within their human hosts, and this requires pairing between males and females. For any mean worm load m, let $p(m)$ be the probability that a given female will be paired; then the mean number of paired female worms per host is $mp(m)/2$ (assuming a 50:50 sex ratio). If each paired female produces E eggs per unit time, and there are N_1 human hosts, then the total number of eggs being produced per unit time is $N_1 Emp(m)/2$. If the probability of a given egg's infecting a snail is P_2, then the number of snails infected per unit time is $P_2 N_1 Emp(m)/2$, which we will abbreviate h_2 and call the force of infection per snail.

Let y be the fraction of the snail population that is infected, hence shedding cercariae. Then $1 - y$ is the fraction of the snail population that is not shedding cercariae. The rate of change of y is a balance between new infections and deaths:

$$dy/dt = h_2(1 - y) - q_2 y \qquad (2.11)$$

where the force of infection h_2 was discussed in the preceding paragraph and q_2 is the instantaneous mortality rate of infected snails. [In case some snails recover from the infection, this recovery rate should be included in q_2, but in most systems death is far more common. Also, (2.11) assumes that the total snail population remains more or less constant.]

Nasell and Hirsch (1973) define the convenient transmission parameter

$$T_2 = P_2 N_1 E/q_2 \qquad (2.12)$$

Assume the system reaches equilibrium. At equilibrium the fraction of infected snails will be constant ($dy/dt = 0$) and we can solve equation (2.11) immediately to obtain

$$y = [T_2 mp(m)/2]/[1 + T_2 mp(m)/2] \qquad (2.13)$$

Exercise 2.3. Derive (2.13).

Students of biology often find mathematical expositions like that in the last paragraph baffling: "How did Nasell and Hirsch ever decide to define a 'transmission parameter' by the obscure formula (2.12)? Where does this expression come from? It all seems so capricious." The problem is, in mathematical writing things are often described in a different order from the way they were originally done. The typical mathematician's paragraph above might be taken to suggest that *first* Nasell and Hirsch came up with T_2 somehow, *then* they used it to solve (2.11).

In fact, it was surely the other way around. First they solved (2.11) (with $dy/dt = 0$), finding

$$y = h_2/(h_2 + q_2)$$

Substituting for h_2 from three paragraphs ago, this is

$$y = [P_2N_1Emp(m)/2]/[P_2N_1Emp(m)/2 + q_2]$$

Now, *dimensionless* combinations of parameters are often significant, precisely because they are dimensionless—"absolute" in the sense that their numerical value is independent of the units in which the various quantities in them are measured. In the above equation, m and $p(m)$ are dimensionless, but q_2 is not, and neither is the combination P_2N_1E. But if we divide numerator and denominator by q_2, we get

$$y = [(P_2N_1E/q_2)mp(m)/2]/[1 + (P_2N_1E/q_2)mp(m)]$$

Since $mp(m)$ is dimensionless and so is 1, it has to be that the batch of things multiplying $mp(m)$ is dimensionless, too. So this batch of things—which is just the transmission parameter T_2—probably has some significance, and in any case we can write the equilibrium y in the tidy form (2.13) by giving this batch of things a name: T_2.

Exercise 2.4. Prove directly from (2.12), using the definitions of the parameters in that equation, that T_2 is dimensionless.

But why call T_2 a transmission parameter? Well, we suspect it has some neat significance, because it is dimensionless and occurs in the solution (2.13) so prominently. What could that significance be? One notes that if P_2 increases in value, so does T_2, if N_1 increases so does T_2, if E increases so does T_2, and if q_2 *decreases* T_2 increases. Now, any one of the named parameter changes will alter the biological situation by causing an increased transmission of schistosomes from humans to snails. So T_2 is a transmission parameter: larger T_2 corresponds to more schistosomes transmitted.

It is customary in mathematical exposition to sometimes "rewrite history" in this way, without warning, and I will sometimes do so in this book, for one of my major goals is to enable you to read the primary theoretical literature for yourself. In reading mathematical descriptions, in general, whenever something seems to just pop up out of nowhere, read further, and try to follow the logic of the calculations themselves rather than the rhetoric of the description.

Similarly to the argument leading up to (2.11), the average number m of worms per human represents a dynamic balance between infection and worm death:

$$dm/dt = P_1CN_2y - q_1m \qquad (2.14)$$

where P_1 is the probability of any given cercaria infecting a human host, C is the number of cercariae produced by an infected snail per unit time, N_2 is the total number of snails, and q_1 is the mean instantaneous death rate of worms in hosts. Nasell and Hirsch (1973) define another transmission parameter,

$$T_1 = P_1CN_2/q_1 \qquad (2.15)$$

in terms of which (2.14) can be written

$$dm/dt = q_1(T_1y - m) \tag{2.16}$$

Exercise 2.5. Derive (2.16).

At equilibrium we will have $dm/dt = 0$, with y given by equation (2.13). Using (2.13) in the right-hand side of (2.16), we have at equilibrium

$$q_1m\left(\frac{T_1T_2p(m)}{2 + T_2mp(m)} - 1\right) = 0 \tag{2.17}$$

Exercise 2.6. Derive (2.17).

The trivial solution $m = 0$ will always be a possibility, regardless of any parameter values. This is not a very interesting solution; it corresponds to absence of the disease. But there will also be a solution with schistosomes present, if the equation obtained by setting the quantity in parentheses in (2.17) equal to zero has a solution with m positive.

The pairing factor $p(m)$ now assumes an obvious importance. It will depend upon how the worms are distributed among their hosts. In his pioneering paper, MacDonald (1965) assumed a random distribution, and Nasell and Hirsch (1973) followed his lead. Bradley and May (1978) considered the effects of aggregated distributions. This is more realistic, but it turns out that aggregation does not alter the essentials of the problem, and I shall consider here only the case where the schistosomes are randomly distributed among their hosts.

The following derivation of $p(m)$ is due to May (1977b). Assume a monogamous breeding system, and assume all possible pairs manage to find each other (so the number of mated pairs in each host is equal to the total number of males present in that host or to the total number of females present, whichever is smaller). These assumptions are believed to be realistic for schistosomes.

Suppose a host contains i worms, with i an even number: $i = 2j$, where j is a non-negative integer. Suppose further that the probability for a given worm to be a male is .5 (so the probability for it to be a female is also .5). MacDonald (1965) has shown that, subject to the assumptions about breeding just named, the average fraction of worms that are *not* paired is

$$(2j)!2^{-2j}/(j!)^2 \tag{2.18}$$

He has also shown that the same formula applies if the total number of worms in the host is an odd number $i = 2j + 1$, with j a non-negative integer.

The expected number of paired worms is

$$mp(m) = m - \sum_{i=0}^{\infty} iP(i)(\text{fraction not paired in a host with } i \text{ worms})$$

where $P(i)$ is the probability for a host to contain i worms. The sum over all integers i is certainly equal to the sum over all even i plus the sum over all odd *i.* Since any even integer *i* is equal to $2j$ for some integer *j*, and any odd *i* is equal to $2j + 1$ for some *j*, this last statement is equivalent to

$$mp(m) = m - \sum_{j=0}^{\infty} 2jP(2j)(2j)!2^{-2j}/(j!)^2$$

$$- \sum_{j=0}^{\infty} (2j + 1)P(2j + 1)(2j)!2^{-2j}/(j!)^2$$

using (2.18).

Since we are assuming that the worms are randomly distributed among the hosts, with *m* the mean number per host, $P(i)$ is a Poisson distribution:

$$P(i) = m^i e^{-m}/i!$$

Therefore

$$mp(m) = m - \sum_{j=0}^{\infty} \{2j[m^{2j}e^{-m}/(2j)!](2j)!2^{-2j}/(j!)^2$$

$$+ (2j + 1)[m^{2j+1}e^{-m}/(2j + 1)!](2j)!2^{-2j}/(j!)^2\}$$

Using the fact that for any positive integer *i*

$$(i + 1)! = (i + 1)i!$$

together with the fact that for any real numbers *x, a, b*

$$x^{ab} = (x^a)^b$$

one can reduce the last expression to

$$mp(m) = m - \sum_{j=0}^{\infty} (2j + me^{-m})e^{-m}(m/2)^{2j}/(j!)^2 \qquad (2.19)$$

May (1977b) gives an equivalent expression involving integrals. Figure 2.3 is a plot of $p(m)$. The qualitative form of this graph is just as you would expect intuitively: the pairing probability $p(m)$ increases monotonically as the mean worm load *m* increases; for *m* less than about 2 the pairing probability is small, and $p(m)$ quickly approaches an asymptotic value of 1 (quantitatively, it is around 0.85 by the time $m = 5$).

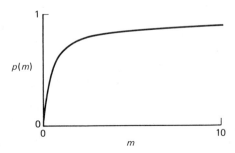

Figure 2.3   The pairing probability $p(m)$ as a function of mean worm load *m*.

One fairly obvious control measure that one might adopt would be to keep people out of the water in which the snails are releasing cercariae. However, agricultural activities [to say nothing of ambient temperatures sometimes in excess of 110 degrees Fahrenheit (43 degrees Celsius)] render this impractical for much of the world's population. Another possibility might be to keep the snail populations down. To see whether this idea stands any chance at all, at least on the basis of the present model, we can ask how the equilibrium mean worm load m obtained from (2.17) varies as we vary the snail density N_2, which will, through (2.15), affect the transmission parameter T_1.

Picking $T_2 = 1$, just to see what kind of behavior to expect, and using (2.19) to evalute $p(m)$, one gets Fig. 2.4. The qualitative form of this graph follows directly from equation (2.17), which we can write (with $T_2 = 1$)

$$T_1 = [2/p(m)] + m$$

together with the form of the graph for $p(m)$. When $m < 1$, $p(m)$ is small relative to 1; indeed as $m \to 0$, $p(m) \to 0$. So for small m the term $2/p(m)$ in the preceding equation is large; therefore, T_1 (horizontal axis in Fig. 2.4) is large. This gives us the lower, dashed branch of the curve in the graph. For m bigger than about 5, $p(m)$ is approximately constant; it varies from about 0.85 to 1 as m goes from 5 to infinity. So the $2/p(m)$ term in the preceding equation is approximately constant (at about 2 or a little more), and the variation in T_1 comes from the second term m in the preceding equation. That gives the upper, solid branch in the graph.

Again we have a breakpoint, this time in mean worm load (plotted vs. T_1 by the dashed curve in Fig. 2.4), and a threshold value E for T_1. The "lower equilibrium curve" of our previous examples has moved down to $m = 0$ here, but if immigration is added to the model the lower equilibrium is again at some finite value.

The threshold E in T_1 [which we can translate into a threshold in snail density N_2 using equation (2.15)] suggests that controlling snails is at least a

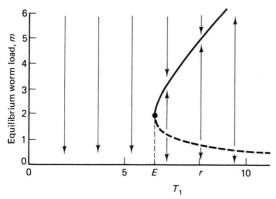

Figure 2.4 Equilibrium worm load as a function of the transmission parameter T_1. (From Bradley and May 1978.)

thinkable policy for controlling schistosomiasis, for it tells us that once we get the snail density below a certain value, the snail population will die out—we don't necessarily have to kill every last snail. To decide whether this is practical or not would require a lot more work.

The breakpoint in m is also thought-provoking. It suggests the possibility that perhaps by eradicating the adult worm population, at least in most of the human population, one could eliminate the disease. The medicines presently available for killing schistosomes in people have dangerous side effects, and they are expensive. Considerable work is, however, underway to find better remedies.

Those medicines may be useful for individual travelers from the world's rich countries, but they do not seem a very practical approach for eliminating the disease where it is endemic, for the breakpoint in m occurs at a very low *mean* worm load m: of the order of 1. However, at such low values of m stochastic effects may be important anyway (Section 2.5), so the present model cannot be considered very reliable near the breakpoint.

Clearly there is a great deal more to modeling schistosomiasis than we can touch upon here. (For more details, see Cohen 1976, 1977, Anderson and May 1985.) As you can well imagine, breakpoints and thresholds are crucial in all kinds of epidemiology.

2.3 STRUCTURAL STABILITY (A FOOTNOTE)

I mentioned on page 9 that, for models of the form (2.2), an equilibrium is *almost* always a point at which the curve $f(N)$ crosses the N-axis, and then proceeded to ignore equilibria for which this curve does not cross the axis. Was this some kind of a swindle, or is there a good reason for ignoring those other equilibria?

To answer this question, let's see what those other equilibria look like. Suppose, then, that N_e is an equilibrium point [that is, $f(N_e) = 0$], but suppose further that the curve $f(N)$ does not cross the N-axis at N_e. Then, assuming that f is a differentiable function of N, there are seven possibilities for the shape of f near N_e.

They are:

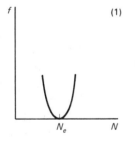

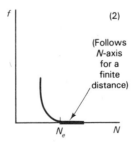

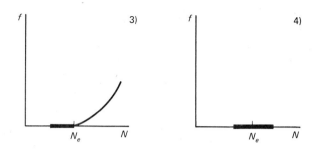

plus the three that are obtained by turning 1 to 3 upside down.

In each of these cases the following is true: if the growth rate $f(N)$ is changed by the *slightest* amount at (hence, by continuity of f, also near) N_e, then the qualitative structure of the system becomes completely different. For instance, take case 1. If we change f near N_e a little bit, we get things like

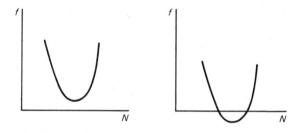

In the first alteration there is no longer an equilibrium; in the second there are two equilibria instead of one. The *qualitative* structure of the system is different, and these kinds of changes can be brought about by an *arbitrarily small* change in f. (For the mathematically minded, "structure" here means precisely: topology of the system trajectories in phase space; "different" structures are nonhomeomorphic in a certain natural sense.)

Notice that small changes in f do *not* lead to such structural changes for those equilibria where the f-curve crosses the N-axis at N_e (with nonzero slope). For instance, if we have a locally stable equilibrium

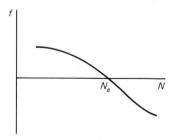

a slight change in f may change the position of the equilibrium a little bit, but the basic qualitative structure remains the same:

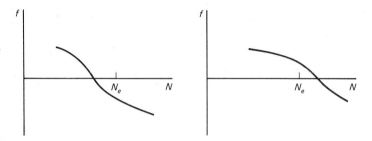

(Again for the mathematically minded: in this discussion a "small" change in f is to be construed as small in a C^1 topology on the space of growth-rate functions.)
A system of the form of equation (2.2):

$$dN/dt = f(N)$$

for which sufficiently small but otherwise arbitrary changes in the function f do not alter the qualitative structure of the system is called *structurally stable*.

Now, we can never know the growth rate of any real population exactly; in view of the numerous sources of more or less random variability associated with biological populations one might go so far as to question whether a real population can be said to *have* a growth rate of *exactly* this or that form. Therefore, a model for which even the qualitative structure of the system depends on the *exact* form of the growth function is not going to be a sensible representation of the growth of a real population.

Thus, I ignored the "other" equilibria on page 9 in order to restrict the discussion to structurally stable models.

It is important to understand that structural stability is, like local stability, local in nature: it requires only that qualitative structure is preserved under *sufficiently small* changes in the shape of f. Structural changes caused by "large" changes in f can certainly occur in realistic models and can even be of great biological importance. We studied examples of exactly this in Section 2.2.

2.4 RESPONSE TO DISTURBANCE

For a real population, the tidy dynamics expressed by a model of the form (2.2) is only part of the story. It describes processes that are intrinsic to the population, but real populations are also subject to all kinds of random extrinsic influences: disturbances from sudden changes in abiotic factors such as temperature or moisture, or sudden encounters with other species not normally encountered, for instance. If such disturbances are too big or too frequent, a model of the form (2.2) may not be sensible. But how big is "too big," how frequent is "too frequent," and what are we to do when environmental variability renders deterministic models like (2.2) unworkable?

These are difficult and profound questions, which theorists have not yet fully answered. I will sketch here and in Section 3.6 some of the ideas that people are thinking about.

2.4.1 A Local Plausibility Argument

Consider a locally stable equilibrium of a model of the form (2.2):

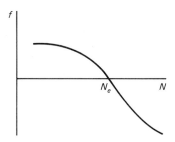

We know that if the density is perturbed away from its equilibrium value N_e by some small amount, it will return to N_e. Now let us go on to ask: How quickly will the density return to equilibrium?

Biological systems tend to find mathematical expression in terms of nonlinear models, such as the logistic, for which the growth rate is a quadratic function of the densities. Nonlinear mathematics is challenging, and it is also rewarding in terms of interesting new phenomena such as those we have studied in Section 2.2. But linear models [$f(N) = aN + b$, with a and b constant, in the present context] are much easier to analyze.

Sometimes it is possible, and sensible, to convert a nonlinear problem into a linear one by the method of *linearization*. For instance, we can do this for our present problem, because we are only going to consider very small displacements from equilibrium.

The point is, we can approximate the function f, *for values of N which are very near to* N_e, by a straight line (drawn as a dashed line in the following sketch) through N_e, whose slope is the same as that of the tangent to f at N_e:

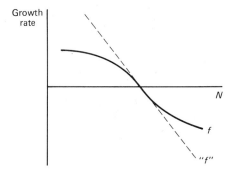

The equation of this straight line is

$$\text{``}f\text{''}(N) = \frac{df}{dN}\bigg|_{N_e} (N - N_e)$$

Exercise 2.7. Convince yourself that this last equation is correct.

If N remains sufficiently close to N_e, it is a good approximation to replace f by "f." [This approximation is equivalent to retaining only the lowest-order term in the Taylor's series (dust off the old calculus textbook!) about N_e for f.] Then equation (2.2) becomes

$$dN/dt = \frac{df}{dN}\bigg|_{N_e} (N - N_e) \qquad (2.20)$$

This equation is called the linearization of equation (2.2) about the point N_e. The method of linearization is discussed further by, for instance, Batschelet (1971, Sec. 9.9).

Defining the constant

$$\Lambda = - \frac{df}{dN}\bigg|_{N_e} \qquad (2.21)$$

and writing (2.20) as

$$d(N - N_e)/dt = -\Lambda(N - N_e)$$

we can immediately integrate it to find the general solution

$$N - N_e = Ce^{-\Lambda t} \qquad N(t) = N_e + Ce^{-\Lambda t} \qquad (2.22)$$

for some constant C. When $t = 0$, we have

$$N(0) = N_e + C$$

so C is the initial displacement away from equilibrium.

Recalling equation (2.3), we observe that Λ is positive for a locally stable equilibrium. So for a locally stable equilibrium, after a small displacement away from equilibrium the density returns to equilibrium exponentially [equation (2.22)]. The characteristic half-life for this exponential return is (Batschelet 1971, pp. 267–268)

$$-\ln(0.5)/\Lambda = 0.69315/\Lambda$$

but it is customary to discard the messy factor $-\ln(0.5)$ and to define the *characteristic return time* to equilibrium (sometimes called the equilibrium's natural response time) simply as

$$T_R = 1/\Lambda \qquad (2.23)$$

For instance, in the case of the logistic equation (2.1)

$$T_R = 1/r \qquad (2.24)$$

for the equilibrium at $N = K$.

Exercise 2.8. Prove (2.24).

The characteristic return time provides a partial answer to our earlier query about the allowable frequency of (small) disturbances (May 1973). Suppose the system is subject to small random disturbances on a time scale T_D, meaning that T_D is the average time between disturbances. Then if $T_R < T_D$, the density will have a chance to return to equilibrium between disturbances, and it will spend most of its time near the equilibrium, something like this:

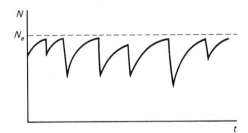

Under these circumstances the disturbances do not play any essential role and a model of the form (2.2) may well provide a good representation of the system. On the other hand, if $T_R > T_D$, the density may get pushed rather far away from equilibrium:

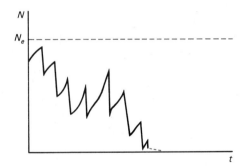

This is not a rigorous proof, but rather a "plausibility argument." The reason it is not a proof is that we derived the return time T_R from the assumption of "sufficiently small" displacements from equilibrium. But now we have started talking about displacements *far* from equilibrium (the above picture even hints at the possibility of extinction). We are in danger of confounding the *global* and the *local*. A "global" property or statement involves densities of all possible values. To talk about going from a finite equilibrium density all the way to zero, or to some very small value, is global. A "local" property or statement just involves densities in a "sufficiently small" neighborhood of some point; such as local stability or T_R.

Holling (1973) coined the term *resilience* to refer to the (global) property of a population system, associated with a given domain of attraction, that the density tends to remain within that domain of attraction in the face of environmental fluctuations. Our understanding of this concept remains sketchy at best, for it involves many factors, which interact in a complicated way.

Clearly the return time is one of these factors. If we have sufficiently small disturbances, on a time scale $T_D > T_R$, then it is very plausible that we have a high degree of resilience. What is not so clear is, exactly what happens if this condition fails; for then we depart from the local realm and our linear approximation is unreliable. Unfortunately, it has become fairly common usage in the literature to call the parameter Λ of equation (2.21) "resilience." That gives us two different (though somewhat related) usages for the same word—a deplorable situation.

Finally, we may note that the equilibrium density N_e itself may fluctuate— for instance, if food supplies vary. If these fluctuations are small enough or slow enough, the density will never wander very far away from equilibrium, even though "equilibrium" is moving around. In such a case we say that the density *tracks* the moving equilibrium. Grant (1986) has documented a beautiful example of tracking.

2.4.2 Environmental Variability and Multiple Domains of Attraction

Many pelagic fish stocks experience rapid changes in abundance, separated by periods of relative constancy, with a period of 50 years or so. Steele and Henderson (1984), who offer the data in Fig. 2.5 to illustrate the effect, suggest it is unlikely that these population fluctuations are caused by any straightforward "tracking" of environmental fluctuations by the animals, for while the physical and chemical marine environment does vary considerably at all time scales, these changes (excluding daily, lunar, and seasonal cycles) are never as pronounced as are the regional biological changes. We are, then, confronted by a mystery. Steele and Henderson propose an explanation involving the action of environmental fluctuations on a system with multiple domains of attraction.

The system they consider is, by now, familiar to us (from Sections 2.2.1 and 2.2.2): a population with density N, which is consumed by predators with a Type III functional response:

$$dN/dt = rN(1 - N/K) - CN^2/(N_0^2 + N^2) \tag{2.25}$$

where r is the population's intrinsic growth rate, K is its carrying capacity, $C = EP$ is the product of the predator's saturation rate of consumption E times the number P of predators, and N_0 is the half-saturation level of prey density.

We are, of course, free to measure both the population density N and the flow of time in whatever units we please, and Steele and Henderson simplify this equation further by choosing units in which the half-saturation prey density $N_0 = 1$ (this is a choice of units for N) and the intrinsic growth rate $r = 1$ (this is a choice of units for time). We are left with two parameters K and C:

$$dN/dt = N(1 - N/K) - CN^2/(1 + N^2) \tag{2.26}$$

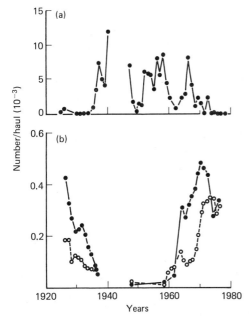

Figure 2.5 Changes in fish populations off the coast of Plymouth, England, measured on the basis of weekly plankton samples. (a) Pilchard eggs; (b) postlarval telecosts (ex cluding clupeids) divided into spring (●) and summer (○) spawners. (From Steele and Henderson 1984. Copyright © 1984 by the AAAS.)

Exercise 2.9. If we change the units in which we measure N, this is equivalent to multiplying all N-values by some constant, say A:

$$N' = AN$$

where N' is the population density measured in the new units. Similarly, a change in time units amounts to a transformation

$$t' = Bt$$

for some constant B. Prove that if we rewrite (2.25) in terms of the new units for density and time, by making the substitutions $N = N'/A$ and $t = t'/B$ in (2.25), then there exists a choice of units for density and time (that is, particular values for the constants A and B) such that our dynamical equation takes the form (2.26) (if we drop the primes in the new equation: $N' \to N$, $t' \to t$, in order to save writing).

As we know from our experience in Section 2.2, for certain parameter values the system specified by (2.25) will have three equilibria with $N \neq 0$, resulting in two domains of attraction separated by a breakpoint. The shaded region in Fig. 2.6 indicates the parameter values for which this occurs.

Steele and Henderson subject this system to environmental fluctuations by letting the parameter C fluctuate randomly in computer solutions of (2.26).

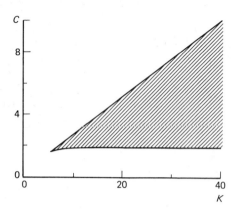

Figure 2.6 Breakpoint structure in relation to the parameters C and K. When parameter values lie in the shaded region, there is a breakpoint. (From Steele and Henderson 1984. Copyright © 1984 by the AAAS.)

The fluctuations they use are of a particular kind, called "red noise" by Steele and Henderson, and motivated by observations of the marine environment.

Environmental fluctuations are modeled by most authors using "white noise." One can model the temporal variation in any quantity as a mixture of oscillations at different frequencies ("Fourier analysis"; for details consult Champeney 1973). In white noise, the magnitude of each frequency component is the same as that of any other frequency component (just as white light is a mixture of all colors). In the marine environment, though, according to Steele and Henderson, fluctuations in properties such as temperature and sea level, for which thorough records have been kept for a long time, tend to vary much more strongly at low frequencies, and this is what Steele and Henderson call "red noise" (since, in the visual spectrum, the lower frequencies correspond to red color).

Indeed, Steele (1985) has gone so far as to suggest that a major difference between terrestrial and marine systems is that random variation in terrestrial environments tends to be well approximated by white noise, whereas random variation in marine environments tends to be well approximated by red noise (specifically, with the variance per unit frequency interval proportional to f^{-2}, where f is frequency). For example, he offers the data in Fig. 2.7.

Steele's generalization is a bold one, which will no doubt be hotly contested by some. For now, let us continue with the analysis of the system (2.26) in a fluctuating environment.

Steele and Henderson studied this system by means of computer simulations, choosing the red noise variation in C so that the fluctuations would move C across the shaded region in K–C "parameter space" (Fig. 2.6) where there is a breakpoint. Some typical solutions are displayed in Fig. 2.8.

The behavior of the solution depends on two parameters: the carrying capacity K and the lowest frequency f in the red noise variation of C. Steele and Henderson find in their computer solutions of (2.26) the following trend. For any given value of K, there is a critical value f_c such that for values of f greater than f_c the density N fluctuates around a single equilibrium value (as in cases a and c in Fig. 2.8), while for f less than f_c, the solution switches rather periodically

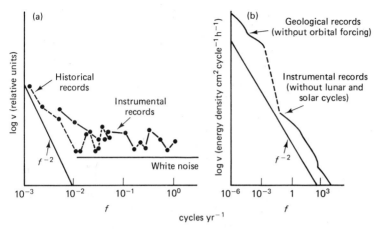

Figure 2.7 Frequency spectra of variance for atmospheric temperature in England (a) and at sea level (b). The log of variance per unit frequency interval, v, is plotted vs. the frequency f. (From Steele 1985. Reprinted by permission from *Nature* Vol. 313, p. 355. Copyright © 1985 Macmillan Magazines Ltd.)

between the two domains of attraction of (2.26) (as in plots b and d). Steele and Henderson find that f_c depends on K as in Fig. 2.9. For larger values of K, f_c is more or less constant. Recalling that the intrinsic growth rate r of the population is equal to 1 in the chosen time units, we see that f_c is rather small compared with the population's intrinsic growth rate. Thus the time between alterations in equilibrium state, which is of the order of f^{-1}, will normally be long relative to the population's generation time.

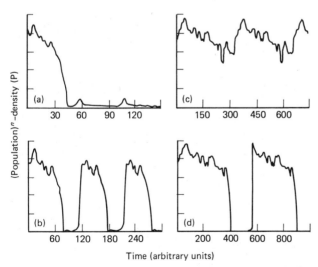

Figure 2.8 Computer simulations with (a) $K = 15$ and $f = 0.02$; (b) $K = 15$ and $f = 0.01$; (c) $K = 30$ and $f = 0.003$; and (d) $K = 30$ and $f = 0.002$. Runs were over several cycles to test for system equilibration. Note the changes in time scale between all of the runs. (From Steele and Henderson 1984. Copyright © 1984 by the AAAS.)

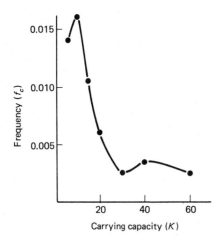

Figure 2.9 The relation of K to f_c, the critical value of f at which the system jumps between the two equilibrium states. (From Steele and Henderson 1984. Copyright © 1984 by the AAAS.)

Exploitation of the population will cause, in effect, K to decrease. This can have the effect of increasing the critical frequency f_c by a factor of 6 or 7 (Fig. 2.9). Thus heavily expoited stocks may have a particularly "jumpy" temporal behavior. Steele and Henderson suggest that we might be seeing just such a jumpy dynamic in the rapid succession of dominant species every few years in the Georges Bank and North Sea waters (Horwood 1981).

It is interesting to see what happens if we use white noise (truncated from below at a frequency f) instead of red noise (Steele 1985). There are two differences. First, f has to be much lower in order to get transitions between the two domains of attraction. Second, instead of the regular flips at rather low frequencies encountered with red noise, with white noise the jumps are much more irregular, and faster. These points are illustrated in the following two solutions shown in Fig. 2.10, with the same values of K and f, but red noise in the upper solution and white noise in the lower:

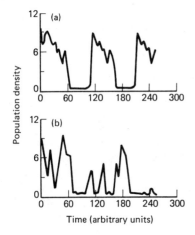

Figure 2.10 Response of N to stochastic forcing by red noise (a) and white noise (b). (From Steele 1985. Reprinted by permission from *Nature* Vol. 313 p. 357. Copyright © 1985 Macmillan Magazines Ltd.)

In summary, this kind of environmental-fluctuation-driven flipping between domains of attraction can cause large, rather regular population fluctuations, on time scales of the order of 50 years or so, when driven by relatively low amplitude red noise environmental fluctuations. A case can be made for a match with marine data, but of course very long time series are needed to do stringent tests. Environmental white noise, on the other hand, at least in the model (2.26), does not seem capable of producing either regular fluctuations in population density or fluctuations at a low enough frequency to match the marine data.

These are only the first investigations of environmental fluctuations and multiple domains of attraction, and the conclusions discussed here should be regarded as highly tentative.

2.5 THE MEANING OF CONTINUOUS POPULATION GROWTH

Now that I have (as I shall permit myself to assume) convinced you that differential-equation population models are interesting, you are probably wondering: yes, but do they make sense?

After all, differential equations were invented to describe the continuous motions of physical objects in continuous space and time. But biological populations do not grow continuously. The basic underlying processes of birth and death are by their very nature *discrete.* And once we're thinking about fundamentals, let's note as well that these processes are not deterministic, either— they are *stochastic* in nature. That is, we cannot say for sure that so many animals will be born, or die, or immigrate, or emigrate in such and such a time interval; all we can realistically hope to say is that there are certain *probabilities* for these things to happen. And yet our differential-equation models are deterministic.

The underlying randomness, or stochasticity, of population processes just alluded to is called *demographic stochasticity.*

In this section I am going to show that, while the objections to deterministic continuous-growth population dynamics I have just sketched are perfectly valid, nevertheless the differential-equation models of which we have by now become so fond are perfectly meaningful under certain circumstances, if we understand them as describing the dynamics of the *average* population density with respect to a certain probability distribution. I will illustrate this in the particularly simple case of exponential growth

$$dN/dt = rN \qquad (2.27)$$

Consider a population of individuals in an area A of space. Let $P_n(t)$, where $n = 0, 1, 2, \ldots$, be the probability that there are n individuals in the population at time t. Describing the states of a population with a probability distribution in this way takes into account both the discrete nature of the population and the stochastic nature of the processes underlying population growth.

This approach to population growth goes back to work by McKendrick (1914) and Yule (1924); a more recent, standard reference is Feller (1968).

Assume that in each infinitesimal time interval δt there is a probability b δt per individual in the population that a new individual will be born, and a probability $d\,\delta t$ per individual in the population that an individual will die. The per capita birth and death rates b and d are functions of the number n of individuals, and of time t.

Suppose the population size at some time t is n. What will it be after a small increment δt in time? Call births and deaths "events." Then the population size at the later time $t + \delta t$ depends on which events occur during the small time interval δt. Namely:

$$P_{n+1}(t + \delta t) = \text{probability(population size} = n + 1 \text{ at time } t + \delta t)$$

$$= \text{probability[a birth in the time interval } (t,\ t + \delta t)]$$

$$= bn\,\delta t$$

$$P_{n-1}(t + \delta t) = \text{probability(population size} = n - 1 \text{ at time } t + \delta t)$$

$$= \text{probability[a death in the time interval } (t,\ t + \delta t)]$$

$$= dn\,\delta t$$

$$P_n(t + \delta t) = \text{probability(population size} = n \text{ at time } t + \delta t)$$

$$= \text{probability(neither of the preceding)}$$

$$= 1 - (b + d)n\,\delta t$$

for δt sufficiently small. Also, for δt sufficiently small the probability that we will have more than one event will be negligible compared with the above probabilities for one event. We are soon going to take the limit $\delta t \to 0$, so we can be confident that δt is indeed sufficiently small.

Now let us turn this around and ask, for given n, what is the probability $P_n(t + \delta t)$ that the population size will be n at time $t + \delta t$? According to the analysis we have just done, there are three circumstances that could result in a population size n at time $t + \delta t$: either (1) the population size was $n - 1$ at time t and there was a birth in the time interval $(t,\ t + \delta t)$, or (2) the population size was $n + 1$ at time t and there was a death in the interval $(t,\ t + \delta t)$, or (3) the population size was n at time t and there was neither a birth nor a death in the interval $(t,\ t + \delta t)$. Each of the three circumstances is itself a conjunction of two independent events; therefore, the probability of each circumstance is the product of the probabilities of those two independent events:

$$\text{Probability[circumstance (1)]} = P_{n-1}(t)b(n - 1)\delta t$$

$$\text{Probability[circumstance (2)]} = P_{n+1}(t)d(n + 1)\delta t$$

$$\text{Probability[circumstance (3)]} = P_n(t)[1 - (b + d)n]\delta t$$

where we have used our earlier calculations for the probabilities of various events in the interval $(t,\ t + \delta t)$.

   The probability that the population size is n at time $t + \delta t$ is the probability for some one of these (mutually exclusive) circumstances to occur, which is the sum of the three probabilities:

$$P_n(t + \delta t) = P_{n-1}(t)b(n - 1)\delta t + P_{n+1}(t)d(n + 1)\delta t$$
$$+ P_n(t)[1 - (b + d)n\ \delta t].$$

   Therefore

$$[P_n(t + \delta t) - P_n(t)]/\delta t = P_{n-1}(t)b(n - 1)$$
$$+ P_{n+1}(t)d(n + 1) - P_n(t)(b + d)n$$

Now take the limit $\delta t \to 0$. Then the left-hand side is nothing other than the derivative $(dP_n/dt)(t)$. So

$$dP_n/dt = P_{n-1}b(n - 1) + P_{n+1}d(n + 1) - P_n(b + d)n \qquad (2.28)$$

Equation (2.28)—which is really a set of infinitely many equations, one for each nonnegative integer n—gives the dynamics of discrete, stochastic population growth, as conceived of in the two paragraphs following equation (2.27).

   Let us consider now the particular case of constant per capita birth and death rates: assume b and d constant.

   The mean population size at any time t is

$$m(t) = \sum_{n=0}^{\infty} nP_n(t) \qquad (2.29)$$

and from (2.28)

$$dm/dt = \sum_{n=0}^{\infty} ndP_n/dt$$

$$= \sum_{n=0}^{\infty} n[P_{n-1}b(n - 1) + P_{n+1}d(n + 1) - P_n(b + d)n] \qquad (2.30)$$

Consider the term

$$\sum_{n=0}^{\infty} nP_{n-1}b(n - 1)$$

If we define a new summation variable $q = n - 1$, we can write this sum as

$$\sum_{q=-1}^{\infty} (q + 1)P_q bq = \sum_{q=0}^{\infty} (q + 1)P_q bq$$

since the term with $q = -1$ is anyway equal to zero. In this last sum we can replace the name q by n to get

$$\sum_{n=0}^{\infty} (n + 1)P_n bn \qquad (2.31)$$

We can do a similar transformation on the second term of the sum:

$$\sum_{n=0}^{\infty} n P_{n+1} d(n+1) = \sum_{n=0}^{\infty} (n-1) P_n dn \qquad (2.32)$$

Exercise 2.10. Prove (2.32).

Using (2.31) and (2.32) in (2.30), we get

$$dm/dt = \sum_{n=0}^{\infty} [(n+1) P_n bn + (n-1) P_n dn - n P_n (b+d) n]$$

$$= \sum_{n=0}^{\infty} (b-d) n P_n = (b-d) \sum_{n=0}^{\infty} n P_n$$

But remember (2.29); using it in this last equation, and setting $r = b - d$, we get

$$dm/dt = rm \qquad (2.33)$$

Recall that m is the mean total population size. We can convert this to a density if we divide by the total area A:

$$d(m/A)/dt = r(m/A)$$

This is identical with the usual equation (2.27) for continuous exponential growth of a population, if we identify the "density" N with the mean density m/A, in the precise sense of equation (2.29). This demonstrates that, at least in the case of exponential growth, the use of a deterministic, differential equation to describe the underlying stochastic and discrete processes of population growth has a rigorous foundation.

Density-dependent models such as the logistic (2.1) or the other models we have studied in this chapter also can be formulated in terms of underlying stochastic models, though these can be very difficult to work with (for some details, see Ludwig 1974, Nisbet and Gurney 1982). But still the basic point remains that what is intended by density N in these models is mean density in the sense of (2.29), for some appropriate distribution $\{P_n\}$.

Of course, the full stochastic theory (2.28) contains a lot more information than just the mean. Are we losing anything essential if we look *only* at the mean? Obviously I think the answer is that *for the most part* we don't lose anything essential, or else it would have been pretty silly of me to spend so much time in this chapter looking just at means. Now all I have to do is to convince you of this, and to explain what I have in mind with the qualifier "for the most part."

First, let us investigate the coefficient of variation s/m, where s^2 is the variance of the distribution $\{P_n\}$:

$$s^2 = \sum_{n=0}^{\infty} n^2 P_n - m^2$$

The coefficient of variation is a measure of how much the actual individual populations are expected to fluctuate around the mean.

Proceeding exactly as we did in going from (2.30) to (2.33), we can show that if

$$Q = \sum_{n=0}^{\infty} n^2 P_n$$

then

$$dQ/dt - 2rQ = (b + d)m \qquad (2.34)$$

Exercise 2.11. Prove (2.34).

To solve (2.34), we use an *integrating factor*. That is, we seek a function $f(t)$ such that

$$[d(Qf)/dt]/f = dQ/dt - 2rQ$$

Expanding the left-hand side, we want

$$[f\, dQ/dt + Q\, df/dt]/f = dQ/dt + [(df/dt)/f]Q = dQ/dt - 2rQ$$

so we want

$$(df/dt)/f = -2r \qquad (2.35)$$

Thinking through the list of elementary derivatives, one realizes that

$$f = e^{-2rt}$$

satisfies this. [Alternatively, you could rewrite (2.35) as $df/f = -2r\, dt$ and integrate both sides to get the same answer.]

Therefore, we can write (2.34) as

$$d(e^{-2rt}Q)/dt = e^{-2rt}(b + d)m$$

Consider a population that begins with exactly n_0 individuals at time 0. Then from (2.33)

$$m = n_0 e^{rt}$$

So

$$d(e^{-2rt}Q)/dt = n_0(b + d)e^{-rt}$$

Hence (taking the indefinite integral of the right-hand side)

$$e^{-2rt}Q = n_0(b + d)(C - e^{-rt}/r)$$

where C is a constant of integration. Therefore

$$Q = n_0 e^{2rt}\{D - [(b + d)/r]e^{-rt}\} \qquad (2.36)$$

where $D = C/(b + d)$ is a constant.

The variance s^2 is

$$s^2 = Q - m^2 = n_0 e^{2rt}\{(D - 1) - [(b + d)/r]e^{-rt}\}$$

We are considering a population that began with exactly n_0 individuals at time 0. So $s^2(t = 0) = 0$, which fixes D in the preceding equation, resulting in

$$s^2 = n_0 e^{2rt}[(b + d)/r](1 - e^{-rt}) \tag{2.37}$$

Therefore, the coefficient of variation is

$$s/m = [(b + d)(1 - e^{-rt})/n_0 r]^{1/2} \tag{2.38}$$

The coefficient of variation is always finite, even though both the mean and the variance grow without bound, and it is proportional to $n_0^{-1/2}$. Unless the population starts out at an extremely small value n_0, the coefficient of variation will always be small.

Small population sizes are associated with large coefficients of variation. These large coefficients of variation come about mainly because the probability for a population to go extinct becomes significant. Averaging over many populations, some growing without bound and some going extinct, will result in a large variance even if each individual population does not fluctuate all that much.

To verify this, let us calculate the probability X_n for a population that has n individuals at some time to eventually go extinct. Consider the first change in this population's size: it comes about either from a birth [with probability $b/(b + d)$] or from a death [with probability $d/(b + d)$], resulting in an extinction probability from then on of X_{n+1} or X_{n-1}, respectively. Therefore

$$X_n = X_{n+1} b/(b + d) + X_{n-1} d/(b + d) \tag{2.39}$$

Of course

$$X_0 = 1 \tag{2.40}$$

a population that has $n = 0$ at some time is sure to go extinct. As well, it must be that a population that grows without bound never goes extinct:

$$\lim_{n \to \infty} X_n = 0 \tag{2.41}$$

Equation (2.39) is a difference equation (since it relates X_n, X_{n+1}, and X_{n-1}), it is linear in the X's, and it has constant coefficients multiplying the X's: it is a linear difference equation with constant coefficients. This type of equation can always by solved by exponentiating appropriate constants. That is, try the solution

$$X_n = a^n \tag{2.42}$$

for some a. If you substitute (2.42) into (2.39), you will get a quadratic equation for a whose two roots are 1 and d/b.

Exercise 2.12. Prove the preceding sentence true.

Therefore, two solutions of (2.39) are $X_n = 1$ and $X_n = (d/b)^n$. Since (2.39) is linear, any linear combination of solutions is also a solution, so if A and B are any two constants,

$$X_n = A + B(d/b)^n \qquad (2.43)$$

solves (2.39). In fact, *any* solution must be of this form, for if we know X_0 and X_1, then we can generate all the other X's one at a time using (2.39), and we could get anything we wanted for X_0 and X_1 by choosing A and B appropriately in (2.43).

As it happens, we have instead the two *boundary conditions* (2.40) and (2.41). Applying these two conditions to (2.43) yields immediately

$$X_n = (d/b)^n \qquad (2.44)$$

Now, $d/b < 1$. [Otherwise we have exponentially *declining* populations, and of course all of these go extinct, so the boundary condition (2.41) does not apply.] Hence the extinction probability X_n will decline very rapidly as n increases. This reinforces the indication we got from the coefficient of variation that the deterministic solutions are good approximations unless population sizes get too small. It also shows that the large coefficients of variation associated with very small populations come about largely because a significant fraction of individual populations are going extinct.

We can conclude that *for the most part the deterministic mean density N of our differential equation model (2.27) is a good approximation. "For the most part" means: unless the density becomes very small.*

Similar results are obtained for logistic growth (Ludwig 1974, Nisbet and Gurney 1982), and it is clear that they extend to rather general models.

2.6 DENSITY DEPENDENCE, DENSITY VAGUENESS, AND "REAL BIOLOGY"

We have done much in this chapter on the basis of deterministic dynamics of the form (2.2). I think it is honest to acknowledge that many observationally oriented ecologists are uncomfortable with this kind of deterministic thinking. In the "real" systems they work with, they see a lot of seeming indeterminacy. How does that relate to the theorist's tidy determinism?

For instance, at the end of Section 2.1 I drew some nice-looking curves to represent density-dependent natality and mortality. Figure 2.11 gives the mortality (expressed as a "k-value", i.e., $\log_{10}(N_t/N_s)$, where N_t and N_s are the numbers entering and surviving the instar III stage) of late-instar nymphs of the bug *Leptoterna dolobrata* vs. density. It will be seen that, while there is a clear *trend* in the relationship, there is also a lot of scatter around the trend.

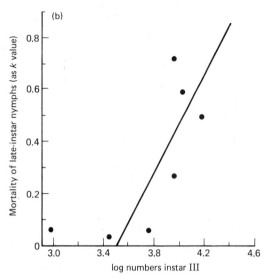

Figure 2.11 Mortality of late-instar nymphs of *Leptoterna dolobrata* vs. density. (From McNeill 1973.)

The trend is the theorist's idealized "density dependence"; the scatter is what Strong (1983), who has forcefully and cogently revived these age-old issues, calls "density vagueness."

Density vagueness can have many sources, which fall basically into two categories: extrinsic and intrinsic.

Vagueness is often caused by chance variations in some extrinsic factor. For instance, the scatter in the above graph is thought to be due primarily to variations in temperature. As I have tried to indicate in Section 2.4, extrinsically driven random variation can indeed have profound effects on population dynamics, but it also can merely have the effect of superimposing "noise" on an underlying deterministic "signal."

As well, there is demographic stochasticity: the intrinsic vagueness, due to the fundamentally probabilistic nature of population processes such as natality and mortality, which I discussed in Section 2.5. In normal, run-of-the-mill, reasonably large populations, the coefficient of variation associated with demographic stochasticity will be small and populations will fluctuate, not too violently, around tidy deterministic means.

However, demographic stochasticity will become important in any situation where population sizes become unusually small. This could happen in colonization, marginal environments, or overexploited populations, to name a few situations. For example, MacArthur and Wilson (1967) discuss demographic stochasticity in their classic work on colonization and extinction on islands. Unfortunately, the study of demographic stochasticity with density dependence is very complicated mathematically, so progress has been slow in these areas.

But the main point is, we have a pretty good idea of what are the situations where this source of density vagueness is likely to be of concern.

In a great many cases, density vagueness simply will not matter. We need to know how much vagueness in density relationships is enough to have significant population dynamical effects. The relationships are often tighter than the example at the beginning of this section, which was chosen from a group (insects) whose dynamics is notoriously density-vague (if not density-independent). Density vagueness may well be important for insects (Strong et al. 1984) and some other organisms (Strong 1985), but for the time being there is little reason to doubt that the idealization of density dependence is appropriate for many natural populations.

We should all keep our minds open to both possibilities. If this book emphasizes deterministic dynamics, it is because (1) while environmental and demographic stochasticity are exciting and lively current research topics in theoretical ecology, our understanding of deterministic dynamics is presently much more fully developed; (2) there is good reason to believe that deterministic dynamics is frequently, maybe even very frequently, a sensible approximation, in the way and for the reasons described above.

ADDITIONAL EXERCISES

2.13. Consider the functional response

$$F(N) = EN/(N_0 + N)$$

Analyze it along the lines of Exercise 2.1. What is its Holling type?

2.14. Analyze the model

$$dN/dt = rN(1 - N/K) - EHN/(N_0 + N)$$

along the lines of Section 2.2.1. Contrast the conclusions arrived at from this model with those arrived at from equation (2.6).

2.15. Consider a parasite whose transmission dynamics is exactly like the transmission dynamics of schistosomiasis, but which causes mortality in its definitive host, this mortality being proportional to the worm load. Imagine that the definitive host population N_1 grows exponentially in the absence of parasites, so that the host dynamics is given by

$$dN_1/dt = rN_1 - q_3 m$$

where m is the mean worm load and q_3 is a constant. The set of three equations consisting of the above, (2.11), and (2.14) summarize the host-parasite interaction. Keep in mind that h_2 in (2.11) involves N_1, which is now no longer a given constant. As well, P_1 in (2.14) will depend on N_1: assume $P_1 = kN_1$, with k = constant. Use the above equation to eliminate N_1 from the new versions of (2.11) and (2.14), and analyze these equations along the lines of Section 2.2.3. Do you still get a threshold behavior? What are the critical parameters that determine whether or not there is a positive equilibrium mean worm load m?

2.16. Simulate the stochastic exponential model of Section 2.5 on a computer. Compare the simulated population growth with the predicted exponential mean $m(t)$. Do this for a selection of initial population sizes n_0 which correspond to a wide range of predicted coefficients of variation s/m.

Chapter 3

Discrete Time

Section 2.5 shows that continuous-time, differential-equation models provide sensible approximations to the discrete and stochastic process of population growth, at least for constant per capita birth and death rates b and d. What about more general forms of these functions?

As mentioned in Section 2.5, b and d will generally be functions of population size n and time t. The general conditions that these functions need to satisfy in order for a differential equation to be a good approximation to the full stochastic model have yet to be formulated. Basically, it's plausible that differential equations will make sense when the functions $b(n, t)$ and $d(n, t)$ are in some sense "sufficiently smooth."

In think the per capita death rate d will quite frequently be "sufficiently smooth." But I am less confident about the per capita birth rate b. There is one quite common circumstance under which this function is decidedly "rough," namely, seasonal breeding. An organism that reproduces only at a certain time of year, for example, has a per capita birth rate that is zero most of the year and is nonzero for a relatively short time. One could incorporate this sort of thing into the formalism of Section 2.5, but the formalism would become rather forced, the mathematics would be awfully messy, and it is really just not a very natural way to proceed.

A more natural thing to do here is to accept that births come in truly discrete pulses, and to take as one's dynamical variable the density just after, or perhaps just before (whichever is more convenient with respect to the particularities of the biology) each breeding occasion. Then density is a real-valued function N_t of a *discrete* variable t, where the discrete index $t = 0, 1, 2, \ldots$ labels the different breeding seasons. One is measuring time in whole-number multiples of some basic time interval Δt: the integer label t for a time means t times the basic interval Δt. As for the basic time interval itself, it can be anything that is appropriate to the problem at hand; it might be a year, or it could be any other interval of time.

51

In this framework, the simplest form of dynamical law corresponding to equation (2.2) will be a *difference equation*

$$N_{t+1} = F(N_t) \qquad t = 0, 1, 2, \ldots \tag{3.1}$$

relating the density at each breeding season to the density at the previous breeding season through some function F.

Seasonal migration could also make a discrete-time model desirable; for that matter, though I don't know offhand of an example, I have no doubt that mortality is sometimes also sufficiently sharply pulsed to call for a discrete-time model. As well, one might sometimes want to represent a basically continuous dynamics in discrete form, for instance, if one is sampling a population at discrete intervals. I will say more about the relation between continuous and discrete models in Section 3.5.

3.1 STOCK-RECRUITMENT MODELS

A classic example of this kind of model is the *stock-recruitment* model that is used by fisheries managers. "Stock" refers to adult fish. I will denote the stock at time t by N_t. "Recruits" are new additions to the parental stock from previous reproduction. I will denote the number of recruits at time t by R_t. Then one assumes (not entirely without justification: Cushing 1971, Cushing and Harris 1973) that there is a well-defined relationship between this year's recruits and last year's parental stock. In mathematical language, one assumes that $R_{t+1} = R(N_t)$, which simply says that R_{t+1} is a function of N_t.

Let S be the probability for an adult to survive from one breeding season to the next. Then the parental stock at time $t + 1$ will consist of recruitment from the previous breeding, plus surviving adults:

$$N_{t+1} = R(N_t) + SN_t \tag{3.2}$$

In case $S = 0$ we have simply

$$N_{t+1} = R(N_t) \tag{3.3}$$

We can see how stock-recruitment relations come out of the underlying biology if we analyze larval mortality from one breeding season to the next using simple continuous-time models. Let $L(t)$ be the number of larvae. (I will talk about larvae here, but of course these ideas extend beyond fishes, so these "larvae" could be other sorts of juveniles as well.) Let continuous time $t = 0$ correspond to a breeding occasion. Then continuous time $t = \Delta t$ will be the next breeding occasion. So in the continuous-time function $L(t)$, $L(0)$ is the number of larvae produced by the parental stock and $L(\Delta t)$ is the number of recruits. If each parent produces b offspring (assumed constant), then

$$L(0) = bN \tag{3.4}$$

where N is the parental stock. Thus the relationship between $L(\Delta t)$ and $L(0)$ is, through (3.4), the stock-recruitment relation. To get it, we need a model for larval mortality.

One commonly used model for larval mortality is due to Beverton and Holt (1957) and looks like this:

$$(dL/dt)/L = -(m_1 + m_2 L) \tag{3.5}$$

The left-hand side here is the per capita rate of increase, so the right-hand side is the negative of the per capita death rate. There is an extrinsic component of mortality m_1, and a component $m_2 L$ which increases as larval density increases.

If we write (3.5) as

$$dL/[L(m_1 + m_2 L)] = -dt$$

we can integrate it using indefinite integrals:

$$-\{\ln[(m_1 + m_2 L)/L]\}/m_1 = -t + C$$

where C is a constant of integration. Therefore

$$(m_1 + m_2 L)/L = e^{m_1(t-C)} \tag{3.6}$$

Taking $t = 0$ in (3.6),

$$[m_1 + m_2 L(0)]/L(0) = e^{-m_1 C}$$

which determines the constant of integration C in terms of $L(0)$. From (3.4), this is

$$e^{-m_1 C} = (m_1 + m_2 bN)/bN \tag{3.7}$$

Recruitment R is $L(\Delta t)$. If we take $t = \Delta t$ in (3.6) and solve for $L(\Delta t)$ using (3.7), we get

$$R(N) = c_1 N/(1 + c_2 N) \tag{3.8}$$

where c_1 and c_2 are positive constants:

$$c_1 = be^{-m_1 \Delta t} \qquad c_2 = (1 - e^{-m_1 \Delta t})bm_2/m_1 \tag{3.9}$$

Exercise 3.1. Prove (3.8) and (3.9).

Equation (3.8) is the Beverton-Holt stock-recruitment relation. In this relation, recruitment increases monotonically from zero, with the rate of increase slowing down the larger N is. Recruitment approaches the finite value c_1/c_2 in the limit as stock approaches infinity, and it is equal to stock when $N = (c_1 - 1)/c_2$:

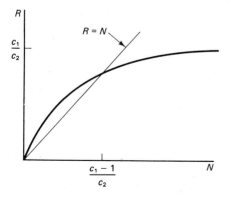

When the stock-recruitment relation increases monotonically with ever-decreasing slope, such as the above, this is called *normal compensation* (Clark 1976).

Another commonly used stock-recruitment relation is that of Ricker (1954, 1958). This relation is based on the well-known circumstance that predation in aquatic environments tends to be almost purely size-selective; thus many fishes inadvertently cannibalize their own eggs and larvae. This can be expressed by replacing equation (3.5) for the larval mortality with

$$(dL/dt)/L = -[k_1(t)N + k_2(t)]$$

Here the per capita mortality rate of larvae consists of a component due to predation from the parental stock, which is taken proportional to the size of the parental stock, $k_1(t)N$; and a component from other sources, $k_2(t)$. Ricker allows for the possibility that the intensities k_1 and k_2 of the two mortality factors may vary through the year. However, he does not allow for parental mortality through the year; such an allowance would make the expression for cannibalistic mortality more complex than $k_1 N$.

We can integrate this equation by writing it as

$$dL/L = -[k_1(t)N + k_2(t)]dt$$

whence

$$\ln[L(\Delta t)/L(0)] = -d_1 N - d_2$$

where

$$d_1 = \int_0^{\Delta t} k_1(t)dt$$

$$d_2 = \int_0^{\Delta t} k_2(t)dt$$

Therefore

$$L(\Delta t) = L(0)e^{-d_1 N - d_2}$$

But $L(\Delta t) = R$, recruitment at the next breeding season, and from (3.4), $L(0) = bN$. So

$$R(N) = Ne^{r(1 - N/K)} \tag{3.10}$$

where

$$r = \ln(b) - d_2 \qquad K = d_1/[\ln(b) - d_2]$$

Equation (3.10) is the Ricker form for the stock-recruitment relation. We will study this function in some considerable detail in Section 3.3. For now, let us just note that rather than increasing monotonically like the Beverton-Holt form, the Ricker stock-recruitment relation has a peak:

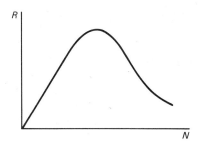

This kind of "peaked" form is called *overcompensation* (Clark 1976).

As we have seen, one mechanism that can lead to overcompensation is cannibalism of juveniles by adult fish. Of course, we can extend the concepts of stock and recruitment to other taxa besides fish. Then we might expect that any situation in which juveniles are hindered by adults will lead to overcompensation. For instance, particularly in the absence of parental care, juveniles will often have to compete with adults for food or other requisites, and in such cases the juveniles will often be at a disadvantage.

The simplest difference-equation models are those in which adults breed only once [equation (3.3)]. Then the stock-recruitment relation tells the whole story; the growth function F of equation (3.1) is just the recruitment function R:

$$N_{t+1} = F(N_t) = R(N_t)$$

For instance, using the Beverton-Holt form in this way, we get

$$F(N) = c_1 N/(1 + c_2 N) \tag{3.11}$$

and using the Ricker form gives

$$F(N) = Ne^{r(1-N/K)} \tag{3.12}$$

We have seen that certain specific density-dependent processes in recruitment can lead to growth rates like (3.11) or (3.12). But I do not want to leave the impression that these growth rate forms are tied to the particular mechanisms I have used to motivate them. For instance, density-dependent adult mortality might very well give rise to the same or very similar growth rates. I pointed out in Section 2.1 that many different biological processes can produce logistic-type population growth (or even precisely logistic growth). The same is true here: equations (3.11) and (3.12) ought really to be thought of as archetypal forms, like the familiar continuous-time logistic, which will tend to result from a diversity of underlying biological causes.

3.2 FIRST TRY AT A QUALITATIVE THEORY OF DIFFERENCE EQUATIONS

In Section 2.1 we had no difficulty whatsoever in formulating a tidy and complete qualitative theory for simple differential equations of the form (2.2). Will it be just as easy to do this for the (even simpler) difference equations of the form

(3.1)? As it turns out, the answer is: no! The behavior of difference equations is much more complicated.

To be sure, the five "parts" of our qualitative theory in Section 2.1 can easily be extended to difference equations, and we can even add to them an interesting sixth part. But the whole story of difference equations is more than the sum of these parts.

First, the parts. In this section, assume that $F(N)$ is a continuous function of N, with continuous first derivative.

1. If N_t lies in a region of the N-axis where $F(N) > N$, so that the graph of F in this region lies above the straight line through the origin with slope = 1, then N will increase in the next basic time period (that is, $N_{t+1} > N_t$)

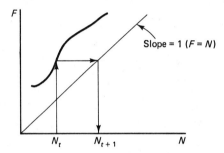

Notice how we obtain N_{t+1} graphically from N_t by following the arrows in the above graph.

2. If N_t lies in a region of the N-axis where $F(N) < N$, and the graph of F in this region is below the slope = 1 line, then N will decrease in the next basic time period (that is, $N_{t+1} < N_t$)

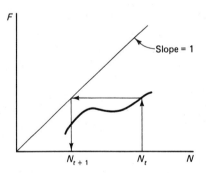

3. If $F(N_e) = N_e$ for some density N_e, then the value N_e of the density is called an *equilibrium value*. If N has initially the value N_e, then it will remain constant [since $N_{t+1} = F(N_t) = F(N_e) = N_e$] until it is displaced away from this value by some external influence. An equilibrium is almost always a point at which the curve $F(N)$ crosses the straight line through the origin having slope 1.

4. Let

$$\lambda = \frac{dF}{dN}\bigg|_{N_e} \tag{3.13}$$

This is the slope of the curve $F(N)$ at an equilibrium N_e. In the continuous case the sign of a corresponding slope determined local stability of equilibria (Section 2.1). In the discrete case, the *magnitude* of this slope is the crucial thing.

In particular, suppose the absolute value of λ is less than 1:

$$|\lambda| < 1 \qquad (3.14)$$

Then the equilibrium is *locally stable,* in precisely the same sense that this term was used in Section 2.1: if the density is displaced away from equilibrium by a sufficiently small amount, it will subsequently return to equilibrium.

For a locally stable equilibrium of a one-dimensional *differential* equation, the return to equilibrium after a small disturbance is always *monotonic:* as time increases the density steadily gets closer and closer to its equilibrium value. In the present context, this same behavior is seen when (3.14) holds, and when in addition $\lambda > 0$:

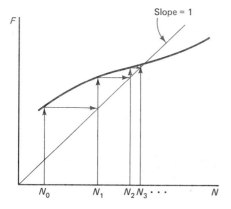

Notice in this picture how I have abbreviated the sequence of going from N_0 to N_1 to N_2 and so on by skipping the intermediate steps in which first N_0, then N_1, and so on, is brought back down to the N-axis (as was done in the preceding two graphs). Without this abbreviation, the above graph would have looked like this:

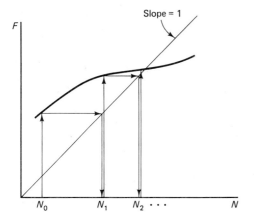

except that the two vertical arrows I have drawn "at" N_1, and the two I have drawn "at" N_2, would really overlap. The abbreviated form is easier to look at, and I will use it from now on.

Now, getting back to our discussion of stability: if together with (3.14) we have $\lambda < 0$, then the return to equilibrium takes the form of *damped oscillations*

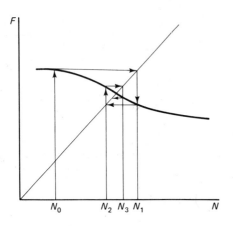

5. If

$$|\lambda| > 1 \qquad\qquad (3.15)$$

for some equilibrium, then that equilibrium is *locally unstable:* as in the continuous case discussed in Section 2.1, the density will tend to move farther away from such an equilibrium after the *slightest* initial disturbance. If $\lambda > 0$ together with (3.15), the density tends to move monotonically away from equilibrium, as in the continuous case:

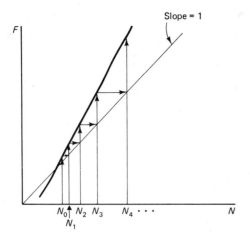

But if we have (3.15) and $\lambda < 0$, the local behavior of the density takes the form of *divergent oscillations:*

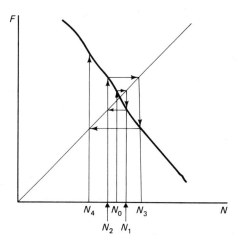

6. Notice that

$$N_{t+2} = F(N_{t+1}) = F(F(N_t)) = F^{(2)}(N_t)$$

in an obvious notation for the "composite function" $F(F(N))$. Similarly,

$$N_{t+3} = F(N_{t+2}) = F(F(F(N_t))) = F^{(3)}(N_t)$$

and, in general, by "composing" k times the function F we can calculate

$$N_{t+k} = F^{(k)}(N_t)$$

There are no quantities in the continuous theory of Chapter 2 that are analogous to the $F^{(k)}$.

These quantities are of great interest and utility, because of the following. Suppose there exists a value of N, call it N_c, such that

$$F^{(2)}(N_c) = N_c$$

and suppose further that at some time t we have $N_t = N_c$. Then

$$N_{t+2} = F^{(2)}(N_t) = F^{(2)}(N_c) = N_c = N_t$$

But that's not all. We have also

$$N_{t+4} = F^{(2)}(N_{t+2}) = F^{(2)}(N_c) = N_c = N_t$$

and I think it will be obvious to you that in a similar fashion we have

$$N_{t+2n} = N_c \qquad n = 1, 2, 3, \ldots$$

In words: every two basic time units, the density returns again to the value N_c. The system has a *cycle*, a *sustained oscillation*, whose *period* is equal to two basic time units. If we were to draw a line graph of N_t versus t, it might look something like this:

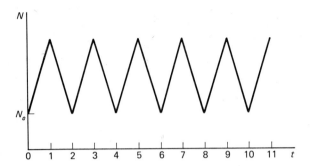

Reasoning in the same way, it is easy to see that, for any k, if there exists a value N_c such that $F^{(k)}(N_c) = N_c$, then there is a cycle with period equal to k basic time units:

$$N_{t+kn} = N_c \qquad n = 1, 2, 3, \ldots \tag{3.16}$$

(You should convince yourself of this.) Under these circumstances, we call N_c a *fixed point of period k*.

Suppose the density starts out at a value that is *near* a fixed point of period k. Will the density tend to move into the cyclic solution, or will it wander away from the cycle? This is a question of local stability, and it is easily answered on the basis of what we have already done.

The composite function $F^{(k)}$ defines a difference equation just like (3.1), except that it involves a basic time unit k times as long as the one we started out with:

$$N_{t+k} = F^{(k)}(N_t)$$

A fixed point of period k is just an ordinary everyday equilibrium of this difference equation. If that equilibrium is stable in the sense of (3.14) [where of course λ is calculated using $F^{(k)}$ in (3.13)], then the corresponding cyclic solution of the original equation, $N_{t+1} = F(N_t)$, is a *stable cycle* in the sense that if the density gets close to one of the values making up the cycle, then the density will tend to move into the cyclic solution. Otherwise the cycle is an unstable one.

So discrete-time models have a lot more oscillations than do continuous-time models—basically because they contain a built-in time delay in the influence of density on population growth. There are damped or divergent oscillations associated with equilibria, and there are also the sustained oscillations associated with fixed points of period $k > 1$. (Of course, a fixed point of period 1 is just an equilibrium point.)

We have, then, what appear to be the elements of a nice simple qualitative theory of difference equations. Why is it not straightforward to assemble these elements into a coherent theory, as we did for differential equations? Well, sometimes it *is* straightforward. For example, consider the Beverton-Holt growth function (3.11). Because of the monotonic increase of this function, the density approaches the equilibrium at $N = (c_1 - 1)/c_2$ monotonically, no matter what the initial value of density:

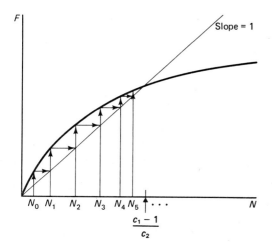

In fact, this is exactly the same qualitative behavior that we see in the solutions of the logistic differential equation.

But what about a growth curve with overcompensation, such as the Ricker form (3.12)? Suppose the density starts out with some value N_0 in the interval $(0, K)$. What can we say about the future history of the density?

Since $F(N) > N$ for all values of N in the interval $(0, K)$, we know that in the next time interval the density will jump to some value that is higher than the initial value N_0. For instance, if N_0 is chosen as in the following diagram,

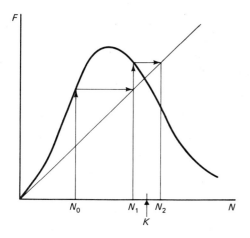

then in the next basic time unit the density will have the value N_1 shown in the diagram. It happens that $N_1 < K$. But it needn't have been. For instance, although $N_1 < K$, the next value N_2 taken on by the density is *greater* than K. In its next step, it must jump to a smaller value [since $F(N_2) < N_2$], but in order to know whether this next value is going to be bigger or smaller than K we would have to laboriously check the result for just the right value N_2 of density.

Thus, while our local bits of information numbered 1 to 5 above tell us in which direction the system will jump in any given step, it is harder than it was in the continuous-time case to put together all these possible individual jumps to get a total picture of the development of the system in time. Item 6 above, the possibility of cyclic solutions, is some help in sorting this out, as we will see in the following section; but there is still more to it than that (as we will also see in the following section).

3.3 A SECOND TRY: CHAOS

In this subsection we analyze more fully the difference equation (3.1)

$$N_{t+1} = F(N_t) \tag{3.1}$$

with the Ricker form (3.12)

$$F(N) = Ne^{r(1-N/K)} \tag{3.12}$$

for the growth function, following May and Oster (1976). I've already sketched the form of $F(N)$ in Section 3.1, and used this in Section 3.2, but it's worth recalling how one does go about sketching the form of an unfamiliar function.

The first question to ask is: For which values of its argument is the function zero? In the present instance, this question is easy to answer: $F(N)$ is zero when $N = 0$, and it approaches zero as a limit as N approaches infinity.

Next question: what is the sign of F? Answer: $F > 0$ for all N between 0 and infinity.

Since the straight line through the origin with unit slope plays such a central role in the graphical theory of difference equations, we ought to know also for which values of N the relation $F(N) = N$ is fulfilled. The answer is: $N = 0$ and $N = K$.

Exercise 3.2. Prove this.

Finally, we need to look for the extrema (maxima and minima) of F. Differentiating, we find that

$$dF/dN = (1 - rN/K)e^{r(1-N/K)} \tag{3.17}$$

This is zero when

$$N = N_m = K/r \qquad (3.18)$$

(It also approaches zero as N approaches infinity.) When $N < N_m$, $dF/dN > 0$; and when $N > N_m$, $dF/dN < 0$. Therefore, F has a maximum at N_m.

So F looks like this:

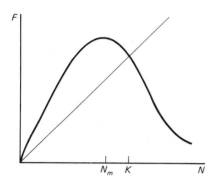

We will be interested only in values of r that are bigger than 1. This implies $N_m < K$, as in the above figure.

The equilibrium value of N, given by $F(N) = N$, is, of course, always $N = K$, no matter what the value of r. However, from (3.18) we see that N_m decreases monotonically as r increases. The maximum value of F is

$$F(N_m) = Ke^{r-1}/r \qquad (3.19)$$

Quite clearly this increases as r increases. Since F always crosses the line through the origin with unit slope at the same two places $N = 0$ and $N = K$, but the maximum value taken on by F between those two values increases as r increases, we may say that F becomes more *sharply peaked* as r increases.

Exercise 3.3. Prove (3.17), (3.18), and (3.19).

Local stability of the equilibrium at $N = K$ is determined by the condition (3.14). In the present case, the equilibrium is stable if $r < 2$ and it is unstable if $r > 2$ (with $\lambda = -1$ when $r = 2$).

Exercise 3.4. Prove the last sentence.

This is no surprise: we expect that the equilibrium will become unstable as we increase r, for as we increase r the function F becomes more sharply peaked, and the absolute value of its slope at the equilibrium becomes steeper, and we know that when this absolute value exceeds 1 the equilibrium will be unstable.

How does the density behave if $r > 2$ and there is no stable equilibrium? It cannot drop down to zero from any finite value, for there is no finite value N such that $F(N) = 0$. So it must be doing something else. What about those cyclic solutions associated with fixed points of period k, as in equation (3.16)?

Let's take a look at the function $F^{(2)}(N) = F[F(N)]$, and see whether we have cycles of period 2. We can construct this function graphically as follows. First, for any density N_t, we can map $F(N_t)$ from the vertical axis to the horizontal axis by using the line of unit slope, as we have been doing all along in this section:

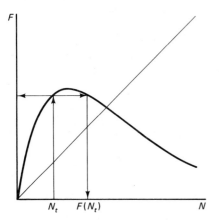

Then, from that value $F(N_t)$ on the horizontal axis, we can find $F(F(N_t)) = F^{(2)}(N_t)$ on the vertical axis, just by using F again:

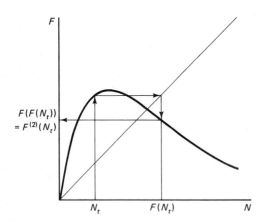

Now, we can extend the N- and F-axes through the origin, as well as the slope $= 1$ line, and we can draw in the slope $= -1$ line as well (as in the following graph). Having done that, we can duplicate any distance up from the origin along the F-axis [for example, $F(F(N_t))$] as a distance *down* from the origin along the F-axis, by bouncing it through each of the two 45-degree lines, like this:

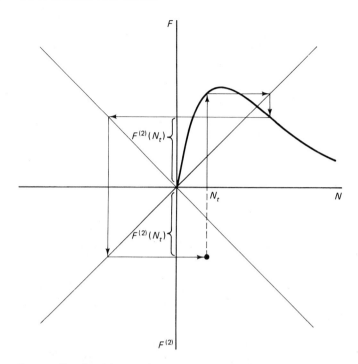

Proceeding in this way for each N on the (positive) horizontal axis, we can get the whole graph of $F^{(2)}$:

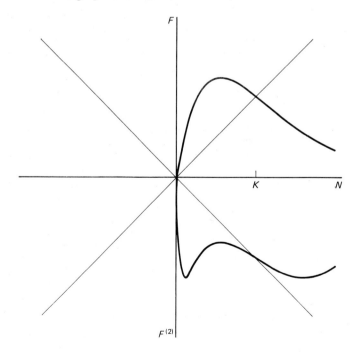

The resultant graph of $F^{(2)}$ is upside down, but that needn't trouble us.

Notice first of all that $F^{(2)}$ has two peaks. This is not a special property of the choice made here for r (which was $r = 1.8$); nor is it even a special property of the functional form (3.12). It is, rather, a very general property: $F^{(2)}$ will have two peaks for *any* F satisfying the following conditions: (1) F has a single peak, (2) $F(0) = 0$, (3) F approaches zero as N approaches infinity. The proof is easy: under these assumptions, there have to be *two* (and only two) N-values that both result in the maximum value (3.19) for $F^{(2)}$, as shown in the following graph:

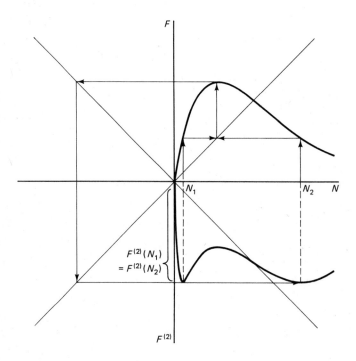

Now, let us inquire into the fixed points of $F^{(2)}$, those points where $F^{(2)}(N) = N$. Obviously, $N = K$ will be a fixed point of $F^{(2)}$, for $F^{(2)}(K) = F(F(K)) = F(K) = K$. What is the slope of $F^{(2)}$ (when plotted right side up) at this point? From the chain rule for derivatives,

$$dF^{(2)}/dN = F'(F(N))F'(N)$$

where ' means the derivative of a function with respect to its argument. Since $F(K) = K$, the slope of $F^{(2)}$ at $N = K$ is, then,

$$dF^{(2)}/dN\Big|_{N=K} = [F'(K)]^2 \qquad (3.20)$$

The right-hand side here is just the square of the slope of F at $N = K$. So *the absolute value of the slope of $F^{(2)}$ at $N = K$ is less than (or greater than) 1 exactly* *when the absolute value of the slope of F at N = K is less than (or greater than) 1.*

Now that we know generally what it looks like, from the previous graph, let's turn $F^{(2)}$ right side up. When $r < 2$, the absolute value of the slope of F at $N = K$ is less than 1, so the absolute value of the slope of $F^{(2)}$ at $N = K$ is also less than 1. So $F^{(2)}$ looks like this:

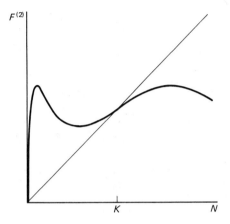

It only has the one fixed point at $N = K$. When $r = 2$, the absolute value of the slope of F at $N = K$ is equal to 1, so the absolute value of the slope of $F^{(2)}$ at $N = K$ is equal to 1. This makes $F^{(2)}$ tangent to the unit slope line at $N = K$, like this:

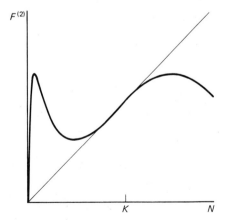

When $r > 2$, the slope of $F^{(2)}$ at $N = K$ is bigger than 1. In order for this to happen, two new fixed points of $F^{(2)}$ have to appear, as the "squiggle" in $F^{(2)}$ becomes more pronounced:

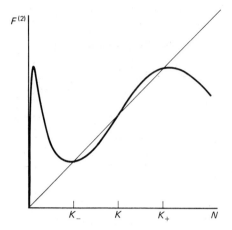

The fixed point at $N = K$ has to be unstable, since the slope there is bigger than 1. But if r is only slightly bigger than 2, the other two fixed points, at $N = K_-$ and $N = K_+$, will be stable since the absolute value of the slope of $F^{(2)}$ will be less than 1 at those points, as I hope will be geometrically obvious to you if you think about the preceding graph and the "squiggling" process that leads up to it.

As we know from Section 3.2, these two stable fixed points of period 2 correspond to a stable, periodic solution, with period 2, of the original difference equation $N_{t+1} = F(N_t)$: the density will tend to approach the condition of oscillating back and forth between K_- and K_+.

To summarize our story thus far: as r increases through the value 2, the stable fixed point $N = K$ of period 1 of F becomes unstable but is replaced by two stable fixed points $N = K_-$ and $N = K_+$ of period 2. One can think of the stable fixed point of period 1 as "splitting" into the pair of stable fixed points of period 2, for K_- and K_+ grow out from the value K as r increases through the value 2: if we plot the values of N corresponding to stable fixed points of F vs. r, we get

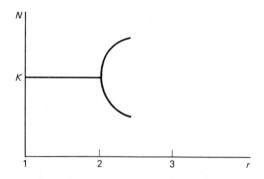

Here the lower branch corresponds to $N = K_-$, the upper branch to $N = K_+$. This kind of phenomenon is called a *bifurcation*.

Instead of talking about fixed points, we can talk about the corresponding

solutions of (3.1) and (3.12): as r increases through the value 2, the stable equilibrium at $N = K$ bifurcates into a stable cycle of period 2.

What happens as we increase r still further? I will describe what happens but will no longer try to sketch the proof of it, as I have been doing thus far. More details, and further references, can be found in the papers by May (1975, 1976, 1981), May and Oster (1976), Guckenheimer et al. (1977), and Guckenheimer (1979).

As r increases and the squiggles in $F^{(2)}$ become more pronounced, the peaks in $F^{(2)}$ will be getting steeper, so that eventually its equilibria will all be unstable, and the stable cycle of period 2 will become unstable. When this happens [at $r = 2.526$ for the growth curve (3.12)], each of the two stable fixed points of $F^{(2)}$ bifurcates into a pair of fixed points of $F^{(4)}$, and all four of these fixed points of $F^{(4)}$ are stable. So the original system has a stable cycle of period 4, as well as unstable cycles of periods 1 and 2.

As r increases still further, we run through a whole infinite sequence of such bifurcations, thus through an infinite sequence of stable cycles of period 2^n of the original system:

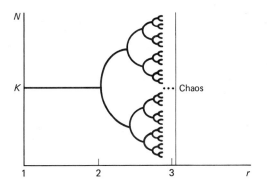

In this diagram, a vertical line drawn at any value of r that is less than r_c intersects the depicted curve at 2^n points, where n depends on the chosen value of r. The values of N on the vertical axis corresponding to these 2^n points are the 2^n values of N through which the density repeatedly moves in the stable cyclic solution of period 2^n. Any other solution will approach the stable cycle asymptotically: in the language of Section 2.1, the domain of attraction of the stable cycle is the set of all N-values greater than 0.

The system runs through this whole infinite sequence of bifurcations in a finite range of values for r, up to a limiting value r_c [=3.102 for the growth function (3.12)]. If $r > r_c$, the system behaves rather amazingly.

It has an infinite number of different cyclic solutions, one for each integral period, but only one of them is stable at each value of $r > r_c$. But that is not the amazing part. The amazing part is that, while most initial values for the density lead to solutions that approach the stable cycle, there are also (infinitely many) initial values that lead to solutions that do not ever settle into an equilibrium, or a cycle, or any other familiar asymptotic behavior.

In these solutions, the density is never greater than N_m or less than $F(N_m)$. Within these bounds, the density seemingly just wanders around, in a way that sometimes looks remarkably like random noise, even though it is obeying the completely deterministic dynamical law (3.1), (3.12)! This kind of behavior is called *chaos*.

For instance, Fig. 3.1 shows some actual solutions of (3.1), (3.12), worked out numerically on a computer by May (1981). In this figure, r increases from bottom to top. Solution (a), with $r < 2$, approaches a stable equilibrium. Solution (b), with r just above 2, has a stable cycle of period 2. Solution (c) shows a stable cycle of period 4. The top three solutions, with $r > 3.102$, are chaotic.

Like random noise, chaotic solutions do not have any *strict* periodicities,

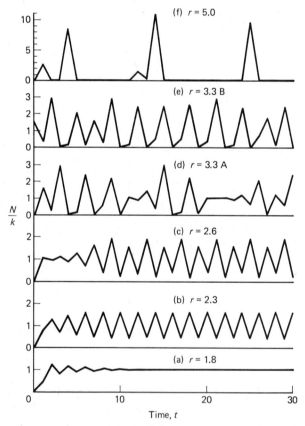

Figure 3.1 The spectrum of dynamical behavior of the population density, N_t/K, as a function of time, t, as described by the difference equations (3.1), (3.12), for various values of r. Specifically: (a) $r = 1.8$, stable equilibrium point; (b) $r = 2.3$, stable two-point cycle; (c) $r = 2.6$, stable four-point cycle; (d to f) in the chaotic regime, where the detailed character of the solution depends on the initial population value, with (d) $r = 3.3$ ($N_0/K = 0.075$), (e) $r = 3.3$ ($N_0/K = 1.5$), (f) $r = 5.0$ ($N_0/K = 0.002$). (From May 1981.)

but they do have certain probabilistic regularities that may be quite useful for biology. For instance, as we move well into the chaotic regime (r well above r_c), the chaotic solutions tend to take the form of long stretches of time during which the density is very low, with occasional sudden eruptions to large density and crashes back to very low density. This can be seen in solution (f) above. As pointed out by May (1975), these eruptions tend to be approximately periodic. As r increases, the eruptions become larger each time, but more scarce.

The study of regularities within chaos is an active field of current research.

3.4 CHAOS AND BIOLOGY

We are conditioned to have certain expectations about how the world works. One of the most exciting aspects of mathematical theory is that it opens up a whole new universe of possibilities, *real* possibilities, beyond our mundane expectations. I've already indicated at the beginning of Section 2.2 how breakpoints and thresholds challenge our expectation that small causes ought to have small effects. Chaos is similarly mind-expanding.

We tend to expect that simple, deterministic processes ought to result in simple behavior. Chaos shows that extremely simple processes can lead to extremely complicated behavior. To put it another way: when we look at data with lots of "noise" in them, we tend to think that there must be some kind of random process at work, some kind of chance environmental fluctuations. Chaos shows that "noisy"-looking data can result from completely deterministic, and even very simple, processes.

If you think about that, I believe you will agree that chaos could have tremendous ramifications for our understanding of biological phenomena.

First, let's try to get some notion of what mathematical models tell us about how widespread chaos might be. I suggested in Section 3.1 that there are good reasons to believe that overcompensation will occur fairly commonly, which could (given high enough r's as well) lead to chaos. Alarmingly, chaos appears in population genetics models as well [Oster et al. 1976)]. Chaos is also seen in continuous-time models when more than two populations are present (Section 6.2). Chaos turns up in membrane physiology (Chay 1986), cell biology (Mackey et al. 1986), and neurophysiology (Rapp et al. 1986), to name but a few biological examples. We may note in passing that not only biological models, but also physical models, can exhibit chaos. For instance, certain chaotic solutions to the equations of fluid dynamics suggest that it might well be impossible to rigorously predict the weather (Lorenz 1963). Perhaps the most familiar example of chaotic dynamics is the dripping water faucet (Shaw 1985).

But do natural populations actually display chaotic dynamics?

One wants to analyze population-density time-series data in a way that emphasizes the particular regularities and irregularities of chaos. Early attempts at this (Hassel et al. 1976, Thomas et al. 1980) found scant evidence of chaos. More recently, a new method of analysis has been applied to putative multispecies chaos by Schaffer (1984, 1985, 1986) and Schaffer and Kot (1985a, 1985b,

1985c). I will say a little bit about the technique used by these investigators in Section 6.3.2, after we have made the aquaintance of multispecies chaos in Section 6.2. But for now, let me just mention that this work has revealed pretty clear evidence of chaos in small-mammal population dynamics, measles epidemics, and outbreaks of *Thrips imaginis*—the last of which has long been viewed as the definitive, classic example of density-independent, extrinsically driven population dynamics (Andrewartha and Birch 1954)!

Before we go on, I should mention to you one more important property of chaotic solutions: *unpredictability*. We would like to be able to use population models to predict what will happen in the future. A rather strong form of predictability would be: given the density at some time $t = 0$, what will its value be at some time in the future? Now, strictly speaking, chaotic solutions are predictable in this way, because they are the result of a completely deterministic dynamics, so the density at each later time is fixed once its value at time $t = 0$ is given. But these solutions have an extremely sensitive dependence on the initial value chosen for density. For instance, Fig. 3.2 gives $N(30)$ plotted vs. $N(0)$ for the model consisting of equations (3.1) and (3.12), with $r = 3.3$.

It will be seen that a very tiny change in $N(0)$ can result in a huge change in $N(30)$. Actually, this graph is an oversimplification. It is a line graph plotted for 768 (the horizontal resolution of my graphics) equally spaced values of N between 0 and 1. This loses a lot of fine structure. For instance, if we do the same thing with 768 values of N between 0.5 and 0.51, we get Fig. 3.3.

Now, in practice we can never know *exactly* what the density is at time $t = 0$. Normally this isn't a problem—small changes have small effects. But because chaotic solutions are so sensitive to small changes in the initial conditions, *in practice* they become unpredictable, at least if you want strong predictions

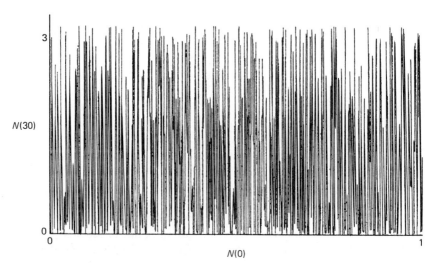

Figure 3.2 The density $N(30)$ after 30 time units as a function of the initial density $N(0)$, for a chaotic solution of equations (3.1), (3.12).

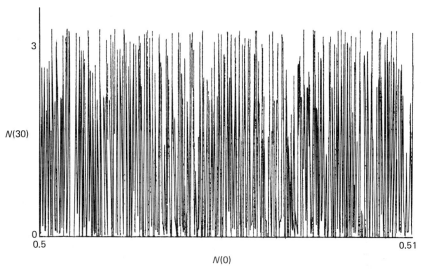

Figure 3.3 Same as Fig. 3.2, for a smaller range of initial densities $N(0)$.

like $N(30)$ in terms of $N(0)$. If all you know is that $N(0)$ lies in a certain small interval, then even if this interval is *quite* small, the resultant $N(30)$ could be just about anything (recall Fig. 3.3). In working with chaotic systems over the next few years, it will be important for us to understand what kind of predictions we can and what kind we can't sensibly expect to make.

3.5 HOMOLOGY

We can write the logistic differential equation (1.1) as

$$dN/N(1 - N/K) = r \, dt$$

which we can integrate from some initial time t_0 to an arbitrary later time t:

$$\int_{N(t_0)}^{N(t)} dN/N(1 - N/K) = \int_{t_0}^{t} r \, dt$$

Carrying out the integrations, one obtains

$$N(t) = K/\{1 - [1 - K/N(t_0)]e^{-r(t-t_0)}\} \qquad (3.21)$$

Exercise 3.5. Prove (3.21).

We can turn (3.21) into a difference equation by taking $t - t_0$ equal to one basic time unit. Thus the solutions of the difference equation

$$N_{t+1} = F(N_t) = K/[1 - (1 - K/N_t)e^{-r}]$$

are guaranteed to behave exactly like solutions of the continuous-time logistic.

It is a little tidier to write this growth function as

$$F(N) = \lambda N / [1 + (\lambda - 1)N/K] \tag{3.22}$$

where $\lambda = e^r$. In this form, we recognize it as our old friend the Beverton-Holt stock-recruitment model, equation (3.11), with $c_1 = \lambda$, $c_2 = (\lambda - 1)/K$.

The growth function (3.22) gives the unique difference equation which is *homologous* to the continuous-time logistic, in the sense of having the same solutions. Even apart from its incarnation as the Beverton-Holt model, it has been widely used in the ecological and genetic literature, particularly in the fifties and sixties.

Obviously, every differential equation of the form (2.2) has a unique homologous difference equation of the form (3.1), which corresponds simply to censusing the continuous population growth at discrete intervals. Is it true, conversely, that every single-species difference equation has a homologous single-species differential equation? Obviously, this cannot be the case. No single-species differential equation can be homologous to a difference equation that has chaotic solutions, for no single-species differential equation has chaotic solutions (recall Section 2.1).

3.6 ENVIRONMENTAL FLUCTUATIONS AND THE STORAGE EFFECT

The study of environmental fluctuations is much more straightforward for difference equations than it is for differential equations, so it will be worth our while to return briefly to that topic here. I will first discuss an analysis originally due to Lewontin and Cohen (1969).

Suppose

$$N_{t+1} = \lambda_t N_t \tag{3.23}$$

for some numbers λ_t. If these numbers were all the same, we would just have geometric growth. We can express environmental fluctuation by drawing the λ_t independently from some distribution.

If we start out at some initial density N_0, then

$$N_1 = \lambda_1 N_0$$

$$N_2 = \lambda_2 N_1 = \lambda_2 \lambda_1 N_0$$

$$N_3 = \lambda_3 N_2 = \lambda_3 \lambda_2 \lambda_1 N_0$$

and in general

$$N_t = \prod_{i=1}^{t} \lambda_i N_0 \tag{3.24}$$

where the uppercase pi symbol means product of the indexed quantities over the specified range:

$$\prod_{i=1}^{t} \lambda_i = \lambda_1 \lambda_2 \lambda_3 \cdots \lambda_t$$

The expected density satisfies

$$E(N_t) = E\left(\prod_{i=1}^{t} \lambda_i\right) N_0$$

where E is expectation value. Since we have assumed the λ_i are all drawn independently from the same distribution,

$$E(N_t) = \lambda^t N_0 \tag{3.25}$$

where λ is the arithmetic mean of the distribution from which the λ_i are drawn. Thus, if the average value of the growth rate is bigger than 1, the expected value of population density grows exponentially, but if the average growth rate is smaller than 1, the expected population density shrinks eventually to zero.

Now let us consider the extinction probability. First, we will calculate the probability that N_t lies between two values K_1, K_2. To begin with, notice that

$$P(K_1 \leq N_t \leq K_2) = P[\ln(K_1) \leq \ln(N_t) \leq \ln(K_2)]$$

since the logarithm is a monotonic function. From (3.24),

$$\ln(N_t) = \ln(N_0) + \sum_{i=1}^{t} \ln(\lambda_i)$$

so

$$P(K_1 \leq N_t \leq K_2) = P\left[\ln(K_1/N_0) \leq \sum_{i=1}^{t} \ln(\lambda_i) \leq \ln(K_2/N_0)\right]$$

$$= P\{\ln(K_1/N_0)/t \leq \overline{[\ln(\lambda)]}_t \leq \ln(K_2/N_0)/t\}$$

where $\overline{[\ln(\lambda)]}_t$ is the arithmetic mean of the logarithms of the λ_i over the previous t generations.

If the λ_i are drawn independently from some distribution, then so are the quantities $\ln(\lambda_i)$ drawn independently from some distribution. Let m and s^2 be the mean and variance of the distribution from which the quantities $\ln(\lambda_i)$ are drawn. Then $\overline{[\ln(\lambda)]}_t$ is a sample mean from this distribution. As you will probably recall from a basic statistics course, for large sample sizes the sampling distribution for just about any underlying distribution is well approximated by a normal distribution with mean m and variance s^2/N, where m and s^2 are the mean and variance of the underlying distribution and N is the sample size (central limit theorem, for instance, Sokal and Rohlf 1981). Therefore, $\overline{[\ln(\lambda)]}_t$ is approximately normally distributed, with mean m and variance s^2/t.

Set

$$T_1 = [(\ln(K_1/N_0)/t - m]/(s/\sqrt{t})$$
$$T_2 = [(\ln(K_2/N_0)/t - m]/(s/\sqrt{t})$$

Then

$$P(K_1 \le N_t \le K_2) = P(T_1 \le T \le T_2)$$

where T is a standardized normal variate. This last probability can, of course, be looked up in any standard collection of statistical tables.

Lewontin and Cohen (1969) go on to make the following amusing point: it is entirely possible in this context to have a situation in which the expected density grows without bound, but at the same time the extinction probability approaches 1!

For instance, suppose that λ_i is 0.5 or 1.7, with equal probability. Then the mean growth rate λ is 1.1, so the expected density grows geometrically, as in (3.25). After 100 generations, say, the expected density is $E(N_{100}) = 13781 N_0$. But the mean and variance of the logarithm of the growth rate are $m = -0.08126$ and $s^2 = 0.3744$. Therefore, the probability that the population density exceeds the original value N_0 after time t is obtained by taking $K_1 = N_0$, $K_2 = $ infinity. After 100 generations this is (from tables of the standardized normal distribution) only 0.092.

In general, if $m < 0$, then T_1 will be positive no matter what K_1 is, and will grow without bound as t increases. In the limit as t approaches infinity, T_1 also approaches infinity. Therefore, the normal integral from T_1 to T_2 will approach zero, no matter what K_2 is. So in the limit as t approaches infinity, the probability of finding the population at any nonzero density is zero: the extinction probability approaches 1.

On the other hand, if $m > 0$, the extinction probability approaches 0 as t approaches infinity.

Exercise 3.6. Prove the last sentence, by taking $K_2 = N_0$.

At first it seems contradictory to have the expected density grow without bound, and at the same time the extinction probability approach 1. Now, as we scrutinize theoretical developments, we should always check whether what we are seeing makes sense. In case it doesn't, there are two possibilities. The first possibility is that something is seriously wrong with the theory (of which there are two subcases: the problem could be in the formulation of the theory, or there could be a mistake in the reasoning). The second possibility is that something is seriously wrong with our idea of what makes sense.

It is always delightful to encounter possibility number two, and to have to revise one's notion of what makes sense. That is what we are faced with here. Mean values can do some strange and misleading things. To illustrate with a simple example, let X be a variate that can be either N^2 with probability $1/N$ or 0 with probability $(N - 1)/N$. Then

$$E(X) = N^2(1/N) + 0[(N - 1)/N] = N$$

yet the probability that X takes the value 0 approaches 1 as N approaches infinity.

This is why I didn't end my investigation of demographic stochasticity in Section 2.5 with equation (2.33). While the mean was doing something attractive and plausible, it was necessary to check that this really was a reliable indication of the behavior of the system. (It turned out that it was, for the most part.)

The argument of Lewontin and Cohen shows that under certain well-defined circumstances, environmental fluctuations are likely to drive a population to extinction, *and* under certain other well-defined circumstances they are not. Basically, this reiterates the hand-waving argument of Section 2.4, from a more rigorous point of view. (A "hand-waving argument" is one that lacks rigor. In order to convince people despite one's lack of rigor, one waves one's hands in a way that signals one's earnestness.)

The important question, then, is: Under *realistic* conditions, how likely is it that environmental fluctuations will cause extinction? Now that we are out of the domain of hand waving, we can hope to address this question. To be sure, it is very hard to say what are realistic environmental fluctuations. But in at least one important class of fluctuations, Chesson (1983, 1986) has shown that extinction is quite unlikely.

Chesson points out that frequently it is the juveniles that are sensitive to environmental fluctuations, with adults being relatively unaffected. Under these circumstances, in a model with adult survival such as (3.2):

$$N_{t+1} = R(N_t) + SN_t \qquad (3.2)$$

it is in recruitment R that the effects of fluctuations will be felt. For instance, if in the example of Lewontin and Cohen it is recruitment that fluctuates between 0.5 and 1.7 (times N_t), with adult survival S pretty much constant at 0.1, then the growth rate fluctuates between 0.6 and 1.8 with equal probability, and the mean of the logarithm of the growth rate, m, 0.0385 is positive. So extinction is very unlikely. Chesson shows that, given relatively modest adult survival, populations can withstand quite considerable fluctuations in recruitment. This phenomenon he calls the *storage effect*.

ADDITIONAL EXERCISES

3.7. If you have access to a computer with graphics, use it to explore further the Ricker model of Section 3.3. Plot $F(N)$, $F^{(2)}(N)$, and $F^{(4)}(N)$ vs. N, with N varying from 0 to 2, for $r = 1.8, 2.3, 2.6, 3.3, 5$. For these same values of r, plot N_t vs. t, for $t = 0$ to 30, for several initial values N_0. For those who enjoy an extra challenge: write a program that determines, to arbitrary accuracy (within the limitations of number representation on your machine), the bifurcation value of r, for the bifurcation from stable cycle of period 2 to stable cycle of period 4.

3.8. For a peaked growth function,

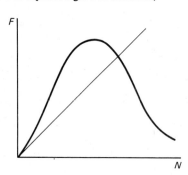

even though the density might start out at arbitrarily large or arbitrarily small values, after a while it will be confined below a certain maximum value N_+ and above a certain minimum value N_-. Even chaotic solutions will eventually be confined between N_- and N_+. Can you name a density N such that $N_+ = F(N)$? Can you name a density N such that $N_- = F^{(2)}(N)$? As we move through the sequence of bifurcations discussed in Section 3.3, what will happen to N_- and N_+?

3.9. Consider an Allee effect (Section 2.1) within the context of discrete-time population dynamics:

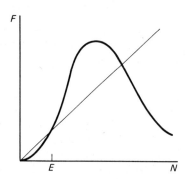

If the density ever falls below the threshold value E, the population will go locally extinct. Can you name a density N such that if E is greater than or equal to N, the population is certain eventually to go extinct?

3.10. Investigate further the storage effect, which is introduced at the end of Section 3.6. In the model

$$N_{t+1} = (R_t + S)N_t$$

suppose that $S = 0.1$ and R_t fluctuates between 0.5 and 1.7, with probabilities $P_{0.5}$ and $P_{1.7}$. What must be the upper bound on $P_{0.5}$ in order to avoid extinction? What is this same number in case $S = 0.9$? Suppose instead that R_t fluctuates between X and 1.7, with equal probability. For $S = 0.1$, what is the lower bound on X to prevent extinction? With $S = 0.9$?

PART TWO

POPULATION INTERACTIONS

We are now ready to undertake the study of interactions between and among populations. The vast majority of published work in this area is formulated in continuous time rather than discrete time, basically because it is simpler; and we will follow suit.

We gradually build interactions together in a way that is directed toward a community/ecosystem viewpoint. First, in Chapter 4, we consider the most elemental ecosystem "building block," the pairwise relationship in which members of one population eat members of another (consumption). This leads quite naturally to the notion of competition for food among consumers, which gets one thinking about other forms of competition as well (Chapter 5). As a further development in building up ecosystems, we contemplate in Chapter 6 the effect on competitive relationships of predation, disturbance, or other mortality factors.

Chapters 7 and 8 are concerned with whole ecological communities. The main focus of Chapter 7 is the attempt to identify functional subunits of communities—guilds—that sensibly can be studied in isolation. This issue is addressed in Chapter 7 from the standpoint of perturbation experiments, because of the importance of such experiments both from a research-methodological and from a practical standpoint. The chapter begins by developing a tool, loop analysis, which is useful in this and other contexts. Chapter 8 reviews recent work, both empirical and theoretical, on food webs, an approach to whole communities that emphasizes trophic relationships.

Chapter 4

Consumption

We begin our study of species interactions with that most elemental of inter-specific relationships, between the eater and the eaten (much of what we do here will apply as well to host-parasite interactions). This topic usually goes by the name "predation," and that is certainly an important kind of consumption, but the ideas that we discuss here apply just as well to other forms of consumption such as herbivory.

In this chapter we are going to consider the situation of a single consumer species feeding on a single resource. More complicated systems involving consumption will be treated in later chapters.

4.1 FUNCTIONAL RESPONSE AND NUMERICAL RESPONSE

Consider a population, called the resource, with density R, whose growth has the form

$$dR/dt = f(R)$$

if it lives alone. But suppose that instead of living alone, the resource is consumed by another population, called the consumer, with density N. If the average individual consumer devours $F(R, N)$ resource individuals per unit time, and there are N consumers per unit area, then the growth of the resource population will become

$$dR/dt = f(R) - NF(R, N)$$

The function $F(R, N)$ is called the *functional response* of the consumer. Notice that it can depend on both population densities.

Similarly, the per capita growth of the consumer population will depend, in general, on the two population densities:

$$dN/dt = NG(R, N)$$

The function $G(R, N)$ is called the *numerical response* of the consumer population.

Putting these two equations together, we get

$$dR/dt = f(R) - NF(R, N)$$
$$dN/dt = NG(R, N)$$

(4.1)

This *pair* of equations, unlike either of them alone, forms a closed "dynamical system": there is an equation for the time derivative of each quantity that can change with time. Just about any consumer-resource model will be of the form (4.1).

The simplest case, dubbed "laissez faire" by Caughley (1976), is that in which individual consumers do not interfere with one another's activities; we then have $F(R, N) = F(R)$ and $G(R, N) = G(R)$. Direct interactions between individual consumers manifest themselves as N-dependence of the functional and/or numerical response.

We have already seen typical examples of functional responses (the three Holling types) in Section 2.2.1. As for numerical response, most published work uses either the form

$$G(R, N) = -d + cF(R, N)$$

(4.2)

or the form

$$G(R, N) = r[1 - N/aF(R)]$$

(4.3)

The idea of (4.2), in which d and c are positive constants, is that when no resource individuals are present, the consumer population dies out at a per capita rate d, owing, of course, to starvation. [Note that by definition $F(0, N)$ must be equal to 0.] When resource individuals are present and being consumed at a rate $F(R, N)$ per consumer, each resource individual consumed is thought of as being "converted" into c consumer individuals.

This line of reasoning can be made more precise by stating it in energetic terms. One can view an animal as an energy processor (Lavigne 1982, Peters 1983): it ingests a certain amount of energy per unit time, of which a fraction is assimilated, and this assimilated energy goes into three categories: respiration, or maintenance (just keeping the animal's own metabolism ticking over); (somatic) growth; and reproduction. [Some energy is stored for later use rather than being used immediately in any of these three ways, but a suitable time average will take that into account.] I will discuss the optimal allocation of energy among these three categories in Section 10.3.

Growth and reproduction are commonly lumped together in the term *production*. So, writing A (= constant) for assimilation efficiency,

$$Ai = r + p$$

where i is ingestion, r is respiration, and p is production of an individual. The units of i, r, and p are energy per unit time; A, being an efficiency, is dimensionless.

If a population has N members, then multiplying both sides of this equation by N gives

$$AI = R + P$$

where $I = Ni$, $R = Nr$, and $P = Np$ are ingestion, respiration, and production for the population. We can also write this as

$$P = -R + AI$$

Let B stand for total population biomass. What is its time derivative? Biomass increases through production, and it decreases through death. So

$$dB/dt = P - (\text{losses to mortality})$$

$$= -R + AI - (\text{losses to mortality})$$

$$= B(-T + AJ) - (\text{losses to mortality})$$

where $T = R/B$ is the *specific respiration* (respiration per unit biomass), and $J = I/B$ is specific ingestion. If W is the mass of an average individual, then the number of animals is $N = B/W$. Dividing both sides of this last equation by W,

$$dN/dt = N(-T + AJ) - (\text{losses to mortality})$$

Mortality might come from predation, accident, disease, or starvation. At the moment we are restricting our attention to the interaction between consumer and resource, so we are neglecting other populations that would account for disease and predation (on the consumers). Starvation is already accounted for in the combination $(-T + AJ)$, which becomes negative if the energy intake AJ is too small relative to the metabolic requirement T. If the probability of a fatal accident per unit time is constant over time and for each member of the population, we can account for that by adding a suitable constant to T. But this constant will generally be quite small relative to metabolism. Then we get

$$dN/dt = N(-T + AJ)$$

where T is a constant approximately equal to specific respiration and AJ is the assimilated energy intake per unit time per unit biomass. But this AJ is proportional to the functional response F, so we have arrived once more at the numerical response (4.2).

It was a little bit crude to divide by the average body mass W, since there will generally be quite a lot of variation in W within a population: this model does not handle growth very well. It may have been better to just stay with the population biomass B as the basic variable: not only does the above derivation then make more sense, but if we are to model in continuous time, biomass is a much more smoothly varying quantity than is number! But it is traditional to talk of numbers in population models, and I will honor tradition here.

In (4.2), if $F(R, N) = F(R)$ (no dependence of functional response on consumer density), each consumer functions completely independently of all the others. But it is often the case that, in feeding on the same resources, different consumer individuals interfere with one another's activities. This can be expressed through the functional response in various ways. For instance, in the Type III functional response (2.4), consumer interference might be expressed by having the half-saturation density R_0 a monotonically increasing function of consumer density N. For example, we might have

$$F(R, N) = ER^2/[(a + bN)^2 + R^2] \tag{4.4}$$

Then for each resource density R, the rate of consumption per consumer will be lower the more consumers are present.

In equation (4.3), where r and a are positive constants, the consumer population is thought of as growing logistically, with intrinsic growth rate r and carrying capacity $aF(R)$—proportional to the consumption rate $F(R)$. Here, consumer interference does not have any effect on the per consumer rate of consumption, since the functional response F is independent of N. But consumers do interfere with one another in some other way, as expressed by the term proportional to N^2 in the growth rate $NG(R, N)$.

One can distinguish as well two kinds of resource growth rate $f(R)$. One possibility is to have a self-renewing, biotic resource, with $f(R)$ having logistic form or something of the sort. The other possibility is to have a resource that flows into the system from outside. This could be due to immigration of biota, or it could correspond to abiotic resources, as in a chemostat, or an aquatic system where phytoplankton consume dissolved nutrients. Typically in such a case one uses

$$f(R) = a - bR$$

where a is the rate of inflow and b is the rate of depletion due to causes other than consumption by the consumer—it could be death or outflow, for example. There is quite a substantial literature on this case, which has been reviewed by Tilman (1982). But I will not touch upon it here.

The reader will have noticed that the above energetic justification for (4.2) is a little different from most of the other arguments in this subsection: it is more *mechanistic,* in that it deduces the form of the numerical response from underlying biological processes (mechanisms). This kind of reasoning, in which the forms of population models are derived from the behavior, physiology, or morphology of individuals, has been applied rather extensively to the functional and numerical responses (for instance, Abrams 1982, Holt 1983, Sih 1984).

4.2 THE ANALYSIS OF TWO-SPECIES INTERACTIONS

I am going to have to take some space here to develop methods for the analysis of two-species interactions. I will motivate the discussion by using as an example the particular consumer-resource model

$$dR/dt = f_R(R, N) = rR(1 - R/K) - ENR^2/(R_0^2 + R^2)$$
$$dN/dt = f_N(R, N) = N[-d + cER^2/(R_0^2 + R^2)] \tag{4.5}$$

which you will recognize as a laissez-faire model with Type III functional response (recall Section 2.2.1). But I will develop sufficient general concepts around this example so that once you have studied this section, you should be able to analyze any other two-species system.

In general, the growth rates will be functions of *state variables* [R and N in the system (4.5)] and of *parameters* [such as r, K, E, R_0, d, c in the system (4.5)]. A point that sometimes bothers students is: What's the difference between state variables and parameters? How do you tell them apart?

The difference is certainly clear within the pair of equations (4.5). The state variables are the quantities for which (4.5) specifies a dynamics, by which is meant a way that the state variables change in time. In (4.5) this specification is done by giving the time derivatives as functions of the state variables and parameters. Equations (4.5) tell us how the state variables R and N change in time; the temporal behavior of the parameters r, K, E, R_0, d, c has to be given from somewhere outside the mathematical system (4.5).

But in going from the biological situation to its mathematical representation (4.5), how do we know which quantities to treat as state variables and which quantities to treat as parameters? The answer to this is that the numerical values of parameters are determined entirely by factors that are extrinsic to the system, while the numerical values of state variables are determined in large part by factors that are intrinsic to the system. What I mean by "intrinsic" here is: having to do with relationships among the various quantities (state variables and parameters) that characterize the system. Thus in (4.5) it is the relationship among the values of R, N, r, K, E, and R_0 expressed by the function on the right-hand side of the first equation that determines how R will change in the next infinitesimal time period (dR/dt).

Anything that remains constant in time within a given biological instance corresponding to a mathematical system is clearly a parameter. In (4.5), we are assuming that once we have chosen a definite pair of species in a definite location, the values of all the parameters are pretty much fixed as constants. That much is easy. But let's suppose that in some system the carrying capacity K for the resource is significantly different in different years, because of variations in climate. Does that make K a state variable?

No, it does not, because variations in climate are *extrinsic* to the system. The climate is unaffected by the density N, say, or the intrinsic growth rate r. So we would have to express this kind of variation in K by making K a *time-varying parameter,* a function of t that would have to be simply plugged into (4.5) everywhere that we see K.

Differential equations with time-varying parameters are perfectly respectable mathematical entities, and in some cases are necessary to represent properly the biological system. However, I will not discuss them in this book, because the mathematics is more difficult.

Finally, we may contemplate yet another possibility. Suppose the resource carrying capacity K varies significantly, not because of climate but because the resource species is itself consuming some other species S (whose density determines K), which perhaps has other consumers $C_1, \ldots, C_n$ as well. It would be difficult to express this by giving K as a specified function of t, because of the *interaction* between the system as we have specified it in (4.5) and the other species $S, C_1, \ldots, C_n$. So it might be better to enlarge our conception of "the system" to include the densities of these other species as state variables.

4.2.1 Phase Space

In general, we want to be able to analyze interactions of the form

$$dN_1/dt = f_1(N_1, N_2)$$
$$dN_2/dt = f_2(N_1, N_2)$$

(4.6)

between two species with densities N_1, N_2. Our example (4.5) is of this form, if we make the identification $N_1 = R, N_2 = N$.

For any system of the form (4.6), the state of the system at any time t is completely specified by giving the two densities $N_1(t), N_2(t)$; these are our state variables. So if we create a two-dimensional Euclidean "space" with axes N_1 and N_2,

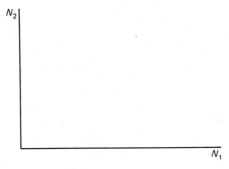

each point in the space corresponds to a possible instantaneous state of the system. This space is called the *phase space* for the system (4.6). Since population densities can never be negative, the phase space for a population model will always consist of the quadrant $N_1 \geq 0$ and $N_2 \geq 0$, as suggested by the above sketch.

If we are given initial values $N_1(t_0), N_2(t_0)$ of the densities at some initial time t_0, then the values $N_1(t), N_2(t)$ of the densities for all subsequent times $t > t_0$ are determined by the equations (4.6). I think it will be clear to you that a pair of functions of time $N_1(t), N_2(t)$, given for all times $t \geq t_0$, corresponds geometrically to a *curve* in phase space:

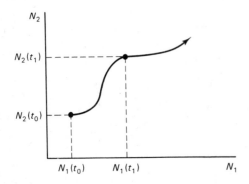

If you pick any time t later than t_0, say $t = t_1$, the curve will pass through some unique point $N_1(t_1), N_2(t_1)$ in phase space. In this way, the curve depicts succinctly how the densities will behave all the way into the infinite future. It's customary, as I've done above, to draw in little arrowheads to indicate the direction along this curve that the densities will move as time progresses into the future.

Similarly, we can extend the curve into the infinite past, for all times earlier than t_0, by solving (4.6) for times $t < t_0$. This tells us what values of the densities would have been necessary at any time in the past in order for the densities to evolve, under the influence of the biological processes embodied in (4.6), to the stated values at t_0. Such a solution curve, extended into the infinite future and the infinite past, is called a system *trajectory* in phase space.

Pick any point on a system trajectory, corresponding, say, to time t. Let δt be an infinitesimal time interval. Then there is another point on the trajectory corresponding to the time $t + \delta t$. If we draw a little arrow from the first point to the second,

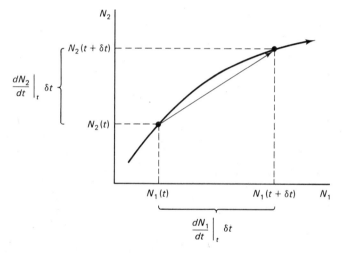

and take its projections onto the two axes (as above), then these projections are, to first order in δt, nothing but

$$\left. \frac{dN_1}{dt} \right|_t \delta t$$

and

$$\left. \frac{dN_2}{dt} \right|_t \delta t$$

In the limit as $\delta t \to 0$, this vector will be *tangent* to the trajectory at the point corresponding to time t. So *at each point (N_1, N_2) in phase space, the tangent vector to the trajectory through that point has components $f_1(N_1, N_2), f_2(N_1, N_2)$ given by the right-hand sides of (4.6)*.

It is evident that for each point in phase space, there must be a trajectory through that point: for we are perfectly free to construct such a trajectory by taking $N_1(t_0), N_2(t_0)$ in the above discussion to be the densities corresponding to any point in phase space we please. However, since the equations (4.6) have a *unique* solution for any given initial values for the densities, there can be only *one* trajectory through each point in phase space.

The actual proof of this uniqueness is fairly involved mathematically. But we can make it plausible as follows. Suppose two trajectories cross at some point in phase space:

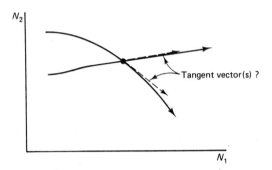

Then there are *two* tangent vectors at this point. Since the tangent vector at each point is determined by the (unique) right-hand sides of (4.6), this cannot happen.

So the system of equations (4.6) determines a whole family of trajectories in phase space, one (and only one) of which passes through each point in phase space. This family of trajectories is called the *phase portrait* of the system. The phase portrait summarizes, in a very compact depiction, every possible temporal behavior of the system.

If this all sounds a bit abstract, let's make it concrete by constructing the phase portrait of the particular system (4.5).

It is best to begin by locating those regions in phase space where dR/dt is positive, negative, and zero; and the same for dN/dt. In particular, the set of points in phase space where $dR/dt = 0$ is called the *R-isocline,* and the set of points where $dN/dt = 0$ is called the *N-isocline.*

We've already worked out the *R*-isocline for this system on page 19:

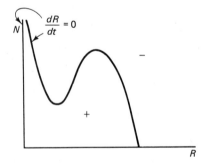

Notice that the *N*-axis is also part of the *R*-isocline, because $dR/dt = 0$ when $R = 0$ as well as on the "bent" curve depicted. The + sign marks the region where $dR/dt > 0$, and the − sign the region where $dR/dt < 0$. In the above picture, the axes have been "switched" here relative to their positions on page 19. The reason for the "switch" is that it is customary when working with consumer-resource systems to make the "resource" axis horizontal.

Exercise 4.1. Check that I have correctly labeled the $+$ and $-$ regions in the preceding sketch.

From the second of equations (4.5), we see that $dN/dt = 0$ if $N = 0$ or

$$d/cE = R^2/(R_0^2 + R^2)$$

This last equation is equivalent to

$$R = [R_0^2/(cE/d - 1)]^{1/2} \qquad (4.7)$$

which represents, of course, a vertical straight line in phase space:

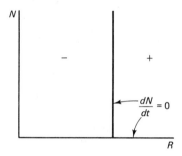

where again the $+$ and $-$ signs give the sign of dN/dt off the isocline.

Exercise 4.2. Again check the labeling of the $+$ and $-$ regions.

Now we know what the R-isocline looks like and what the N-isocline looks like. Next, we want to draw both of them in the same picture. There are seven qualitatively different relative positions of the two isoclines, namely,

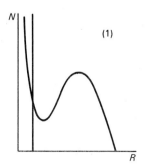

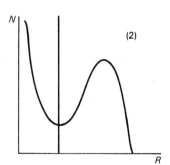

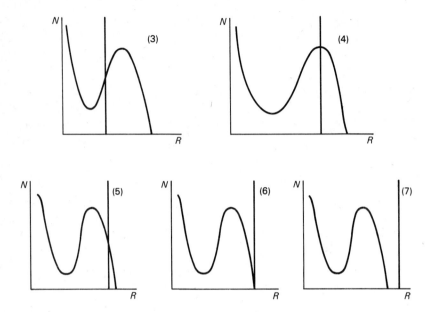

Clearly, any one of these possibilities could crop up, depending on the parameter values. (Just to make sure I'm not swindling you with my facile "clearly," you should have a look at how the positions of the isoclines depend on the parameters, to verify my statement.)

Of these seven possibilities, three can immediately be ruled uninteresting, on the basis that they are structurally unstable (Section 2.3): numbers 2, 4, 6. I will leave the rigorous proof of this as an exercise for the mathematical fans among you; basically it is "obvious," because each of these is transformed into one of the other four remaining possibilities if the position of the N-isocline along the R-axis changes by the *slightest* amount.

I will begin by considering possibility 5:

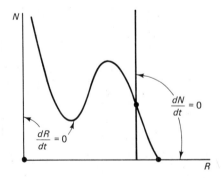

Notice that I have drawn three solid circles in the above picture. These are points that lie on *both* the R-isocline *and* the N-isocline; that is, they are the points in phase space where $dR/dt = 0$ and $dN/dt = 0$. Such points are *equilibrium* points for our system (4.5), just like the equilibria we discussed for single-species systems on page 9.

If the densities have initially the values corresponding to such an equilibrium point, they will remain at those values until they are displaced away from them by some external influence. So an equilibrium is, strictly speaking, itself a trajectory, albeit of a very special kind. An equilibrium is almost always a point at which the two isoclines cross. (Equilibria where the two isoclines just touch each other without crossing are, obviously, structurally unstable.)

Having located the isoclines and the equilibria, and having noted the signs of the growth rates dR/dt and dN/dt in different regions of phase space, we can start to fill in trajectories. It is best to begin with the axes.

On the R-axis, $N = 0$ and (4.5) becomes

$$\begin{cases} dR/dt = rR(1 - R/K) \\ dN/dt = 0 \end{cases}$$

That is, when no consumers are present, the resource population grows logistically, and the consumer population remains at 0 (we have not included migration in the model, and there is no spontaneous creation of life). Hence there are two trajectories that follow along the R-axis; they are essentially the dotted arrows in the sketch at the top of page 12:

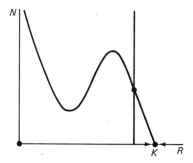

On the N-axis, when $R = 0$, equations (4.5) reduce to

$$\begin{cases} dR/dt = 0 \\ dN/dt = -dN \end{cases}$$

These equations say that there is no immigration of resource individuals and that in the absence of food, the consumer population dies off at a per capita rate d per unit time. In the absence of food, the consumer population will always approach the equilibrium at the origin in phase space, which corresponds to a trajectory on the N-axis approaching the origin:

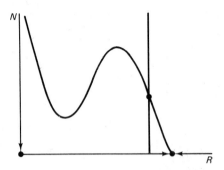

Any trajectory that is directed toward an equilibrium only approaches the equilibrium asymptotically; it never actually intersects the equilibrium. This is in accord with my earlier statement that there is only one trajectory through each point in phase space (if you recall as well my earlier remark that an equilibrium is itself a trajectory). For instance, solving the previous pair of equations for the densities as a function of time on the trajectory that follows the N-axis, we find

$$R(t) = 0$$

$$N(t) = N(0)e^{-dt}$$

from which we see that N approaches 0 asymptotically.

Our next step in sketching out the phase portrait is to see how the trajectories cross the isoclines. Recall the statement earlier in this subsection that at each point in phase space, the tangent vector to the trajectory through that point has components (f_1, f_2), where f_i are the growth rates in (4.6). Since (in an obvious notation) $f_R = 0$ on the R-isocline, the trajectories have to be vertical whenever they cross that isocline, and since $f_N = 0$ on the N-isocline, the trajectories have to be horizontal whenever they cross that isocline. Thus, we can fill in little arrows on the isoclines to indicate how the trajectories cross the isoclines:

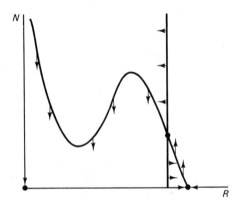

Recall that the two components of the little arrow at a point (R, N) are given by $f_R(R, N)$, $F_N(R, N)$ [right-hand sides of (4.5)]. So the arrows on the $R-$ $(N-)$ isocline are vertical (horizontal), because f_R (f_N) is zero there. But:

Exercise 4.3. Why do they point sometimes up and sometimes down (or sometimes to the right and sometimes to the left)?

Once you've thought about that exercise, you can probably sketch in whole trajectories in phase space. However, this might get a little tricky near an equilibrium. Before we can go much further, we're going to have to look more closely at equilibria, which we do in the next subsection.

4.2.1.1 Two-Dimensional Equilibria

Consider a system of the form (4.6), and assume that f_1 and f_2 are C^1 functions of N_1 and N_2 (that is, f_1 and f_2 have continuous first derivatives with respect to N_1 and N_2). Any point (N_{1e}, N_{2e}) in phase space such that

$$f_1(N_{1e}, N_{2e}) = f_2(N_{1e}, N_{2e}) = 0 \qquad (4.8)$$

is, as we have already remarked, an equilibrium of our system. I am sure you will recall from Section 2.1 that for a one-dimensional system $dN/dt = f(N)$, the derivative df/dN determines whether an equilibrium is locally stable or unstable. A similar statement is true in the two-dimensional case that we are now interested in, but now we have four derivatives to think about, not just one, and the connection between these derivatives and local stability is not as obvious as in the one-dimensional case.

The four derivatives in question are

$$A_{ij} = \left.\frac{\partial f_i}{\partial N_j}\right|_{N_{1e},N_{2e}} \qquad (4.9)$$

for $i, j = 1, 2$. I am going to discuss later, in Sections 5.1.1 and 7.1.3, why they affect local stability in the way that they do. For now, I am just going to state that the equilibrium is locally stable if

$$I_e < 0 \quad \text{and} \quad \Omega_e > 0 \qquad (4.10)$$

where

$$I_e = A_{11} + A_{22} \qquad \Omega_e = A_{11}A_{22} - A_{12}A_{21} \qquad (4.11)$$

Local stability means here exactly what it did in Section 2.1: an equilibrium is locally stable if, after a sufficiently small but otherwise arbitrary displacement of the densities away from equilibrium, the densities return to equilibrium.

In fact, the quantities I_e and Ω_e tell us quite a lot more about two-dimensional equilibria than just whether they are locally stable. They also tell us the form of the trajectories in a sufficiently small neighborhood of equilibrium, assuming that the system we are talking about is structurally stable, in the sense of Section 2.3. One can show that, for two-dimensional systems, structural stability implies that every equilibrium is an isolated point and that at every equilibrium $I_e \neq 0$ and $\Omega_e \neq 0$. The following catalog of structurally stable equilibria is standard material which can be found, for instance, in Sansone and Conti (1964).

$$I_e^2 - 4\Omega_e < 0 \qquad I_e < 0: \quad \text{stable focus}$$

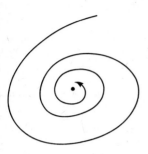

$$I_e^2 - 4\Omega_e < 0 \qquad I_e > 0: \quad \text{unstable focus}$$

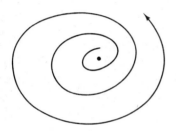

$$I_e^2 > 4\Omega_e > 0 \qquad I_e < 0: \quad \text{stable node with two tangents}$$

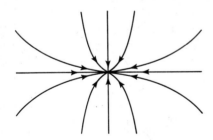

$$I_e^2 > 4\Omega_e > 0 \qquad I_e > 0: \quad \text{unstable node with two tangents}$$

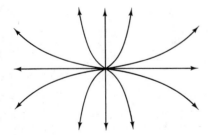

$$\Omega_e < 0: \quad \text{saddle point}$$

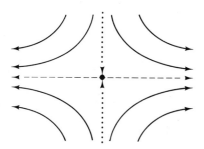

Notice that there are exactly two trajectories (drawn with dotted lines in the above sketch) that approach a saddle point (asymptotically, of course) and exactly two trajectories (drawn with dashed lines in the above sketch) that radiate out from a saddle point. These four special trajectories are called *separatrices*. All other trajectories in a neighborhood of a saddle point enter the neighborhood from outside, swing more or less past the saddle point, and then depart from the neighborhood.

$$I_e^2 - 4\Omega_e = 0 \qquad I_e < 0: \quad \text{stable point}$$

(may be a stable focus, stable node with two tangents, or some other stable node, such as:)

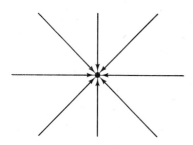

$$I_e^2 - 4\Omega_e = 0, \qquad I_e > 0: \quad \text{unstable point}$$

(may be an unstable focus, unstable node with two tangents, or some other unstable node, such as:)

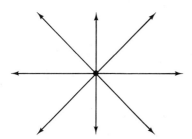

Now we can investigate the "off-axis" equilibrium in the picture on page 92. Solving first for the equilibrium values of the densities, we find from (4.7)

$$R_e = [R_0^2/(cE/d - 1)]^{1/2} \qquad (4.12)$$

and from the first of (4.5)

$$N_e = r(1 - R_e/K)(R_0^2 + R_e^2)/ER_e \qquad (4.13)$$

If we identify R with N_1 and N with N_2 in the preceding discussion of equilibria, we can calculate I_e and Ω_e for this equilibrium from equations (4.9) and (4.11). If in this process we use (4.13) to eliminate N_e in favor of R_e, we will obtain

$$I_e = -rR_e/K + r(1 - R_e/K)(R_e^2 - R_0^2)/(R_0^2 + R_e^2) \qquad (4.14)$$

$$\Omega_e = 2cER_0^2 \, rR_e^2(1 - R_e/K)/(R_0^2 + R_e^2)^2 \qquad (4.15)$$

Exercise 4.4. Prove (4.14) and (4.15).

Since $R_e < K$, we see immediately from (4.15) that $\Omega_e > 0$. What is the sign of I_e? We could "grind this out" numerically using (4.14), but there's an easier way. Because $\partial f_N/\partial N$ [equation (4.5)], evaluated at the equilibrium, is zero (as you will have noticed while doing the above exercise), I_e is simply equal to $\partial f_R/\partial R$, evaluated at the equilibrium. In taking the partial derivative of f_R with respect to R, we hold N constant. So that derivative uses values of f_R along a horizontal straight line through the equilibrium:

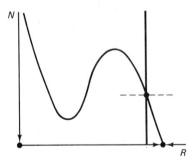

From the bottom sketch on page 88, we know that f_R is positive to the left of the equilibrium, and negative to the right. So in a neighborhood of the equilibrium, f_R decreases as R increases, with N held fixed. Therefore, $\partial f_R/\partial R < 0$ at the equilibrium. So $I_e < 0$.

Hence, using (4.10), our equilibrium is locally stable. From the above catalog of equilibria, we see that it is either a stable focus or a stable node with two tangents, depending upon the sign of $I_e^2 - 4\Omega_e$. This sign can in fact be either positive or negative, depending upon the parameter values. Notice especially the role of the parameter c in (4.14) and (4.15), with all other parameters in those equations held fixed: if c is large, $I_e^2 - 4\Omega_e$ will be negative and the equilibrium will be a focus, and if c is small, $I_e^2 - 4\Omega_e$ will be positive and the equilibrium will be a node with two tangents. It follows from (4.12) that in order to keep the other parameters in (4.14) and (4.15) fixed as we vary c, we have to vary d at the same time.

What does large c and d mean in biological terms? Both of these parameters scale rates in the consumer population: d is the instantaneous mortality rate when no resource individuals are available, and c is the rate of conversion of consumed resource individuals into consumer individuals. So large c corresponds to "fast" consumer dynamics, small c to "slow" consumer dynamics.

4.2.1.2 Completing the Picture

Adding the information about the signs of the growth rates contained in the sketches on pages 88 and 89 to the sketch on page 92, we get

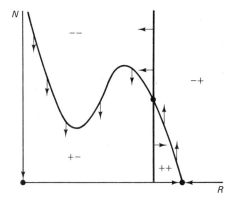

The first sign here refers to f_R, the second to f_N. Therefore, for example, in the region where the signs are $-+$, trajectories move to the left ($f_R < 0$) and up ($f_N > 0$). If we assume "fast" consumer dynamics, we know the equilibrium is a focus. So we'll have trajectories like this:

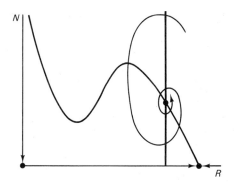

Now let's look near the coordinate axes. Using the signs of f_R and f_N near the axes, we can see that near the axes, we must have something like this:

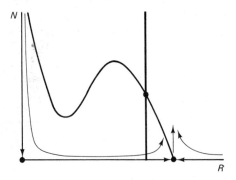

There has to be one trajectory (and only one) that emanates out from the equilibrium at $R = K$, in order to make the transition between the two other types of trajectory shown here. The equilibrium at $R = K$ is a saddle point, and this trajectory is one of its separatrices. The other separatrix emanating out from the equilibrium would go into the region of negative N if our system had any biological meaning there. The two separatrices that approach the equilibrium lie on the R-axis. Basically, this is all obvious geometrically; if you are still not convinced, you can prove that the equilibrium is a saddle point by doing the calculation of its I and Ω.

    The origin is also a saddle point, with two separatrices lying on coordinate axes, and the other two in the biologically meaningless region where $R < 0$ or $N < 0$.

    Now we can fill in the whole picture:

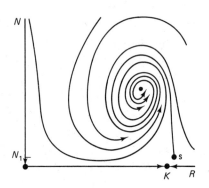

    This picture summarizes every possible behavior of the system. For instance, suppose we think of introducing a *wild* vertebrate grazer [so N obeys the second of (4.5) rather than being held by us at a fixed value, as in Section 2.2.1] into a new area, with N the density of herbivores, R the density of plants. Then at first N will have some small value, say N_1 in the above picture, and R will be near K. So the system will follow the trajectory that starts at point s in the above picture. We can get the behavior of just the herbivore density by projecting that trajectory onto the N-axis, which will give us something like this:

for N as a function of time t: at first an eruption to quite high density, followed by a dropping back and eventual oscillatory approach to equilibrium.

This behavior is familiar to wildlife managers with experience of large ungulates. For instance, Fig. 4.1 shows an eruption of sheep introduced into New South Wales. Perhaps the most spectacular example on record is that of reindeer introduced onto St. Matthews Island in the Bering Sea. Figure 4.2 gives a fit of a laissez-faire model similar to the one we've been discussing to data for this eruption.

Such eruptions have often been seen as "ecological disasters," with all kinds of remarkable explanations offered for them. Caughley (1976, 1979) has made the point that this is simply the natural dynamics of such a system, that it is in reality an orderly approach to equilibrium, and that there is nothing at all arcane about it.

4.2.1.3 Limit Cycles and Kolmogorov's Theorem

As you see, figuring out what the phase portrait of a system looks like is basically pretty straightforward. There is, however, one thing that can be difficult to cope with: the system may have a limit cycle.

I remarked earlier that there can be only one trajectory through each point

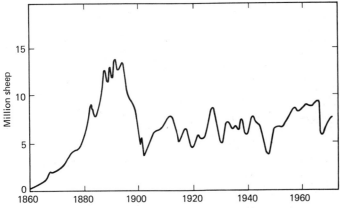

Figure 4.1 Sheep numbers in the Western Division of New South Wales, Australia, between 1960 and 1972. (From Caughley 1976.)

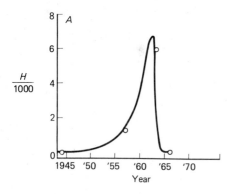

Figure 4.2   Reindeer numbers on St. Matthews Island between 1944 and 1966. (From Caughley 1976.)

in phase space; trajectories can't cross over each other, and, in particular, a trajectory can never cross over itself, like this:

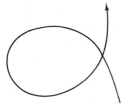

However, a trajectory *can* make a nice smooth closed curve in phase space, like this:

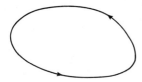

(It could just as well circulate in a clockwise manner.) Such a trajectory is called a *periodic trajectory*. If you think of projecting a periodic trajectory onto the two axes, you can see that the two densities N_1 and N_2 will undergo sustained oscillations (with the two populations somewhat out of phase, that is, having their maxima at different times).

Periodic trajectories are special trajectories, in much the same way that equilibria are special trajectories: other trajectories can approach (either in the future or in the past) a periodic trajectory asymptotically. In particular, a periodic trajectory may be a *stable limit cycle*

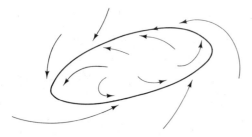

or an *unstable limit cycle*

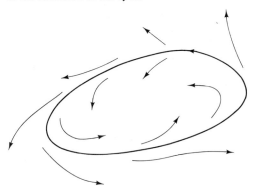

depending upon how the neighboring trajectories behave. (There are other possibilities, too, which I will not go into.)

Analogously to local stability for equilibria, a periodic trajectory is a stable limit cycle if, after sufficiently small perturbations of the densities away from the trajectory, the densities tend to return to the trajectory. (There's not too much danger in not qualifying the word "stability" in this context, since this is just about the only kind of stability to which one alludes for periodic trajectories.)

A closed curve in a two-dimensional space divides that space into two distinct pieces: one piece "inside" the curve, the other piece "outside." This seemingly banal observation has far-reaching consequences. Since a trajectory can never cross another trajectory, any trajectories inside a periodic trajectory can only run around in there. If you think about how they can possibly be arranged in there, you will probably be ready to agree that every periodic trajectory must surround at least one equilibrium point, in a two-dimensional system such as we are discussing now. There are many possible configurations, but by far the most common are to have a stable focus inside an unstable limit cycle

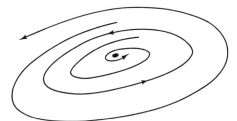

or to have an unstable focus inside a stable limit cycle

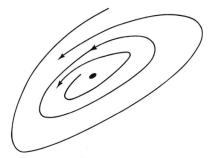

This is our first hint that things are going to be more complicated when we consider systems of three or more species, for a closed curve does *not* divide a three- or higher-dimensional space into two distinct pieces.

It can be difficult to *prove* that a system has a periodic trajectory, although usually when such a trajectory is present, one has very good reason to suspect it, just from sketching the trajectories as in the preceding section. In the case of consumer-resource systems, there is a theorem originally due to Kolmogorov (1936), and elaborated by Scudo (1971), Rescigno and Richardson (1967), and May (1972), which says that essentially every consumer-resource model that is at all realistic has *either* a stable equilibrium *or* a stable limit cycle.

Specifically, *Kolmogorov's theorem,* as stated by May (1972), is the following. Represent the consumer-resource model in the form

$$dR/dt = RH(R, N)$$

$$dN/dt = NG(R, N)$$

instead of the form (4.1). Suppose that for all $R \geq 0, N \geq 0$

(i) $\partial H/\partial N < 0$

(ii) $R(\partial H/\partial R) + N(\partial H/\partial N) < 0$

(iii) $\partial G/\partial N < 0$

(iv) $R(\partial G/\partial R) + N(\partial G/\partial N) > 0$

Suppose in addition that

(v) $H(0, 0) > 0$

and that there exist positive real numbers A, B, C such that

(vi) $H(0, A) = 0$

(vii) $H(B, 0) = 0$

(viii) $G(C, 0) = 0$

(ix) $B > C$

Then the system has either a stable equilibrium point or a stable limit cycle.

These conditions have the following simple biological interpretations. For any given population sizes, it is the case that (i) the per capita rate of increase of the resource density is a decreasing function of the number of consumers, and (iii) the rate of increase of the consumer population decreases as the consumer density increases. As well, (ii) the rate of increase of the resource density is a decreasing function of both densities, while (iv) the rate of increase of consumer density is an increasing function of both densities.

In addition, (v) when both densities are low, the resource has a positive rate of increase. However, (vi) there is a consumer density that is big enough to stop resource growth, even when the resource is very scarce. On the other hand, (vii) even in the absence of consumers, the resource will not grow without bound. For its part, (viii) the consumer population, when rare, cannot grow at arbitrarily small resource densities. Finally, (ix) the minimum resource level that will permit an extremely sparse consumer population to grow must be a level at which the resource is also capable of growth.

The conclusion of the theorem usually goes through even if some of the inequalities in the hypotheses are replaced by equalities. In these sorts of cases, where the theorem "almost applies," we have strong reason to suspect the presence of either a stable equilibrium or a stable limit cycle. For more discussion of these cases, see May (1974). In many cases when Kolmogorov's theorem does not quite apply, we can resort to a more powerful but more complicated method known as Hopf bifurcation theory (e.g., Iooss and Joseph 1980).

Getting back to our canonical example (4.5), suppose R_e [equation (4.12)] falls in a position like this (possibility 3 in the catalog of possibilities back on page 90):

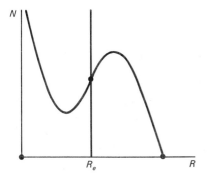

Then the discussion surrounding equations (4.14) and (4.15) immediately tells us that the equilibrium is an *unstable* focus. The only change is that now $\partial f_R / \partial R > 0$ at the equilibrium (same reasoning as before).

Exercise 4.5. Show that the hypotheses of Kolmogorov's theorem apply here, except that we have equality in condition (iii), and conditions (i), (ii), (iv), and (vi) fail for $R = 0$, but hold for $R \neq 0$ and sufficiently small. Exercise 4.5 leads us to strongly suspect the presence of a stable limit cycle, making the phase space like this:

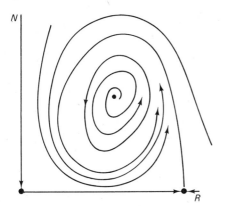

I think you could easily go back and take care of possibility 1 of page 89—
it is similar to possibility 3. I should say a few words about possibility 7. In that
case, the resource simply does not produce enough energy to support a consumer
population at all, and the consumer population will die out for any initial values
of the densities. The isoclines look like this

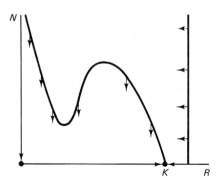

and the phase portrait looks like this

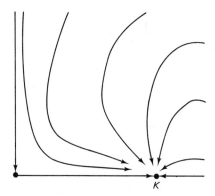

There will always be parameter values that correspond to cases like this,
in which the two-species system just is not viable and collapses down to a system
in which one or both species are absent. The biological meaning of such cases
is usually not hard to figure out.

4.3 HOW INSECTICIDES AFFECT THE SPRUCE
BUDWORM SYSTEM

In Section 2.2.2 I discussed the spruce budworm system, and at the end of that
section I said a little bit about the effect of insecticides. We now have the mathematical apparatus with which to pursue those remarks a little more deeply.
    We will add more detail to the model in Section 2.2.2, in the form of a

dynamical equation for the leaf area R. This approach, due to May (1977), is enough to get at the essentials, though it is still a cruder model than that of Ludwig et al. (1978).

May assumes that the growth of leaf area is logistic, with a loss to budworms that is linearly proportional to the budworm density N:

$$dR/dt = sR(1 - R/R_{max}) - cN$$
$$dN/dt = rN(1 - N/kR) - EPN^2/(n^2R^2 + N^2)$$

(4.16)

with s, R_{max}, and c positive constants. The second equation here is the budworm equation (2.8) [using (2.9, 2.10)]. The pair of equations (4.16) describes the interacting dynamics of budworms and foliage. We have already worked out the N-isocline in phase space; it can be seen on page 22.

From (4.16), the R-isocline $dR/dt = 0$ is a parabola:

$$N = sR(1 - R/R_{max})/c$$

(4.17)

with R_{max} lying somewhere to the right of T_1 (p. 22). So the isoclines look like this

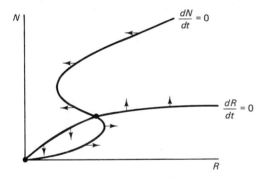

resulting in the following trajectories (which include a stable limit cycle, corresponding to the periodic budworm eruptions discussed in Section 2.2.2):

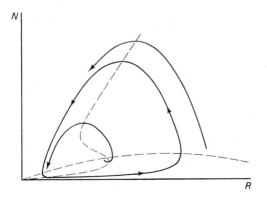

Now suppose we try to keep the budworm population down by spraying with insecticides. If the insecticides kill a proportion i of the budworm population per unit time, then the second of equations (4.16) becomes

$$dN/dt = rN(1 - N/kR) - EPN^2/(n^2R^2 + N^2) - iN \qquad (4.18)$$

which we can rewrite as

$$dN/dt = r'N(1 - N/K') - EPN^2/(N_0^2 + N^2) \qquad (4.19)$$

with

$$r' = r - i \qquad K' = kR(r - i)/r \qquad (4.20)$$

Equation (4.19) is the same as our original budworm equation (2.8), except that r and K are replaced by r' and K' as given by (4.20).

What is the effect of this rescaling of r and K? The rescaled budworm growth rate $r'N(1 - N/K')$ has a zero at K' and has its peak at $K'/2$, at which point the growth rate has the value $r'K'/4 = rK'^2/4K$ [using (2.9) and (4.20)]:

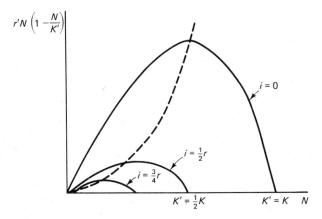

Exercise 4.6. Prove that the sentence leading up to the above sketch is correct, hence that the sketch is correct.

Now we can rethink the N-isocline. We need to go all the way back to the sketch on page 17. The effect of the above-depicted shrinking of the budworm growth curve (without predation) will be to shift the "saturation" point in the harvesting term to the right, relative to the budworm growth curve. Magnifying the scale of the sketch on page 17 to make up for the above-depicted shrinkage, we will, if i is big enough, have something like this:

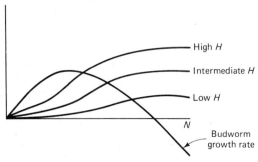

There is now only one equilibrium, whatever the value of *H!* So the "kink" in the curve on page 19 will be "straightened out." It's a little tricky to translate this to our budworm density-leaf area phase space, because of the messy dependence on *R* in the second of equations (4.19). But again, the "kink" in the budworm isocline is straightened out, as follows:

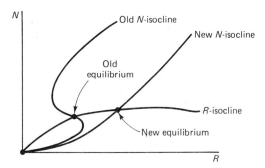

The new equilibrium is stable:

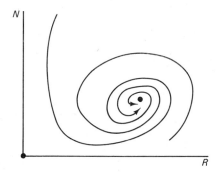

Of course, if one could manage to get *i* larger than *r*, the budworms would be (locally) eradicated altogether [from (4.20)], but this would involve massive spraying and does not really come into question.

The spraying does eliminate the limit cycle, and with it the budworm outbreaks. Instead, the system will sit at the new equilibrium, with budworm density *N* well below the former "outbreak" level and leaf area *R* at a healthy level. However, *N* is above the former "usual" low level (on the lower branch of the old isocline).

It seems like a reasonable enough situation. So much so that we might consider taking a break in the spraying, having got things under control. But if we do this, the budworm isocline will revert to its old form, and the densities will be sitting at the point in phase space previously occupied by the new equilibrium. But *this point is now in a region of positive budworm growth* (recall the top picture on page 105), so the budworms will immediately explode to "outbreak" levels!

The new stable equilibrium created by insecticide use has a fatal flaw: it can be maintained only by continuing to spray forever, and a cessation of spraying brings one immediately back to the "worst case" of a budworm outbreak. The environmental (particularly human) costs of such massive and ceaseless insecticide use are likely to be too high to accept.

I think this is a nice illustration of the kinds of insight that one can gain from tinkering with models. But, please do not take the conclusions reached here as definitive. *If* the biology is more or less as indicated in Section 2.2.2 and here, we might expect the system to behave like the model. At least one highly respected authority on the budworm (Royama 1984) has questioned the role of natural enemies of the budworms, which is so central to the working of this model. The model still needs a lot of testing, in terms of its predictions and of its biological foundations.

ADDITIONAL EXERCISES

4.7. Work out the possible phase portraits for a laissez-faire consumer, with Type II functional response, of a logistic resource. That is, replace $R^2/(R_0^2 + R^2)$ in (4.5) by $R/(R_0 + R)$. You will find your results from Exercise 2.13 helpful.

4.8. Replace the logistic, self-renewing resource of (4.5) with a resource that flows into the system from outside. That is, replace $rR(1 - R/K)$ in (4.5) by $a - bR$, where a and b are positive constants. Work out the possible phase portraits. Comment on their biological meanings.

4.9. Investigate the effect of consumer interference by replacing the constant R_0 in (4.5) by a function $a + bN$, with a and b positive constants. Work out all possible phase portraits. Comment on their biological meanings.

4.10. The biological idea behind modeling interference in Exercise 4.9 is that interference may distract the consumers sufficiently from their foraging activities to cause them to saturate at a higher resource density. Another way that interference might work is for the activity of interfering and defending against interference to itself use up a noticeable amount of energy. One could model this effect by adding a term $-iN^2$ to the right-hand side of the second of equations (4.5). Work out the possible phase portraits and comment on their biological meanings.

4.11. Because of the health problems associated with extensive use of insecticides, management of the spruce budworm has tended recently to shift to the use of biological control agents. As a first rough estimate of how this might work, we could think of increasing the number P of budworm predators per unit area of forest, in (4.16). How would an increase in P affect the phase space, and what does this mean for the behavior of the system?

Chapter 5

Competition

In Chapter 4 we studied the interaction of a single consumer species and a single resource type. However, most consumers in nature consume more than one resource, and most resources are consumed by more than one species of consumer. So the next logical step for us is to contemplate systems that consist of a consumer species consuming several resources, or a resource consumed by several consumer species, or, in general, systems consisting of n consumer species and k resource types, for any positive integers n and k.

Again let me remind you that I am using the words "consumer" and "resource" in the generalized sense indicated at the very beginning of Chapter 4. In particular, the resources might conceivably be species of plants or other primary producers; then the consumers would be primary consumers (herbivores)—and we would be embarking upon the construction of ecosystem models "from the bottom up."

Our system of resources and consumers exists, of course, within some area of space. I am going to assume throughout this book that the resources in question are pretty much evenly distributed within this spatial area—the habitat looks *homogeneous* to our consumer species. Also, for the sake of this chapter, let us assume that none of the consumers predate or parasitize any of the others, and that there are no mutualistic interactions among them. A set of consumers satisfying these conditions is often referred to as a *competitive community*.

It is possible that the resources are so plentiful that the consumer species are limited by other factors. For instance, the consumers may suffer so much mortality that they never become abundant enough to tax the supply of resources. In such a case the consumers may have very little, if any, effect on each other. On the other hand, since any resource is, ultimately, limited in supply, we expect that in many cases resources will be in short supply and the consumer species will have to *compete* for those resources.

Both of these situations undoubtedly occur in nature. It is very difficult to say which is more common, and in fact this very question is itself a topic of considerable current research interest (Connell 1983, Schoener 1983). It will be interesting to see what the answer turns out to be, but whatever it may be, my purpose in this chapter is to discuss the case where competition *does* occur.

There are basically two ways—two *fundamentally different* ways—that an individual organism may go about getting its required share of the available resources (Yodzis 1986). One way is to collect a fraction of the resources from the whole area. The other way is to collect all the resources from a fraction of the area. (And of course, there is a continuum of intermediate strategies between these two extremes.)

These are two different strategies of utilizing space in the acquisition of resources. I will call the two strategies *collectivism* and *monopolism,* respectively. They lead to very different kinds of competition.

In collectivist consumption, each individual ranges more or less freely through the whole area, collecting resources as it wanders. Different individuals may very well try to avoid one another as much as possible, and if they are successful in this avoidance we will have pure exploitative or consumptive competition (Section 5.2): each individual hinders the others solely by consuming resources that they might otherwise have consumed. There may in addition be an element of direct interference between individual consumers (Section 5.3).

In monopolist consumption, some essential resource can be obtained only by occupying, more or less exclusively, some portion of space. This leads to competition for space (Section 5.4). The essential resource may be space itself, as in attachment sites for sessile filter feeders or nest sites for hole nesting birds. Most plants, on the other hand, need to occupy a certain amount of space below ground in order to obtain water and nutrients, and a certain amount of space above ground in order to obtain light.

Again we are going to have to take time out from our development of the biological models themselves to fill in a bit of mathematical background. I introduced certain mathematical ideas in Sections 2.1, 2.3, 2.4.1, 3.2, and 3.3 which proved useful for discussing the growth of single populations, and I added to that mathematical framework in Section 4.2 in a way that enabled us to contemplate systems consisting of two species. Now that we want to treat systems of more than two species, we will need to elaborate our mathematical framework still further.

5.1 MULTISPECIES INTERACTIONS

Consider a system of s species, with densities $N_1, N_2, \ldots, N_s$. Such a system might, for instance, consist of n consumer species and k resource species, as suggested above, with $s = n + k$; or it could even consist of all the species present in some habitat. I will take those s densities to be the state variables (Section

4.2) for our system, so the instantaneous growth rate dN_i/dt, $i = 1, \ldots, s$, of each species is some function f_i of all the densities:

$$dN_i/dt = f_i(N_1, \ldots, N_s) \qquad i = 1, \ldots, s \qquad (5.1)$$

For the time being, let us assume that the densities are the only quantities that vary significantly in time—I will say a little bit about environmental variation later on.

We can save ourselves a lot of writing, and also achieve a certain economy of thought, by regarding the whole *set* of densities $N_1, N_2, \ldots, N_s$ as *one* mathematical object. I will represent this object by a boldface letter: $\mathbf{N}$. (If you need to write down $\mathbf{N}$ with pencil and paper, you can just underline the N.) Should you want to visualize $\mathbf{N}$ as somehow made up of its components N_i, you can think of it as a *column vector:*

$$\mathbf{N} = \begin{bmatrix} N_1 \\ N_2 \\ \vdots \\ N_s \end{bmatrix}$$

Similarly, we can think of the s growth rates $f_1(\mathbf{N}), f_2(\mathbf{N}), \ldots, f_s(\mathbf{N})$ as the component parts of a column vector $\mathbf{f}(\mathbf{N})$:

$$\mathbf{f}(\mathbf{N}) = \begin{bmatrix} f_1(N_1, \ldots, N_s) \\ f_2(N_1, \ldots, N_s) \\ \vdots \\ f_s(N_1, \ldots, N_s) \end{bmatrix}$$

Then we can write (5.1) as

$$dN/dt = \mathbf{f}(\mathbf{N}) \qquad (5.2)$$

where the components of the derivative of a column vector are defined to be the derivatives of the components:

$$d\mathbf{N}/dt = \begin{bmatrix} dN_1/dt \\ dN_2/dt \\ \vdots \\ dN_s/dt \end{bmatrix}$$

If $s = 1$ equation (5.2) is just equation (2.2), and if $s = 2$ it is none other than equation (4.6).

As we did in Section 4.2 for $s = 2$, we can construct a *phase space* for the system. This space will have s axes, each labeled with one of the s densities N_i, $i = 1, \ldots, s$. Of course, when $s > 2$ (and especially if $s > 3$) it's no longer so easy to draw a picture of this space, but nevertheless s-dimensional phase space certainly exists as a mental construct, and it is a useful one.

   As in the two-species case, each point in phase space represents an instantaneous state of the system, and each solution $N(t)$ of (5.2), extended to infinite
past and future times, gives us a curve in phase space, which we will again call
a *trajectory*. There is one and only one trajectory through each point in phase
space, just as in the two-species case.

   Biological population densities can never have negative values, nor can
they ever become infinite. So each trajectory is confined within a finite region
of phase space as it evolves into the future. And yet, the trajectory extends to
the infinite temporal future. So each trajectory moves about within a finite region
of phase space for an infinite time. If you think about this, I believe it will
become evident to you that this can only happen if each trajectory approaches
some sort of limit as it evolves into the future.

   The next four paragraphs may seem a little abstract, but please persevere!
We are going to arrive at a very important concept.

   If N, M are two points in phase space, we can define the distance between
them to be

$$d(\mathbf{N}, \mathbf{M}) = [(N_1 - M_1)^2 + (N_2 - M_2)^2 + \cdots + (N_s - M_s)^2]^{1/2}$$

In one, two, and three dimensions, this is just the ordinary Euclidean distance
of everyday intuition. If N is a point in phase space and E is a subset of points
in phase space, we can define the distance between N and E to be the shortest
distance between N and a point of E:

$$d(\mathbf{N}, E) = \text{Min}\{d(\mathbf{N}, \mathbf{N}_E); \quad \mathbf{N}_E \text{ in } E\}$$

   Let N_0 be any point in phase space, and let $N(t)$ be the solution
of (5.2) that passes through N_0. We say that $N(t)$ approaches E as $t \rightarrow \infty$ if
$d(N(t), E) \rightarrow 0$ as $t \rightarrow \infty$. We can always find at least one set E that $N(t)$
approaches, namely, the whole phase space! But that is rather trivial. The smaller
E is, the more information we are getting from the statement that $N(t)$ approaches
E. The *smallest* closed set that $N(t)$ approaches as $t \rightarrow \infty$ is called the *omega-
limit set* of N_0 and denoted $\omega(N_0)$. (If the word "closed" doesn't mean anything
to you in this context, just ignore it.) The smallest closed set that $N(t)$ approaches
as $t \rightarrow -\infty$ is called the *alpha-limit set* of N_0, and denoted $\alpha(N_0)$.

   The omega-limit sets include some very important objects that we have
encountered already. For instance, a stable equilibrium (Sections 2.1 and 4.2.1.1)
is the omega-limit set of every point in its domain of attraction. Also, a stable
limit cycle is the omega-limit set for every point in its domain of attraction.
These are examples of limit sets that attract trajectories "from all around them."
Consider, on the other hand, the saddle point (page 95). This is the omega-limit
set of each point on the two separatrices that approach the saddle point asymptotically, but if you move the least bit off these separatrices, the saddle point is
no longer your omega-limit set.

   Those special omega-limit sets that are omega-limit sets for points "all
around them," like stable equilibria and stable limit cycles, are called "attractors."
More precisely: an omega-limit set A is an *attractor* if there exists a real positive

number ϵ such that for every N in phase space with $d(N, A) < \epsilon$, A is the omega-limit set of N.

I promised we would arrive at an important concept: the notion of attractor is it. Now, why are attractors so important? It's because when we go out and observe a population system, we are usually going to find it near some attractor. The attractors are the places in phase space where trajectories tend to end up; and it often doesn't take a system at all long to get pretty close to some attractor. *In a very real sense, we can, and do, observe attractors.*

Indeed, just by going out and looking at lots of population systems, we can "discover" attractors. Arguably, this is why the basic attractors—equilibrium points and limit cycles—are such easy concepts to assimilate: we already have an intuitive feeling for them before we do the mathematics. There are lots of systems for which the densities do not vary a great deal: thinking about systems like this amounts to an empirical discovery of *point attractors* (a term that I will frequently use as a synonym for stable equilibria). There are other cases where the densities undergo sustained oscillations: through these we could empirically discover stable limit cycles (also known as *periodic attractors*).

On the other hand, there are systems that do not seem to fit either of these paradigms very well. What about them? There are several possibilities, including:

1. It could be that our assumption thus far in this section of a constant environment is violated. This could result in so much "noise" in the dynamics that any underlying attractors are obscured, or it could be that the populations "track" environmental variation, by staying close to an attractor that is itself moving around in phase space owing to environmental change. [For some data that very much suggest this kind of "tracking," see Grant (1986).]

2. It could be that the system under observation has been moved far away from any attractor by some large disturbance, or that the system was recently initiated far from any attractor (via, say, colonization) and is moving toward an attractor but is not yet close to it. This is called *transient* behavior. [The ungulate eruptions of Section 4.2.1.2 are examples. For other data in which transients seem to play an important role, see Brown et al. (1986).]

3. It could be that the system is near an attractor that is neither an equilibrium point nor a limit cycle. Such "strange attractors" exist! I am going to discuss them in Section 6.2.

The vast majority of theoretical ecology that has been done up to now assumes the existence of a stable equilibrium. I will discuss this assumption, and alternatives to it, later in this chapter, and in Chapters 6 and 8. For now, let's look a little more closely at equilibria.

5.1.1 Equilibria

Consider again the system (5.2). Any point N_e in phase space such that $f(N_e) = 0$ is an equilibrium of our system, in exactly the same sense that we've discussed in Sections 2.1 and 4.2.1.1. In a structurally stable system, only single isolated points can be equilibria. An equilibrium that is locally stable in the sense of Sections 2.1 and 4.2.1.1 is an attractor in the sense of the previous section. Therefore, it is important to be able to determine whether an equilibrium is stable or not.

I glossed over this point in Section 4.2.1.1, stating conditions for stability (in the two-dimensional case) without attempting to make them make sense. To be quite honest, I did this because I was afraid that if I took you on too many mathematical side excursions at that point, you might get bored and give up on this whole enterprise. Now that you've stuck with me this long, I'm going to permit myself to assume that you are beginning to see the point of mathematical thinking and maybe even enjoying it; and that you want to at least understand the basic ideas behind any "cookbook" that might be thrown at you.

In case you're willing to settle for the intuitive grasp of local stability that, I hope, you've got by now, and don't care about how one actually determines stability of multidimensional equilibria or why it works out that way, you can skip directly to Section 5.2 with no loss of continuity. You can always come back and finish this section if, someday, you need to understand stability calculations.

I am going to use complex numbers and matrices in what follows. In case these topics are unfamiliar to you, or you need to review them, the essential ideas that we will need here are sketched in the Appendix. Even if you know all about matrices, you should at least skim Section A.2 to familiarize yourself with my notational conventions. I will assume you have done so.

Step 1: Linearize

The first step is to linearize the system (5.2) around the equilibrium point N_e (recall Section 2.4.1). Expanding the components of f in a Taylor's series (that old calculus text again!) we get

$$f_i(N) = f_i(N_e) + \sum_j A_{ij}(N_j - N_{ej}) + \text{terms of higher order in the } (N_j - N_{je})$$

For N sufficiently near N_e, f_i is well approximated by keeping just the linear terms. So we will write

$$f_i(N) = f_i(N_e) + \sum_j A_{ij}(N_j - N_{ej}) = \sum_j A_{ij}(N_j - N_{ej}) \qquad i = 1, \ldots, s \quad (5.3)$$

[since $f(N_e) = 0$]. Here

$$A_{ij} = \left. \frac{\partial f_i}{\partial N_j} \right|_{N_e} \qquad i, j = 1, \ldots, s \qquad (5.4)$$

So in a neighborhood of N_e, we can approximate (5.1) by the linear system

$$dN_i/dt = \sum_j A_{ij}(N_j - N_{ej}) \qquad i = 1, \ldots, s \qquad (5.5)$$

The array A_{ij} of s^2 numbers is often called in the ecological literature the *community matrix* associated with the equilibrium. Solutions to this system of equations approximate, in a neighborhood of equilibrium, the solutions to our original equations (5.2). In particular, one can prove that *if* N_e *is a locally stable equilibrium of* (5.5), *it is also a locally stable equilibrium of* (5.2).

If we denote by **A** the matrix whose elements are the numbers A_{ij},

$$\mathbf{A} = \begin{bmatrix} A_{11} & A_{12} & A_{13} & \cdots & A_{1s} \\ A_{21} & A_{22} & A_{23} & \cdots & A_{2s} \\ & & \vdots & & \\ A_{s1} & A_{s2} & A_{s3} & \cdots & A_{ss} \end{bmatrix} \tag{5.6}$$

we can write (5.5) as

$$d\mathbf{N}/dt = \mathbf{A}(\mathbf{N} - \mathbf{N}_e) \tag{5.7}$$

We can simplify (5.7) just a little bit more if we define

$$\mathbf{X} = \mathbf{N} - \mathbf{N}_e \tag{5.8}$$

Then

$$d\mathbf{X}/dt = d\mathbf{N}/dt$$

(since $\mathbf{N}_e$ is a constant column vector), so (5.7) is

$$d\mathbf{X}/dt = \mathbf{A}\mathbf{X} \tag{5.9}$$

This looks simple, but deceptively so. If we write it out in terms of the components of **X**,

$$dX_i/dt = A_{i1}X_1 + A_{i2}X_2 + \cdots + A_{is}X_s \qquad i = 1, \ldots, s$$

we see that the s individual differential equations are highly coupled (meaning that the derivative of X_i involves not just X_i but all the other X's as well).

Step 2: Solve This Linear System

Assume that **A** is diagonalizable (as almost always turns out to be the case in ecology). Let $\{ \mathbf{v}_i, i = 1, \ldots, s \}$ be s linearly independent eigenvectors of **A**. It is shown in Section A.2 that any column vector can be written as a linear combination of the s eigenvectors. So in particular, this is true of $\mathbf{X}(t)$ at each time t:

$$\mathbf{X}(t) = \sum_i a_i(t)\mathbf{v}_i \tag{5.10}$$

Therefore

$$d\mathbf{X}/dt = \sum_i da_i/dt\,\mathbf{v}_i \tag{5.11}$$

and

$$\mathbf{AX} = \sum_i a_i \mathbf{Av}_i = \sum_i a_i \lambda_i \mathbf{v}_i \tag{5.12}$$

where λ_i is the eigenvalue corresponding to $\mathbf{v}_i$. Putting these into (5.9),

$$\sum_i (da_i/dt - \lambda_i a_i)\mathbf{v}_i = 0 \tag{5.13}$$

Since $\{\mathbf{v}_i\}$ is linearly independent, the sum can be zero only if each coefficient is zero:

$$da_i/dt = \lambda_i a_i \qquad i = 1, \ldots, s$$

This we can easily solve:

$$a_i(t) = c_i e^{\lambda_i t} \qquad i = 1, \ldots, s$$

where c_i is a constant of integration. Therefore

$$\mathbf{X} = \sum_i c_i e^{\lambda_i t} \mathbf{v}_i$$

and from (5.8)

$$N_j(t) = N_{ej} + \sum_j c_i(v_i)_j e^{\lambda_i t} \qquad j = 1, \ldots, s \tag{5.14}$$

where the number $(v_i)_j$ is the jth component of the vector $\mathbf{v}_i$.

At $t = 0$ we have

$$N_j(t) = N_{ej} + \sum_i c_i(v_i)_j$$

so choosing the s constants c_i, $i = 1, \ldots, s$, amounts to choosing an initial displacement away from equilibrium.

Step 3: Stability

The equilibrium will be locally stable if for any initial displacement (that is, for any choice of c_i), all the densities approach $\mathbf{N}_e$ as $t \to \infty$. In order for this to be the case, the summation over i in equation (5.14) must approach 0 as $t \to \infty$, for *any* choice of the s numbers c_i. This will happen if and only if each individual factor $e^{\lambda_i t}$ vanishes as $t \to \infty$.

The eigenvalues λ_k are, in general, complex numbers. Write $\lambda_k = \mu_k + i\nu_k$, where $i^2 = -1$, and the real numbers μ_k and ν_k are, respectively, the real and imaginary parts of λ_k. It is a basic property of exponentiation that $e^{a+b} = e^a e^b$. So

$$e^{\lambda_k t} = e^{(\mu_k + i\nu_k)t} = e^{\mu_k t} e^{i\nu_k t} \tag{5.15}$$

According to de Moivre's theorem (A.11),

$$e^{i\nu_k t} = \cos(\nu_k t) + i \sin(\nu_k t)$$

So the imaginary part v_k of an eigenvalue λ_k, when it is nonzero, produces *oscillations* in the solution. In particular, whatever the value of v_k, the factor $e^{iv_k t}$ in (5.15) will not vanish as $t \to \infty$. Therefore, if $e^{\lambda_k t}$ is to vanish as $t \to \infty$, it has to be that the factor $e^{\mu_k t}$ vanishes as $t \to \infty$. This will happen if and only if μ_k, the real part of λ_k, is negative.

In order to have local stability, we need to have this for each k. So, *the condition for local stability of an equilibrium is that all the eigenvalues of the community matrix corresponding to that equilibrium have negative real parts.*

Let us calculate the eigenvalues for a two-species system ($s = 2$). An eigenvalue λ satisfies the equation $\mathbf{Av} = \lambda\mathbf{v}$ for some vector $\mathbf{v}$. Writing this out in components, as in (A.23), we have

$$\sum_{j=1}^{2} A_{ij}v_j = \lambda v_j \qquad i = 1, 2$$

These two equations are

$$A_{11}v_1 + A_{12}v_2 = \lambda v_1$$

$$A_{21}v_1 + A_{22}v_2 = \lambda v_2$$

It must be that either $v_1 \neq 0$ or $v_2 \neq 0$ (for otherwise $\mathbf{v}$ is identically $\mathbf{0}$). Suppose $v_1 \neq 0$. Then dividing by v_1 in both of the above equations,

$$A_{11} + A_{12}(v_2/v_1) = \lambda$$

$$A_{21} + A_{22}(v_2/v_1) = \lambda(v_2/v_1)$$

These are two simultaneous equations for the two quantities λ, (v_1/v_1).

Exercise 5.1. Show that it follows from the above two equations that λ satisfies

$$\lambda^2 - (A_{11} + A_{22})\lambda + A_{11}A_{22} - A_{12}A_{21} = 0$$

Show that the same equation results if we assume that $v_2 \neq 0$ instead of assuming $v_1 \neq 0$.

In terms of the notation that we used in Section 4.2.1.1, the quadratic equation obtained in the above exercise is

$$\lambda^2 - I_e\lambda + \Omega_e = 0$$

where I_e and Ω_e are defined in equations (4.11).

Therefore, the eigenvalues are

$$\lambda = [I_e \pm (I_e^2 - 4\Omega_e)^{1/2}]/2$$

The equilibrium is stable if both of these roots have negative real parts. If $I_e^2 \geq 4\Omega_e$, both roots are real. They have the same sign only if $\Omega_e > 0$, and that sign is negative only if $I_e < 0$. On the other hand, if $I_e^2 < 4\Omega_e$ (whence $\Omega_e > 0$), the two roots are complex conjugates of one another, with (common) real part I_e. So we need $I_e < 0$ for stability.

So in any case, the condition for local stability is

$$I_e < 0 \quad \text{and} \quad \Omega_e > 0$$

which is identical with (4.10).

When there are more than two species, the calculation of eigenvalues can be very messy. In Section 7.1.3 I will indicate how to do it for relatively simple systems, say $s \leq 5$. I will also give conditions for determining whether all the eigenvalues have negative real parts without actually calculating the eigenvalues themselves, but the use of these conditions, too, is practicable only for relatively simple systems. Beyond that, one has to resort to some rather complicated numerical methods, which can only be carried out on a computer. Most packages of scientific computer subroutines include programs for the computation of eigenvalues.

As in Section 2.4.1, we can define a parameter Λ that provides a rough measure of how quickly the densities return to equilibrium after a sufficiently small perturbation:

$$\Lambda = \text{Min}\{-\text{Re}(\lambda_i); \quad i = 1, \ldots, s\} \tag{5.16}$$

where $\text{Re}(\lambda_i)$ means the real part of λ_i. The return time will be at most of the order of $T_R = 1/\Lambda$.

5.2 COLLECTIVISM: PURE CONSUMPTIVE COMPETITION

Now we are ready to begin our study of competition. If two or more consumer species share (one or more) resources, and if they are limited by those resources, then the consumer species will hinder each other (as will the individual members of each of those species) through this dependence on shared resources. Quite simply, each resource item that is consumed by consumer 1 is thereby rendered unavailable to consumer 2.

This kind of competition has traditionally been called *exploitation*. However, some authors have used the term in the context of competition for space, which is monopolist, so Schoener (1983) introduced the term *consumptive competition* to mean pure exploitation with a collectivist spatial utilization, and I will use that term here.

A pair of species can engage in consumptive competition even if neither species is aware of the other's existence. For example, one species might utilize a resource during the day, and the other species during the night. They could still hinder each other through their mutual dependence on the same resource.

5.2.1 The Classical (Equilibrium) Theory

The "classical" theoretical ecology of the sixties and seventies emphasized very strongly the role of competition in structuring the systems we see in nature.

However, this classical theory construed competition almost exclusively in the specific sense of consumptive competition, and its theory of consumptive competition was an equilibrium theory. We will see in the rest of this chapter that there is a lot more to competition than that. Nevertheless, the classical work was a valuable start, and its basic paradigm—that competing species cannot be too similar in their ecology—is still very much with us.

Let us consider, with MacArthur (1972), a "laissez-faire" system (Section 4.2) of n consumer species, with linear functional responses and k resource types:

$$dN_i/dt = C_iN_i\left(-T_i + \sum_J a_{iJ}w_JR_J\right) \qquad i = 1, \ldots, n$$

$$dR_I/dt = s_IR_I(1 - R_I/L_I) - \sum_j a_{jI}N_jR_I \qquad I = 1, \ldots, k \tag{5.17}$$

Here N_i is the density of consumer species i and R_I is the density of resource type I. Notice that I am using lowercase subscripts for consumers and uppercase subscripts for resources.

One item of resource type I has nutritional value w_I (assumed to be the same for all consumers), and C_i is a conversion factor for the transformation of nutritional intake into individuals of species i. The probability that during a unit of time, a member of consumer species i captures and consumes an item of resource J is a_{iJ}. The starvation rate of consumer species i is T_i. Resource type I grows logistically with intrinsic growth rate s_I and carrying capacity L_I in the absence of all consumers.

Notice that we have assumed the nutritional value of a resource item is a fixed constant, independent of a consumer's overall diet. Resources like this are called *substitutable* (Tilman 1982). I will discuss other nutritional possibilities in Section 5.4.2.1.

Assume the system has an equilibrium point with all n consumers present at nonzero density. Then, from the first set of equations comprising (5.17),

$$0 = -T_i + \sum_J a_{iJ}w_JR_J \qquad i = 1, \ldots, n$$

at equilibrium. These are n linear equations for the k resource densities R_I, $I = 1, \ldots, k$.

Suppose there are more consumer species than resource types: $n > k$. What will happen? To investigate this question, let's take the particular case $n = 3$, $k = 2$. Then we have

$$\left.\begin{array}{l} 0 = -T_1 + a_{11}w_1R_1 + a_{12}w_2R_2 \\[4pt] 0 = -T_2 + a_{21}w_1R_1 + a_{22}w_2R_2 \\[4pt] 0 = -T_3 + a_{31}w_1R_1 + a_{32}w_2R_2 \end{array}\right\} \tag{5.18}$$

We can solve the first two of these equations for R_1 and R_2. The answer is

$$R_1 = (a_{12}T_2 - a_{22}T_1)/[w_1(a_{12}a_{21} - a_{11}a_{22})]$$

$$R_2 = (a_{21}T_1 - a_{11}T_2)/[w_2(a_{12}a_{21} - a_{11}a_{22})]$$

Exercise 5.2. Prove these last two equations correct.

Both unknowns are determined, but we still have one equation left, namely, the third of (5.18). Putting our solutions for R_1 and R_2 into this, we get

$$(a_{32}a_{21} - a_{31}a_{22})T_1 + (a_{31}a_{12} - a_{32}a_{11})T_2 + (a_{11}a_{22} - a_{12}a_{21})T_3 = 0$$

This is a relation involving nothing but parameters. There is no reason for it to hold in general. Moreover, should the parameters happen to be such as to satisfy this relation, then the very *slightest* change in a parameter will destroy this concordance. So for most parameter values there is no solution, and whenever there is a solution, the resulting system (5.17) is structurally unstable.

This kind of situation is called *overdetermination.* We have more equations than we need to determine all the unknowns. Whenever $n > k$ in (5.17), the equilibrium equations (5.18) are overdetermined. There will be no solution, unless just the right $n - k$ relations among the parameters happen to hold, and then the model will be structurally unstable. As indicated in Section 2.3, a structurally unstable model is as good as no model.

If we insist upon equilibrium solutions, as does the classical theory, we have to conclude that, at least on the basis of this model, there cannot be more consumer species than resource types. The impossibility of equilibrium coexistence of n consumer species on $k < n$ resources has been proved for a very general class of models by McGehee and Armstrong (1977), who also provide references to earlier work on this question.

This is our first indication that coexisting competitors cannot be too similar. If there is not in the habitat a sufficient variety in resource types for the consumers to have sufficiently different diets (and thereby avoid competition), coexistence (at least in the sense of a point attractor) is not possible.

Let us, then, suppose instead that there are at least as many resource types as there are consumer species: $k \geq n$. Let us further suppose that the resource dynamics is much faster than the consumer dynamics. Then the resource densities will "track" the demands made on them very precisely; at all times the resources will be essentially in equilibrium. These equilibrial resource levels are obtained by setting $dR_I/dt = 0$ in (5.17):

$$R_I = L_I\left[1 - \left(\sum_j a_{jI}N_j\right)\middle/ s_I\right] \qquad I = 1, \ldots, k$$

We can substitute these relationships into the first set of equations in (5.17) to eliminate all R's from them. If we then group the various terms together in the appropriate way, we will obtain

$$dN_i/dt = r_iN_i\left(K_i - N_i - \sum_{j \neq i} \alpha_{ij}N_j\right)\middle/ K_i \qquad i = 1, \ldots, n \qquad (5.19)$$

where

$$\left.\begin{array}{ll}
r_i = C_i\left(\sum_J a_{iJ}w_J L_J - T_i\right) & i = 1, \ldots, n \\[3mm]
K_i = \left(\sum_J a_{iJ}w_J L_J - T_i\right) \bigg/ \left(\sum_J L_J w_J a_{iJ}^2/s_J\right) & i = 1, \ldots, n \\[3mm]
\alpha_{ij} = \left(\sum_K L_K w_K a_{iK}a_{jK}/s_K\right) \bigg/ \left(\sum_K L_K w_K a_{iK}^2/s_K\right) & i, j = 1, \ldots, n
\end{array}\right\} \quad (5.20)$$

Exercise 5.3. Prove (5.19) and (5.20).

I trust that you will recognize (5.19) as the Lotka-Volterra competition equations. You will have encountered these equations in elementary ecology courses, and you will have studied the behavior of solutions to these equations for the case $n = 2$ in those same courses.

For the most part, classical competition theory uses the Lotka-Volterra equations (5.19) rather than equations like (5.17) which explicitly model the resource dynamics. However, the resource dynamics are taken into account (subject to our assumption that they are "fast enough") rather elegantly in the relationships (5.20), through the L's and s's.

The α's, which quantify the strength of competition, express overlap in resource utilization. To see this, notice that, on the one hand, if consumer species i and j have no overlap in diet, so that for every K either $a_{iK} = 0$ or $a_{jK} = 0$, then $\alpha_{ij} = 0$; while on the other hand, if consumers i and j have identical diets, so that $a_{iK} = a_{jK}$ for all K, then $\alpha_{ij} = 1$. For situations intermediate between these two extremes α_{ij} lies between 0 and 1.

Equations (5.20) relate the parameters in the Lotka-Volterra equations to the dynamics of a discrete set of exploited resources and to the patterns of exploitation of those resources. But what is a "resource"?

To begin with, one might say that a resource corresponds to a biological species. This will frequently be a sensible way of looking at things, but there are exceptions. For instance, the roots and leaves of a single plant species may well be viewed as distinct resources by two different consumer species. Or, different life stages of a single species may serve as distinct resources (Haigh and Maynard Smith 1972).

Another aspect of the problem can be illustrated through seed-eating birds. Are all the seeds in their habitat one resource? Certainly not: some birds prefer large seeds, some prefer small seeds. (Let's neglect, for the moment, differences in hardness of seed husks.) But how large is large? Seeds do not come in two or three distinct sizes, but rather in a continuum of sizes. So it is appropriate to think of them as comprising a one-dimensional *resource continuum*.

We can easily generalize (5.20) to apply to such a resource continuum. Let x be a continuously varying resource label (seed size, or whatever), and let $w(x)$, $s(x)$, and $L(x)$ be the nutritional value, intrinsic growth rate, and carrying capacity, respectively, of resources of type x. Let $a_i(x)dx$ be the probability that, during a unit interval of time, a given individual of consumer species i captures and consumes a resource item whose type lies in the interval $(x, x + dx)$. Define (with MacArthur and Levins 1967) the *resource-availability spectrum*

$$P(x) = [L(x)w(x)s(x)]^{1/2} \qquad (5.21)$$

and the *resource-utilization spectrum* of species i

$$u_i(x) = [L(x)w(x)/s(x)]^{1/2} a_i(x) \qquad (5.22)$$

Then converting the sums in (5.20) to integrals [or, indeed, by starting from scratch with the appropriate continuous analogs to (5.17)], we obtain (if we regard T_i, $i = 1, \ldots, n$, as negligibly small)

$$
\left.
\begin{aligned}
r_i &= C_i \int dx P(x) u_i(x) & i &= 1, \ldots, n \\[2mm]
K_i &= \int dx P(x) u_i(x) \Big/ \int dx u_i(x)^2 & i &= 1, \ldots, n \\[2mm]
\alpha_{ij} &= \int dx u_i(x) u_j(x) \Big/ \int dx u_i(x)^2 & i, j &= 1, \ldots, n
\end{aligned}
\right\} \qquad (5.23)
$$

The integrals are to be taken over the entire range of x for which $P(x)$ and $u(x)$ are defined.

Exercise 5.4. Prove (5.23).

Not all continuous resources can be represented in a one-dimensional space like this. Take seeds, for instance. They vary not only in size but in the hardness of their husk and in their content of specific nutrients. If these other factors were important for the seed consumers being studied, one would have to work with a multidimensional resource space. Not much theory has yet been done in this setting, but the interested reader can consult May (1974b), Yoshiyama and Roughgarden (1977), and Rappoldt and Hogeweg (1980).

5.2.1.1 Limiting Similarity

With discrete resources, we found that (at least from an equilibrium point of view), n consumer species cannot coexist if they jointly exploit $k < n$ resources. Under these circumstances, there is not enough scope for dissimilarity among the consumers. What is the corresponding statement for consumers sharing a continuous resource spectrum? This question was considered by MacArthur and Levins (1967) as follows.

A given feeding apparatus is going to be more effective at processing some food types than others. For instance, each avian beak size will be inefficient at processing seeds that are too large or too small. So we expect the resource-utilization functions (5.22) to be peaked in some way. In many cases, a Gaussian function

$$u_i(x) = U_i \, e^{-(x-x_i)^2/2\sigma_i^2}$$

(5.24)

will be appropriate. Here x_i is the position of the peak, U_i is its height, and σ_i, one standard deviation, provides a measure of its width.

Consider two species, with utilization functions of the same height U and width σ, but at different positions x_1 and $x_2 = x_1 + d$.

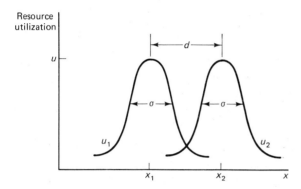

Then

$$\alpha_{12} = \frac{U^2 \int_{-\infty}^{\infty} dx \, e^{-(x-x_1)^2/2\sigma^2} e^{-(x-x_1-d)^2/2\sigma^2}}{U^2 \int_{-\infty}^{\infty} dx (e^{-(x-x_1)^2/2\sigma^2})^2}$$

Introducing a new variable of integration $y = x - x_1$, we can write this as

$$\alpha_{12} = \frac{\int_{-\infty}^{\infty} dy \, e^{-y^2/2\sigma^2} e^{-(y-d)^2/2\sigma^2}}{\int_{-\infty}^{\infty} dy (e^{-y^2/2\sigma^2})^2}$$

Now

$$e^{-y^2/2\sigma^2} e^{-(y-d^2)/2\sigma^2} = e^{-[y^2+(y-d)^2]/2\sigma^2}$$

and

$$y^2 + (y-d)^2 = 2y^2 - 2yd + d^2 = 2[y^2 - yd + (d/2)^2 + d^2/4]$$
$$= 2(y - d/2)^2 + d^2/2$$

so

$$e^{-y^2/2\sigma^2} e^{-(y-d)^2/2\sigma^2} = e^{-d^2/4\sigma^2} e^{-(y-d/2)^2/\sigma^2}$$

Therefore

$$\alpha_{12} = \frac{e^{-d^2/4\sigma^2} \int_{-\infty}^{\infty} dy \, e^{-(y-d/2)^2/\sigma^2}}{\int_{-\infty}^{\infty} dy \, e^{-y^2/\sigma^2}}$$

If we define a new variable of integration $z = y - d/2$, and write the top integral here in terms of z, then it will be identical to the bottom integral. So

$$\alpha_{12} = e^{-d^2/4\sigma^2}$$

If we calculate α_{21} using similar methods, we will find $\alpha_{21} = \alpha_{12}$. So long as the utilization spectra differ only in their positions, not in their heights or widths, the pairwise competition coefficients will depend only on the distance between peaks. We can denote this coefficient by

$$\alpha(d) = e^{-d^2/4\sigma^2} \tag{5.25}$$

Actually, this is only an approximation, because a realistic utilization function will be truncated at some lower limit of resource variable x, and at some upper limit, while the Gaussian extends all the way to plus and minus infinity. This can make a difference in quantitative applications. For instance, Pulliam (1975, 1983) performs such truncations in his calculations on sparrow coexistence. But for the qualitative use we will make of it, (5.25) is an adequate approximation.

Figure 5.1 is a plot of (5.25), with the horizontal axis scaled in units of d/σ.

Getting back to our pair of competitors, we want to take in the Lotka-Volterra equations (5.19) $n = 2$ and $\alpha_{12} = \alpha_{21} = \alpha(d)$. Then if we set the right-hand sides of (5.19) equal to 0 to solve for the equilibrium densities, we obtain

$$N_{e1} = [K_1 - \alpha(d)K_2]/[1 - \alpha(d)^2]$$
$$N_{e2} = [K_2 - \alpha(d)K_1]/[1 - \alpha(d)^2] \tag{5.26}$$

Exercise 5.5. Prove (5.26).

You can readily verify, using the methods of Chapter 4, that this equilibrium is stable for any parameter values. However, in order for it to correspond to co-existence of our two species, both densities need to be greater than zero at equi-

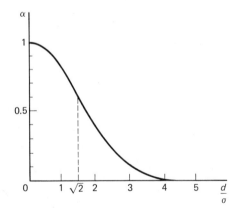

Figure 5.1 Alpha vs. d/σ, according to equation (5.25). (From MacArthur 1972. *Geographical Ecology*, Harper & Row, New York.)

librium. So we need $K_1 > \alpha(d)K_2$ and $K_2 > \alpha(d)K_1$. Translating this into a constraint on $\alpha(d)$, the condition for coexistence of two species is

$$\alpha(d) < \text{smaller of } K_1/K_2, K_2/K_1 \qquad (5.27)$$

Again, the competitors cannot coexist if they are too similar: coexistence implies an upper limit on α, hence a lower limit on d [from (5.25)], although this lower limit collapses to zero if $K_1 = K_2$, since then $\alpha(d)$ need only be smaller than 1.

The situation is different if we have three or more competitors. Suppose we have three consumer species, with identical Gaussian utilization spectra $u_i(x)$, except for the positions of the peaks. Assume the peaks are equally spaced at a distance d, and number the species 1, 2, 3 in order as the value of x at the peak increases:

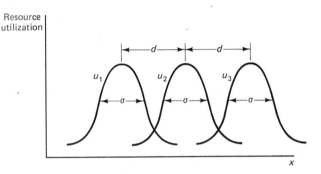

Then applying (5.25) to each pair of peaks, and remembering that the peaks of species 1 and 3 are separated by a distance $2d$ on the resource axis x, we get

$$\alpha_{12} = \alpha_{21} = \alpha_{23} = \alpha_{32} = \alpha(d)$$

$$\alpha_{13} = \alpha_{31} = \alpha(d)^4$$

Assume the outer two species have the same carrying capacity $K_1 = K_3 = K$. Putting all this into the Lotka-Volterra equations (5.19) (with $n = 3$) and solving for the equilibrium densities, we get

$$N_{e1} = N_{e3} = [K - \alpha(d)K_2]/[1 - \alpha(d)^2]^2 \qquad (5.28)$$

$$N_{e2} = \{[1 + \alpha(d)^4]K_2 - 2\alpha(d)K\}/[1 - \alpha(d)^2]^2$$

Exercise 5.6. Prove (5.28).

Again this equilibrium is always stable (May 1974). But in order for all equilibrium densities to be positive we need

$$2\alpha(d)/[1 + \alpha(d)^4] < K_2/K < 1/\alpha(d) \qquad (5.29)$$

Now, unlike with two competitors, there is always a finite lower limit on d that will permit coexistence. For instance, if $K_2 = K$, we need $\alpha(d) < 0.544$, corresponding [through (5.25)] to $d > 1.56\sigma$. We can do a similar calculation for more than three species. Thus with four species we need $d > 1.1\sigma$; with five species we need $d > 1.5\sigma$; with six species we need $d > 1.3\sigma$ for coexistence; and so on.

With minor variations depending on the number of species, $d \gtrsim \sigma$ is an approximate condition for coexistence.

This kind of lower limit on the similarity of coexisting competitors is one of the major results of classical competition theory. It is called *limiting similarity*. A corollary of limiting similarity is the notion of *ecological character displacement* (Brown and Wilson 1956, Fenchel 1975), which you will recall from elementary ecology courses.

The fact that limiting similarity is less severe when there are only two species (and even vanishes when $K_1 = K_2$) is a simple example of *diffuse competition,* in which "several competitors can much more easily outcompete and eliminate a species than a single competitor can" (MacArthur 1972, Pianka 1975).

The condition $d \gtrsim \sigma$, as an approximate criterion for limiting similarity, has often been stated as a sweeping generalization. However, the above calculations make quite a few assumptions about details, and this is not a good basis for generalization. We need to ask how *robust* the condition $d \gtrsim \sigma$ is, meaning how insensitive it is to details in the underlying model.

For instance, we may ask whether the shape of the resource-utilization curves influences the result significantly. We did the calculation above for Gaussian utilization spectra u_i. Roughgarden (1974) has investigated other shapes.

Specifically, he treats the family of curves

$$u(x) = c_2 \exp[-c_1(x/\sigma)^n]$$

where

$$c_1 = [\Gamma(3/n)/\Gamma(1/n)]^{1/2} \qquad c_2 = c_1/[2\sigma\Gamma(1/n + 1)]$$

and $\Gamma(x)$ is the gamma function (e.g., Copson 1935). For $n = 2$ this is the Gaussian distribution. In each case the curve has its peak at $x = 0$, and has standard deviation σ.

However, the curves have different kurtosis, depending on the value of n. Kurtosis is the extent to which a peaked distribution is concentrated in the central regions within a standard deviation of the peak. For $n > 2$, these curves are *platykurtic* (broad peak, thin tails) relative to the Gaussian; for $n < 2$, we get *leptokurtic* (narrow peak, thick tails) distributions, relative to the Gaussian (Fig. 5.2).

Equation (5.29) is still the condition for coexistence, with $\alpha(d)^4$ in that equation replaced by $\alpha(2d)$. However, now $\alpha(d)$ is to be calculated from (5.23) using the new utilization spectra. With $K_2 = K$, Roughgarden (1974) finds the following conditions for limiting similarity:

Kurtosis parameter n	Lower limit on d/σ
0.5	0.15
1.0	0.90
2.0	1.56
∞	1.67

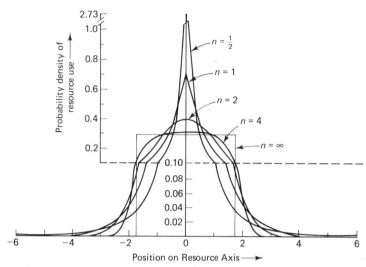

Figure 5.2 Family of resource-utilization functions that vary in kurtosis; the variance of each curve is 1. The curves are leptokurtic for $n = \frac{1}{2}$ and $n = 1$ and are playtkurtic for $n = 2$, $n = 4$, and $n = \infty$. Note the change of scale at bottom of figure. (From Roughgarden 1974.)

Recall that $n = 2$ is the Gaussian. Platykurtosis ($n = \infty$) has no significant influence on limiting similarity, but leptokurtosis can make quite a difference. The thick-tailed distribution with $n = 0.5$ still yields the qualitative effect of a lower limit on the allowable similarity, but the numerical value for the limiting similarity is an order of magnitude smaller than the Gaussian value.

The other major assumption we have been making so far is the use of linear functional responses in the underlying consumer-resource model (5.17). Abrams (1980) has investigated the use of other functional responses, and finds that this can have significant effects on the outcome. In particular, he finds that when the steady-state resource density is relatively low, with a Type II functional response the competition coefficient corresponding to a given overlap can be many times larger than the coefficient obtained from a linear functional response, given the same overlap.

So the criterion $d \geq \sigma$ for limiting similarity is *not* robust. This means that the study of how closely species can be "packed" into niche space (Hutchinson 1978, Chap. 5) is more complicated than early workers in the field had hoped it would turn out to be. A *quantitative* science of limiting similarity, while possible in principle (given unlimited grant support and vast armies of ecologists to carry out the necessary field and theoretical work), does not appear to be a practical goal at present. This may seem a negative result to many. But let me suggest that to comprehend that this is true, and *why* it is true, as I believe we do on the basis of existing theory, is a positive result in the sense of a genuine understanding of how nature is put together.

Besides, limiting similarity remains a valid and important *qualitative* insight into the structure of nature.

5.2.2 Nonequilibrium Coexistence

I argued in Section 5.2.1 that n consumer species cannot coexist in equilibrium if they share $k < n$ distinct resource types, and this has been proved under rather general assumptions by McGehee and Armstrong (1977). Is the assumption of equilibrium coexistence a mere technical detail, or can we get coexistence with nonpoint attractors?

We should start by stating exactly what we mean by "coexistence." Essentially what we want to mean is that two or more species can coexist if their densities remain positive for all times. But there is a problem with this definition if we are to judge coexistence on the basis of solutions to completely deterministic systems like the ones we are considering here. This is one place where we have to be careful about possible effects of demographic stochasticity.

In Section 2.5 I showed that under most circumstances we can ignore the statistical fluctuations in population density due to demographic stochasticity. The circumstances under which we cannot ignore those fluctuations are when a population density becomes extremely small—then the probability of a fluctuation to extinction becomes significant. Solutions of our deterministic systems in which the densities become arbitrarily small (though never zero) will generally not correspond to real biological coexistence.

Therefore, as a criterion for ecological coexistence we will require not only that all densities remain positive forever, but in addition that they remain bounded away from zero (that is, for each density N we require the existence of a positive number η such that $N > \eta$ for all t). This requirement is called *persistence* in most of the ecological literature.

In most systems of coexisting species, a property called *mutual invasibility* holds. It works as follows. Suppose we remove one species, say S, from the system, and let the remaining species reach an attractor. Then if we replace a few individuals of species S to this system, the density of species S will increase (and the system will approach a new attractor): species S is able to invade a "reduced" system consisting of all the other species under consideration, when that reduced system is near an attractor in its "reduced" phase space (which is missing the dimension corresponding to species S).

The condition of mutual invasibility says that this kind of invasion works, no matter which species S you remove from the system.

For instance, consider the pair of Lotka-Volterra competitors that we discussed in Section 5.2.1.1. If we remove species 1 from the system, the reduced system of species 2 alone will approach the point attractor at $N_2 = K_2$ (in its reduced phase space: the N_2-axis). Now if species 1, with some small density ϵ, tries to invade that system, it will have the Lotka-Volterra growth rate

$$dN_1/dt = r_1 N_1 [K_1 - N_1 - \alpha(d)N_2]$$

which is, with $N_1 = \epsilon$, $N_2 = K_2$,

$$dN_1/dt = r_1 \epsilon [K_1 - \epsilon - \alpha(d)K_2]$$

Species 1 can invade if this is positive for any $\epsilon > 0$, no matter how small. So we need $\alpha(d) < K_1/K_2$. Similarly, the condition for species 2 to be able to invade when rare is $\alpha(d) < K_2/K_1$. So the conditions for mutual invasibility are exactly the same as (5.27), the conditions for coexistence!

Actually, it is very plausible that mutual invasibility implies coexistence, in the sense of persistence (isn't it?), and usually one finds that it does. There are, however, exceptional cases in which mutual invasibility holds, but persistence does not (Armstrong and McGehee 1980 discuss an example), so establishing mutual invasibility is not a rigorous proof of persistence. Nevertheless, mutual invasibility is relatively easy to check and is a strong "plausibility argument" for coexistence. This is the spirit in which we will use it in this section.

Studying computer simulations of the solutions to differential equations for two consumers sharing one resource, Koch (1974) found solutions in which both consumers, as well as the resource, seemed to persist indefinitely, with the densities appprearing to oscillate. One can only carry on a simulation for a finite time, so rigorously speaking this could conceivably have been a rather amazing transient behavior of a system in which a species would eventually go extinct after all. However, McGehee and Armstrong (1977) subsequently proved analytically that these solutions really do remain bounded away from zero forever.

The method of their proof was to construct an attractor block for the system. An *attractor block* is a closed surface in phase space, bounded away from zero for all densities, such that everywhere on this surface, the trajectories cross the surface toward the inside. Clearly such a surface must surround some kind of attractor (Section 5.1), and equally clearly any solution for which the densities are initially in the domain of attraction of this attractor will persist.

However, I am not going to discuss the rigorous proof here. Instead I would like to show you a proof of mutual invasibility later formulated by Armstrong and McGehee (1980) as a plausibility argument for persistence. This argument has the virtue of giving some insight into the biological basis for coexistence.

The example treated by Armstrong and McGehee is the following laissez-faire (Section 4.1) system of two consumers and one resource:

$$dN_1/dt = N_1[-d_1 + c_1 E_1 R/(R + R_0)]$$
$$dN_2/dt = N_2(-d_2 + c_2 E_2 R) \tag{5.30}$$
$$dR/dt = rR(1 - R/K) - E_1 N_1 R/(R + R_0) - E_2 N_2 R$$

Suppose first that consumer 2 is absent. Then the system consisting of consumer 1 and the resource has an equilibrium at, say, (N_1^*, R^*). Setting dN_1/dt and dR/dt equal to zero in (5.30), with $N_2 = 0$, the equilibrium densities have to obey

$$-d_1 + c_1 E_1 R^*/(R^* + R_0) = 0 \tag{5.31}$$
$$r(1 - R^*/K)/K - E_1 N_1^*/(R^* + R_0) = 0$$

This equilibrium may be stable or unstable, depending on parameter values.

Now suppose consumer 1 is absent. Then the system of consumer 2 and the resource has an equilibrium at (N_2^{**}, R^{**}), where

$$-d_2 + c_2 E_2 R^{**} = 0 \tag{5.32}$$
$$r(1 - R^{**}/K) - E_2 N_2^{**} = 0$$

Within the two-dimensional phase space defined by $N_1 = 0$, this equilibrium is stable.

Now let us check invasibility for consumer 1. Suppose that consumer 2 and the resource are near the equilibrium point at (N_2^{**}, R^{**}), and a small number of consumer 1 individuals appear on the scene. They can invade if dN_1/dt is positive when N_1 is small and (N_2, R) is near (N_2^{**}, R^{**}). From the first of equations (5.30), we see that this condition for invasion is

$$-d_1 + c_1 E_1 R^{**}/(R^{**} + R_0) > 0$$

One can easily see that the growth rate of consumer 1 is a monotonically increasing function of R. This growth rate is 0 when $R = R^*$ [first of equations (5.31)], and positive when $R > R^*$. So the invasion condition is simply $R^{**} > R^*$.

But using precisely the same argument to check for invasibility by consumer 2, we can show that if $R^{**} > R^*$, the growth rate of consumer 2 will be *negative* if N_1 and R are near the equilibrium given by (5.32), with only a few members of species 1 present. So it would appear that consumer 1 will not only invade the system but will eliminate consumer 2 by driving the system toward that equilibrium. Indeed, if the parameters are such that the equilibrium expressed by (5.32) is stable, that is exactly what will happen.

But suppose that equilibrium is unstable. Then the system will not approach it. We know from Kolmogorov's theorem (Section 4.2.1.3) that when the equilibrium is unstable, the system of consumer 2 and the resource has a stable limit cycle. One can show (Armstrong and McGehee 1980) that the condition for a few individuals of consumer 2 to invade a system of consumer 1 and the resource, moving near this limit cycle, is $R_c > R^{**}$, where R_c is the average resource density over one cycle; and one can show that $R_c > R^*$.

Therefore, let us choose the parameters such that $R_c > R^{**} > R^*$ (this can be done; Armstrong and McGehee 1980). Since $R^{**} > R^*$, consumer 1 can, when rare, invade a system of consumer 2 and the resource when that system is near its (point) attractor; and since $R_c > R^{**}$, consumer 2 can, when

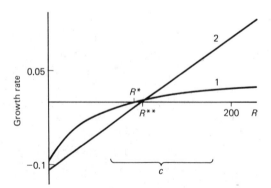

Figure 5.3 Growth rates of the predators of equations (5.30) as functions of prey density R. The region C represents the approximate range of variation of R over one cycle in the three-species system. (From Armstrong and McGehee 1980.)

rare, invade a system of consumer 1 and the resource when that system is near its (limit cycle) attractor. The condition of mutual invasibility is met.

Figure 5.3, which plots the per capita growth rates of the two consumers as functions of R, with parameter values that yield coexistence, gives some feeling for the condition $R_c > R^{**} > R^*$ that we need in this context for coexistence. Basically what is happening is that the resource cycles through a range of values such that consumer 1 exploits the resource more efficiently at low resource levels, and consumer 2 is more efficient at high levels:

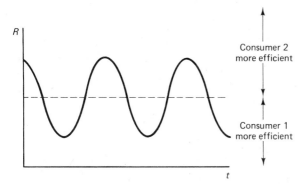

There is still a significant vestige here of the old notion of limiting similarity. Although the two consumers coexist while exploiting what is clearly one simple structureless resource, now they need to exploit it in a sufficiently different *way* in order to coexist. These results have been extended by Zicarelli (1975) to show that not only two but any number of consumers can coexist on one resource.

Ecologists have not yet assimilated these ideas enough for us to judge how much they have to do with what we see in nature. The conditions for coexistence seem to require a fairly delicate balance among parameters (for instance, the double inequality $R_c > R^{**} > R^*$ in the example we have just looked at), suggesting that we might not observe this kind of coexistence very often.

5.2.3 Environmental Variability and Competitive Coexistence

There is quite a wide variety of results concerning the influence of environmental variability on competitive coexistence. Although this is an important topic, I am not going to discuss it in detail. For one thing, it is still a very unsettled field, with many contrasting results, some of them tentative in nature. For another, much of the controversy in this field involves rather technical mathematical questions of exactly what is the appropriate way to model random variation (environmental stochasticity).

However, the basic ideas involved are not difficult to grasp, and what I am going to do here is to give brief verbal descriptions of these ideas.

The intuitive view of random environmental fluctuations as tending to destabilize equilibria, sketched in Section 2.4.1, was formalized and applied to the problem of limiting similarity of competitors by May and MacArthur (1972). They found that even very weak environmental stochasticity can destabilize equilibria among competitors sharing a one-dimensional continuous resource (as in Section 5.2.1.1) if those competitors are too similar. In this way, they "rediscovered" the classical condition $d \gtrsim \sigma$ for limiting similarity.

However, several authors criticized assumptions made by May and MacArthur. This side of the dispute is ably summarized by Turelli (1978a), who found under somewhat different biological assumptions and mathematical methods that weak to moderate random environmental variation has no significant effect on limiting similarity (Turelli 1978b).

All this work involves adding some sort of random variation to parameters in models rather like those considered in Section 5.2.1.1. Meanwhile, another tradition was developing, centered around the intuitive idea, apparently first offered in print by Hutchinson (1961), that environmental variability could actually *promote* competitive coexistence, by preventing the attainment of an equilibrium in which one or more species were excluded. If nothing else, the May-MacArthur-Turelli line of thought makes it clear that this kind of coexistence will require some kind of special structure, rather like what we have seen in Section 5.2.2 for a constant environment, in the patterns of resource exploitation.

One possibility is for different consumer species to be particularly efficient resource exploiters at different resource levels, as in the sketch on page 131. Stewart and Levin (1973) showed that this could enable coexistence of two competitors on one resource whose abundance varies seasonally. A variation on this theme is for different consumers to specialize in exploiting the resource primarily during a particular interval of time in each seasonal resource cycle. Armstrong and McGehee (1976) showed that this allows coexistence of any number of consumers on one seasonally varying resource.

It is not implausible that the same mechanisms will work in an environment where resource abundance varies randomly, and this has indeed been demonstrated by Levins (1979) and Abrams (1984).

This Hutchinsonian tradition of "temporal partitioning of resource utilization" (in which we can well include the models discussed in Section 5.2.2) can be viewed as an extension of the traditional notion of limiting similarity in the partitioning of resources themselves (Section 5.2.1.1). Basically what we seem to be finding out is that consumptive competitors cannot coexist if they are too similar *both* in the resources they exploit *and* in the temporal patterns of their exploitation of those resources.

Studies of this extended principle of limiting similarity in the field are going to be difficult but fascinating, particularly since coexistence through temporal partitioning of resource utilization seems to call for some kind of non-equilibrium dynamics, either driven by extrinsic temporal variation of the environment, as in this section, or embodied in the intrinsic dynamics of the populations themselves, as in Section 5.2.2. Relatively long term field projects would seem to be indicated.

5.3 COLLECTIVISM: INTERFERENCE

Mutual exploiters of the same resources, if they are limited by those resources, are going to hinder each other, willy-nilly, through the indirect effect that we call consumptive competition. An indirect effect of one species on another is an effect that takes place by virtue of a mutual interaction with other species (general definition in Section 7.2.2). Consumptive competitors hinder each other indirectly, through their (direct) effects on resource levels.

But sometimes competition takes the form of direct, aggressive interactions between members of the competing species themselves. This kind of competition is called *interference*.

Interference can very well occur together with consumptive competition; indeed, mutual exploitation of the same resources is definitely a situation with the potential for aggressive behavior. But interference can also occur without a significant component of consumptive competition. For instance, many sessile fauna are probably limited by the availability of attachment sites rather than by food, resulting in more or less pure interference. But I will get to that in Section 5.4. Here I want to consider interference in conjunction with consumptive competition, in a collectivist framework.

Consider a set of consumer species that compete for shared resources, and suppose this consumptive aspect of their dynamics can be described by Lotka-Volterra equations (5.19), with the parameters in those equations determined by consumptive interactions through relations (5.20) or (5.23) or something like them. Suppose in addition that acts of interference occur between individuals of different species, and perhaps among individuals of the same species as well. Case and Gilpin (1974) have modified equations (5.19) to take this into account, as follows.

If individuals of species i interfere with individuals of species j, what will the consequences of this be?

First, it will involve two kinds of cost to species i. Each act of interference will cost species i something in terms of the rate of resource consumption and hence of population growth, because each such act will require a certain amount of time or energy that could have been used for resource acquisition instead; also each act of interference could result in injury to the interfering individual. Second, there could be a generalized cost, not dependent on the number of actual acts of interference, if interference requires morphological or physiological modifications to the interfering organisms.

Also, interference by individuals of species i directed against individuals of species j will have a negative effect on the growth rate of species j.

Finally, we may note that if species i behaves aggressively toward species j, then individuals of species i may also very well behave aggressively toward each other. This would be yet a third cost to species i of interference by members of that species.

Putting this all together, Case and Gilpin modify equations (5.19) as follows:

$$dN_i/dt = r_i N_i \left[K_i - (1 + f_i)N_i - \sum_j (\alpha_{ij} + c_{ij} + e_{ij})N_j \right] \Big/ K_i$$

$$i = 1, \ldots, n \tag{5.33}$$

where c_{ij} is a measure of the per-act-of-interference cost to species i of an act of interference by a member of species i against a member of species j, f_i includes both the generalized cost to species i of interference on the part of species i and the per-act-of-interference cost of intraspecific interference of species i, and e_{ij} is a measure of the cost to species i of an act of interference by a member of species j. The interference parameters c_{ij}, f_i, and e_{ij} are all positive numbers.

We can get an appreciation for the kinds of things that can happen if we think of a pair of species: $n = 2$.

First, let us recall from elementary ecology that the Lotka-Volterra equations (5.19) can describe three kinds of competitive interactions, as follows:

$$\alpha_{12} < K_1/K_2 \text{ and } \alpha_{21} < K_2/K_1 \Rightarrow \text{coexistence}$$

$$\alpha_{12} > K_1/K_2 \text{ and } \alpha_{21} < K_2/K_1 \Rightarrow \text{species 2 dominates species 1}$$

$$\alpha_{12} < K_1/K_2 \text{ and } \alpha_{21} > K_2/K_1 \Rightarrow \text{species 1 dominates species 2}$$

$$\alpha_{12} > K_1/K_2 \text{ and } \alpha_{21} > K_2/K_1 \Rightarrow \text{contingent competition}$$

(The two middle possibilities correspond, of course, to one kind of competition, namely, dominance.)

In the case of coexistence, there is a stable equilibrium with both densities greater than zero. When species 1 dominates species 2, there is *no* equilibrium with both densities positive, and all trajectories in phase space approach asymptotically the point attractor at $(N_1, N_2) = (K_1, 0)$. In what I call *contingent competition*, there is an equilibrium with both densities positive, but it is a saddle point; the phase space has two (point) attractors, at $(N_1, N_2) = (K_1, 0)$ and $(N_1, N_2) = (0, K_2)$; the ultimate outcome of competition is contingent upon the initial density (that is, upon which domain of attraction it happens to be located in).

Each isocline is a straight line in phase space, which intersects both axes. As you can easily see from the Lotka-Volterra equations (5.19), the N_1-isocline intersects the N_1-axis at $N_1 = K_1$ and the N_2-axis at $N_2 = K_1/\alpha_{12}$; while the N_2-isocline intersects the N_1-axis at $N_1 = K_2/\alpha_{21}$ and the N_2-axis at $N_2 = K_2$. The relative locations of these points of intersection with the axes determine the above conditions for the outcome of competition, as follows:

Coexistence

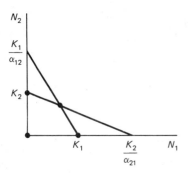

Species 1 dominates species 2

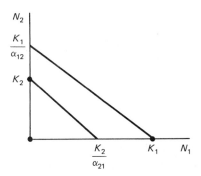

Species 2 dominates species 1

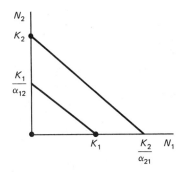

Contingent competition

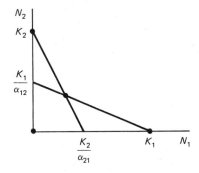

With the Case-Gilpin equations (5.33), the isoclines will still be straight lines, and each isocline will still intersect both axes. But now the N_1-isocline will intersect the N_1-axis at $N_1 = K_1/(1 + f_1)$ and the N_2-axis at $N_2 = K_1/(\alpha_{12} + c_{12} + e_{12})$; while the N_2-isocline will intersect the N_1-axis at $K_2/(\alpha_{21} + c_{21} + e_{21})$ and the N_2-axis at $K_2/(1 + f_2)$. Using the relationships among these intersections exactly as in the Lotka-Volterra case, we can immediately infer the effect of any interference parameters on the outcome of competition.

One can show that the purely consumptive forms (5.20) or (5.23) for the competition coefficients imply that $\alpha_{ij}\alpha_{ji} \le 1$, no matter what parameters we use in those expressions. This would seem to rule out the possibility of contingent competition, which requires $\alpha_{12}\alpha_{21} > 1$, within a framework of pure consumptive competition. Thus, observations such as those of Park (1954) on flour beetles, which plainly indicate contingent competition, would seem to indicate that more is going on than pure consumptive competition.

Exercise 5.7. Prove that (5.20) or (5.23) implies $\alpha_{ij}\alpha_{ji} \le 1$.

Actually, it is not quite true that contingent competition is impossible in consumptive competition. Recall that (5.19), (5.20), and (5.23) were obtained from (5.17) by assuming that the resource dynamics is so much faster than the consumer population dynamics that the resources are always essentially in equilibrium. If one drops this assumption and treats the full set (5.17) of four dynamical equations, one finds that contingent competition can occur under certain circumstances (Hsu and Hubbell 1979).

Interference can easily result in contingent interactions. For instance, imagine that in terms of pure consumptive competition, species 2 dominates species 1. Can species 1 improve its lot by interfering with species 2? Graphically it is easy to see that in this situation, unilateral interference by species 1 can produce contingent competition (which is an improvement in species 1's lot), but species 1 can neither dominate species 2 nor transform the interaction into a coexistent one:

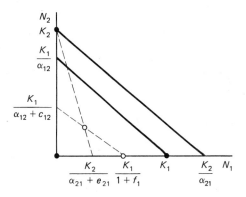

In this figure, the solid lines indicate the isoclines for pure consumptive competition, and the dashed lines indicate the isoclines that result from adding interference. The open circles indicate new equilibria.

Interference can also promote coexistence (Schoener 1976, Vance 1984). We have seen above that interference on the part of the subdominant species cannot transform a dominant consumptive interaction into one that permits coexistence; the only way that we can get coexistence is if both species are aggressive, in such a way as to transform the phase space like this:

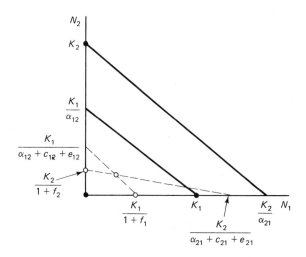

However, it is not obvious without a little algebra that this is really possible. Let's do the algebra.

Without interference, species 2 dominates species 1, so $K_2 > K_1/\alpha_{12}$ and $K_1 < K_2/\alpha_{21}$, which we can rewrite as

$$K_2/K_1 > 1/\alpha_{12} \quad \text{and} \quad K_2/K_1 > \alpha_{21}$$

Assume $1/\alpha_{12} > \alpha_{21}$. (The following argument, and its conclusions, are essentially the same if we assume $1/\alpha_{12} \leq \alpha_{21}$.) Then we have only one condition

$$K_2/K_1 > 1/\alpha_{12} \tag{5.34}$$

Now add interference. This will produce coexistence if (previous figure)

$$K_2/K_1 < (1 + f_2)/(\alpha_{12} + c_{12} + e_{12})$$
$$(\alpha_{21} + c_{21} + e_{21})/(1 + f_1) < K_2/K_1 \tag{5.35}$$

Can we satisfy (5.34) and (5.35) simultaneously? Comparing the first of (5.35) with (5.34), we see that no matter what, f_2 must be big enough. The second of (5.35) says that in addition either $\alpha_{21} + c_{21} + e_{21}$ must be small enough, or else f_1 must be large enough.

So, under the right conditions interference can convert a dominant consumptive interaction into a coexistent one. In order for this to happen, a number of conditions must be met, but of these, the only one that *always* has to be satisfied is that f_2 must be large enough: there must be either a large generalized cost or a lot of intraspecific interference in the consumptively dominant species.

This seems implausible from an evolutionary standpoint: one would expect that a more efficient resource exploiter would experience weaker selection for any kind of interference ability, since the only point of evolving such ability (at least within the present framework) would be to acquire more resources. However, more study of this issue is certainly called for.

5.4 MONOPOLISM: COMPETITION FOR SPACE

At the very beginning of this chapter, I drew a fundamental distinction between collectivist and monopolist utilization of space in the process of resource acquisition: individual collectivists utilize a fraction of the resources from the whole area occupied by the system, while individual monopolists utilize all the resources from a fraction of the area. Monopolist consumers capture resources by capturing the space containing those resources. Competition among monopolists is competition for space.

Competition for space often occurs on a seasonal basis. For example, many bird species establish and defend territories during the breeding season but range freely during the rest of the year. This could have important implications for community structure, if the populations in question are limited by processes that occur during the period of spatial competition. However, I am going to discuss here the more clear-cut situation in which each individual occupies a unit of space for pretty much its whole lifetime. The most obvious instances of this kind of competitor are sessile organisms. Motile organisms may also sometimes appropriately be thought of in this fashion, if they live in an environment consisting of several habitable "islands" in a "sea" of uninhabitable space.

It is essential for a spatial competitor to be able to occupy any vacant space that may become available, and this requires a degree of mobility. Usually there is a definite dispersal phase in the life cycle: seeds, spores, and larvae are examples. The scale of dispersal may not be much greater than the size of an adult, or it may be over whole geographic regions.

Competition for space is primarily interference competition, since each competitor is seeking to monopolize a portion of space, rather than to share resources.

Less work has been done on modeling competition for space than on modeling consumptive competition, and it is a far more difficult task. All the existing models have serious faults. And yet, a general picture of competition for space seems to be emerging, which stands a reasonable chance of surviving more thorough scrutiny. I am going to briefly sketch that picture here.

Because I want to abstract out certain features that are characteristic of competition for space, I am going to discuss competition for space in its purest form: there will be no spatial heterogeneity of the habitat, and there will be only a very small probability of local coexistence of the kind discussed in Section 5.2.

5.4.1 Reaction-Dispersal Theory

As indicated in the preceding discussion, the dynamics of competition for space consists of two aspects, which take place on two different spatial scales. Competition itself—the monopolizing of space—takes place on a relatively small spatial scale (locally). Dispersal, on the other hand—the finding of space to monopolize—takes place on a relatively large spatial scale. The particular character of competition for space comes from the interplay of these two aspects.

Reaction-dispersal theory takes as its starting point the contrast in spatial scales. In this approach, the area of space under consideration is thought of as being divided into a number of "cells," with competition occurring *within* each cell and dispersal *among* the cells. The dynamical equations compound these two processes as follows. If there are n species and m cells,

$$dN_i^a/dt = f_i^a(N_1^a, \ldots, N_n^a) + J_i^a(N_1^1, \ldots, N_n^m)$$

$$i = 1, \ldots, n \qquad a = 1, \ldots, m \qquad\qquad (5.36)$$

where N_i^a is the density of species i in cell a, f_i^a is the growth rate of species i in cell a in the absence of dispersal, and J_i^a is the net contribution to the growth rate of species i in cell a due to dispersal of species i to and from cell a. Note that the local growth rate f_i^a depends only on densities in cell a, while the dispersal term J_i^a can depend on densities throughout the system. Thus the functions f_i^a describe the small-scale process of competition within cells, while the functions J_i^a describe the large-scale process of dispersal among cells.

Let us assume that the within-cell dynamics is Lotka-Volterra in form:

$$f_i^a = r_i N_i^a \left(K_i - \sum_j \alpha_{ij} N_j^a \right) \bigg/ K_i \qquad i = 1, \ldots, n \qquad a = 1, \ldots, m \qquad (5.37)$$

If the area of space occupied by the system is inhomogeneous, the parameters in (5.37) might be different for different cells. By writing, for instance, K_i instead of K_i^a in (5.37), I have assumed that the habitat in question is homogeneous. This is an idealization which isolates competition for space in its purest form.

The dispersal functions J could reflect a wide variety of behaviors. The simplest, and most studied, possibility is a passive migration of each species from cells with a relatively high density of that species to cells with a relatively low density of that species, which is expressed by the form

$$J_i^a = \sum_b D_i^{ab}(N_i^b - N_i^a) \qquad i = 1, \ldots, n \qquad a = 1, \ldots, m \qquad (5.38)$$

In particular, I have assumed the system is closed: any migration into a cell must come from some other cell, not from somewhere outside the system.

This formalism applies most clearly to a system of discrete units of habitat (such as islands) linked by migration, or to a system of distinct patches linked by local dispersal. One would like as well for many applications (such as plant or epifaunal communities) to be able to think of the cells as portions of continuous space. The present formalism caricatures such a system rather poorly, and yet I believe that it captures the essential features of the resultant communities, for two reasons. First, the results obtained from this formalism (including the effect of disturbance, to be discussed in Chapter 6) seem to match observations well. Second, computer simulations that do more closely mimic processes in continuous space (Botkin et al. 1972, Moser 1972, Shugart et al. 1973, Maguire and Porter 1977, Karlson 1981, Karlson and Jackson 1981, Karlson and Buss 1984) yield similar results.

The first application of this formalism to competition for space was by Levin (1974), who analyzed the case of two species in two cells. He assumed the two species to be identical in their local dynamics and in their dispersal rates between the two cells, so that $r_1 = r_2 = r$, $K_1 = K_2 = K$, $\alpha_{12} = \alpha_{21} = \alpha$, $D_i^{ab} = D$ for all i, a, b. It will be convenient to introduce a new notation for the densities. Let X_i denote the density of species i in cell 1, and let Y_i denote the density of species i in cell 2. Then

$$dX_1/dt = rX_1(K - X_1 - \alpha X_2)/K + D(Y_1 - X_1)$$
$$dX_2/dt = rX_2(K - X_2 - \alpha X_1)/K + D(Y_2 - X_2)$$
$$dY_1/dt = rY_1(K - Y_1 - \alpha Y_2)/K + D(X_1 - Y_1)$$
$$dY_2/dt = rY_2(K - Y_2 - \alpha Y_1)/K + D(X_2 - Y_2)$$

$$(5.39)$$

Let us suppose that the two species cannot coexist within a collectivist context, that is, locally, within a cell. With the assumption of dynamical identity made in the preceding paragraph, if $\alpha < 1$ the two species can coexist locally, while if $\alpha > 1$ they cannot—their interaction is contingent in the sense explained in Section 5.3. So we will assume $\alpha > 1$. The question is, can the two species coexist within the framework of (5.39).

First, suppose there is no dispersal: $D = 0$. Then each cell functions completely independently of the other. In cell 1 there are two stable equilibria: $(X_1, X_2) = (K, 0)$ and $(X_1, X_2) = (0, K)$. Similarly in cell 2 there are the two stable equilibria $(Y_1, Y_2) = (K, 0)$ and $(Y_1, Y_2) = (0, K)$. That is, only one species is going to be present in each cell. There are two stable equilibria of the system as a whole with both species present in the system: the equilibrium with species 1 present in cell 1 and species 2 in cell 2, $(X_1, X_2) = (K, 0)$ and $(Y_1, Y_2) = (0, K)$; and the equilibrium with species 2 in cell 1 and species 1 in cell 2, $(X_1, X_2) = (0, K)$ and $(Y_1, Y_2) = (K, 0)$. Notice that in both of these equilibria there is the symmetry $Y_1 = X_2$, $Y_2 = X_1$.

What happens if $D \neq 0$? Let us assume we still have the symmetry

$$Y_1 = X_2 \qquad Y_2 = X_1 \qquad (5.40)$$

Using this in (5.39), we get

$$dX_1/dt = rX_1(K - X_1 - \alpha X_2)/K + D(X_2 - X_1)$$
$$dX_2/dt = rX_2(K - X_2 - \alpha X_1)/K + D(X_1 - X_2)$$

plus the identical pair of equations with (Y_1, Y_2) in place of (X_1, X_2). At equilibrium, then,

$$0 = rX_1(K - X_1 - \alpha X_2)/K + D(X_2 - X_1)$$
$$0 = rX_2(K - X_2 - \alpha X_1)/K + D(X_1 - X_2)$$

$$(5.41)$$

with Y_1 and Y_2 given by (5.40).

Adding together the two right-hand sides in (5.41), we get

$$X_1^2 + X_2^2 - KX_1 - KX_2 + 2\alpha X_1 X_2 = 0 \qquad (5.42)$$

Subtracting the two right-hand sides in (5.41), we get

$$X_1 + X_2 = K(r - 2D)/r \qquad (5.43)$$

Equation (5.42) describes a hyperbola (solid curve in the following sketch) in the phase space for cell 1, (5.43) a straight line (dashed lines for various values of D)

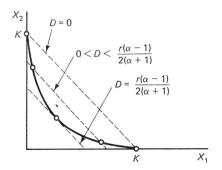

When $D = 0$ we have the two equilibria $(X_1, X_2) = (K, 0)$ and $(X_1, X_2) = (0, K)$ [with Y_i given by (5.40)] corresponding to the presence of only species 1 or only species 2 in cell 1. As D increases from 0, these equilibria move along the hyperbola, with both densities positive, until they coalesce with $X_1 = X_2$. From (5.42) and (5.43), at this point of coalescence $X_1 = X_2 = K/(1 + \alpha)$ and $D = r(\alpha - 1)/2(\alpha + 1)$.

The equilibria are stable when $D = 0$, so one might expect them to remain stable for sufficiently small D. One can show that this is the case. However, the equilibria become unstable before they coalesce at $D = r(\alpha - 1)/2(\alpha + 1)$; specifically they become unstable for $D > r(\alpha - 1)/2(2\alpha + 1)$ (Levin 1974).

What this all means is that for sufficiently small dispersal rates, the two species can coexist even though the dynamics in the two cells are coupled as in (5.39). Each cell will have predominantly one species or the other, but both species will be present throughout the system. In biological terms, each species initially captures a unit of space and is able to maintain itself there despite the presence in the system of dispersers of both species.

When dispersal rates become too high, the distinction between cells is lost, and spatial utilization is, in effect, collectivist. This is called "complete mixing" in the reaction-dispersal context. Under these circumstances, coexistence is no longer possible if $\alpha > 1$, at least in a constant environment.

5.4.2 Competition for Space and Community Structure

The reaction-dispersal system (5.36) to (5.38) has been studied for more than two species by Yodzis (1978 and other works cited there). I will not go into the mathematics here but will just describe the results. Unless otherwise indicated,

I will assume throughout this section that dispersal rates are low enough to avoid "complete mixing" of cells.

One can generate model communities of spatial competitors by letting a number of species, chosen at random from some "pool," colonize an area of empty space. Then one can let the system develop under the dynamics (5.36) to (5.38), and see what kinds of communities result.

The pool of potential colonizers is specified if we give probability distributions for all relevant parameters of those species. In the work that I am going to describe, each parameter was chosen at random from some fixed interval of real numbers. It turns out that all the interesting results depend on the value of just one parameter, which I will denote by C. It is the probability for a competition coefficient α_{ij} to be greater than K_i/K_j. The probability for a randomly chosen pair of species to coexist locally (within a cell) is then $(1 - C)^2$ (recall page 134). Since our present purpose is to see what happens when this kind of coexistence is rare, C will never be taken less than 0.9 in what follows. Then only one pair of species in a hundred can coexist locally.

Larger values of C correspond to larger competition coefficients. Therefore, I will call C the *strength of competition.*

If $C = 1$, then all pairwise interactions are contingent. Once a species has become established in a cell, it cannot be eliminated by dispersers from other cells. Community structure is a relict of the original colonization episode, so I call such a community "founder controlled."

If $C < 1$ there will still be some contingent pairwise interactions, but there will also be some functional dominance. Therefore, an initial colonizer cannot necessarily maintain its predominance in a cell; intercell dispersal will bring on a "reshuffle" of cell occupants, with some species possibly being eliminated from the system entirely. Dominant interactions are crucial for this process, and, as we will see below, the overall prevalence of such interactions in the community as a whole strongly affects the outcome. Therefore, I call such a community "dominance controlled."

5.4.2.1 Dominance Control

Assume first that $C < 1$. Then the probability for a randomly chosen colonizing species to dominate another colonizing species, chosen at random, is the probability for a randomly chosen competition coefficient α_{ij} to be $> K_i/K_j$ times the probability for α_{ji} to be $< K_j/K_i$. This product is $C(1 - C)$. The degree of dominance [as measured by $C(1 - C)$] is the crucial factor in determining community structure, so I call these communities *dominance controlled.*

After the original colonization episode, there will be a sequence of intercell invasions due to dispersal, with some species being eliminated from the system entirely. This process will often terminate in an equilibrium, but in certain communities an equilibrium is never attained. Rather, in some cells the identity of the locally numerically dominant species repeatedly cycles through a subset of the colonizing species. I call this kind of behavior a *quasicycle.* A similar behavior in Lotka-Volterra systems with immigration has been studied by Gilpin (1975) and May and Leonard (1975). [I should warn the reader that the term "quasi-cycle" has also been used by Nisbet and Gurney (1982) to refer to another, completely unrelated form of cyclic population dynamics.]

Quasicycles result from intransitive dominance relationships. The simplest example occurs if three colonizing species A, B, C are such that A dominates B which dominates C which dominates A. This kind of relationship was first observed by Jackson and Buss (1975) among the epifauna that inhabit the under-surfaces of certain foliaceous corals. Subsequent observations are detailed by Buss (1986).

For the model communities being described here, the fraction of communities with a quasicycle is plotted vs. the number of colonizing species for several different values of the competition strength C in Fig. 5.4. It will be seen that there is quite a potential for this sort of thing, particularly in species-rich systems with weak competition. A number of investigators have explored the possibility of quasicycles in communities of sessile fauna (Buss 1986 and other works cited there, Quinn 1982, Karlson and Buss 1984, Paine 1984).

For now, let us consider the communities that do approach an equilibrium. In the approach to equilibrium, the number of species in the community will at first increase steadily as more and more species arrive, then decrease steadily to an equilibrium value as subdominant species are eliminated. A plot of species richness vs. time will, then, have a "peak." This behavior is often seen in studies of succession in plant communities, and Dayton (1973a) has portrayed such a process in considerable detail, for the epifauna in a rocky intertidal zone.

Equilibrium species richness is plotted vs. the number of colonizing species for a number of different values of the competition strength C, in Fig. 5.5. As

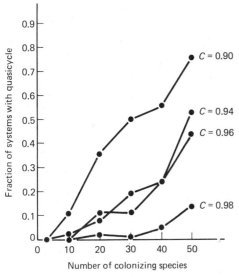

Figure 5.4 Probability of a quasicycle vs. the number of colonizing species, for several values of the competition strength C, in reaction-dispersal systems. (From Yodzis 1978. *Competition for space and the structure of ecological communities.* Springer-Verlag, Berlin.)

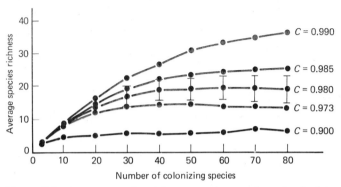

Figure 5.5 Average species richness vs. the number of colonizing species, for several values of the competition strength C, in equilibrium reaction-dispersal systems. (From Yodzis 1978. *Competition for space and the structure of ecological communities.* Springer-Verlag, Berlin.)

the number of colonizing species increases, equilibrium species richness at first also increases. However, equilibrium species richness eventually levels off at a value determined by the competition strength C, and once this saturation value is reached, further increases in the number of species available for colonization have a negligible effect on the number of species actually present in the community.

So long as the supply of potentially colonizing species is adequate, equilibrium species richness is determined by the competition strength C, not by the number of colonizing species. If competition is stronger (as expressed here by a larger value of C), contingent interactions are more likely and dominance is less common. So *the stronger the competition, the more diverse the community* (which is, of course, the exact opposite of what we expect in collectivist competition).

Up to now, I have in this section considered an idealized homogeneous habitat. What about an inhomogeneous habitat? In the present formalism, this would correspond to different local parameters r_i^a, K_i^a, α_{ij}^a in different cells a. The effect would be to allow different species to dominate in different cells, and so to increase the number of species that can coexist. Undoubtedly this is an important force at work in nature. To assess the relative importance of this mechanism for coexistence on the one hand, and of contingent interactions on the other is a formidable task for future field work.

Tilman (1982), following up on earlier work of MacArthur and Levins (1964) and MacArthur (1972), has done some theory that relates to this issue. His approach stresses the role of nutritional physiology in competition for resources.

Recall the model (5.17) of competition for substitutable resources. We can rewrite the first set of equations (5.17) as

$$dN_i/dt = C_i N_i g_i(R_1, \ldots, R_k)$$
$$g_i(R_1, \ldots, R_k) = -T_i + \sum_J a_{iJ} w_J R_J$$

Notice that the sign of each consumer growth rate depends only on the resource densities, through the function g_i. Therefore, it is natural to think in terms of a space whose axes correspond to the k resource densities R_J, $J = 1, \ldots, k$.

For the sake of simplicity, consider just two resources. Then this "resource space" looks like

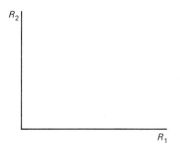

and for the above consumer dynamics, consumer i has zero growth when the resource densities fall on the straight line plotted here:

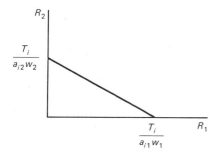

This line—the set of resource densities corresponding to zero consumer growth—is called the consumer's *isocline* in resource space. The consumer has negative growth when the resource densities lie below the isocline, and positive growth when the resources lie above it.

Depending on the nutritional physiology of the consumer species, the function g_i, and the resultant isocline in resource space, could have different forms from the above linear form. These have been cataloged by Tilman as follows.

In general, the resources are *substitutable* if each can sustain reproduction when the other is lacking. In this case the isocline intersects both coordinate axes, so that each resource alone supports positive population growth (when its density is above the intersection point). The above linear form corresponds to *perfectly substitutable* resources. Substitutable resources may also be *complementary*, if a diet including both resources is more beneficial than a diet consisting of either resource alone,

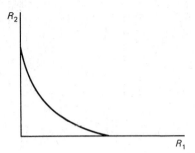

or *antagonistic,* if the consumer requires proportionately more total resource when the two resource types are consumed together than when either is consumed alone:

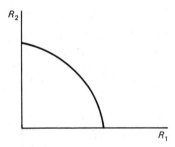

The extreme case of perfectly antagonistic resources,

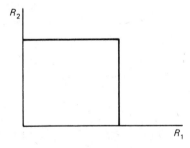

corresponds to consumer *switching* behavior: the consumer always consumes either one resource or the other (depending on their relative abundance), but never both together.

The next major category is the *essential* resources. Essential resources are not substitutable: the consumer must have a certain minimum intake of both essential resources in order to reproduce. Therefore, the isocline does not intersect either axis. In the case of *perfectly essential* resources, the isocline consists entirely of parts parallel to each axis:

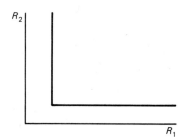

There may be a gradual transition from limitation by one resource to limitation by the other, with partial substitutability in the transition, which Tilman calls the *interactive-essential* case:

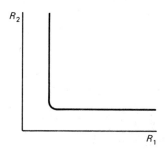

Finally, if only one resource is essential, and the other not, we have the *hemi-essential case;* an intersection with only one axis:

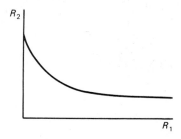

Now, if one is willing to assume equilibrium dynamics within a cell, one can explicate the within-cell dynamics by plotting the isoclines for the various different consumers together in resource space. Tilman (1982) has studied this approach in considerable depth, and the reader is referred to his book for further detail. Tilman's major result is the following. For *essential* resources, the identity of the species dominant in each cell is very sensitive to the relative resource concentrations in each cell. Therefore, if the within-cell dynamics is determined by essential resources, a small inhomogeneity in the distribution of resources over a habitat can result in a large increase in the number of species that can coexist within the habitat. Tilman maintains that this is the primary mechanism governing the diversity of plant guilds.

5.4.2.2 Founder Control

If $C = 1$, there is no functional dominance in the pool of colonizing species. All interactions are contingent. In this case, community structure is governed by the colonization process rather than by processes intrinsic to the community, so I call the resulting communities *founder controlled.*

There are no quasicycles in founder controlled communities. In the approach to equilibrium, species richness simply increases steadily until the entire area is occupied, instead of "peaking" as in the case of dominance control. Equilibrium species richness depends on the number of species in the pool of colonizers and on the size of the area under consideration. For a given number of potential colonizing species, species-area curves will level off at larger areas for founder controlled communities than for dominance controlled communities.

Most natural communities involving competition for space show clear signs of dominance control. But founder control, or something very close to it (perhaps dominance control with C very close to 1) is also sometimes observed. The best-known examples are probably the marine fouling communities studied by Sutherland (1974), Sutherland and Karlson (1977), and Schoener and Schoener (1981), among others. Neither Porter (1974) nor Bak and Luckhurst (1980) found any evidence of functional dominance in coral reefs in the Caribbean, though many other reefs do exhibit dominance. Similarly, Sammarco (1982) did not find evidence of dominance in Caribbean macroalgal communities, though other such assemblages have shown strong dominance. Lowland tropical rain forests also have many features of founder control (Yodzis 1978, Hubbell 1986).

In the "complete mixing" domain of high dispersal rates, the local character of competition breaks down and the ideas appropriate to collectivist spatial utilization apply: coexistence in a constant environment is, with contingent pairwise interactions, impossible, and all species but one must go extinct. Chesson and Warner's (1981) "lottery model" and Hubbell's (1986) "community drift model" are two very similar models which, while not expressing dispersal explicitly, seem to address this situation.

In these models (which are formulated in discrete time) it is assumed that in each annual recruitment to the adult population, every individual that has died since the last recruitment is replaced by an individual chosen at random from the species present. In a constant environment, this leads to a "random walk" of community composition, in which eventually all species but one go extinct (Hubbell 1986). Hubbell shows that the time scale for this process can, however, be very long—on the order of thousands of generations. This means that for organisms with long generation times relative to our own (such as the tropical trees studied by Hubbell), we may perceive such a system as permitting "coexistence."

When there is environmental variability that mainly affects recruitment, true coexistence for indefinite periods of time is possible (Chesson and Warner 1981). Basically this is a version of Hutchinson's idea (1961), already discussed in Section 5.2.3, that environmental variability can promote coexistence by preventing any one species from gaining a particularly strong position. In Chesson and Warner's formulation, however, the storage effect of Section 3.6 plays an essential role by moderating the more extreme effects of variability in a way that is insensitive to particularities of the species; thus neither does any one species wind up in a particularly *weak* position.

5.5 HOW COMPETITION CAN CONTROL COMMUNITY STRUCTURE

On page 109 I defined the concept of competitive community. We have seen in this chapter that competition imposes certain structural features on these communities. In this section I am going to briefly bring together what we have learned.

But first, I should say a few words about the use of the word "community" in ecology. The word is used in three distinct ways in the ecological literature:

1. The set of all species in a given area.
2. A functionally defined subset of 1.
3. A taxonomically defined subset of 1.

The notion of competitive community defined on page 109 is an instance of usage 2. Things like "fish community" or "bird community" are examples of usage 3. "Seed-eating bird community" is a mix of usage 2 and usage 3. Clearly we would be much better off to use different words for different concepts, particularly if the alternative is to apply theory developed under usage 2 to data based on usage 3. (Those who do this are hoping, of course, that the two usages are more or less equivalent.)

Distinct terms for usages 2 and 3 exist in the literature, and I would be remiss if I did not plead (with Hutchinson 1978, pp. 166, 168) for the consistent use of these terms, in order to avoid potentially serious confusion. The term *guild* has been suggested (Root 1967) for usage 2, and *taxocene* has been suggested (Chodorowski 1959, Hutchinson 1967) for usage 3. With these conventions, *community* could be reserved for usage 1.

By talking about competitive communities I am, then, sinning, like practically everybody else. I am going to reform right here and now, before your very eyes. Henceforth, I will call the notion introduced on page 109 a *competitive guild*.

We have seen three different ways that competition can control the structure of competitive guilds:

Collectivist spatial utilization. When there is pure consumptive competition, the structure of competitive guilds springs from sharing resources through niche differentiation.

Monopolist spatial utilization, dominance control. When there is pure competition for space, with some species capable of functional dominance, the structure of competitive guilds springs from dominance relationships.

Monopolist spatial utilization, founder control. When there is pure competition for space, with no functional dominance, the structure of competitive guilds springs from the colonization process.

I believe that most natural competitive guilds fall rather clearly into one of these three categories, but there is certainly a degree of blurring. Thus founder control can be viewed as a limiting case of dominance control, and guilds that are close to, but not quite, founder controlled might more appropriately be thought of as founder controlled than dominance controlled. On the other hand, colonization events will often play some role in the structure of dominance controlled guilds. In a basically consumptive context, interference may produce a degree of dominance (and spatial segregation). Niche differentiation will sometimes enable a degree of local coexistence among competitors for space (for example, vertical stratification in a forest), and spatial heterogeneity as well as differences in regeneration niche (Grubb 1977) undoubtedly augment diversity in plant guilds. Indeed, dominance relationships themselves may sometimes relate to an underlying niche structure.

So the threefold classification I am suggesting may be too simplistic, and a finer classification may need to be articulated. However, a *less* finely differentiated view is certainly too simplistic.

Some guilds, rather than blurring these distinctions, seem to neatly combine two or more categories. Grubb (1986) provides a nice example. In his chalk grasslands, the perennials, viewed as a guild in themselves, are dominance controlled. This guild is "perceived" by the annuals as a matrix of openings, which are occupied in a founder controlled fashion. Each year the matrix (which itself changes from year to year as the perennial guild develops) is occupied by a fresh founder controlled guild of annuals. Similar processes operate on other time scales for other short-lived plants. This sort of combination may well be quite common for plants.

5.6 JUST PLAIN COMPETITION

Throughout this chapter I have taken a "mechanistic" view of competition, attempting to relate the effects of competition to underlying biological processes. In this section I am going to describe another viewpoint that is sometimes adopted.

This other point of view is "phenomenological" in nature. It sees competing species quite simply as species that hinder one another, without worrying about how this mutual hindrance comes about. Particularly if one's goal is simply to detect the presence of competition, this viewpoint would seem a natural one to adopt.

For example, suppose we want to know whether a pair of species in some community are in fact competitors. Most ecologists would consider perturbation experiments, in which the abundances of one or more of the putative competitors are manipulated in some way, to be a sound approach to testing for the presence of competition.

Suppose the two species do in fact compete. If the density of either competitor is kept at an artificially low level for a period of time, the density of the other competitor should increase. If the density of either competitor is kept at an artificially high level for a period of time, the density of the other competitor should decrease. These are examples of what Bender et al. (1984) call *press perturbations.*

Conversely, one might suppose that if one observes this kind of response to press perturbations, then competition is present. There is a sizable body of field work in which press perturbations are used to test for the presence of competition, summarized by Schoener (1983) and Connell (1983). In this methodology, it is generally not considered necessary to demonstrate what the competitors are competing *for.*

I would like to consider how the results of press perturbation experiments relate to the structure of underlying models. I want to do this partly because perturbation experiments are of interest in a lot of other contexts besides just this one (I will return to this topic later, in Chapter 7), and partly because there is an interesting surprise in store for us here.

Consider a pair of species, with densities N_1, N_2, and growth rates

$$dN_1/dt = f_1(N_1, N_2)$$
$$dN_2/dt = f_2(N_1, N_2)$$

(5.44)

Suppose we do an experiment in which we add individuals of species 1. We can add the new individuals in one batch and then watch the resultant transient behavior ("pulse perturbation" in the terminology of Bender et al. 1984), or we can keep adding new individuals to actually change the phase space and move the system to a new attractor ("press perturbation"). Because the second manipulation involves a discrete change of the system from an initial state to a different final state, and because we don't have to try to follow the transient behavior in between, it will usually be more practicable, despite the possible practical difficulties associated with continual addition of organisms.

In a press perturbation experiment, the dynamics (5.44) is transformed into

$$dN_1/dt = f_1(N_1, N_2) + I_1$$
$$dN_2/dt = f_2(N_1, N_2)$$

(5.45)

where I_1 is the rate of addition of members of species 1. Assume the system has a single, point attractor for all relevant values of I_1. How will the addition affect the equilibrium density N_{2e}?

The equilibrium densities will depend on I_1, so I will write them $N_{1e}(I_1)$, $N_{2e}(I_1)$. For any I_1, at equilibrium we have, from the first of (5.45)

$$f_1[N_{1e}(I_1), N_{2e}(I_1)] + I_1 = 0$$

$$f_2[N_{1e}(I_1), N_{2e}(I_1)] = 0$$

Differentiating with respect to I_1,

$$A_{11} \, dN_{1e}/dI_1 + A_{12} \, dN_{2e}/dI_1 + 1 = 0$$

$$A_{21} \, dN_{1e}/dI_1 + A_{22} \, dN_{2e}/dI_1 = 0$$

where

$$A_{ij} = \left. \frac{\partial f_i}{\partial N_j} \right|_{N_{1e}(I_1), N_{2e}(I_1)} \qquad i, j = 1, 2$$

are the elements of the community matrix (recall Section 5.1.1). We can solve these two equations for

$$dN_{2e}/dI_1 = A_{21}/(A_{11}A_{22} - A_{12}A_{21}) \tag{5.46}$$

Exercise 5.8. Prove (5.46).

In Section 4.2.1.1 I stated as a condition for stability of an equilibrium $A_{11}A_{22} - A_{12}A_{21} > 0$ (4.10). Therefore, so long as we still have a stable equilibrium, the denominator of the right-hand side of (5.46) is positive. Now, if species 1 and 2 are competing, we expect that the outcome of our addition experiment will be $dN_{2e}/dI_1 < 0$: the continual addition of members of species 1 causes a decrease in the density of species 2. Therefore, "competition" corresponds in this context to $A_{21} < 0$.

Exercise 5.9. Prove that $A_{21} < 0$ for the Lotka-Volterra equations (5.19), for any value of $I_1 \neq 0$.

So the Lotka-Volterra equations predict the expected outcome of a press addition experiment. Indeed, all competition models that I am aware of predict this result. (Of course, if we continually remove organisms instead of continually adding them, we will get the opposite result.)

On the other hand, one can still get the "competition" outcome from press perturbations, even if the two species in question do not compete for anything! Consider, for example, two species, with densities N_1 and N_2, which grow completely independently of one another: they exploit entirely separate resources, and engage in no interference whatever. Just for the sake of concreteness, assume each species grows logistically:

$$dN_1/dt = r_1 N_1 (1 - N_1/K_1)$$

$$dN_2/dt = r_2 N_2 (1 - N_2/K_2)$$

Certainly in a press addition or removal experiment, one would find no effect at all; these two species function completely independently.

Now imagine that a predator, with density P, consumes these two species, with a simple linear functional response:

$$dP/dt = CP(-T + a_1w_1N_1 + a_2w_2N_2)$$
$$dN_1/dt = r_1N_1(1 - N_1/K_1) - a_1N_1P + I_1$$
$$dN_2/dt = r_2N_2(1 - N_2/K_2) - a_2N_2P$$

(5.47)

where a_i, $i = 1, 2$, is the predator's consumption rate of species i and w_i, $i = 1, 2$, is the nutritional value for the predator of an individual of species i.

Anticipating that we are going to perform a press addition *Gedankenexperiment* (German: thought-experiment), I have added an addition rate I_1 to species 1's growth equation. Again, we can assume equilibrium, set the right-hand sides of (5.47) equal to zero, differentiate the three equations with respect to I_1, and solve for

$$\frac{dN_{2e}}{dI_1} = -\frac{1}{\dfrac{a_2w_2}{a_1w_1}\left(\dfrac{I_1}{N_{1e}} + \dfrac{r_1}{K_1}N_{1e}\right) + \dfrac{a_1r_2}{a_2K_2}N_{1e}}$$

(5.48)

Exercise 5.10. Prove (5.48).

But the right-hand side is negative: which means that according to the experiment, the two species are competing!

This result is not difficult to understand. By adding more species 1 individuals to the system, we increase the predator population, hence the predation pressure on species 2. Clearly this mechanism will operate whenever the two species in question limit the predator population. This is our second example of an indirect effect (the first was consumptive competition, you will recall from the first paragraphs of Section 5.3).

This phenomenon has been studied in considerable detail by Holt (1977, 1984), who calls it *apparent competition.* I do not think that anyone would want to claim that species in apparent competition are "really competing," but certainly they cannot be distinguished from "real competitors" through press perturbation experiments alone.

For our purposes, we can conclude three things from the present discussion. First, it's a jungle out there. Second, there's a lot more to perturbation experiments than casual thought might lead one to expect. Third, predators can have profound effects on the interactions of their prey. I am going to turn now to the third point, and will return to the second in Chapter 7.

ADDITIONAL EXERCISES

5.11. Work out the phase space trajectories for the four Lotka-Volterra types whose isoclines are sketched on pages 134–135. You will probably be able to sketch the trajectories right away simply using the signs of the growth rates in different regions of phase space; but check the behavior near a few of the equilibria by calculating I_e and Ω_e.

5.12. Computer project. Integrate the Armstrong-McGehee equations (5.30) numerically, with

$$d_1 = 0.1$$

$$c_1 = 0.3$$

$$E_1 = 0.5$$

$$R_0 = 50$$

$$r = 0.1$$

$$K = 300$$

$$d_2 = 0.11$$

$$c_2 = 0.33$$

$$E_2 = 0.003$$

Use $N_1 = 1$, $N_2 = 0.01$, $R = 400$ as initial values for the densities. If you do not already have access to a good subroutine for integrating differential equations, try RKF45 of Forsythe, Malcolm, and Moler (1977).

Experiment with the parameters to see how sensitive coexistence is to their values.

5.13. Replace the logistic resources of equations (5.17) by resources that flow into the system from outside. That is, replace the second of (5.17) by

$$dR_I/dt = b_I - c_I R_I - \sum_j a_{jI} N_j R_I \qquad I = 1, \ldots, k$$

Assuming that the resource dynamics is much faster than the consumer dynamics, use $dR_I/dt = 0$ for all I to eliminate the R's from the first of (5.17), as we did in getting the Lotka-Volterra equations (5.19) and the constitutive relations (5.20). Take $n = 2$, $k = 3$ and work out the phase spaces for these systems.

5.14. Replace the linear functional responses in (5.17) with Type II functional responses. Again work out the consumer-consumer interaction that replaces (5.19), assuming fast resource dynamics.

5.15. Obviously, the Lotka-Volterra equations (5.19) are not the only consumer-consumer equations that describe competition. Exercises 5.12 and 5.13 are examples of alternative equations. (Other examples, nicely motivated from biological considerations, are given by Schoener 1976, 1978.) However, any consumer-consumer model that has a point attractor can be linearized around that attractor, and the linearized model will behave, in a neighborhood of the point attractor, exactly like some Lotka-Volterra system. This is one possible way to generalize the notion of "competition coefficient α_{ij}" beyond Lotka-Volterra models.

Work out the community matrix (5.4) for a Lotka-Volterra model (5.19). Show that

$$\alpha_{ij} = A_{ij}/A_{ii} \qquad i, j = 1, \ldots, s$$

Therefore, this expression gives "competition coefficients," in the sense of local behavior near a point attractor, for general consumer-consumer models. Work out these coefficients for the model of Exercise 5.12.

5.16. In Section 5.3 I showed, in a collectivist framework, that if species 2 dominates species 1 in terms of consumptive competition, then species 1 cannot achieve dominance by interfering with species 2, nor can it even coexist with species 2 in this way. Thus in collectivist competition, it is more important to be good at resource utilization than at interference.

Consider this same issue in a monopolist framework. We found in Section 5.3 that species 1 can convert species 2's dominance into a contingent interaction through interference. Will this promote coexistence in a monopolist framework? Does this suggest a tradeoff in spatial competition between efficiency at resource utilization on the one hand and at interference on the other? Can you cite evidence for such a tradeoff, in terms of alternative strategies adopted within habitats, for plants? For sessile fauna? For (nonterritorial) fishes?

Chapter 6

Mortality and Competition

Changes in mortality factors such as predation, grazing, physical disturbance, and toxic pollution can have a profound effect on the coexistence of competing species. Indeed, there is a rich empirical tradition of studying the influence of some single mortality factor on the structure of competitive guilds, at least for sessile organisms.

For instance, Darwin (1859, Chap. 3) allowed a lawn that had long been mown to grow freely, and found that "out of twenty species growing on a little plot of mown turf (three feet by four) nine species perished, from the other species being allowed to grow up freely." In another classic study, Paine (1966) found that removal of the top predator from an intertidal guild resulted in a decrease in the number of major space-utilizing species in the assemblage from 15 to 8 (see also Paine 1974).

There have been quite a few theoretical studies on this topic as well, and I will discuss some of them in this chapter. We are going to encounter some new and rather weird attractors in this context, which necessitates yet another mathematical excursion (Section 6.1). But first, let's think a little bit about methodology.

Often in field studies, intermediate levels of mortality have been found to permit higher species richness (= total number of species) in the competitive guild, as in the two examples cited above. On the other hand, some studies (cited in Section 6.4) find lower species richness. Different outcomes are possible under different circumstances. So we need to explicate which outcomes we should expect under which circumstances.

"Circumstances" here might be specified quantitatively, but they might also be specified qualitatively. A qualitative specification involves *drawing a distinction* or a series of distinctions.

For example, in order to understand the effects of mortality on competitive coexistence, we need to draw at the very least the following distinctions.

First, we need to distinguish among collectivist consumption, monopolist consumption with dominance control, and monopolist consumption with founder control in the competitive guild.

Second, we need to categorize the species selectivity of the mortality factor. I will distinguish four forms of selectivity in this chapter: no preference, preference for one or more functionally dominant species, preference for one or more functional subdominants, and switching (a disproportionate preference for the most abundant prey species at any time).

With three forms of guild control and four forms of selectivity, we can distinguish 12 different cases (actually 10, since the two selectivity categories involving dominance are meaningless in founder control). In each case, we can work out theoretically how the mortality factor affects species richness. Then, if our distinctions have been appropriately and sharply enough drawn, we can, given the requisite information (namely, the information required to specify which of the 10 cases is at hand), predict the effect of any given particular mortality factor in the field. This is a methodology that enables us to make theoretical predictions that are at once nontrivial (i.e., not patently obvious), exact, and qualitative.

Early in its development, theoretical ecology had a tendency to see the exact *quan*titative predictions of physics as a methodological exemplar. As it became clear that many, if not most, of the insights into ecology that one could realistically hope for were *qual*itative in character (recall, for instance, our discussion of limiting similarity), a tendency to attempt sweeping generalizations appeared (for instance, the "intermediate disturbance hypothesis," universally associating intermediate mortality levels with enhanced species richness). But ecology is too subtle for sweeping generalizations to be of much use.

The *pluralistic* methodology of drawing distinctions that I sketched above is one possible way out of this methodological impasse, one possible way to formulate a nontrivial, exact, qualitative theory. This methodology is implicit in a great deal of the theoretical ecology of the last decade, and it is not uncommon for theorists to adopt it quite explicitly (e.g., Schoener 1983, 1986, Toft 1986, Yodzis 1986). A subsidiary purpose of this chapter is to discuss the pluralistic methodology through an example.

After working out some of the underlying theory, I will confront the resulting scheme of predictions with a survey of the observational literature in Section 6.4, where I will also add a few more remarks to this methodological discussion.

6.1 CONTINUOUS CHAOS

You will, I am sure, recall the important notion of attractor, introduced in Section 5.1. As emphasized there, most of our observations of population systems (except for systems very much subject to extrinsic influences) are going to be, in effect, observations of attracting sets in phase space. We are by now well familiar with point attractors, and we have had a little bit of experience with limit cycles. I am going to discuss here another class of attractors, the chaotic attractors.

These are very strange objects indeed, and it will take a little work merely to describe them. The approach that I am going to take here is based on that of Abraham and Shaw (1983). I will presuppose that you have a pretty good recollection of Sections 3.2, 3.3, 4.2, and 5.1. You may find that you want to refresh your memory of that material.

6.1.1 Limit Cycles and Poincaré Sections

It will be helpful to start by looking a little more closely at limit cycles. Think first of a two-dimensional system (two species), and suppose it has a stable limit cycle:

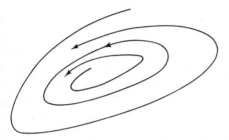

Pick a point on the limit cycle, say P, and look at a small neighborhood of that point:

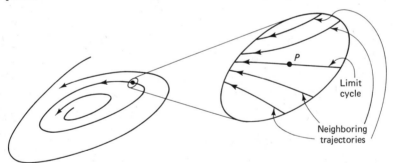

Draw a small segment of a straight line through P, perpendicular to the limit cycle. Denote this line segment S:

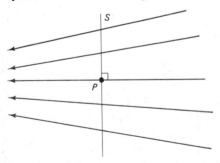

Such a little line segment is called a *Poincaré section* (as in "cross section"), after the nineteenth century French mathematician Henri Poincaré, who was the first to think of limit cycles in this way.

There will be a trajectory crossing through each point of the Poincaré section S, and each of these trajectories will cross S again at some (generally other) point. For any point x on S, denote the point of first return to S of the trajectory through x by $R(x)$:

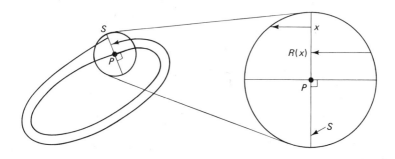

The mapping R is called a *first return map.*

Since R simply maps the one-dimensional line segment S into itself, we can graph it:

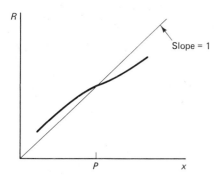

Of course, from the graph you can read off the point $R(x)$ to which any point x on S will first return if we follow the trajectory through x. And then by using the mapping R again on the point $R(x)$, you can find the second return point to S, and so on. We have reduced the dynamics in a neighborhood of the limit cycle to something very much like the discrete-time single population systems that we discussed back in Chapter 3!

For a stable limit cycle, each subsequent return of a trajectory to S will be closer to P than the last, so the graph of R will have positive slope, less than 1 (compare the sketches on page 57):

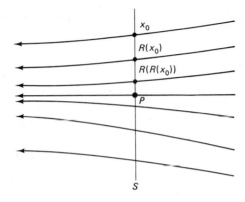

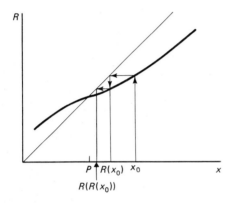

We can construct Poincaré sections for other kinds of periodic trajectories, too. If we do this with an unstable limit cycle, for instance, each subsequent return of a trajectory to S will be farther away from P than the last, so the graph of R will have a positive slope, greater than 1 (compare the lower sketch on page 58):

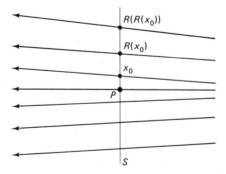

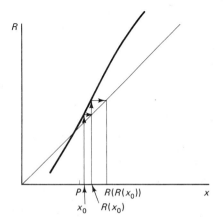

P $R(R(x_0))$ x
x_0 $R(x_0)$

What if the graph of R has negative slope? Then (recalling the upper sketch on page 58, for instance) each time a trajectory returns again to S, it is on the other side of the periodic trajectory from where it was at the previous return. This is clearly quite preposterous if phase space is a two-dimensional Euclidean space (as it is for two-species population systems). However, for a limit cycle that lies in a Möbius band like this (note the 180° twist),

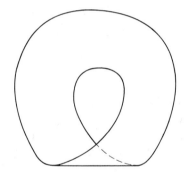

neighboring trajectories will behave in exactly this way, moving from one side of the limit cycle to the other in each circulation, without ever intersecting the limit cycle or any other trajectory:

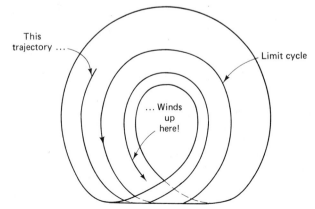

This trajectory ...

Limit cycle

... Winds up here!

In principle, this kind of thing can happen for population systems with more than two species, but I do not know of an explicit example where it does.

6.1.2 Chaotic Attractors

Pursuing the analogy with the discrete systems of Chapter 3 still further, what would it mean if a first return map had a peak in it, like the chaotic systems studied in Section 3.3?

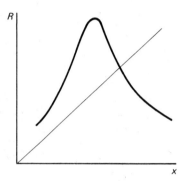

Well, for one thing, each point of return $R(x)$ will have *two* points x mapped into it:

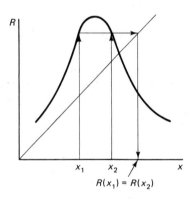

Geometrically, this kind of mapping, where two points are carried into the same point as the trajectories flow along, has got to involve some kind of *folding*. There are various ways that this can happen, of which the following is about the simplest.

Imagine that the trajectories lie within a ribbon and that they expand within this ribbon:

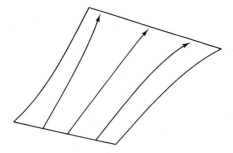

However, as this expansion takes place, the ribbon begins to fold over

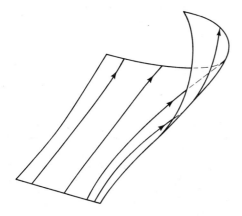

finally folding back "on itself":

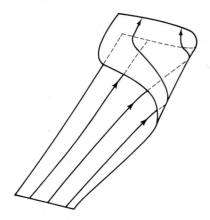

At the same time, the ribbon bends around in a circle

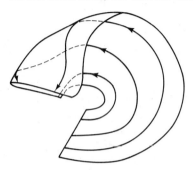

eventually joining back up with the end from which the trajectories "originated":

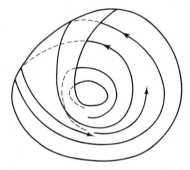

Actually, since the "ribbon" we are talking about is made up of trajectories, and trajectories can never cross, it can't join back up with itself if it is a rigorously two-dimensional surface. Rather, the ribbon is a "thick surface," made up of infinitely many layers of normal two-dimensional surfaces, like a strudel or croissant dough (in the pithy analogy of Abraham and Shaw 1983). Abraham and Shaw explicate this microstructure with wonderful clarity (using lots of pictures—printed in two colors!). The final picture above, though, gives a pretty reasonable idea of the attractor first discovered by Rössler and called by him *spiral chaos* (1976).

The reason for the name "spiral chaos" becomes clear if you view the object in the preceding picture "from directly above":

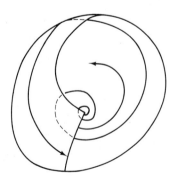

In this view you can see the spirals clearly. Another way to conceive of this object is to start with an unstable focus in a "thick" plane, and let the trajectories move up out of the plane as they expand out, then fold back and bend down into the plane. This is the "reinjection principle" of Rössler (1979).

If you take a section across the ribbon about here

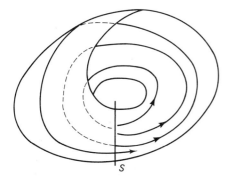

and construct a first return map, it will have a peaked graph just like the chaotic discrete maps that served as our starting point in this subsection.

In the discussion of limit cycles in the preceding subsection, the (simple two-dimensional) ribbon of trajectories that produce the first return map are neighboring trajectories to the attractor itself, which is just the limit cycle. Those neighboring trajectories enter the ribbon from outside. In the case of spiral chaos, the *whole object* pictured above, embedded in some phase space with at least three dimensions, is the attractor. This object is a self-contained bundle of trajectories: no trajectories enter from outside. However, neighboring trajectories *do* approach the bundle of trajectories asymptotically—which is just saying that the bundle of trajectories is indeed an attractor.

There are many other chaotic attractors, still being explored and classified by mathematicians, but I am not going to discuss any other than spiral chaos.

The amazing thing about these attractors is that they can occur in the phase spaces of very simple systems. For instance, in the next section we will see that spiral chaos can occur in the simplest model one can think of in which two competitors are consumed by a single predator species, with the predator limited by these prey. Even the Lotka-Volterra competition equations themselves, for more than three species, have chaotic attractors for certain parameter values (Arneodo et al. 1982; see also Smale 1976).

In view of the very close relationship between discrete and continuous chaos (via the first return map), you will not be surprised if I tell you that they have many properties in common. Thus, while the densities of a population system near a point attractor are more or less constant, and the densities of a population system near a limit cycle are more or less cyclic, the densities of a population system near a chaotic attractor vary in an extremely complicated way which can be difficult to distinguish from random noise! (We will see examples of this in the following section.)

6.2 MORTALITY AND CONSUMPTIVE COMPETITION

6.2.1 A Predator That Is Limited by Its Prey

Consider a pair of competing species, with densities N_1, N_2, which utilize space in a collectivist fashion and whose dynamics obey the Lotka-Volterra equations. Add to that system a predator, with density P and a linear functional response:

$$\left.\begin{array}{l} dN_1/dt = r_1 N_1 (K_1 - N_1 - \alpha_{12} N_2)/K_1 - a_1 N_1 P \\ dN_2/dt = r_2 N_2 (K_2 - N_2 - \alpha_{21} N_1)/K_2 - a_2 N_2 P \\ dP/dt = P(-T + w_1 a_1 N_1 + w_2 a_2 N_2) \end{array}\right\} \quad (6.1)$$

This system has been analyzed by Parrish and Saila (1970), Cramer and May (1972), Fujii (1977), Vance (1978), Gilpin (1979), Takeuchi and Adachi (1983), and Schaffer and Kot (1985a). I am going to summarize these results here, without going into mathematical details.

Throughout the following, *predation level* on prey species i will refer to a_i/r_i: the capture frequency per unit time, scaled to the intrinsic growth rate. In particular, when I speak of *preferences* of the predator for one prey or the other, I will mean it in the sense of the scaled capture frequency a_i/r_i.

This way of stating things is "natural" from the standpoint of the theory, in the sense that it enables the simplest statements of the results. It is not necessarily a "natural" way to report observations; this would normally be done in terms of the capture frequencies a_i, scaled to a common "clock time." Fortunately, the difference will seldom obtrude in a practical sense, as the r_i associated with prey that share a predator will usually be comparable.

Obviously, if the predation level on any species is high enough, then it will be eliminated from the system despite any competitive interactions. This kind of "overharvesting" certainly changes the nature of the system, but in a rather trivial way. I will not mention these overharvesting effects in the following.

Suppose first that the competitors can coexist in the absence of predation: $\alpha_{12} < K_1/K_2$ and $\alpha_{21} < K_2/K_1$. If the predator has no preferred prey, it will have no effect on coexistence: as the level of predation on both prey increases, the equilibrium prey densities will decrease, and they will both approach zero as the predation level approaches infinity. If the predator has a preferred prey, this prey will be eliminated at sufficiently high predation levels, so the competitive interaction will be converted to functional dominance of the less preferred prey at sufficiently high predation levels.

Now suppose the competitive interaction is contingent if the predator is absent: $\alpha_{12} > K_1/K_2$ and $\alpha_{21} > K_2/K_1$. If the predator has no preference, the interaction will remain contingent. A strong enough preference for either species can lead to functional dominance of the other. There is a small region in (harvesting level) parameter space in which stable limit cycles, with all three species present, exist.

Finally, suppose one competitor dominates the other in the absence of predation: $\alpha_{12} < K_1/K_2$ and $\alpha_{21} > K_2/K_1$. If the predator has no preference, there are two possibilities: (1) if $\alpha_{12} + \alpha_{21} < 2$, the dominance remains, (2) if $\alpha_{12} + \alpha_{21} > 2$, the dominant interaction is transformed into a contingent one at high enough predation levels. If the subdominant competitor is preferred, predation yields no change in the outcome of competition. If the dominant competitor is preferred, all three species can coexist in the system if the predation levels are high enough.

This coexistence is at a point attractor if $\alpha_{12}\alpha_{21} < 1$. If $\alpha_{12}\alpha_{21} > 1$, the attractor can be a point, a limit cycle, or (as first realized by Gilpin 1979) the spiral chaos of Section 6.1.2.

For instance, Figs. 6.1 to 6.4 are numerical simulations of equations (6.1) with the parameter values: $r_1 = r_2 = T = K_1 = K_2 = 1$, $w_1 = w_2 = 0.5$, $\alpha_{12} = 1$, $\alpha_{21} = 1.5$, and $a_2 = 1$. The predation level a_1 on the dominant species changes from one figure to the next, taking on the values 6 (yielding a periodic solution), 8 (doubly periodic), 10 (spiral chaos), and 13 (spiral chaos), in that order. The first of the above chaotic solutions (Fig. 6.3) is "kind of cyclic," while the second (Fig. 6.4) is markedly noisy.

How might one verify that one is observing some sort of multispecies chaos? At first, this seems a daunting task, for the coherent structure of the chaotic attractor is evident only in the phase space portrayal of the population dynamics: to measure a phase space trajectory one has to measure, with sufficient accuracy and over a long enough period of time, all the relevant densities. One is confronted, then, with two difficulties. First, one has to know enough about the interactions taking place to know which densities are the relevant densities. Second, one has to get time series for all those densities—and it's already difficult enough to get a good long-term time series for *one* population density.

Both these problems are alleviated by a discovery of Packard et al. (1980) and Takens (1981), who showed that one can reconstruct a multispecies attractor from the time series for only one species density. If N is the density to be used for this purpose, the procedure is to plot, for each time of observation t, $N(t)$ versus $N(t + T)$ versus $N(t + 2T)$ versus ... versus $N[t + (m - 1)T]$, for some fixed positive time delay T and for some positive integer dimension m. The result is an m-dimensional plot which reveals the coherent structure of any attractor that may be present.

Packard et al. and Takens were interested in the physics of turbulence. Schaffer has applied their method to ecological systems. He suggests that the Canadian lynx "cycle" is probably doubly periodic, rather like Fig. 6.2 (Schaffer 1984, 1985), while the histories of human measles in New York City and in Baltimore provide rather clear examples of spiral chaos (Schaffer and Kot 1985a, 1985b). Some of the data behind the controversial "three-year cycles" of microtine rodents look chaotic in Schaffer's (1986) analysis. And startlingly, that classic example of "density-independent regulation," the seemingly irregular outbreaks of *Thrips imaginis,* may actually be an instance of (density-regulated) chaos (Schaffer and Kot 1985c).

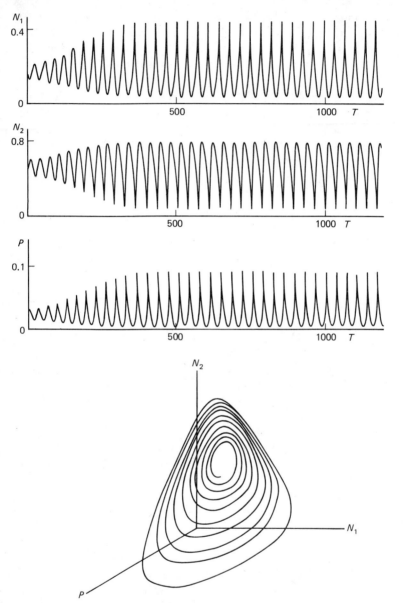

Figure 6.1 Numerical solution of the system (6.1) with $a_1 = 6$: singly periodic. (From Takeuchi and Adachi 1983. Reprinted with permission from *Bulletin of Mathemetical Biology*, Volume 45, Existence and bifurcation of stable equilibrium in two-prey, one-predator communities, 1983, Pergamon Press, Inc.)

6.2.2 No Feedback from Guild Densities to Level of Mortality

Let us consider next a mortality factor whose level is not linked to the state of the competitive guild. This could be a predator that is limited by some other

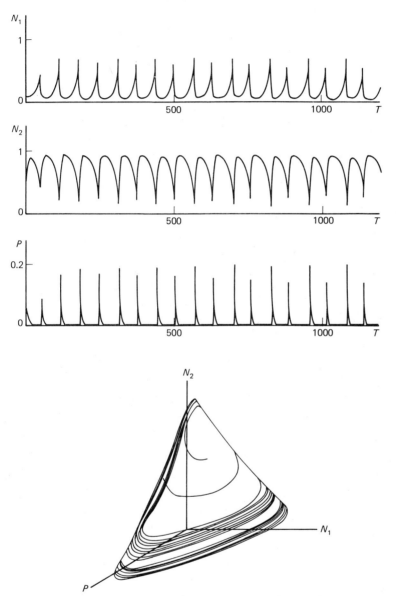

Figure 6.2 Numerical solution of the system (6.1) with $a_1 = 8$: doubly periodic. (From Takeuchi and Adachi 1983. Reprinted with permission from *Bulletin of Mathematical Biology*, Volume 45, Existence and bifurcation of stable equilibrium in two-prey, one-predator communities, 1983, Pergamon Press, Inc.)

factor than food, or it could be physical disturbance, or pollution by some toxic substance, for example.

Suppose first that the mortality rate per individual is constant. Then we are talking about the first two of equations (6.1), with P constant. This case is

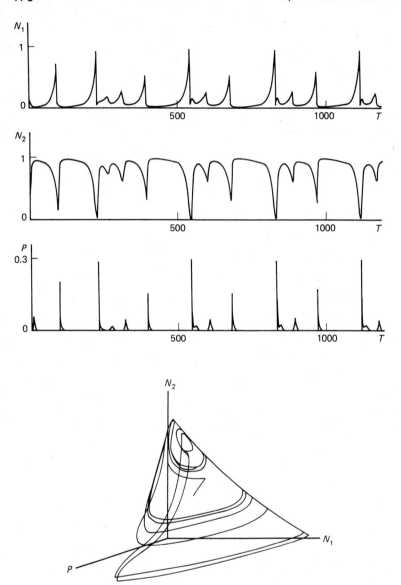

Figure 6.3 Numerical solution of the system (6.1) with $a_1 = 10$: mild spiral chaos. (From Takeuchi and Adachi 1983. Reprinted with permission from *Bulletin of Mathemetical Biology*, Volume 45, Existence and bifurcation of stable equilibrium in two-prey, one-predator communities, 1983, Pergamon Press, Inc.)

very simple to deal with, for we can immediately rewrite the first two equations of (6.1) as

$$dN_1/dt = r_1 N_1 [K_1(1 - a_1/r_1) - N_1 - \alpha_{12} N_2]/K_1$$

$$dN_2/dt = r_2 N_2 [K_2(1 - a_2/r_2) - N_2 - \alpha_{21} N_1]/K_2$$

(6.2)

where I have taken $P = 1$ without loss of generality (for instance, by a suitable redefinition of a_i). Clearly, the outcome of competition is determined exactly

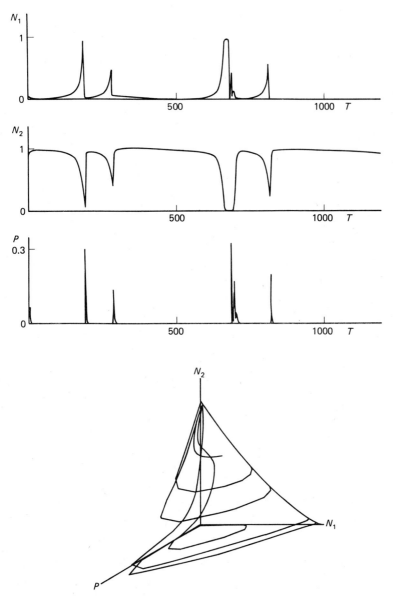

Figure 6.4 Numerical solution of the system (6.1) with $a_1 = 13$: more severe spiral chaos. (From Takeuchi and Adachi 1983. Reprinted with permission from *Bulletin of Mathemetical Biology,* Volume 45, Existence and bifurcation of stable equilibrium in two-prey, one-predator communities, 1983, Pergamon Press, Inc.)

as on page 134, except that instead of looking at the relationships between α_{ij} and K_i/K_j, we need to compare α_{ij} with K'_i/K'_j, where $K'_i = K_i(1 - a_i/r_i)$.

Again I will call the mortality rates a_1/r_i (scaled to the intrinsic growth rates) the *mortality levels.* One can show the following.

If the mortality level is the same for both species, adding the mortality factor makes no difference at all in the outcome of competition.

Suppose coexistence is possible without the mortality factor. Then if the mortality factor acts preferentially on either competitor, that competitor will be eliminated for sufficiently high mortality level (the competitive interaction will become dominant); at lower levels coexistence will be maintained.

If the competition is contingent without the mortality factor, it will remain so at low mortality levels, but if one species suffers a higher level of mortality, it will become subdominant at high enough levels.

Finally, suppose there is functional dominance without the mortality factor. If the mortality factor acts preferentially on the subdominant, the competitive relationship will remain unchanged for all levels. If the factor acts preferentially on the dominant competitor, then we need to distinguish two cases. If $\alpha_{12}\alpha_{21} < 1$, we may have no change in the qualitative nature of the interaction, coexistence, or a reversal of dominance, depending on the value of $(1 - a_1/r_1)/(1 - a_2/r_2)$. If $\alpha_{12}\alpha_{21} > 1$, we may have no change, contingent competition, or a reversal of dominance.

Exercise 6.1. Prove the statements in the preceding four paragraphs.

Another possibility is for the level of mortality on each population to be constant, or essentially constant. For instance, if a predator saturates at a low prey density relative to the prey growth curve,

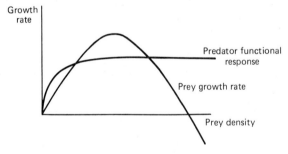

then the prey population experiences, in effect, constant mortality. This case has been treated by Yodzis (1976, 1977b) and Abrams (1977). The results are similar to those for system (6.1), except that all attractors are point attractors.

Everything we have done so far in this chapter has been for two competing species. Let us briefly consider the effect of mortality on diffuse Lotka-Volterra competition. Generally the effects of selective mortality tend to be rather obvious; the nontrivial case is mortality that acts at about the same level on all species. Let us consider that case here.

When the mortality rate per individual is constant, it follows very quickly as above that adding the mortality factor has no effect on diffuse competition (Holt 1985). Let us consider the effect of a constant population mortality rate on the three-species model of Section 5.2.1.1:

$$dN_1/dt = rN_1(K - N_1 - \alpha N_2 - \alpha^4 N_3)/K - a$$

$$dN_2/dt = rN_2(K - \alpha N_1 - N_2 - \alpha N_3)/K - a$$

$$dN_3/dt = rN_3(K - \alpha^4 N_1 - \alpha N_2 - N_3)/K - a$$

I have taken all three carrying capacities and intrinsic growth rates as equal. I have also taken the three mortality rates as equal, as we want to consider non-selective mortality. Notice that the first and third of these equations are identical. We can seek an equilibrium of the two-dimensional system consisting of the first two equations, with $N_3 = N_1$.

Solving for equilibrium, one finds from the second equation

$$N_1^* = (K - N_2^* - aK/rN_2^*)/2\alpha \qquad (6.3)$$

Substituting this into the first equation yields

$$(KN_2^* - N_2^{*2} - aK/r)[2\alpha KN_2^* - (1 + \alpha^4)(KN_2^* + N_2^{*2} + aK/r)$$
$$- 2\alpha^2 N_2^{*2}] - 4aK\alpha^2 N_2^{*2}/r = 0 \qquad (6.4)$$

This is a quartic equation for the equilibrium density N_2^*. While there are closed expressions for the roots of quartics (unlike polynomials of degree 5 or higher), in practice they are too complicated to be of much use, and one has to find the roots numerically, on a computer. In order to avoid clumsiness in those numerical computations, we want to have as few parameters in our equations as possible. We can eliminate the carrying capacity K right away, by choosing units of density in which $K = 1$; this is no loss in generality. We are left with two parameters: a/r and α.

For each pair $(a/r, \alpha)$, we can solve (6.4) for N_2^*, by a systematic computer search for zeros of the left-hand side. Then we can use (6.3) to get N_1^* and N_3^* $(=N_1^*)$. If both N_1^* and N_2^* are positive, we have an equilibrium. Using the methods of Section 5.1.1 we can check whether it is stable. For each mortality level a/r, we can then search for the largest α, say α_L, such that the system has a stable equilibrium with positive densities. This is the alpha that corresponds to limiting similarity.

One obtains Fig. 6.5. The upper limit α_L decreases with increasing mortality level. Through (5.25), this means that adding the mortality factor causes limiting

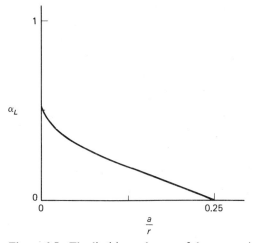

Figure 6.5 The limiting value α_L of the competition coefficient that allows coexistence vs. the scaled mortality rate a/r, for diffuse competition.

similarity to increase. In particular, if the three species are near their limiting similarity, adding the mortality factor will cause the middle species to be eliminated from the system.

This is, to be sure, a very rough and ready calculation, with lots of special assumptions. Nevertheless, it is useful to see that, at least in this simple case, our expectation from the more extensive two-species work (that added nonselective mortality will tend to have an adverse effect on competitive coexistence) extends to diffuse competition.

6.2.3 Summary

The results of this section can be summarized as follows. Suppose we vary a particular mortality factor on a competitive guild of collectivist consumers. Of course, very high levels of mortality will commonly be associated with low species richness; at sufficiently high mortality levels, the entire guild will be eliminated. And of course at very low levels of mortality any difference from the state of the guild when the mortality factor is absent will be too small to observe. At intermediate levels of mortality, *if* there is a change in species richness, relative to the species richness when the mortality factor is absent, we expect it to be as follows.

If the mortality is nonselective, or if its level is higher for less abundant species, it will be associated with a decrease in species richness. If the mortality factor acts preferentially on more abundant or functionally dominant species, it will be associated with an increase in species richness.

There is one result in Section 6.2.1 that does not fit the preceding statement. It is the possibility of a stable limit cycle in the case of a contingent competitive interaction. This does require rather particular values of the mortality levels (Takeuchi and Adachi 1983)—in particular it does not occur for nonselective mortality—but it can occur. If we have this situation, then removal of the mortality factor will cause a decrease in species richness.

Researchers have still not considered by any means all the possible models that come into question here, so it may be necessary at some point to refine the scheme just suggested.

6.3 MORTALITY AND COMPETITION FOR SPACE

If we adopt the reaction-dispersal viewpoint of Section 5.4.2, we can easily infer what happens in the case of spatial competition from the results of Section 6.2, by applying those results to local, within-cell, interactions (Yodzis 1978, Chap. 5).

Consider, for example, the case of nonselective mortality. It does not affect the qualitative character of a contingent pairwise interaction, but it can transform a dominant interaction into a contingent one. For a dominance controlled guild, any reduction in dominance allows more species to coexist. Therefore, although nonselective mortality tends to hinder coexistence in the context of collectivism (Section 6.2), it facilitates coexistence in dominance control.

In founder control, on the other hand, nonselective mortality will bring about, if any change, a decrease in species richness, by reducing the effective area occupied by the guild.

6.4 THE DATA

Table 6.1 summarizes a fairly thorough survey of the literature, carried out sporadically over a period of years. In each case the "effect on S" (S = species richness) is the one that the cited theoretical works predict will occur, *if* there is any change in S. There was, inevitably, a degree of ambiguity in assigning observational papers to these categories (particularly where selectivity is concerned), and someone else might have made other assignments. The treatment of the data for Table 6.1 is discussed in detail by Yodzis (1986).

TABLE 6.1 EFFECT ON SPECIES RICHNESS S OF INCREASING THE INTENSITY OF A PARTICULAR MORTALITY FACTOR (AT "INTERMEDIATE" LEVELS OF MORTALITY)

Guild control	Selectivity	Effect on S	Theory	Observation
Collectivist	None	Decreases	1, 32, 38	2, 27
	For dominant	Increases	6, 35, 37	
	For subdominant			
	Switching	Increases	28, 35	
Dominance	None	Increases	4, 14, 30, 39	3, 5, 7, 8, 9, 10, 11, 15, 19, 20, 21, 22, 23, 24, 26, 31, 33, 34
	For dominant	Increases	39	13, 18, 25
	For subdominant	Decreases	39	12, 13, 18
	Switching			
Founder	None	Decreases	40	16, 17, 26, 29, 36
	Switching			

Tabulated numbers correspond to these references:

1. Abrams (1977)
2. Addicott (1974)
3. Ayling (1981)
4. Caswell (1978)
5. Connell (1970)
6. Cramer and May (1972)
7. Darwin (1859)
8. Day (1972)
9. Dayton (1971)
10. Dayton (1973b)
11. Dickman and Gochnauer (1978)
12. Glynn (1976)
13. Harper (1969)
14. Hastings (1980)
15. Heinselman (1973)
16. Hunter (1980)
17. Hunter and Russell-Hunter (1983)
18. Lubchenco (1978)
19. Loucks (1970)
20. Menge (1976)
21. Osman (1977)
22. Paine (1966)
23. Paine (1971)
24. Paine (1974)
25. Porter (1972)
26. Porter (1974)
27. Risch and Carroll (1982)
28. Roughgarden and Feldman (1975)
29. Sammarco (1982)
30. Slatkin (1974)
31. Slobodkin (1964)
32. Takeuchi and Adachi (1983)
33. Taylor (1973)
34. Tomkins and Grant (1977)
35. Vance (1978)
36. Waser and Price (1981)
37. Yodzis (1976)
38. Yodzis (1977b)
39. Yodzis (1978)
40. Yodzis (unpublished)

In going through the literature, I have not found any clear conflict between theory and observation, to the best of my ability to interpret the observations in terms of these categories. However, robustness of these theoretical results has not been thoroughly enough studied and, as mentioned already, interpreting the observational literature is anything but straightforward. So the pluralistic scheme represented by Table 6.1 should be regarded as a tentative suggestion. Nevertheless, it can serve for us as an example of the pluralistic methodology.

Notice that in order to arrive at a consistent scheme, both of the distinctions I have used (guild control and selectivity) are necessary. For instance, if one neglects the different kinds of guild control and only keeps the four selectivity categories, then contradictory observations will be found in the case of nonselectivity. On the other hand, if one neglects the different kinds of selectivity and only distinguishes the three categories of guild control, contradictory observations will be found within dominance control.

The scheme needs to be tested more stringently, both observationally and theoretically. Let us imagine what might happen as we accumulate more data. There are two possibilities.

One possibility is to discover a clear contradiction with the scheme. Such a discovery might indicate the need to draw further distinctions. For instance, imagine that we had started out distinguishing only selectivity categories. Then eventually we would discover a contradiction within the existing data, as I mentioned above. One resolution of this difficulty would be to distinguish guild control categories. On the other hand, contradictions with the scheme might indicate that the whole scheme needs to be rethought. For instance, it might turn out that so many distinctions have to be drawn that the scheme becomes too complicated to be of any use—this is another way of looking at the problem of robustness discussed at the end of Section 5.2.1.1.

Everything I have discussed in this chapter is based on Lotka-Volterra systems with their particular (linear) form for the isoclines. There are indications that nonlinearity of the isoclines can have important effects on these conclusions (Abrams 1980; Hanski 1981; Holt 1985; Yodzis 1976, 1977b). Just how significant this nonrobustness is should become apparent over the next few years.

In any case, falsification of a proposed scheme of distinctions (as of any falsifiable theory) is a positive event, not a negative one, because we can learn something from it.

The other possibility—continuing validation of the scheme—seems at first less interesting. But it, too, permits further progress. Supposing that we cannot falsify these predictions, we can tighten up our predictions, by asking for more information in the predicted result (hence in the data as well!). For example, I have been careful to stress that the predicted effect on S in the table is the one we expect to see *if* we see any change in S. Suppose we want to predict as well whether there will be a change or not. This is a stronger prediction, and it requires more information to make it. In particular, at the very least we would have to add as another distinction whether and in what way there is feedback from the state of the guild to the level of mortality (recall our very first result in Section 6.2.2). Should we be so fortunate as to arrive at this state, we will need a whole

new observational base, for it is often difficult to identify such feedback observationally.

ADDITIONAL EXERCISES

6.2. Computer project (if you have access to graphics hardware). Integrate the system
(6.1) numerically. Plot phase space trajectories, using the projection

$$H = 0.707107(N_1 - N_2)$$

$$V = 0.408248(-N_1 - N_2) + 0.816597P$$

where H and V are horizontal and vertical coordinates in the two-dimensional space
where you are plotting. Verify the results stated in the text.

6.3. Computer project (if you have access to graphics hardware). Use the Packard-
Crutchfield-Farmer-Shaw-Takens construction sketched at the end of Section 6.2.1
to reconstruct attractors from time series for one variable, obtained from numerical
solutions to the system (6.1). Take $m = 3$ and use the projection given in Exercise
6.2 with $N_1 \rightarrow N(t)$, $N_2 \rightarrow N(t + T)$, $P \rightarrow N(t + 2T)$. Experiment with different
values of T and with different variables chosen for "N." Do this with parameters
that yield cyclic and chaotic solutions, e.g., those given for Figs. 6.1 to 6.4.

6.4. For the system (6.1), solve for the equilibrium densities in the case $\alpha_{12} < K_1/K_2$,
$\alpha_{21} < K_2/K_1$. Verify the results stated in the text for this case. (We will check stability
of the equilibrium in Exercise 7.7.)

6.5. Computer project. Caswell (1978) has demonstrated a nonequilibrium mechanism
whereby, in a monopolist framework of spatial utilization, a predator can enable a
pair of competitors to coexist within a habitat even if one dominates the other locally.
Duplicate Caswell's results. Extend them by seeing what happens in case the two
competitors *can* coexist in the absence of the predator.

Chapter 7

Generalized Press Perturbations and Guilds

In this chapter we are going to start thinking about whole systems. Most population theory (such as everything we have done up to now), like most observational work, contemplates systems that, in the natural world, do not exist in isolation but rather interact with other populations. Thus, for example, the consumers studied in isolation in Chapter 4 may interact with other consumers to produce the consumptive competition of Section 5.2, and those competitive interactions can be profoundly altered by consumption of the competitors, as we have seen in Chapter 6. And there will be other species present as well.

When can we call a halt to this process of considering more and more interactions? Do we ultimately have no honest recourse but to study nothing less than entire communities in the sense given that term in Section 5.5? In other words: is there anything short of a whole community that we can sensibly regard as a guild, in the sense of Section 5.5?

I am going to consider this issue here from the standpoint of certain perturbations, which are more general versions of the press perturbations described in Section 5.6. I do not claim that this is the only acceptable way to define guilds: the definition one uses in any given situation must take its meaning from the kind of thing one wants to do with that "guild." However, perturbation experiments are widely used in ecological field research. Furthermore, as I will indicate in Section 7.2, generalized press perturbations are of considerable practical interest.

In Section 7.1, which might be viewed as an extension of Section 5.1.1, I am going to develop some more mathematics, this time a computational technique which is quite useful for studying perturbation experiments and, incidentally, lots of other things. Section 7.2 develops the basic theory of perturbation experiments, and Section 7.3 addresses the notion of guild from this standpoint. In order to understand this chapter, you have to study Section A.2 (appendix) first.

7.1 LOOP ANALYSIS

I am going to continue in this section the analysis, started in Section 5.1.1, of point attractors of multispecies systems, and will assume that you recall Section 5.1. What I want to do here is to acquaint you with a graphical representation for community matrices, due to Levins (1974, 1975), which provides a convenient computational tool for certain purposes as well as a helpful way to envision multispecies interactions.

Sections 7.1.1 and 7.1.2 simply establish some notations and conventions. Sections 7.1.3 and 7.1.4 indicate how to use these tools to do certain calculations. Throughout, this discussion has the character of a "cookbook": I indicate how to calculate certain things, but I make no attempt to prove that these procedures really do what I am claiming they do. This is a departure from the basic spirit of this book, which is to try to give you a feeling for why things are done the way they are. However, doing the proofs in Sections 7.1.3 and 7.1.4 would take up too much space, and these are anyway just direct translations into the loop analysis language of standard results from the theory of determinants and cofactors, which you would encounter in any basic book on linear algebra.

7.1.1 Loop Diagrams

Consider a system of the form (5.1),

$$dN_i/dt = f_i(N_1, \ldots, N_s)$$

with an equilibrium point N_e, at which the community matrix has the elements A_{ij} given by equation (5.4):

$$A_{ij} = \left.\frac{\partial f_i}{\partial N_j}\right|_{N_e} \qquad i, j = 1, \ldots, s$$

The first thing we will do is to represent the numbers A_{ij} in a convenient graphical form called a *loop diagram*.

Each density (or other dynamical variable) N_i is represented by a *vertex:*

and each nonzero element A_{ij} of the community matrix by a directed line (called a *link*)

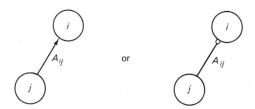

joining the two vertices corresponding to N_i and N_j. If $A_{ij} > 0$, the corresponding link ends (at the vertex corresponding to N_i) in an arrow; if $A_{ij} < 0$, the link ends in a circle. For any $A_{ij} = 0$, nothing is drawn in the diagram.

Translating the above mathematical definition of A_{ij} into words, it is the per capita effect of population j on the growth rate of species i. That is why one wants to think of the link corresponding to A_{ij} as drawn *from* the population j vertex *to* the population i vertex.

For instance, we might have

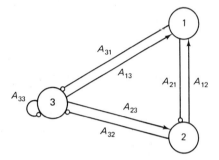

This diagram corresponds to a simple aquatic system of blue-green algae (density N_1) and green algae (density N_2) exploiting the nutrient phosphate (concentration N_3). The green algae produce vitamins which are used by the blue-greens; hence the link corresponding to A_{12} (the effect of 2 on 1, or greens on blue-greens) has an arrow on it because $A_{12} > 0$. The blue-green algae produce a substance which is toxic to greens, so $A_{21} < 0$ and the A_{21} link has a circle on it.

Growth of the phosphate concentration is self-damped: even if there were no algae to consume it, its concentration would grow only a certain amount and then stop—and this self-damping is significant at normal equilibrium densities when the algae are present. So the concentration of phosphate has a negative effect on itself, which is quantified by A_{33} (<0). This gives a link from vertex 3 to itself in the diagram. Such a link is called a *self-loop*. This one ends in a circle because $A_{33} < 0$.

The community matrix corresponding to this loop diagram is

$$\begin{bmatrix} 0 & A & B \\ -C & 0 & D \\ -E & -F & -G \end{bmatrix} = \begin{bmatrix} A_{11} & A_{12} & A_{13} \\ A_{21} & A_{22} & A_{23} \\ A_{31} & A_{32} & A_{33} \end{bmatrix}$$

where $A, B, \ldots, G$ are positive constants. The loop diagram and the community matrix contain precisely the same information, namely, the per capita effect of species j on species i's growth rate, for all pairs i, j of species, in a sufficiently small neighborhood of a point attractor. However, the loop diagram depicts the information in a form which is particularly easy to digest.

Exercise 7.1. Draw the loop diagram corresponding to each of the following community matrices. In each case, a capital letter stands for a positive constant. The symbol 0 is zero, not a letter.

1. Predator-prey system with a self-damped prey (for instance, the system of equations (4.5) at its point attractor with both species present):

$$\begin{bmatrix} -A & -B \\ C & 0 \end{bmatrix}$$

2. Two consumers on two resources, with one resource inhibiting the other:

$$\begin{bmatrix} -J & 0 & A & B \\ -C & -K & D & E \\ -F & -G & 0 & 0 \\ -H & -I & 0 & 0 \end{bmatrix}$$

3. One consumer of two noninteracting resources:

$$\begin{bmatrix} 0 & A & B \\ -C & -D & 0 \\ -E & 0 & -F \end{bmatrix}$$

4. A food chain:

$$\begin{bmatrix} -A & B & 0 \\ -C & -D & E \\ 0 & -F & 0 \end{bmatrix}$$

5. A longer food chain:

$$\begin{bmatrix} -A & B & 0 & 0 \\ -C & -D & E & 0 \\ 0 & -F & -G & H \\ 0 & 0 & -I & 0 \end{bmatrix}$$

6. A cultivated field with crop plant species 1, herbivore species 2 and 3, predator species 4, other plants 5, a parasite 6, and an insecticide 7:

$$\begin{bmatrix} -A & -B & 0 & 0 & 0 & 0 & 0 \\ C & 0 & 0 & -D & 0 & -E & -F \\ 0 & 0 & 0 & -G & H & 0 & 0 \\ 0 & I & J & 0 & 0 & 0 & -K \\ 0 & 0 & -L & 0 & -M & 0 & 0 \\ 0 & N & 0 & 0 & 0 & 0 & -P \\ 0 & 0 & 0 & 0 & 0 & 0 & 0 \end{bmatrix}$$

7.1.2 Loops and Feedbacks

Let V_i denote the vertex corresponding to density N_i. Let $V_{i(1)}, V_{i(2)}, \ldots, V_{i(n)}$ be a sequence of n vertices such that

1. Each neighboring pair $V_{i(j)}, V_{i(j+1)}$ of vertices in the sequence is connected by a link from $i(j)$ to $i(j + 1)$.
2. $i(n) = i(1)$.
3. No two vertex labels other than $i(n)$ and $i(1)$ are the same.

Then the sequence of n links that connect those n vertices in sequence [corresponding to matrix elements $A_{i(j+1)i(j)}$] is called a *loop,* and n is called the *length of the loop.* We can attach a number to each loop, which is just the product of the A_{ij}'s corresponding to all the links in it, and it is convenient when we want to talk about loops to name them by these products as well.

To illustrate these definitions, let's list all the loops that pass through the N_3 vertex in our very first example of a loop diagram, on page 180:

There is a loop of length 1, the self-loop A_{33}.

There are two loops of length 2: $A_{13}A_{31}$ and $A_{23}A_{32}$.

There are two loops of length 3: $A_{13}A_{21}A_{32}$ and $A_{23}A_{12}A_{31}$.

If two loops share no vertices in common, they are called *disjunct.* For instance, in the diagram on page 180 the loops A_{33} and $A_{12}A_{21}$ are disjunct. If two loops have a vertex in common, they are called *conjunct.* The loops A_{33} and $A_{13}A_{31}$ on page 180 are conjunct.

For any loop diagram, let $L(m, k)$ be the sum over all possible products of k links that form m disjunct loops. Set $L(m, k) = 0$ if $m > k$ or if k exceeds the total number of vertices in the system. Then, define the *feedback at level k,* denoted Z_k, to be

$$Z_0 = -1$$

$$Z_k = \sum_{m=1}^{k} (-1)^{m+1} L(m, k), \qquad k > 1 \tag{7.1}$$

(Of course, $Z_k = 0$ if $k >$ total number of vertices in the system.)

I've been throwing a lot of abstract definitions at you. An example will make it all a lot more concrete. Let us calculate the feedbacks for our example loop diagram on page 180.

First, take $k = 1$. Then from (7.1),

$$Z_1 = (-1)^2 L(1, 1) \tag{7.2}$$

since $L(m, k) = 0$ if $m > k$. This is just the sum over all loops of length 1 (self-loops), which in our example is

$$Z_1 = A_{33} \tag{7.3}$$

Now take $k = 2$. Then we will need $L(1, 2)$ and $L(2, 2)$. $L(1, 2)$ is the sum of all loops of length 2:

$$L(1, 2) = A_{12}A_{21} + A_{23}A_{32} + A_{13}A_{31}$$

$L(2, 2)$ is the sum of all possible products of two links that form two disjunct loops, that is, the sum of all possible products of two distinct self-loops. Since our example system has only one self-loop,

$$L(2, 2) = 0$$

Therefore

$$Z_2 = (-1)^2 L(1, 2) + (-1)^3 L(2, 2)$$

$$= L(1, 2) - L(2, 2) = A_{12}A_{21} + A_{23}A_{32} + A_{13}A_{31} \tag{7.4}$$

To finish, we compute Z_3. We will need $L(1, 3)$, $L(2, 3)$, and $L(3, 3)$. $L(1, 3)$ is the sum of all loops of length 3:

$$L(1, 3) = A_{12}A_{31}A_{23} + A_{13}A_{21}A_{32}$$

$L(2, 3)$ is the sum of all possible products of two disjunct loops, in which one of the loops is a self-loop and the other has length 2:

$$L(2, 3) = A_{33}(A_{12}A_{21})$$

Finally, $L(3, 3) = 0$ for the same reason that $L(2, 2) = 0$. So

$$Z_3 = L(1, 3) - L(2, 3) + L(3, 3)$$

$$= A_{12}A_{31}A_{23} + A_{13}A_{21}A_{32} - A_{33}A_{12}A_{21} \qquad (7.5)$$

Since our example system has only three vertices, there are no more nonzero feedbacks.

Exercise 7.2. Calculate the feedbacks Z_k for systems 1 to 5 of exercise 7.1.

7.1.3 Local Stability

In Section 5.1.1 I argued that a point attractor is locally stable if all the eigenvalues of the community matrix corresponding to that equilibrium have negative real parts. For each diagonalizable s by s matrix there is a polynomial, called the *characteristic polynomial*, whose roots are the s eigenvalues of the matrix. We can use loop analysis to get the characteristic polynomial. In fact, it is just

$$P(\lambda) = \lambda^s - \sum_{k=1}^{s} Z_k \lambda^{s-k} \qquad (7.6)$$

where Z_k is the feedback at level k, given by equation (7.1). For a proof of this, see Levins (1975).

To calculate the eigenvalues, one has to find the s roots of the polynomial (7.6). Often, one just wants to know whether the equilibrium is locally stable or not, and to find this out one does not have to actually work out all the eigenvalues; one just has to know whether or not all s roots of (7.6) have negative real part. There is a set of conditions on the coefficients Z_k, known as the *Routh-Hurwitz conditions*, which enable one to check whether all the roots have negative real parts, without actually solving for those roots (Frazer et al. 1960).

First, construct the following sequence of test functions. Set $R_0 = Z_0$, and derive R_1 from R_0, R_2 from R_1, and so on, by writing the lower element for the upper element in columns of the following chart:

Z_0	Z_1	Z_2	Z_3	Z_4	Z_5	etc.
Z_1	$Z_2 - Z_0Z_3/Z_1$	Z_3	$Z_4 - Z_0Z_5/Z_1$	Z_5	$Z_6 - Z_0Z_7/Z_1$	etc.

Remember that $Z_k = 0$ for all $k > s$. Now, the Routh-Hurwitz conditions for local stability of the equilibrium are: $R_k < 0$ for all $k = 0, \ldots, s$.

For instance, if $s = 4$ we start out with

$$R_0 = Z_0$$

Then to get R_1, we substitute for Z_0 in the above expression, using the table:

$$R_1 = Z_1$$

To get R_2, we substitute for Z_1 in the above expression, using the table:

$$R_2 = Z_2 - Z_0 Z_3 / Z_1$$

To get R_3, we substitute for Z_0, Z_1, Z_2, and Z_3 in the above expression, using the table. Since $Z_k = 0$ for all $k > s$ (which is 4 in the present instance), the table tells us to substitute Z_4 ($= Z_4 - Z_0 Z_5 / Z_1$, with $Z_5 = 0$) for Z_3:

$$R_3 = Z_3 - Z_1 Z_4 / (Z_2 - Z_0 Z_3 / Z_1)$$

$$= (Z_1 Z_2 Z_3 - Z_0 Z_3^2 - Z_1^2 Z_4) / (Z_1 Z_2 - Z_0 Z_3)$$

Finally, to get R_4 we substitute in the above expression. This is actually very simple, for the table tells us to substitute $Z_5 = 0$ for Z_4. Therefore, the last term in the numerator of the above expression will drop out. But without that term, the numerator is just the denominator times Z_3, so all the other stuff will cancel out, leaving just Z_3, for which we are to substitute Z_4:

$$R_4 = Z_4$$

(*Caution:* In doing these calculations, you might be tempted to simplify things by using the fact that $Z_0 = -1$. But you must not set $Z_0 = -1$ until you have finished working out all the R's, since in constructing each next R you have to substitute Z_1 for Z_0!)

The Routh-Hurwitz conditions $R_k < 0$ for $k = 0, \ldots, s$ will always imply that $Z_k < 0$ for all $k = 1, \ldots, s$: if any one feedback is positive, the equilibrium is unstable. Starting at $s = 3$, there will be additional conditions for stability. For $s = 3, 4, 5$ they are

$$s = 3: \quad Z_1 Z_2 + Z_3 > 0 \tag{7.7}$$

$$s = 4: \quad Z_1 Z_2 Z_3 + Z_3^2 - Z_1^2 Z_4 < 0 \tag{7.8}$$

$$s = 5: \quad Z_1 Z_2 Z_3 + Z_3^2 - Z_1^2 Z_4 < 0 \quad \text{and}$$

$$(Z_1 Z_4 - Z_5)(-Z_1 Z_2 Z_3 - Z_3^2 + Z_1^2 Z_4)$$

$$+ Z_5 (Z_1 Z_2 + Z_3)^2 + Z_1 Z_5^2 > 0 \tag{7.9}$$

Exercise 7.3. Find the stability conditions for the systems 1 to 3 of Exercise 7.1.

7.1.4 The Inverse Matrix

If the community matrix $\mathbf{A}$ is nonsingular (which it always will be for structurally stable systems), then it has a unique inverse $\mathbf{A}^{-1}$: $\mathbf{A}\mathbf{A}^{-1} = \mathbf{A}^{-1}\mathbf{A} = \mathbf{I}$ (= the unit matrix), as you will recall from Section A.2 (Appendix), or perhaps from else-where. One can use loop analysis to calculate the elements $(\mathbf{A}^{-1})_{ij}$ of the inverse matrix. I am now going to state the recipe for doing this, for future reference. (The future of which I speak is not distant: we will find in the next section that the inverse matrix plays an important role in practical community studies.)

For any pair of vertices V_i, V_j, suppose there is a sequence $V_{k(1)}$, $V_{k(2)}$, ..., $V_{k(n)}$ of vertices such that

1. $k(1) = j$
2. $k(n) = i$
3. $A_{k(h+1)k(h)} \neq 0$ for all $h = 1, \ldots, n - 1$

Then the sequence of $n - 1$ links corresponding to $A_{k(h+1)k(h)}$, $h = 1, \ldots,$ $n - 1$, is called a *path* from vertex V_j to vertex V_i. The *length* of the path is $n - 1$.

Notice that, just as in a loop, in a path the links are all *directed* such that as you move along each link in the sequence of links from V_j to V_i, you are always going from the unmarked end of the link to the end of the link that has either a circle or an arrow on it.

With each path we can associate a number $p_{ij}^{(n)}$, which is simply the pro-duct of the $n - 1$ A's associated with the $n - 1$ links in the path:

$$p_{ij}^{(n)} = A_{ik(n-1)}A_{k(n-1)k(n-2)} \cdots A_{k(2)j} \qquad (7.10)$$

For algebraic consistency we have to define

$$p_{ii}^{(1)} = 1 \qquad \text{for all } i \qquad (7.11)$$

If in addition to the above three conditions for a path we have

4. No two vertices in the sequence $V_{k(1)}, \ldots, V_{k(n)}$ are the same

then the path is called a *simple open path.*

For any simple open path p, let the *complementary subsystem to p* be the system (loop diagram) obtained by deleting the n vertices involved in the path p. Denote the feedback at level $s - n$ of the complementary subsystem to p by $Z_{s-n}^{(p-)}$, where, as always, s is the total number of vertices in the original loop diagram.

Using these concepts, we can write the elements of the inverse matrix as follows:

$$(\mathbf{A}^{-1})_{ij} = -\sum_p p_{ij}^{(n)} Z_{s-n}^{(p-)}/Z_s \qquad (7.12)$$

The sum here is over all simple open paths from vertex j to vertex i; for each simple open path p, $p_{ij}^{(n)}$ is given by (7.10), where $n - 1$ is the length of the path p. Like (7.6), this formula is by no means obvious; Levins (1975) derives it. As well as explaining why we want to be able to calculate the inverse matrix, I will in Section 7.2.1 run through an example of using equation (7.12) to com-pute the inverse.

7.2 PERTURBATION EXPERIMENTS

The growth rates in equations (5.1) depend on all kinds of parameters as well as on the densities. We can make this explicit by writing those equations

$$dN_i/dt = F_i(N_1, \ldots, N_s; C_1, \ldots, C_p) \qquad i = 1, \ldots, s \qquad (7.13)$$

where C_a, $a = 1, \ldots, r$, are parameters. Normally those parameters just have fixed values, which is why we didn't make the dependence on them explicit in Section 5.1.

A very important class of problems has to do with the response of a population system to a change in the parameter values from one fixed set of numbers to a different fixed set of numbers. For the sake of simplicity we will consider here a change in just one parameter, but it is trivial to extend our methods and conclusions to multiparameter changes.

This class of problems includes a lot of the experimental manipulations that field ecologists do, such as stocking or erecting exclosures (the "press" experiments introduced in Section 5.6). It also includes changes in human harvesting of populations, for instance, increasing fishing quotas. As well, it includes an enormity of unwitting human influences, such as changing the level of sewage discharge, regularly leaking or dumping toxins into the environment, or changing the levels of pesticide application.

Another important class of problems that can be related to generalized press perturbations are *coevolutionary* problems, in which one contemplates the effects of interacting populations on the evolution of each other's population parameters. I will not go into this interesting field here, but Levins (1975) and Roughgarden (1977) discuss it from a loop analysis standpoint, and having mastered this chapter you will be able easily to read those works.

The change occurs during some time period (t_1, t_2). Before t_1 the parameter has a fixed (= constant in time) value, and after t_2 it has a new fixed value. The duration $t_2 - t_1$ of the time period during which the change is taking place will usually be relatively small; it will do no harm to think of it as arbitrarily small, so that we need only think about the system "before" and "after" the change.

I will call this kind of perturbation a *generalized press perturbation,* reserving the unqualified term "press perturbation" for the special case where the parameter being altered is an input of members of one of the species in the system, as in Section 5.6. Of course, we can also define generalized pulse perturbations which extend the pulse perturbations mentioned in Section 5.6 to arbitrary parameters. But I am not going to discuss pulse perturbations, as they are conceptually much simpler than press perturbations.

Normally we would expect the system to be near some attractor before the change. The change in a parameter value will change the structure of phase space, so that the location in phase space of the prechange attractor will in general no longer correspond to an attractor. However, the new phase space will have new attractors. Therefore, after the change the system will move toward some new attractor.

We can pose two kinds of questions here. First, we can ask what the system will look like after it has reached a new attractor. This means waiting a sufficient amount of time for the system to reach that new attractor. Second, we can investigate the temporal behavior of the system starting immediately after the change, and look at its *transient* behavior as it moves toward the new attractor.

I will consider both these aspects of the matter here. However, I will make a couple of simplifying assumptions. Now, sometimes simplifying assumptions are harmless (as our restriction above to changes in just one parameter), sometimes they are not. The simplifying assumptions that I am about to introduce are *not* harmless. The reason I am introducing them is that without these assumptions the mathematics gets very difficult, so much so that little of any use is known about what happens.

First, I am going to consider point attractors only. Second, I am going to restrict attention to small parameter changes only—sufficiently small so that a local (= infinitesimal) analysis suffices. In practice, this means that the parameters must not change so much that either the linear approximation fails or a structural change happens to our attractor, such as becoming unstable or ceasing to exist.

I granted in advance that these are not harmless assumptions. But at least they do not fall into a third category of simplifying assumptions, namely, those that are so far removed from reality as to be utterly without interest. There are plenty of important "real world" problems to which our analysis ought to apply.

7.2.1 The New Equilibrium Densities

Suppose the parameter C_m changes, and suppose we wait long enough for the system to reach a new equilibrium. For a small parameter change δC_m, the new equilibrium densities will be

$$N_{ei}(C_m + \delta C_m) = N_{ei} + \left.\frac{\partial N_{ei}}{\partial C_m}\right|_{C_m} \delta C_m$$

To evaluate the required derivative, differentiate the equations (7.13) with respect to C_m:

$$\sum_j \left.\frac{\partial F_i}{\partial N_j}\right|_{N_e} \frac{\partial N_{ej}}{\partial C_m} + \frac{\partial F_i}{\partial C_m} = 0$$

Using (5.4),

$$\sum_j A_{ij} \frac{\partial N_{ej}}{\partial C_m} = -\frac{\partial F_i}{\partial C_m} \tag{7.14}$$

This is a set of s linear equations for the s quantities $\partial N_{ej}/\partial C_m$, which are the quantities we are interested in. The set of equations can be solved if the community matrix $\mathbf{A}$ is nonsingular, which it will be for any structurally stable system: simply multiply both sides of that equation from the left by the inverse matrix $\mathbf{A}^{-1}$:

$$\frac{\partial N_{ei}}{\partial C_m} = -\sum_l (\mathbf{A}^{-1})_{il}\frac{\partial F_l}{\partial C_m} \tag{7.15}$$

For the particular case of a press perturbation, as discussed in Section 5.6, the parameter of interest is an input I_j (which could of course be negative) to some species j:

$$
\begin{aligned}
dN_1/dt &= F_1(N_1, \ldots, N_s)\\
dN_2/dt &= F_2(N_1, \ldots, N_s)\\
&\vdots\\
dN_j/dt &= F_j(N_1, \ldots, N_s) + I_j\\
&\vdots\\
dN_s/dt &= F_s(N_1, \ldots, N_s)
\end{aligned} \tag{7.16}
$$

and

$$\partial F_i/\partial I_j = \begin{cases} 0 \text{ if } i \neq j\\ 1 \text{ if } i = j \end{cases}$$

Then (7.15) is simply

$$\frac{\partial N_{ei}}{\partial I_j} = -(\mathbf{A}^{-1})_{ij} \tag{7.17}$$

To study press perturbations through (7.17), or generalized press perturbations through (7.15), we need to calculate the inverse matrix. My advice here is similar to what I offered in Section 5.1.1 about working out stability. In relatively simply cases one can use loop analysis to calculate the inverse matrix (Section 7.1.4). In more complicated cases, the same packages of computer programs that enable the computation of eigenvalues will also include routines for inverting matrices.

As an example of using loop analysis, consider the agricultural system, part 6 of Exercise 7.1. Introducing more suggestive notations for the variable names, variable 1 = P_1 is a crop plant, self-damped because of crowding, variable 2 = H_1 is a herbivore that feeds on P_1, variable 3 = H_2 is another herbivore that feeds on other plants P_2 (= variable 5), variable 4 = P_r is a generalist predatory insect that feeds on both H_1 and H_2, variable 6 = P_a is a specialized parasitoid (a parasitic insect that generally kills its host, generally another insect species) which attacks H_1, and variable 7 = I is an insecticide that kills all the insects found on the crop plant, namely, H_1, P_r, and P_a.

You've already worked out the loop diagram, in Exercise 7.1, part 6; it's

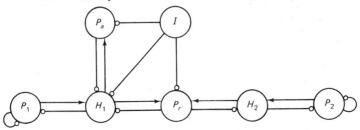

Now, let us see what is the effect of the herbicide on the crop pest H_1. If C_I is an input of herbicide (that is, a change in the amount of herbicide being applied), we want to calculate

$$\frac{\partial H_1}{\partial C_I} = -(\mathbf{A}^{-1})_{H_1 I}$$

First, we need all the simple open paths from I to H_1:

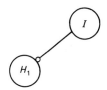

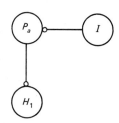

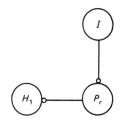

and the corresponding complementary subsystems:

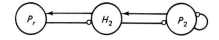

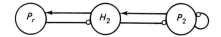

Exercise 7.4. Calculate the feedback $Z_5^{(p-)}$ for the first of these complementary subsystems, and $Z_4^{(p-)}$ for the second and third systems.

In the above exercise you will find that only the second complementary subsystem has nonzero feedback at the appropriate level, and that this feedback is negative. For the associated path, $p_{H_1I}^{(3)} = (-P)(-E)$ is positive. (Use matrix **6** on page 181.) Finally, so long as we have a stable equilibrium, Z_s must be negative. Therefore, from (7.17) $(A^{-1})_{H_1I}$ is negative, so $\partial H_1/\partial C_I$ is positive: adding more insecticide will cause the pest population to increase. The reason, of course, is that the pesticide we have postulated kills insects generally, including the enemies of the herbivore we want to control.

7.2.2 The Transient Behavior

It may well take quite some time for the system to approach the new equilibrium. Thus field experiments (including the unintentional ones where human activity has unwitting environmental effects) will often see the intervening transient behavior. Therefore, we had better see what we can learn about this behavior.

We will consider a change in some parameter C from a value $C_0 + \delta C$ to a value C_0, where δC is small. The transient behavior that we wish to study is the dynamical behavior commencing just after the change in C to the new value C_0, so the system has an equilibrium at the densities $N_e(C_0)$, and the dynamics in a neighborhood of that point in phase space is given by equation (5.14), which is, written in vector form,

$$\mathbf{N}(t) = \mathbf{N}_e(C_0) + \sum_j c_j \mathbf{v}_j \, e^{\lambda_j t} \tag{7.18}$$

Here c_j are arbitrary constants, and $\mathbf{v}_j$ is an eigenvector of the community matrix $\mathbf{A}$ (of the new equilibrium), corresponding to the eigenvalue λ_j.

The following calculation is a little bit more sophisticated mathematically than is most of the rest of this book. For one thing, it requires an understanding of Section A.4, in the Appendix. In case you find that this is more mathematical than you care to get right now, you can skip to equation (7.22) and read on from there without any further loss in continuity.

I am going to assume in what follows that you have read Section A.4, and will freely use notation introduced there, without explanation.

The densities are starting out at the values corresponding to the old equilibrium, $\mathbf{N}_e(C_0 + \delta C)$. Therefore, the constants c_j are determined by the initial condition

$$\mathbf{N}(0) = \mathbf{N}_e(C_0 + \delta C) \tag{7.19}$$

To first order in the small perturbation δC,

$$N_e(C_0 + \delta C) = N_e(C_0) + (\partial N_e/\partial C)\delta C$$

where (throughout this section) all functional evaluations are at the density $N_e(C_0)$ and the parameter value C_0. Using the vector form of (7.15), this is

$$N_e(C_0 + \delta C) = N_e(C_0) - A^{-1}(\partial F/\partial C)\delta C \qquad (7.20)$$

Using (7.18) and (7.20) in (7.19), we obtain

$$\sum_j c_j v_j = -A^{-1}(\partial F/\partial C)\delta C$$

Multiplying from the left with the dual vector $\bar{v}_i$, using (A.41), and carrying out the summation containing the Kronecker delta, this becomes

$$c_i = -\bar{v}_i A^{-1}(\partial F/\partial C)\delta C$$

Therefore, (7.18) is

$$N(t) = N_e(C_0) - \sum_j e^{\lambda_j t} v_j \bar{v}_j A^{-1}(\partial F/\partial C)\delta C \qquad (7.21)$$

We can expand the exponential in the well-known series

$$e^{\lambda_j t} = \sum_{m=0}^{\infty} \lambda_j^m t^m/m!$$

Hence

$$\sum_j e^{\lambda_j t} v_j \bar{v}_j = \sum_j \sum_{m=0}^{\infty} (\lambda_j^m t^m/m!) v_j \bar{v}_j = \sum_{m=0}^{\infty} (t^m/m!) \sum_j \lambda_j^m v_j \bar{v}_j$$

Using (A.50) and (A.43), this is just

$$\sum_{m=0}^{\infty} (t^m/m!) A^m$$

So (7.21) reads

$$N(t) = N_e(C_0) - \sum_{m=0}^{\infty} (t^m/m!) A^{m-1}(\partial F/\partial C)\delta C$$

$$= N_e(C_0) - A^{-1}(\partial F/\partial C)\delta C - \sum_{m=1}^{\infty} (t^m/m!) A^{m-1}(\partial F/\partial C)\delta C$$

where I have separated out the $m = 0$ term from the sum. Using (7.20) on the first two terms in this last expression, we get

$$N(t) = N_e(C_0 + \delta C) - \sum_{m=1}^{\infty} (t^m/m!) A^{m-1}(\partial F/\partial C)\delta C \qquad (7.22)$$

Of course, the first term here is just the initial value of N immediately after the parameter change. The remaining terms give the change in N during the subsequent time. In order to interpret these terms it will be helpful to see how powers of **A** translate into loop diagrams.

For instance, we have from equation (A.27)

$$(\mathbf{A}^2)_{ij} = \sum_k A_{ik} A_{kj}$$

Recall the definition of a path in Section 7.1.4. Each nonzero term in the above sum is the number $p_{ij}^{(3)}$ associated [equation (7.10)] with a path of length 2 from the vertex j to the vertex i. The matrix element $(\mathbf{A}^2)_{ij}$ is just the sum of these numbers over all paths of length 2 from vertex j to vertex i. Similarly, $(\mathbf{A}^n)_{ij}$ is the sum of the numbers $p_{ij}^{(n+1)}$ for all paths of length n from vertex j to vertex i.

Paths of length 1 correspond to *direct* effects of species j on species i; longer paths represent *indirect effects,* in which species j influences species i through a chain $s_1, s_2, \ldots, s_k$ of other species, such that species j directly affects species s_1 which directly affects species $s_2 \ldots$ which directly affects species s_k which directly affects species i.

Turning now to equation (7.22), what happens just after the parameter change, at small values of t? For each species i, the dominant effect on its density N_i early in the transient comes from the nonzero term in the sum for which t is raised to the smallest power (since t is small). There are three possibilities.

In case $(\partial F_i/\partial C) \neq 0$, the lowest-order effect on the density N_i comes from the term with $m = 1$. It is just the effect of the parameter change on the growth rate of species i itself. This will be the dominant short-term effect for all species i whose growth rates depend explicitly on the parameter C. For example, in the case of a press perturbation, this case applies only to the species that itself is being added or removed.

In case $(\partial F_i/\partial C) = 0$ but $\sum_j A_{ij}(\partial F_j/\partial C) \neq 0$, the lowest-order effect on N_i comes from the term in (7.22) with $m = 2$. It comes from the *direct* interspecific effects on species i of those species whose growth rates depend explicitly on the parameter C. In the particular case of a press perturbation, the $m = 2$ term is

$$-t^2 A_{ix} \, \delta C/2$$

where x is the species that is being pressed. So for those species that have direct interactions with the pressed species, the first effects to be seen will come from the direct interactions with the pressed species.

For all remaining species, the first effects to be seen will come from indirect effects.

That is what happens in the short term. As t increases, the dynamics can become quite complicated, as many terms in the sum in (7.22) may come into play. Of course, we know that as t becomes large, **N** approaches the new equilibrium $\mathbf{N}_e(C_0)$. This long-term behavior can be quite different from the short-term behavior just discussed, as the case study in the following section demonstrates.

7.3 IDENTIFYING GUILDS

7.3.1 A Case Study

In studying population systems experimentally, we need to identify true functional guilds, that is, collections of species that function as a unit, without too many external influences. Ever since Section 5.6, we have been learning just how tricky this can be. I would like to give one more example here, partly to bring this undercurrent in what we have been doing to the surface, partly to illustrate the contrast between short-term and long-term effects that I discussed in the preceding section.

J. H. Brown and several coworkers have been studying granivores in the Sonoran desert for a number of years. Both ants and rodents are permanent residents, and major consumers of seeds, in the study area. At first, then, one thinks of a "granivore guild," abstracted from the consumer-resource interaction as in Section 5.2.1.

In removal experiments, both ants and rodents increased in the short term when the other group was removed (Brown et al. 1979). Furthermore, in these manipulations resource levels on experimental and control plots strongly suggested that the granivore interaction was indeed mediated through exploitation of shared (seed) resources. This all fits in very nicely with the notion of a guild of granivores, along the lines of classical competition theory.

However, the experiments were continued for another 4 years, and something rather strange and interesting happened in the long term. Starting about 2 years after the beginning of the experiment, rodents continued to benefit from the absence of ants, but ant populations in the rodent removal plots began to *decline* relative to the control plots. This made it appear as though the ants had been *benefiting* from the presence of their putative competitors, the rodents.

Rethinking the structure of their guild, Davidson et al. (1984) have come up with a simple explanation for this seemingly paradoxical behavior. The granivore guild, as abstracted from the exploitative interaction, looks like this as a loop diagram (A = ants, R = rodents):

If we extend the guild to include the resources in a model something like (5.17), we get

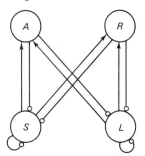

where S = small seeds and L = large seeds. Of course, from the viewpoint of the ant-rodent interaction this much is not going to make any difference. But what if we add to this picture an interaction between the plants bearing large seeds and those bearing small seeds? The former are in general bigger plants, and indeed it turns out that they hinder the small-seeded plants significantly, without any discernible effect in the other direction (Davidson et al. 1984). So really we have

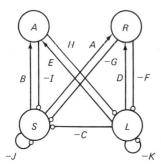

Let us work out the effect on ants of an input of rodents (of course, a removal will have the opposite effect).

Exercise 7.5. Show that $\partial N_A / \partial I_R = (BCF - BGK - EFJ)/(-Z_4)$.

If $BCF > BGK + EFJ$, this is positive. In the long-term removal experiment, one is going to observe $-\partial N_A / \partial I_R$. So a perfectly reasonable explanation for the long-term effect is hindrance of the small-seeded plants by large-seeded ones. The possibility of this kind of effect (in "abstract theory"!) seems to have been first pointed out, almost 10 years earlier, by Levine (1976).

The striking difference between short-term and long-term effects in these experiments is no surprise, in view of the discussion in Sections 7.2.1 and 7.2.2. Equation (7.22) tells us that in the short term we see the effects of the shortest paths from ants to rodents. These are the paths of length 2 that go from ant or rodent vertex to (large or small) seed vertex to rodent or ant vertex. The effects of these paths are competitive, so we see competition in the short-term experiments. Equation (7.17) tells us that in the long term we see the cumulative effects of several (perhaps many) indirect interactions, summarized in the inverse matrix. The result could be in the same direction as the short-term effect, or (as here) completely opposite to the short-term effect. The dependence of the long-term outcome on many different indirect pathways is made very explicit in the loop calculation (7.12) of the inverse matrix.

It is sobering to contemplate the pressures on ecologists to draw conclusions from short-term data. Most academic research projects are constrained in length by the need to produce graduate degrees or to publish sufficiently frequently. Assessments of environmental impacts are often deadlined yesterday. There is little we can do about these constraints themselves, but we should at least be aware of the dangers they pose.

7.3.2 Some Generalities

How are we, then, to go about identifying true functional guilds? One method, as we have seen, is to start with an intuitive notion as to which interactions are the important ones, to test this notion against experiments, possibly to refine the notion, to test it further, and so on. In practice, I think it is always ultimately going to come down to this: trial and error.

But are there any generalities to be gained from theory that might help in this process? This is a question that has not yet received the amount of study that it deserves, but a few things can be said.

First, recall how MacArthur obtained the Lotka-Volterra competition equations (5.19) from consumer-resource models (Section 5.2.1). The assumption there was that the dynamics of the resources were so much faster than that of the consumers that the resource densities just moved along with the consumer densities, always "tracking" equilibrium levels. Schaffer (1981) has extended this idea to a general setting.

Suppose some set of species in a community has much slower dynamics than all the other species with which it interacts. Then, in Schaffer's terminology, we can "abstract" from the dynamical equations for the whole community a smaller set of equations for these "slow" species by exactly the same procedure described in Section 5.2.1 to "get rid of" the resource equations. The abstracted system of equations provides a good approximation for certain purposes, including press perturbation experiments (Bender et al. 1984).

Suppose instead that some set of species has much *faster* dynamics than all the other species with which it interacts. Then, if we want to use either press or pulse experiments to estimate the interaction parameters, we can simply ignore those other species. Surprisingly, use of such estimates at much later times, when the slower species have "caught up" with what is going on, introduces only quite small errors (Bender et al. 1984).

For example, suppose we want to know whether two species of rabbits that both feed on lichens compete. If we perform a press experiment in which the density of one species of rabbit is held at a lower level, the system will reach, on a time scale of rabbit dynamics, a quasi-equilibrium in which the rabbit numbers are relatively stable but the lichens are still adjusting. Conclusions as to the effect of the pressed rabbit species on the other rabbit species drawn from this quasi-equilibrium will not be seriously in error (Bender et al. 1984).

Bender et al. suggest another generalization, which may well be the most useful of all. Consider a community of s species, of which we are interested in studying n particular species. We can number the n species of interest $1, \ldots, n$ and call them the "focal" species; then the other $s - n$ species are numbered $n + 1, \ldots, s,$ and we will call them the "remaining" species.

The community matrix $\mathbf{A}$ can be viewed as a juxtaposition of four "blocks" (Section A.3, Appendix):

$$\mathbf{A} = \begin{bmatrix} \mathbf{A(FF)} & \mathbf{A(FR)} \\ \mathbf{A(RF)} & \mathbf{A(RR)} \end{bmatrix}$$

where $A(FF)$ is an n by n matrix describing direct interactions among focal species, $A(FR)$ is an n by $s - n$ (rectangular) matrix describing direct effects of remaining species on focal species, $A(RF)$ is a $s - n$ by n (rectangular) matrix describing direct effects of focal species on remaining species, and $A(RR)$ is a $s - n$ by $s - n$ matrix describing direct interactions among the remaining species.

Similarly, we can write A^{-1} as

$$A^{-1} = \begin{bmatrix} A^{-1}(FF) & A^{-1}(FR) \\ A^{-1}(RF) & A^{-1}(RR) \end{bmatrix}$$

However, it is important to understand that, for example, $[A(FF)]^{-1}$ is *not* the same as $A^{-1}(FF)$. The inverses here are taken in different senses: $[A(FF)]^{-1}$ is the inverse of an n by n matrix, while $A^{-1}(FF)$ is an n by n matrix which is a submatrix of A^{-1}, which is in turn the inverse of an s by s matrix.

One can see that the two kinds of inverse do not match up by writing the equation $A^{-1}A = I$ as

$$\begin{bmatrix} A^{-1}(FF) & A^{-1}(FR) \\ A^{-1}(RF) & A^{-1}(RR) \end{bmatrix} \begin{bmatrix} A(FF) & A(FR) \\ A(RF) & A(RR) \end{bmatrix} = \begin{bmatrix} I(FF) & 0 \\ 0 & I(RR) \end{bmatrix} \tag{7.23}$$

where $I(FF)$ is the n by n unit matrix and $I(RR)$ is the $s - n$ by $s - n$ unit matrix. The upper left corner here reads

$$A^{-1}(FF)A(FF) + A^{-1}(FR)A(RF) = I(FF) \tag{7.24}$$

If $[A(FF)]^{-1}$ were the same as $A^{-1}(FF)$, then the second term on the left-hand side of this equation would be absent.

The lower left corner of (7.23) is

$$A^{-1}(RF)A(FF) + A^{-1}(RR)A(RF) = 0$$

Therefore

$$A(RF) = -[A^{-1}(RR)]^{-1}A^{-1}(RF)A(FF)$$

Substituting this into (7.24), multiplying from the right with $[A(FF)]^{-1}$, and rearranging a bit, we get

$$A^{-1}(FF) - [A(FF)]^{-1} = A^{-1}(FR)[A^{-1}(RR)]^{-1}A^{-1}(RF) \tag{7.25}$$

The effects of focal species on one another in press perturbation experiments are determined by the *FF* part of the s-dimensional inverse, $A^{-1}(FF)$. However, if we calculate those effects using just the part $A(FF)$ of the community matrix that describes interactions among focal species only (that is, if we completely ignore the presence of the remaining species), then *in those calculations* the effects of focal species on one another in press perturbation experiments will be determined by the (n-dimensional) inverse of that n by n matrix, namely, $[A(FF)]^{-1}$. Therefore, the left-hand side of (7.25) is the error we make in predicting these effects while ignoring the remaining species.

Obviously, if the effect of every remaining species on every focal species is sufficiently small [$A^{-1}(FR)$ sufficiently small] and the effect of every focal species on every remaining species is sufficiently small [$A^{-1}(RF)$ sufficiently small], then all interactions between focal and remaining species are small, and there is no danger in neglecting the remaining species. Equation (7.25) verifies this banality: under the prescribed circumstances the right-hand side of (7.25) is small, so the error is small.

But (7.25) also reveals the following nontrivial insight: if *either* the effect of every remaining species on every focal species is sufficiently small [$A^{-1}(FR)$ sufficiently small] *or* the effect of every focal species on every remaining species is sufficiently small [$A^{-1}(RF)$ sufficiently small], then the right-hand side of (7.25) is small, so the error is small, and there is no danger in neglecting the remaining species.

For instance, suppose we want to study the interaction between two species of ants. Suppose elephants have a big effect on both ant species, by trampling on their colonies. Suppose further that we are confident that neither ant species has a significant effect on elephants. Then the above principle suggests that we may well be justified in ignoring elephants in our studies of the ant-ant interaction, despite the big effect of elephants on ants.

Returning to the question raised in the introductory paragraphs of this chapter: we *can* under certain circumstances sensibly study in isolation smaller units than whole communities. The decision to do this is difficult, and requires quite a lot of knowledge about the community. It would be impractical to suggest that preliminary studies on this specific question become part of standard practice in ecology. But we should all at least be aware of the possible pitfalls in ad hoc definitions of guilds.

ADDITIONAL EXERCISES

7.6. Work out the conditions (4.10) for stability of a two-species equilibrium, using loop analysis.

7.7. Check stability of the equilibrium studied in Exercise 6.4.

7.8. Work out equation (5.48) by using loop analysis instead of the method used in Section 5.6.

7.9. Find the inverse of the following matrix:

$$\begin{bmatrix} -1 & 0 & -1 & 0 \\ 1 & -1 & 0 & 2 \\ 0 & 0 & -1 & 0 \\ 1 & 0 & 0 & -1 \end{bmatrix}$$

using loop analysis.

7.10. Consider a system of two predators on two prey, obeying equations (5.17) with $n = 2$, $k = 2$. Suppose prey species 1 evolves an evasive tactic that works against predator 1 but not against predator 2. That is: suppose that the parameter a_{11} becomes smaller in value. Assuming equilibrium dynamics, how will this affect the density of prey species 2 in the long term? In the short term?

7.11. Computer project (somewhat ambitious). Write down a system of four differential equations for the dynamics of the system of ants, rodents, small-seeded plants, and large-seeded plants, as conceived of by Davidson et al. (1984) and discussed in Section 7.3.1. That is, your equations should have an equilibrium whose community matrix has as its loop diagram the sketch on page 194.

Simulate the experiments of Davidson et al. by suitable numerical integrations, on a computer, of this system of equations. That is, obtain the four densities as functions of time, after press perturbations like those of Davidson et al. If you have chosen your parameters suitably, you should see in your solutions the difference between short- and long-term behavior observed by these authors.

Chapter 8

Whole Communities

In this chapter, we are going to complete our study of population interactions by looking at some recent theories for whole communities, in the sense of Section 5.5: we want here to consider all the species in a habitat. Typically, a community in this sense will consist of hundreds of species, even if we permit ourselves to ignore (possibly at our peril: Ducklow et al. 1986) microorganisms.

In principle, we can directly extend the ideas we have been developing in this part to such a community, conceiving of it as a system of very many interacting species. In practice, such a system is just too vast to work with.

One way to approach such large systems is to study only small parts of them at a time, to study small subsets of species as if they existed in isolation. This is the approach of traditional ecological models such as those we have studied in earlier chapters, and of traditional ecological field study.

The traditional way perceives some subset of a community with very high taxonomic resolution—typically organisms are distinguished right down to the species level. Another approach is to try to study the whole community without omitting any species, but to do so with a low taxonomic resolution. With this standpoint, which will be ours in the present chapter, biospecies are lumped together into relatively few categories, and these categories are made the basic units of study.

I should mention that there are other ways to conceive of communities than as systems of interacting populations. Instead of classifying individual organisms into species (which is the starting point of the population approach) one can, for example, classify them with regard to body size (Isaacs 1972; Kerr 1974; Platt and Denman 1977, 1978; Silvert and Platt 1978, 1980). Or, one can focus on the flows of energy and nutrients within a community (Odum 1983).

I am not going to discuss these other viewpoints—not because of any lack of merit in them, but because they do not relate so organically to the more traditional ecology that I have been discussing in previous chapters as does the population viewpoint.

I have tried for the most part to discuss in this book material that has been around long enough to be fairly well established. In order to round out the story on competition, I deviated somewhat from this conservative approach in Chapter 6.

I am deviating still further from the conservative approach here, in order to round out the story of building up community models from a population viewpoint. I should warn the reader that the material discussed in this chapter is from a relatively new and still unsettled field.

8.1 FOOD WEBS

The first simplification we are going to make is to ignore all interactions other than trophic ones and, for some purposes, intraspecific interference. In other words, we will ignore any direct interactions between species that are not consumer-resource interactions.

Next, we will lump together those biospecies that are trophically similar into *trophospecies*. By "trophically similar" species one means species that have pretty much the same prey *and* pretty much the same predators.

For any community, we can compile a listing of which trophospecies eat which others. If we carry this out comprehensively, for all the trophospecies in a community, the result is a *community food web*. Throughout the rest of this chapter I will use "species" to mean "trophospecies" and "food web" to mean "community food web."

There are conceptual difficulties already at this stage. Real animals can be quite variable in their feeding habits. Quite often diet depends strongly on an animal's age (or at least life stage). Furthermore, should the prey types that it normally prefers be unavailable for some reason, then very often an animal will switch to another prey type. A real community may be a more plastic entity than the notion of food web suggests.

Besides, in lumping trophically similar biospecies together into trophospecies, how do we recognize trophic "similarity"? If we look at the existing food web data, we do not find any consistent procedure for aggregating biospecies into trophospecies. Most of these food webs were explicated by investigators who were really interested in some particular group of organisms, so the aggregation into trophospecies is not even done consistently *within* food webs, much less among them.

Food web theorists are well aware of these difficulties. They are working with the available data anyway, on the basis that it is going to take a very long time to build up a better data base, and in the meanwhile we would be foolish not to get as much as we can out of the data we have.

The "listing" of trophic relationships in a food web can take the form of a diagram such as Fig. 8.1, for Narragansett Bay, Rhode Island (Kremer and Nixon 1978; Briand 1983a, Case 7). Here each vertex represents a trophospecies,

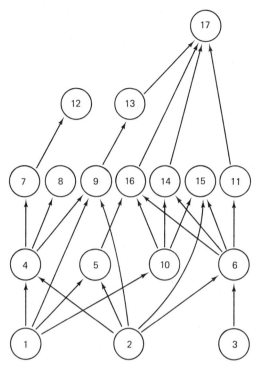

Figure 8.1 Narragansett Bay food web. Legend: 1 = flagellates, diatoms; 2 = particulate detritus; 3 = macroalgae, eelgrass; 4 = *Acartia,* other copepods; 5 = sponges, clams; 6 = benthic macrofauna; 7 = ctenophores; 8 = meroplankton, fish larvae; 9 = Pacific menhaden; 10 = bivalves; 11 = crabs, lobsters; 12 = butterfish; 13 = striped bass, bluefish, mackerel; 14 = demersal species; 15 = starfish; 16 = flounder; 17 = man. (After Kremer and Nixon 1978. *A coastal marine ecosystem,* Springer-Verlag, Berlin.)

and an arrow from vertex *i* to vertex *j* means that species *j* consumes species *i*. I will call such an arrow the food web *link* from species *i* to species *j*.

The species at the bottom of a food web, which feed on no other species, are called *basal species*. In the above example, these are species 1, 2, and 3. Basal species will mostly be primary producers, but it is conventional in current food web research to count detritus as a basal species, as well (species 2 above). The species at the top of a food web, on which no other species feed, are called *top species*. Species that are neither basal nor top are called *intermediate species*.

The food web of Fig. 8.1 is typical of the existing data, in that the basal species are very highly aggregated, the top species are distinguished almost to the biospecies level, and the intermediate species are quite mixed in their degree of aggregation.

For the most part I am in this book assuming that you are familiar with the basic data of ecology from earlier courses, and from your own reading and experience. However, food web data are not yet part of the basic data of ecology. Before I can talk about food web theories, I will have to acquaint you with the kind of structure in the data that these theories are attempting to address.

8.1.1 The Data

This subsection sometimes gets a little tedious. You might want to just skim it on first reading, then come back to it as needed for the subsequent developments.

The food web data base is not a coherent body of work. It is a scattering, throughout the literature, of food webs that were usually put together by biologists who wanted to establish a context for the study of some particular group of organisms. To work out systematically and consistently a food web for any but the most artificially simple systems is an immense task, so understandably, researchers whose real interest lay elsewhere did not produce flawless webs. Someday, we are going to have to undertake the systematic measurement of food webs; before we do so it will be necessary to explicate very carefully the appropriate protocols.

As of this writing, the standard published collection of food web data is to be found in a paper by Briand (1983a). This is a collection of 40 published food webs, from a wide variety of communities, carefully checked and standardized to the limited extent possible given the available information. From Table 8.1 on p. 222 you can see that these food webs come from a wide variety of habitats.

I must explain that two versions of this collection are in use. One version is precisely what appears in Briand's paper. For historical reasons, some of those webs contain trophospecies that feed on the identical species and that are fed upon by the identical species. For instance, the Narragansett Bay food web in Section 8.1 has 20 species, not 17, in Briand (1983a). In that original version, the sponges and clams (species 5 in the above depiction) were assigned as two different trophospecies, and striped bass, bluefish, and mackerel (species 13 in the above depiction) were assigned as three different trophospecies. This reflected the interest of the web's original compilers in these particular groups.

Briand himself in his more recent work has further lumped together all trophospecies with identical prey and identical predators. Applying this procedure to Briand's original collection yields a new, unambiguous collection of webs, which I will call the "rationalized" Briand webs. In the following, unless I specifically refer to the rationalized collection, I mean the original, published collection.

The structures that have thus far attracted attention fall into several categories. (Unless otherwise specified, all the properties and relationships in the following are for the Briand collection.) I will describe some of these structures by saying that certain things are less common, or more common, than one would expect on the basis of chance. I will explain what this means in Section 8.1.2.

1. *Species properties. Species richness* is the number of species in the web. In the Briand collection, it ranges from 5 to 45. Twenty of the webs (half of the 40) have fewer than 15 species; 5 webs have more than 30 species. The distribution of species richnesses may well depend as much on differing degrees of aggregation by different authors as it does on the number of biospecies present.

I have already introduced in Section 8.1 the concepts basal, top, and intermediate species. A *predator* is a species that feeds on some other species in the web and a *prey* is a species that is fed upon by some other species in the web. A *herbivore* is a species that feeds on a basal species (in food web usage current as of this writing, this includes detritivores). A (*dietary*) *specialist* is a predator that feeds on only one prey; the antonym is *generalist*.

Unless it is very sloppily done, aggregation is not likely to mix basal and intermediate species. It would be a peculiar investigator who would lump into the same trophospecies a basal and an intermediate biospecies. Therefore, these are sensible concepts. The same is true of predators and prey, top species and herbivores.

On the other hand, if a predator feeds on several biospecies and these are all lumped into one trophospecies, then a dietary specialist will be created, and this could happen quite frequently. And yet this term still has a relative meaning: a predator that feeds on only one trophospecies is certainly more specialized than a predator that feeds on more than one trophospecies. Or is it? Perhaps the "specialist" predator's prey were subjected to "more aggregation."

We see that when aggregation is taking place, certain concepts become very tricky, if not downright useless, while others remain perfectly sensible. Still others are somewhere in between. We would be imprudent not to temper our confidence in any food web results according to the amount of aggregation dependence in them, pending careful investigations of the aggregation dependence.

Briand and Cohen (1984) have found, in a collection of 62 observed food webs, including the rationalized Briand webs, that the proportion of species within each web that are basal, intermediate, and top, respectively, while varying considerably among webs, appears to be independent of species richness. Stated otherwise, they obtain "scaling laws" $B/S = r, I/S = q, T/S = p$, where S is species richness, B, I, T are the number of basal, intermediate, and top species in a web, respectively, and r, q, p are constants: $r = 0.19, q = 0.53, p = 0.29$. From this it follows that the ratio of number of prey to number of predators among these webs is approximately constant: namely, $(B + I)/(T + I) = 0.88$. This is in accord with an earlier suggestion by Cohen (1977b) to the effect that the prey/predator ratio is constant.

I will discuss the proportion of herbivores in category 5.

2. *Link properties.* I have defined *link* in Section 8.1.

Reported food webs contain virtually no cannibalistic links (that is, no trophospecies that feed on themselves), even though cannibalism within biospecies is by no means rare in nature. For the sake of consistency, the very few reported cannibalistic links have not been included in Briand's webs.

If there are no cannibalistic links, then the number of possible links is $S^2 - S = S(S - 1)$. If L is the total number of links in a food web, then the ratio $C = L/S(S - 1)$ can vary from 0 to 1 and is one measure of how "complex" a web is. This quantity C was dubbed *connectance* by Gardner and Ashby (1970), who were the first to call attention to its significance.

Rejmánek and Starý (1979) found that the product SC was constant in a sample of plant-aphid-parasitoid webs. Yodzis (1980) found this product to decrease with increasing S in Cohen's (1978) collection of webs. Cohen and Briand (1984) found that the number L of links in the same collection of 62 webs used by Briand and Cohen (1984) appears to be proportional to S: $L = 1.86S$, which implies that connectance decreases as S increases. As well, these authors found scaling laws for the number L_{BI} of links from basal to intermediate species, the number L_{BT} of links from basal to top species, the number L_{II} of links from intermediate to intermediate species, and the number L_{IT} of links from intermediate to top species, namely, $L_{BI} = 0.27L$, $L_{BT} = 0.08L$, $L_{II} = 0.30L$, $L_{II} = 0.35L$.

3. *Elementary link relationships.* A *cycle* is the set of links corresponding to a sequence of distinct species $s_1, \ldots, s_k$ such that s_1 feeds on s_2 feeds on $\ldots$ s_k feeds on s_1. (A cycle with $k = 1$ is a cannibalistic link.) Reported food webs contain virtually no cycles, despite the fact that cycles must be quite common in aquatic systems (Isaacs 1972).

A *food chain of length $k - 1$* is a sequence $s_1, s_2, \ldots, s_k$ of species such that s_i feeds on s_{i-1} for all $i = 2, \ldots, k$. A *maximal food chain* is a food chain that links a basal species with a top species. A *loop-forming omnivore link* is a link between two species s_1 and s_2, where s_1 and s_2 are also linked by a food chain of length greater than 1.

Let K be the number of species pairs that either are connected by a link or have a prey species in common. The quantity $C_u = K/S(S - 1)$ was called *upper connectance* by Yodzis (1980). Those species that share a prey are the ones that would be most likely to indulge in significant interference, in the sense of Section 5.3, with one another. Therefore, if we were to calculate connectance from interactions rather than just from direct trophic interactions, what we have called C (which is called *lower connectance* in the present context) would be a lower bound on the fraction of nonzero off-diagonal elements of the community matrix, and C_u would be an upper bound.

Perhaps the most striking and well-known aspect of food web structure is the circumstance that observed maximal food chains tend to be short. Typically maximal food chains have two or three links, though Briand's collection does include chains as long as nine links. However, Pimm (1980) has verified, in an early food web collection, that maximal food chains are generally shorter than one would expect on the basis of chance.

Pimm (1980) showed that loop-forming omnivore links are significantly less common than one would expect on the basis of chance for a certain collection of webs. This result was extended to the Briand webs by Yodzis (1984a). Both these authors also found that, relative to what one would expect on the basis of chance, loop-forming omnivore links with lower values of k (in the above definition of loop-forming omnivore link) are more common than those with higher values of k. Yodzis (1984a) finds as well that omnivore links which correspond to feeding on both plants and animals are especially rare.

I will discuss structure involving C_u under category 5.

4. *The niche overlap graph.* With any food web we can associate a graph which summarizes trophic niche relationships in the web. In this graph there is a vertex for each predator in the web, and each pair of vertices is joined by an (undirected) line, called an *edge,* if and only if that pair of predators has a prey species in common. This is called the *niche overlap graph* by Cohen (1978). The niche overlap graph is an *undirected* graph, because an edge does not have a specified direction, like the links in food webs (which are for that reason *directed graphs*).

The niche overlap graph associated with the Narragansett Bay food web of Fig. 8.1 is shown in Fig. 8.2. Species 4 and 5 both have species 1 as a prey, so vertices 4 and 5 are joined by an edge. We do not draw an additional edge between 4 and 5 because they also share species 2 as a prey, however. Species 4 and 7 do not share a prey, so they are not joined by an edge. Species 12, 13, and 17 each consume only species that have no other predators, so each of these three species is not connected to any others in the niche overlap graph. And so on.

A *clique* is a set of species such that every pair of species in the set has some prey species in common. The corresponding set of vertices in the niche overlap graph are all connected to one another by edges, for instance, vertices 11, 14, and 15 in Fig. 8.2. A *dominant clique* is a clique that is contained in no larger clique, for instance, vertices 11, 14, 15, and 16 in Fig. 8.2.

Certain graphs can be represented in a simpler depiction: as overlaps of subintervals of a straight line. Thus in Fig. 8.3, some of the labeled intervals overlap, for example, 4 and 5. Others, such as 4 and 7, do not. Intervals 12, 13, and 17 do not overlap any others. Indeed, you can easily verify that a pair of intervals in this picture overlaps if and only if the corresponding pair of vertices in the Narragansett Bay niche overlap graph is joined by an edge. An *interval niche overlap graph* is a niche overlap graph which, as in our example, can be

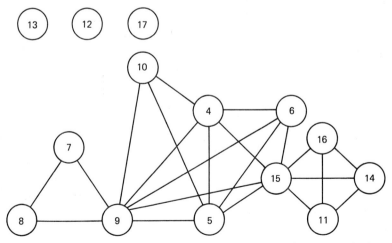

Figure 8.2 Niche overlap graph for the Narragansett Bay food web (Fig. 8.1). Each pair of vertices is joined by an edge if and only if that pair of predators has a prey in common.

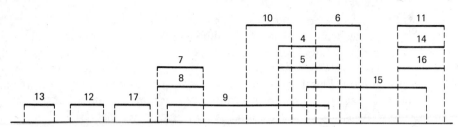

Figure 8.3 Representation of the niche overlap graph of Fig. 8.2 as overlaps of subintervals of a straight line. In this depiction a pair of labeled subintervals overlap if and only if the corresponding pair of vertices in the niche overlap graph (Fig. 8.2) are joined by an edge.

completely represented in this way: as overlaps of subintervals of a straight line. An *interval food web* is a food web whose niche overlap graph is interval.

Not every food web is interval. Cohen (1978) gives the following particularly simple example of a noninterval food web:

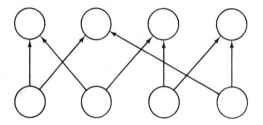

Exercise 8.1. Construct the niche overlap graph for this food web. Verify that it is not interval.

Sugihara (1982, 1984) has called attention to another interesting graph-theoretical property. A *circuit* in an undirected graph is a sequence $V_1, \ldots, V_k$ of distinct vertices such that there is an edge joining V_{i-1} and V_i for all $i = 2, \ldots, k,$ and in addition there is an edge joining V_1 and V_k; k is the *length* of the circuit. A niche overlap graph (or any other undirected graph) is called a *rigid-circuit graph* if every circuit longer than 3 has a chord, that is, an edge that creates a shorter circuit.

For instance, this graph

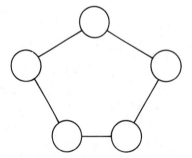

is not rigid circuit, because it has a circuit of length 5 without a chord. Adding one chord to that circuit

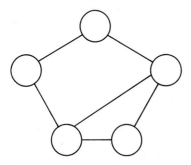

is still not quite enough to produce a rigid-circuit graph. However, the following graph

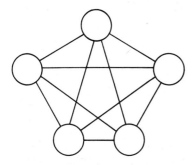

is rigid circuit.

Here are more examples both of rigid-circuit and of non-rigid-circuit graphs:

Rigid circuit

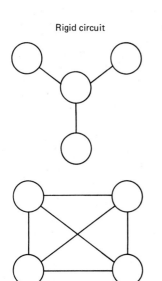

Nonrigid circuit

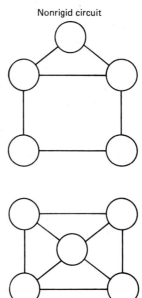

Exercise 8.2. Is the niche overlap graph associated with the Narragansett Bay food web a rigid-circuit graph?

I will sometimes refer to the rigid-circuit property as *rigidity* for short; and I will call a food web a *rigid-circuit food web* if its niche overlap graph has the rigid-circuit property.

Of the 40 Briand food webs, 31 are interval. Cohen (1978) showed that this is a higher incidence of intervality than one would expect on the basis of chance. Of the 40 Briand food webs, 36 have rigid-circuit niche overlap graphs. Sugihara (1982) showed that this is a greater number than one would expect on the basis of chance.

5. *Environmental and other correlates.* Briand has classified the environment in which each food web in his collection was observed as "fluctuating" or "constant." The environment was considered to be fluctuating if the original report indicates temporal variations (be they periodic or random) of substantial magnitude in temperature, salinity, water availability, or any other major physical parameter.

There are structural differences between the webs from these two types of environment. For a given species richness S, food webs in constant environments have higher upper connectance C_u than those in fluctuating environments (Briand 1983a). Since there is no such difference with regard to lower connectance, this means that for a given S and a given number L of trophic links, food webs in constant environments are organized so as to have more trophic niche overlap—more edges in their niche overlap graphs—relative to food webs in constant environments. This tendency is also expressed as follows: for a given species richness S, food webs in constant environments have fewer, but larger, dominant cliques (Yodzis 1982).

Briand (1983b) also classifies environments as to *dimensionality.* He calls an environment *two-dimensional* if it is essentially flat, like a grassland, tundra, lake bottom, or rocky intertidal. A *three-dimensional* environment is one that is clearly solid in its geometry, such as a pelagic water column or a forest canopy. Finally, some habitats are of *mixed* dimensionality; they have both a two-dimensional and a three-dimensional aspect. For instance, many aquatic communities include both pelagic and benthic components. In a collection of 113 observed food webs, Briand and Cohen (1987) find that maximal food chains tend to be longer in three-dimensional than in two-dimensional environments.

Briand has done principal component and cluster analyses involving many environmental and food web properties, extending and rigorizing the informal, preliminary indication of Fig. 3 in Briand (1983a). The only account published as of this writing is Briand (1985), which shows that food webs from three kinds of freshwater environment—lakes and rivers, lake reservoirs, and streams—have significantly different structure in terms of proportion of herbivores, food chain lengths, upper connectance, and trophic specialization.

Food web structure has also been related to the types of organisms in webs. Pimm (1980) found that omnivory is more common in insect-dominated webs than in others. Yodzis (1984c) found differences in vertical food web structure associated with ectotherms as compared with endotherms. I will discuss this work in Section 8.3.

Every ecologist is familiar with the concept of "trophic level." But I have discussed food web structure in some depth without ever mentioning the familiar term "trophic level"! Why? I prefer to avoid this term, because it is ambiguous. For instance, in the Narragansett Bay food web of Fig. 8.1, species 4 feeds on basal species, so it is at "trophic level" 2. But what about species 9? It feeds on basal species, which would put it at "trophic level" 2, but it also feeds on species 4, which ought to put it at "trophic level" 3!

I have been putting "trophic level" in quotation marks, because there are several different ways to define the "trophic level" of a species. For instance:

1. One plus the length of the shortest food chain linking the species to a basal species
2. One plus the length of the longest food chain linking the species to a basal species
3. One plus the modal length of all food chains linking the species to basal species
4. One plus the mean length of all food chains linking the species to basal species
5. One plus the mean length, weighted with respect to energy flows, of all food chains linking the species to basal species
6. In Section 8.3 I am going to give yet another definition.

Of course, one is free to use the term "trophic level" if one wants to, but only if one states exactly what one means by it in that particular context.

8.1.2 Probabilistic Explanation

Many aspects of food web structure assume their significance as structure by comparison with what one expects "on the basis of chance." What exactly does this mean?

Let Q be a system of rules which specifies (1) a set $S(Q)$ of "possible" food webs and (2) a probability distribution $P(Q)$ on this set which gives the probability for each food web to "occur." The specification of $S(Q)$, and sometimes of $P(Q)$, may be in terms of constraints, like having a certain number of species or the rigid circuit property, or it may be in terms of a procedure for constructing food webs, like the assembly rules I will discuss in Section 8.2.2. I will use $U(Q)$ to stand for the pair $\langle S(Q), P(Q) \rangle$—that is, the set $S(Q)$ together with the probability distribution $P(Q)$ on that set—and I will call $U(Q)$ the *universe* of food webs corresponding to the rules Q.

That all may seem a bit abstract, so let's look at a few simple (though admittedly rather artificial) examples.

Let the food web universe $U(Q_1)$ be defined as all those food webs having three species, with no cycles, with every basal species having at least one predator, with every predator having at least one prey, and with any two distinct food webs considered equally likely to occur. Then $S(Q_1)$ is the set of all three-species food webs with no cycles, every basal having at least one predator and every predator having at least one prey; and $P(Q_1)$ is specified by the rule that all members of the set $S(Q_1)$ are equiprobable. So the universe $U(Q_1)$ is as follows:

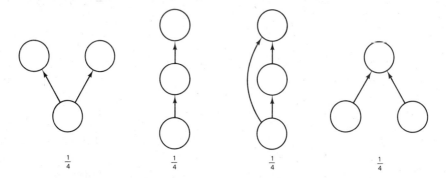

where the number under each food web is its probability of occurrence according to the distribution $P(Q_1)$.

If we add the constraint that no omnivore links can occur, then we obtain a new system Q_2 of rules, corresponding to the universe $U(Q_2)$:

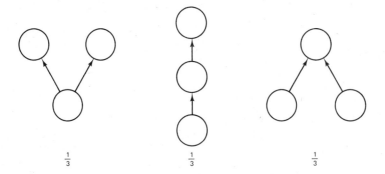

We have a new set $S(Q_2)$. Although $P(Q_2)$ is defined by the same rule (equiprobability) that we used for Q_1, the probability of occurrence for a given food web is different because now there are fewer possible webs.

Keeping the same specification $S(Q_3) = S(Q_2)$, we might want to change the probability distribution P. For instance, suppose we regard it as equally likely that a food web will have one basal species as it is that a web will have two basals, and that any two food webs with the same number of basals are equally likely to occur. With this specification for $P(Q_3)$, we obtain the following universe $U(Q_3)$:

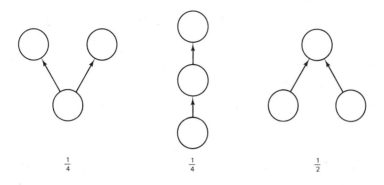

$\frac{1}{4}$ $\frac{1}{4}$ $\frac{1}{2}$

Exercise 8.3. Work out the food web universes $U(Q_1)$, $U(Q_2)$, $U(Q_3)$ from the above statements of Q_1, Q_2, Q_3, and verify that I have done it correctly.

I will use the term "food web characteristic" to mean any number or set of numbers that we can unambiguously calculate given an arbitrary food web. It could be a quantity, like the number L of links, or it might be a property, such as being interval or not. In the latter case, we could agree by convention that our calculation will result in the number 1 if the web is interval, 0 if not. Any food web characteristic has a probability distribution within each universe $U(Q)$. These probability distributions are consequences of the rules Q.

For instance, we may consider the number L of links in the above food web universes. In the universe $U(Q_1)$, the probability is $\frac{3}{4}$ that $L = 2$, $\frac{1}{4}$ that $L = 3$, and 0 that L has any other value. In both $U(Q_2)$ and $U(Q_3)$, $L = 2$ for all food webs. Or, consider the length $l_{\max}$ of the longest food chain in a food web. Within the universe $U(Q_2)$, the probability is $\frac{2}{3}$ that $l_{\max} = 1$, $\frac{1}{3}$ that $l_{\max} = 2$, and 0 that it has any other value. Within the universe $U(Q_3)$ we have a probability $\frac{3}{4}$ that $l_{\max} = 1$ and a probability $\frac{1}{4}$ that $l_{\max} = 2$.

Exercise 8.4. Calculate the probability distributions stated in the preceding paragraph.

With more realistic rules Q it often turns out to be impossible to calculate these probability distributions "in closed form"—with pencil and paper—and one has to calculate them by simulating the universe $U(Q)$ on a computer and working out the distributions by simple counting within this simulated universe. This way of calculating probability distributions is called the *Monte Carlo* method.

The point of all this is that we can compare the theoretical probability distributions I have just been discussing with observed distributions for the same food web characteristics. To get the observed distributions, we need as data a sample from the set of all real food webs. In addition, we need an a priori probability of occurrence for each of those webs. If the sample of real food webs we are working with is large enough and was chosen "at random" [for instance, by a massive survey of the literature, such as that of Briand (1983)], it is not entirely unreasonable to regard any two of the food webs as equally likely to occur, and this is the hypothesis that is usually adopted.[1]

By comparing the resultant observed probability distributions for some particular set of characteristics with the distributions that follow from a theoretical system of rules Q, using suitable statistical tests, we can make certain argumentations.

The argumentation that we will follow depends of course upon whether we are getting a good fit or a bad fit; whether the observed probability distributions seem to agree with the ones that follow from Q or not. In case we are getting good agreement, then we can regard the rules Q as an *explanation* for the observed characteristics. If we get a bad fit, then we can conclude that Q is not an explanation.

A little less obviously, our line of argument also depends on our feelings about the rules Q. There are two relevant possibilities here.

The first possibility is for us to regard the rules Q as serious candidates for an explanation of the characteristics that we observe. In this case we will either accept or reject Q as a viable explanation, depending upon whether or not we get good agreement in our statistical tests.

The other possibility is for us to regard the rules Q as being so weak that they ought to imply practically nothing! Indeed, we may consciously choose Q to be as contentless, as trivial, as neutral as we can manage, while still having enough content to define a relevant context ("minimal conditions"). If this seems strange, bear with me. I will give examples.

Suppose we have chosen Q in this way. What will we conclude, then, if we get good agreement of the data with the consequences of Q? Since we regard Q as trivial, we will regard the data as trivial: that is, any patterns (with respect to the characteristics we are considering) that we might have discerned in the data will be viewed as being devoid of interest, since they can be explained so easily. On the other hand, if we get bad agreement, we will conclude that the patterns we see in the data are significant and interesting: in order to explain them with some system Q of rules, we will have to choose Q to have real content.

In this second argumentation, instead of using the data to test Q, we are using Q to test (our perception of) the data! That is, we are using Q to test the biological significance of some pattern that we perceive in the data.

Consider, for example, the property of being an interval food web that I discussed above. This property is rather abstract and nonintuitive: what should our attitude be when we find that 31 of the 40 Briand food webs are interval? Is this, perhaps, a surprisingly large incidence of intervality, that cries out for an explanation; or is it a triviality, unworthy of comment?

To answer this, we might examine the incidence of intervality in food web universes that are based on minimal conditions such as: fix the total number of predators, the total number of prey, and the total number of links. If we find

---

[1] There are, however, deep philosophical problems with this line of argument, having to do with the meaning of the word "random." Kolata (1986) reviews some thought-provoking recent work.

that the observed proportion of interval food webs is significantly more than the proportion in such universes, perhaps for several quite different seemingly minimal systems of rules, then we may conclude that we *should* be surprised by the observed incidence of intervality; that it *does* cry out for explanation; that intervality in the real world *is* "more common than one would expect on the basis of chance." This is exactly what Cohen (1978) did, for six different simple food web universes.

In Section 8.2.2.1 I will give an example, using these same data, of the other form of argumentation, in which agreement with the observed incidence of intervality is used to test the worth of a system Q of rules.

Of course, in this methodology we can if pressed state *exactly* what we mean by "on the basis of chance," by stating our rules Q and displaying our statistical tests. Indeed, when using this methodology in the primary literature, we are as scientists obliged to provide this information *without* being pressed. This is especially important since the argumentation rests to some extent on a subjective judgment about the appropriateness of Q.

This subjective element is particularly important in the argumentation in which Q is regarded as contentless, or at least minimal. No nonempty set of conditions is *entirely* without content, and, paradoxically, we cannot choose Q to be the empty set of conditions because then we would not know how to construct $U(Q)$!

What one seeks when one wants to invoke this argumentation is a system of rules that does not introduce an automatic bias with respect to the putative patterns in the data, or with respect to a factor whose influence one wants to test for, but which does include enough other factors to ensure that the corresponding universe is a relevant context—the "minimality" referred to above. It can be very tricky to avoid unwanted biases creeping into Q as one tries to define a suitably "neutral" context.

A recent case in point is the controversy over the use of so-called "null models" in testing for putative influences of competition on the structure of certain guilds. In this case, the "null models" corresponded to rules Q not for food webs but for the distribution of species over the islands of an archipelago. The intention was to demonstrate the absence of competition as a causative factor by choosing Q so as to predict the correct distributions, without assuming the presence of competition.

As it turned out, certain of the conditions in Q, meant to establish a context "neutral" with respect to competition, were interpretable as subtle expressions of competition after all. I do not have space to go into the details here, but the papers by Gilpin and Diamond (1984) and by Connor and Simberloff (1984), taken together, summarize the arguments on both sides, and serve as a valuable cautionary tale with regard to this particular methodology.

8.2 FOOD WEB THEORIES

Most current food web theories fall into two classes. One line of reasoning runs that, whatever the processes that might produce communities, the end result will have to be a system that is stable, in at least one of the many senses of that word; so those food web characteristics associated with stability are the ones we should observe. I will call this the "dynamic stability" approach (Section 8.2.1.1).

The other class of explanations involves the genesis of communities. This viewpoint argues that real communities do not simply spring into being, then to persist or not; they are built up in a process of gradual assembly, subject to certain constraints. The assembly process imposes structure, and it is only the systems that have been previously structured in this way whose stability comes into question. In case the assembled communities already possess the kinds of structure that we observe, regardless of stability, then stability becomes irrelevant in terms of determining that structure. I will discuss this "assembly" approach in Section 8.2.2.

The two classes of explanation are not necessarily antagonistic. As I will indicate in section 8.3, it might be necessary to combine the two in order to understand food web structure.

8.2.1 Trophodynamics

A food web expresses the topology of trophic interactions, without reference to any details of those interactions such as functional responses and encounter probabilities. Most research on "food webs" is actually based on adding further structure, of various kinds, to this topological skeleton.

For instance, it is very tempting to think of all the organisms of each trophospecies as comprising a population, and to associate population-dynamical models with food webs. Then if N_i is the density of trophospecies i, we can associate systems of the form we studied in Section 5.1,

$$dN/dt = f(N) \tag{8.1}$$

with food webs. Since our starting point in this whole procedure was to focus on trophic interactions, I will call such models *trophodynamical*. It is within this trophodynamical framework that the dynamic stability argumentation sketched in the first paragraph of Section 8.2 is carried out.

It is important to understand that there are two different kinds of tropho-dynamical models: *local* ones and *global* ones. (We have met this distinction before, in Section 2.4.1.) A global model is a specification of the growth rate vector f throughout all of phase space. A local model specifies these functions only in an infinitesimal little patch of phase space, through the community matrix

$$A_{ij} = \left.\frac{\partial f_i}{\partial N_j}\right|_{N_e} \tag{8.2}$$

at some equilibrium N_e. A global model enables us to reach more conclusions about the behavior of the system than does a local one, but at the cost of having to put in more information when we specify the model.

The global models most commonly used in trophodynamics are *Lotka-Volterra models,* which have the form

$$dN_i/dt = N_i\left(b_i + \sum_j a_{ij}N_j\right) \qquad i = 1, \ldots, s \qquad (8.3)$$

We have already worked with an instance of these equations, in the consumer-resource model (5.17). The b_i are (positive) growth rates for the basal species, and (negative) starvation rates for the nonbasals. The a_{ij} are interaction rates. If species i is a prey for species j, then $a_{ij} < 0$ and $a_{ji} > 0$; otherwise $a_{ij} = 0$ for $i \neq j$.

At any equilibrium $\mathbf{N}_e$,

$$b_i + \sum_j a_{ij}N_{ej} = 0 \qquad i = 1, \ldots, s$$

In vector notation this is [recall equation (A.23)]

$$\mathbf{b} + \mathbf{a}\mathbf{N}_e = 0$$

Multiplying from the left with $\mathbf{a}^{-1}$,

$$\mathbf{N}_e = -\mathbf{a}^{-1}\mathbf{b} \qquad (8.4)$$

So long as the matrix $\mathbf{a}$ is nonsingular, this equation has one, and only one, solution for $\mathbf{N}_e$. The community matrix (8.2) at the equilibrium (8.4) is

$$A_{ij} = N_{ei}a_{ij} \qquad (8.5)$$

Exercise 8.5. Prove (8.5).

In general, to associate a global trophodynamical model with a food web, we need to specify metabolic rates, functional responses, numerical responses, prey preferences, and so on for all the species in the web [as is done in a particularly simple, but not necessarily realistic, way in the Lotka-Volterra models (8.3)]. This is a tall order. Instead, we can build local trophodynamical models, in the following way.

Suppose the system has the general form (8.1), and assume it has a point attractor. Then we know that the associated community matrix (8.2) determines the dynamics in a phase space neighborhood of the attractor (Section 5.1.1). While it is a formidable task to make plausible guesses about all the functional responses and so on for such a large system, it is a much smaller task to guess the elements of the community matrix. Indeed, as we will see in Section 8.2.1.2, one can plausibly guess community matrices that correspond to real, observed food webs.

Since trophodynamics ignores nontrophic interactions, the *signs* of the matrix elements A_{ij} are determined by the food web that underlies the system:

1. If species i is eaten by species j, then $A_{ij} < 0$ and $A_{ji} > 0$.
2. Because of intraspecific interference, $A_{ii} < 0$ for all i.
3. All other matrix elements are zero.

(The second of these statements actually goes beyond purely trophic interactions, but trophodynamical models turn out to be quite pathological if we leave out these "self" interactions.) We need only fill in the magnitudes.

Each global model that has a point attractor implies a unique local model in a neighborhood of that attractor. For instance, each Lotka-Volterra model (8.3) implies a local model based on the community matrix (8.5). But, of course, one could associate infinitely many global models with a given local model.

So long as one is concerned only with the stability of point attractors, there is no need to postulate anything more than a local model. However, if one wishes to discuss global properties such as invasion resistance (Section 8.2.2.2), then one needs to postulate global models.

8.2.1.1 Dynamical Stability and Food Web Structure

Within the trophodynamic framework, communities that persist for long periods of time will be associated with attractors, in the sense of Section 5.1. Therefore, it is natural, as sketched in the first paragraph of Section 8.2, to seek those community properties (including food web properties) that promote the existence of attractors. This program, applied to point attractors, is the dynamic stability approach.

The first application of dynamic stability in trophodynamic models to (what we now think of as) food web structure was a paper by May (1972b). May worked in a certain universe (in the sense of Section 8.1.2) of community matrices. Within this context, he found that the more complex a community is, in the sense of a large product SC (S = species richness, C = connectance), the less likely is its community matrix to be stable. This suggests that it should be very rare for a community to have both many species (large S) and many interactions (large C).

Upon further reflection (DeAngelis 1975, Gilpin 1975b, Lawlor 1978) it became clear that May's community matrix universe lacked a number of essential biological constraints. However, May's work inspired others to develop the dynamic stability viewpoint further. The idea of using the underlying food web topology to constrain the forms of realistic community matrices crystallized in a paper by DeAngelis (1975). Soon thereafter, the dynamic stability approach was applied to a classic problem of whole-system ecology.

In 1977, every schoolperson knew that the length of food chains was determined primarily by energetic considerations: only a fraction (at most 10 percent) of the energy consumed by an animal winds up as biomass, most of the rest being used up in respiration. Therefore, as we move up a food chain, less and less energy is available for the next predator in the chain. Eventually there will be too little energy to support another predator.

Pimm and Lawton (1977) proposed instead a dynamic stability explanation for the length of food chains. These authors studied community matrices associated with the loop diagrams depicted in Fig. 8.4.

With loop diagram d (= 1, . . . , 5) in Fig. 8.4, Pimm and Lawton associated a statistical universe $U(d)$, by choosing the elements A_{ij} of the community matrix

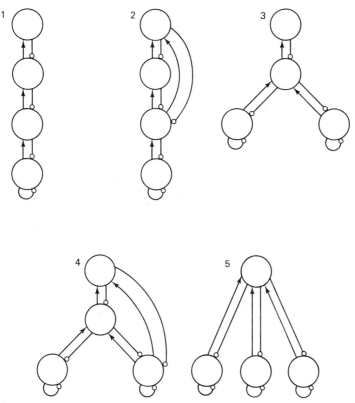

Figure 8.4 Five loop diagrams. (After Pimm and Lawton 1977. Reprinted by permission from *Nature* Vol. 275, p. 329. Copyright © 1977 Macmillan Magazines Ltd.)

from certain intervals of real numbers, as follows. The nonzero elements A_{ii} (self-loops for the basal species) were chosen at random from the interval $[-1, 0)$, elements A_{ij} corresponding to the effects of predators on prey were chosen at random from the interval $[-10, 0)$, and elements A_{ij} corresponding to the effects of prey on predator were chosen at random from the interval $(0, 0.1]$. The self-damping elements A_{ii} for nonbasal species were taken to be zero. For each loop diagram nearly 2000 community matrices were randomly constructed in this way.

The return time T_R (Sections 2.4.1, 5.1.1) for each community matrix was computed, resulting in five frequency distributions, one for each universe $U(d)$, of the return time. These frequency distributions are shown in Fig. 8.5. The models containing longer food chains have longer return times. For instance, in the three models without any omnivory (diagrams 1, 3, 5) the model whose maximal food chains have length 1 (diagram 5) has a return time less than or equal to 5 in almost 50 percent of the random parameter choices. With maximal food chains of length 2 (diagram 3) this drops to 5 percent and with a maximal food chain of length 3 (diagram 1) it drops to less than 1 percent. At the same time, the percentage of return times longer than 150 increases with food chain

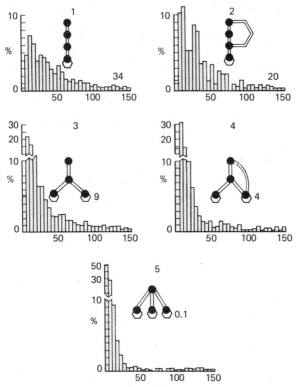

Figure 8.5 Frequency distribution of the return time T_R in each of the five statistical universes $U(d)$ of community matrices. (After Pimm and Lawton 1977. Reprinted by permission from *Nature* Vol. 275, p. 330. Copyright © 1977 Macmillan Magazines Ltd.)

length: it is 0.1 percent with a maximal food chain length of 1, 9 percent with a maximal food chain length of 2, and 34 percent with a maximal food chain length of 3.

I said a little bit in Section 2.4.1 about the relation between the return time T_R and Holling's concept of resilience. Pimm and Lawton adopt the viewpoint that the longer the return time, the less likely is a system to persist in a fluctuating environment. On that basis, the above results show that even in the absence of energetic or any other limitations on food chain lengths, environmental variability alone will limit the length of food chains.

One sees similar trends in the models with omnivory (diagrams 2, 4). But as well, a significant proportion of these models do not have stable community matrices at all: both in case 2 and in case 4, 78 percent of the community matrices are unstable. This has to do with positive feedbacks associated with the new loops, in the sense of Section 7.1, in which the omnivore links participate.

Pimm and Lawton (1978) studied this destabilizing effect of omnivory in more detail. They reached three conclusions:

1. Omnivory should be relatively rare.
2. Omnivores should only rarely feed on species in trophic levels that are not adjacent.

3. Food webs composed of insects and their parasitoids may have much more complex patterns of omnivory than the webs dominated by vertebrates and their prey.

As mentioned in Section 8.3, these predictions concerning omnivory seem to be supported by observations.

However, Yodzis (1984a) has questioned whether the rarity of omnivory should be attributed to the dynamical stability hypothesis. In an analysis of the positioning of omnivore links in observed food webs, he finds that the observed deficit of observed omnivore links relative to Pimm's (1980) "minimal" universe (Section 8.1.2) is fully accounted for by a particular lack of organisms that feed on both plants and animals. This additional pattern is not predicted by the dynamical stability hypothesis.

The omnivory predictions are significantly more robust than are the food chain predictions. Omnivory is destabilizing in a more absolute sense (elimination of a point attractor) than are long food chains (for which there is still a point attractor, but it has a larger return time). One can debate the significance of larger return times for the persistence of communities, but one cannot debate the significance of lack of an attractor.

Moreover, the food chain result depends critically on the assumption that only basal species have significant self-damping, as pointed out by Saunders (1978). If there is significant self-damping of consumer populations, the dependence of the return time on food chain lengths may be much weaker, or even absent.

Nevertheless, the work of Pimm and Lawton does put forward a provocative new *possible* explanation for food chain lengths. When theory provides us with more than one possible explanation for some phenomenon, only further observations can distinguish the competing explanations. In this next step in the process of scientific explanation, theory still has a role to play: it suggests which new data analyses, or new data, are needed. I will summarize the evidence with regard to food chain lengths in Section 8.3.

8.2.1.2 Plausible Community Matrices

The work described in Section 8.2.1.1 applies the trophodynamical viewpoint to idealized food webs that are intended to embody basic features of food webs generally. In this section I will discuss some work with trophodynamical models that are tailor-made for specific observed food webs. Two uses of these models will be described: (1) a test of the validity of the trophodynamical viewpoint itself, (2) an investigation of press perturbations in the whole community context.

In the introductory paragraphs of Section 8.2.1 I sketched the construction of a community matrix associated with a putative point attractor of a trophodynamical model for some food web. I want to pursue that construction further here, with the underlying food web being some observed food web [say, one of the webs in Briand's (1983a) collection]. In the earlier discussion, I pointed out that the signs of the elements of the community matrix are determined by the food web.

Unfortunately, one cannot draw many conclusions just from the pattern of signs of the community matrix elements. We need to be able to say something about the magnitudes as well. Suppose we can "guess" these magnitudes to within an order of magnitude. Then we can view each A_{ij} as chosen at random from some interval $\pm [B_{ij}/10, B_{ij}]$ of real numbers. Indeed, one might argue that this is the best we could ever possibly hope to do, anyway, on two bases:

1. If we were to go out and literally try to measure all these quantities, it would be such an immense and difficult task that we could count ourselves lucky to achieve even this much accuracy.
2. Apart from any attempt to measure these parameters, because of the many sources of variability in natural communities and the complex nature of the trophospecies themselves, these parameters may not possess exact values. It may be meaningless to assert any more than that their values lie in such-and-such intervals of real numbers.

Equation (8.2) tells us that A_{ij} is the *per capita* effect of species j on the growth rate of species i. This enables us to make plausible guesses, based on the nature of the particular organisms involved in a given observed food web, as to the relative magnitudes of some of the bounds B_{ij}. For instance, if insects consume trees, the *per capita* effect of insects on trees will be much smaller than the *per capita* effect of trees on insects.

I call a community matrix that is obtained in this way from a food web for some real community a *plausible community matrix* for that community (Yodzis 1981a). A plausible community matrix embodies not only the topology of trophic interactions in the community, through the pattern of *signs* of its elements, but also the specific organisms in that community, through the pattern of *magnitudes* of its elements.

As for the diagonal matrix elements A_{ii}, these express intraspecific interference, which results in "self-damping" of a population's growth. It is very difficult to decide on reasonable assumptions for these quantities. Most authors agree that primary producers tend to be strongly self-damped, for primary production is commonly observed to be strongly linked to factors like light and nutrient availability. Saunders (1978) and Rejmánek and Starý (1979) have suggested that nonbasal species could also often be significantly self-damped, while Lawton and Pimm (1978) and Pimm (1982, Section 4.2.4) have argued against this view.

I think there is very little real evidence one way or the other, and it is best to regard this question as open for the time being. Anyway, the calculations described in this section produce qualitatively the same result whether or not one assumes self-damping for nonbasal species.

For any given observed food web, we can perform on a computer the following operation. First, generate 100 plausible community matrices as just described, using a random-number generator to draw the values of each matrix element A_{ij} from the interval $\pm [B_{ij}/10, B_{ij}]$. Make a note of the proportion of these that are stable. Then, disrupt each plausible community matrix into a new community matrix, by randomly permuting all positive off-diagonal elements among themselves, and all negative off-diagonal elements among themselves. Note the proportion of these "disrupted" community matrices that are stable.

What is the meaning of such a disruption? A disrupted community matrix describes the same food web as does the plausible community matrix from which it is obtained, for the pattern of signs is unchanged. Moreover, the average strength of interactions within the community is unchanged since we are permuting the interaction strengths among themselves. All that is different is that the detailed pattern of interaction strengths in a disrupted matrix no longer corresponds to the particular organisms in the real community, as does this pattern in the plausible matrix.

If we do this for the 40 observed food webs in the collection of Briand (1983a), we obtain Table 8.1. In these calculations, self-damping was assumed for all species, but the qualitative nature of the results is the same without this assumption. We see in Table 8.1 a very clear pattern: in *every* case where the plausible community matrices have a probability ≥0.01 of stability, the disrupted matrices have a smaller probability.

If local trophodynamical models are not a sensible way to represent the dynamics of these communities, there is no reason for local stability of the community matrix to be associated with those particular patterns of interaction strengths that happen to mirror the particular organisms in the actual community. It seems difficult to escape the tentative conclusion that these highly idealized community representations are, to some extent, appropriate. This includes three elements that have gone into our construction: a dynamical system of the form (8.1), aggregated state variables N_i, and equilibrium dynamics (existence of a point attractor).

One might leap to the conclusion that this work validates as well the dynamic stability argumentation of Section 8.2.1.1. This is not correct. A refutation of the trophodynamical framework would of course also refute the dynamic stability approach to food web structure. But a validation of the trophodynamical framework does not validate the dynamic stability argumentation; that argumentation makes further assumptions beyond the trophodynamical framework. The mere presence of point attractors of real communities does not imply that those point attractors are there because of the structure of the underlying food webs.

We can, however, conclude that what I am calling "plausible community matrices" really are plausible candidates as community matrices for these real communities. So we can use these matrices, or rather their inverses, to study press perturbations [Section 7.2.1, equation (7.17)] in the whole community context.

The interaction strengths A_{ij} in plausible community matrices are, you will recall, determined only to within an order of magnitude. Because of this, one expects a certain amount of random variation in the inverse matrices. What one finds is a great deal of variation. This variation is of three kinds: (1) variation in the strength of effects (i.e., in the magnitude of each element of $\mathbf{A}^{-1}$), (2) variation in the direction of effects (i.e., in the sign of each element of $\mathbf{A}^{-1}$), (3)

TABLE 8.1 STABILITY IN PLAUSIBLE AND DISRUPTED
COMMUNITY MATRICES

Case	Community	Plausible	Disrupted
		Fraction of community matrices that are stable	
1	Cochin estuary	0.12	0.05
2	Krysna estuary	0.64	0
3	Long Island estuary	0.49	0
4	California salt marsh	0.52	0.03
5	Georgia salt marsh	1	0.22
6	California tidal flat	0.07	0
7	Narragansett Bay	0	0
8	Bissel Cove marsh	0.07	0.02
9	Lough Ine rapids	0.43	0.03
10	Exposed intertidal (New England)	0.89	0.15
11	Protected intertidal (New England)	0.59	0.12
12	Exposed intertidal (Washington State)	0.41	0
13	Protected intertidal (Washington State)	0.19	0
14	Mangrove swamp (Station 1)	0.20	0.13
15	Mangrove swamp (Station 2)	0.24	0.09
16	Pamlico River	0.45	0
17	Marshallese reefs	0.39	0
18	Kapingamarangi atoll	0.33	0
19	Moosehead Lake	0.74	0
20	Antarctic pack ice zone	0.09	0
21	Ross Sea	0.12	0
22	Bear Island	0.01	0
23	Canadian prairie	0.19	0
24	Canadian willow forest	0.92	0.04
25	Canadian aspen forest	0.95	0.02
26	Aspen parkland	0.28	0
27	Wytham Wood	0.12	0
28	New Zealand salt meadow	0.78	0
29	Arctic seas	0.07	0
30	Antarctic seas	0.47	0
31	Black Sea epiplankton	0	0
32	Black Sea bathyplankton	0	0
33	Crocodile Creek	0.87	0
34	River Clydach	0.07	0
35	Morgan's Creek	0.71	0
36	Mangrove swamp (Station 6)	0.26	0
37	California sublittoral	0.76	0
38	Lake Nyasa rocky shore	0.63	0
39	Lake Nyasa sandy shore	0.67	0
40	Malaysian rain forest	0.34	0.02

After Yodzis 1981a. Reprinted by permission from *Nature* Vol. 289, p. 676. Copyright © 1981 Macmillan Magazines Ltd.)

variation in the topology of major effects (i.e., in the identity of those matrix elements that are the biggest).

Yodzis (1988a) has studied this variation. For these calculations, all self-damping elements A_{ii} for nonbasal species were taken negligibly small, in order to work with the simplest possible community matrices that are at all plausible.

For each real food web, 100 plausible and stable community matrices were generated. Self-damping contributes very strongly to stability of the community matrix; with only basal species self-damped, it was practicable to compute 100 stable community matrices for only 16 of the 40 rationalized Briand food webs.

In this discussion I will use the term "effect of species j on species i" to mean the effect on species i of an addition of species j in a long-term press perturbation. Call the effect of species j on species i *directionally determined* if at least 95 percent of plausible community matrices $\mathbf{A}$ have inverses in which the element $(\mathbf{A}^{-1})_{ij}$ has the same sign; otherwise call it *directionally undetermined*.

Table 8.2 summarizes directional indeterminacy in the 16 Briand food webs mentioned above. In this table, four types of effect are considered: the effect on the pressed species' own density ("self"), the effect of a pressed predator on one of its prey, the effect of a pressed prey on one of its predators, and effects in which the pressed species does not interact directly with the affected species. The particular indirect case in which two species share a prey is singled out ("competitive").

. We see that there is a great deal of directional indeterminacy in these effects. Furthermore, even when effects are directionally determined, it is not uncommon that they run counter to the seemingly most obvious expectations. For instance, one expects that adding predator individuals will have a negative effect on that predator's prey populations, but in 11 percent of the *determined* predator-prey interactions in these communities, adding predators has a *positive* effect on the prey.

Basically these results show that indirect pathways are very frequently prevalent over direct pathways [recall the discussion of equation (7.22)] in determining the long-term outcomes of press perturbations, at least for this sample of community matrices.

One may well object that in this table strong and weak effects are mixed indiscriminately, and that while it is hardly surprising that weak effects should show this kind of sensitivity to the exact values of the interaction strengths, one would expect the stronger effects (which are anyway the really interesting ones) to be more determinate. As it turns out, this is not the case at all: not even the question of which effects *are* the stronger ones has a simple answer.

TABLE 8.2   DIRECTIONAL INDETERMINACY IN PLAUSIBLE COMMUNITY MATRICES ASSOCIATED WITH 16 OBSERVED FOOD WEBS

Type	N	Proportion directionally undetermined	Among determined, proportion showing reverse effect
Self	223	0.27	0
Predator on prey	317	0.52	0.11
Prey on predator	317	0.54	0.07
Indirect	3423	0.50	—
Competitive	566	0.58	0.29

N is the total number of effects of each type (the number of pairs of species in each type category) in the 16 food webs.

After Yodzis (1988a).

If x is any real number, define mag $x = N$, where N is the (unique) integer such that $10^N \leq x < 10^{N+1}$. Then $10^{\text{mag } x}$ is simply the "order of magnitude" of x, in the usual sense. For a given community matrix $\mathbf{A}$, call the effect of species j on species i a *major effect on i* if, for all k,

$$\text{mag} \, |(\mathbf{A}^{-1})_{ij}| \geq \text{mag} \, |(\mathbf{A}^{-1})_{ik}|$$

and say that it is a *major effect of j* if, for all k,

$$\text{mag} \, |(\mathbf{A}^{-1})_{ij}| \geq \text{mag} \, |(\mathbf{A}^{-1})_{kj}|$$

Call the effect a *major effect* if either of these two conditions is satisfied. These definitions simply identify the major effects as those that are largest in order of magnitude.

There is a startling amount of variation in the identity of major effects. To illustrate this, let us agree to use the standard loop diagram conventions of Section 7.1.1 for the negative inverse matrix $-\mathbf{A}^{-1}$. Of course, the ij element of this matrix gives the effect of each species j on species i in a long-term press addition perturbation [equation (7.17)]. In order to keep our graphs relatively simple, let us also agree to draw in only those links that correspond to the major effects *on* each species.

This kind of graph gives us an overall picture of the sensitivity, in the long term, of each species to presses of other species. The importance of such information from a management viewpoint is obvious. Figures 8.6 and 8.7 show the major effect graphs in this sense for two different plausible community matrices associated with the Narragansett Bay food web of Fig. 8.1.

These two graphs give completely different impressions of how the community would react in the long term to press perturbations. In the first version, for example, the biggest effect on 2 would come from pressing that species itself. In the second version, 11 other species would have comparable (in order of magnitude) effects on 2. On the other hand, there is some constancy: for instance, in both versions species 7 and 12 are each the major influence on the other.

To quantify this variation, call the effect of species j on species i *unimportant* if, in a random sample of plausible community matrices, the probability for it to be major is less than 0.05, and call it *most important* if this probability is greater than 0.95. The effects that are neither unimportant nor most important are *topologically undetermined* in the sense that we cannot decide, at the 95 percent confidence level, whether those effects will be major or not in a given plausible community matrix.

Table 8.3 summarizes the proportion of effects that are topologically undetermined in each of the 16 Briand communities considered. Typically, close to half the effects in a given food web are topologically undetermined. Of the topologically determined effects, the vast majority are unimportant; thus of the potentially "large" effects (those that are not unimportant), only very few are sure to be large (most important). Furthermore, even those few effects that are most important still show a considerable degree of directional indeterminacy, as shown in Table 8.4.

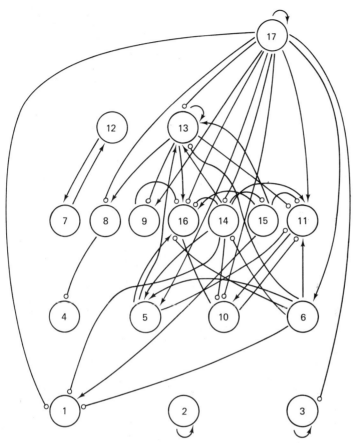

Figure 8.6 Major effects on each species of the Narragansett Bay food web, obtained from a randomly generated plausible community matrix. (After Yodzis 1988a.)

These results, which clearly extend also to generalized press perturbations, carry a very important practical message: *short-term observations are close to useless for predicting the long-term effects of persistent alterations of all kinds of community parameters.* Predicting those long-term effects not only requires data on the strengths of many interactions in the system, it requires very accurate data on many interaction strengths. This is a daunting prospect, particularly where there is risk of environmental damage.

8.2.2 Assembly

In this subsection we are going to consider the second class of food web theories mentioned in the introductory paragraphs to Section 8.2, namely, theories in which food web structure is the outcome of a process of community assembly.

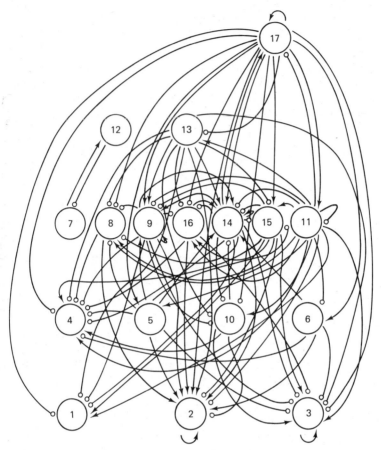

Figure 8.7 Major effects on each species of the Narragansett Bay food web, obtained from another randomly generated plausible community matrix. (After Yodzis 1988a.)

8.2.2.1 Energetic Constraints

An obvious constraint on such a process is the flow of energy through a food web. This constraint acts in two ways: first, in order for a new species to enter the community, its energetic requirements must be met; second, the more energy that a population consumes, the more energy it makes available for its consumers. Energetically constrained community assembly was modeled by Yodzis (1981b, 1984b). In this work, the assembly process is defined through the following set of rules (Yodzis 1984b):

Given three parameters N, P, E, with N a positive integer, P a positive real number, $0 < E < 1$:

1. The community starts with N basal species, each with production P. A sequence of additional species then enters the community.

TABLE 8.3 PROPORTION OF EFFECTS IN PLAUSIBLE COMMUNITY MATRICES
ASSOCIATED WITH A SAMPLE OF 16 OBSERVED FOOD WEBS,
WHICH FALL INTO THREE CATEGORIES (EXPLAINED IN THE TEXT)

Case	S	Proportion unimportant	Proportion most important	Proportion topologically undetermined
3	24	0.727	0.002	0.271
4	13	0.118	0.018	0.864
5	6	0.556	0	0.444
7	17	0.581	0	0.419
8	15	0.573	0.004	0.423
9	9	0.049	0.012	0.939
10	3	0.444	0	0.556
11	5	0.520	0	0.480
14	8	0.578	0.031	0.391
15	7	0.531	0	0.469
16	14	0.577	0.005	0.418
25	24	0.760	0.002	0.238
28	32	0.901	0.002	0.097
29	16	0.598	0.008	0.394
36	19	0.332	0.008	0.660
40	11	0.579	0.017	0.404

The case numbers are those assigned to the 16 webs by Briand (1983); S is species richness.
After Yodzis (1988a).

2. A newly arrived species has a total required rate of energy intake e, chosen from the interval $[1, 10^5]$ according to the probability density

$$p(e) = \begin{cases} C_1(e-1) & 1 < e < 10 \\ C_2/e & 10 < e < 10^5 \end{cases}$$

where the constants C_1 and C_2 are such that $p(e)$ is continuous, with its integral over the interval $[1, 10^5]$ equal to 1.

TABLE 8.4 DIRECTIONAL INDETERMINACY OF MOST IMPORTANT
EFFECTS IN PLAUSIBLE COMMUNITY MATRICES
ASSOCIATED WITH 16 OBSERVED FOOD WEBS

Type	N	Proportion directionally undetermined	Among determined, proportion showing reverse effect
Self	44	0.07	0
Predator on prey	55	0.31	0
Prey on predator	55	0.33	0
Indirect	769	0.30	—
Competitive	28	0.39	0.35

N is the total number of most important effects of each type in the 16 webs.
After Yodzis (1988a).

3. The new arrival chooses as potential prey a sequence $\{s_1, s_2, \ldots\}$ of distinct species already in the community, using the following probabilistic law: at each stage in the sequence, the probability to be chosen next for each species not yet in the sequence is proportional to its total unused production.

For each prey species s_i, the new species is allowed to utilize a randomly chosen fraction f_i, with $0 < f_i \le 1$, of the total production of s_i.

Species s_i may already have other species feeding on it. In case f_i is larger than the fraction of s_i's production that is still unutilized, f_i is set equal to the total unutilized production of species s_i.

Then if P_i is the total production of s_i, the new arrival has available to it an energy $f_i P_i$ per unit time from species i, for each i.

4. The sequence defined in 3 terminates as soon as the cumulative sum $T = f_1 P_1 + f_2 P_2 + \cdots$ exceeds the energy requirement e. In case T never reaches e, even after all species in the community are included in the sequence, the new arrival cannot enter the community, and another new arrival is tried, starting with step 2. If the sequence terminates with $T > 10e$, the last f_i is adjusted so that $T = 10e$.

5. The total energy intake of the new species is T. Every species, except of course for basals, is assumed to have an ecological efficiency E (definition below). So the production of the new species as it functions in the community is ET, which is available to subsequently arriving species.

6. New species continue to enter the community in this way until the total unutilized production of the community is less than 1. This is not sufficient to support any more new species (rule 2); so the assembly process terminates.

The basic idea here is very simple, though its precise statement requires some verbiage. The only rule whose motivation may not be self-evident is the form of the distribution $p(e)$ in rule 2. This distribution is based on a generality suggested by Hutchinson and MacArthur (1959) and May (1978): that the number of species that exist, at least at larger sizes, is proportional to L^{-2}, where L is a measure of linear dimension. Since body mass W goes like L^3, this says that the number of species goes like $W^{-2/3}$.

We want the distribution of ingestion rates (for the quantity e in terms of which rule 2 is phrased is the rate of ingested energy). As you are probably aware from a physiological ecology course, there has been a lot of work in recent years in which all kinds of bioenergetic parameters are allometrically related to body size (for instance, Peters 1983, Calder 1984). In a major review of the literature, Farlow (1976) suggested that ingestion scales like $W^{2/3}$, where W is body mass. Rule 2 is based on Farlow's relationship. There is quite a massive controversy as to whether ingestion might not scale like $W^{3/4}$ instead of $W^{2/3}$ (for instance, Hayssen and Lacy 1985, Heusner 1985), but this would not make a great deal of difference in $p(e)$.

If the number of existing species goes like $W^{-2/3}$ and ingestion e goes like $W^{2/3}$, then the number of existing species, hence the number of potential colonizing species, goes like e^{-1}, at least at the larger end of the spectrum. Rather than just cut the distribution off at the lower end, the stated form for $p(e)$ in rule 2 lets it gradually go to zero as e moves below 10.

The parameter E is the ecological efficiency of Slobodkin (1960). It is the efficiency with which energy flux into a prey population is converted into energy flux into predator populations. This is a product of three factors, each less than 1: the fraction of ingested energy that is converted into a usable form (assimilation efficiency) times the fraction of assimilated energy that is converted into production (production efficiency) times the fraction of production that actually is ingested by predators.

As you may well imagine, the estimation of ecological efficiencies is fraught with complexity, and I will not discuss the matter here. The data are summarized by May (1981b), who concludes that E will seldom be larger than 0.1, and it can be as small as 0.001.

For each given number N of basal species, production P of each basal species, and ecological efficiency E, the stated assembly rules define a universe $U(N, P, E)$ of assembled food webs, in the sense of Section 8.1.2. The question one then wants to pose is whether a given observed food web could plausibly have been drawn at random from the universe $U(N, P, E)$ for some parameter set N, P, E.

In order to address this question, we need to compare the structure of the observed food web with the structure of food webs in the universe $U(N, P, E)$ for various choices of the parameters N, P, E. We will treat *measurement variables* (whose differing states can be expressed in a numerically ordered fashion) differently from *nominal variables,* which correspond to binary properties (in our case, intervality and rigidity) which a food web either possesses or not.

The following list takes into account all measurement variables that have been deemed significant by those authors who have studied food web structure (Section 8.1.1): species richness S, ratio R of the number of predator species to number of prey species, proportion p_h of herbivores, proportion p_s of specialist predators, number L of trophic links, number G of edges in the niche overlap graph, number I_0 of loop-forming omnivore links, lower connectance C, upper connectance C_u, average maximal food chain length K. These will be our test statistics.

To test the hypothesis that a given real web could plausibly have been drawn from the universe $U(N, P, E)$ one can proceed as follows. Generate in a computer simulation 100 assembled food webs with the given parameters (N taken the same as in the real web). Calculate the range of each of the 10 test statistics in this sample of 100 webs. If the value of more than one test statistic lies outside the calculated range for that statistic, reject the hypothesis. Otherwise accept it.

Satisfactory fits were found in this way for 25 of the 28 Briand webs from fluctuating environments, and for 3 of the 12 Briand webs from constant environments, a total of 28 of the 40 Briand webs (Yodzis 1984b). In these fits the ecological efficiency ranged from 0.001 to 0.1, mostly taking the value 0.01— quite reasonable values. Total primary production (NP) ranged over 4 orders of magnitude—which is probably a bit too much, but not outrageously so. In fluctuating environments, these models seem adequate to account for the observed food web structure, with the possible exceptions of the intervality and rigid-circuit properties.

We can use these two nominal properties for a further test. For each of the 28 food webs that were successfully fitted, we can calculate the proportion of webs in $U(N, P, E)$ that are interval and that are rigid. This gives us estimates for the number of interval and the number of rigid food webs to be expected in the sample of 28 observed food webs on the hypothesis that each of these webs was drawn at random from the appropriate $U(N, P, E)$. The expected number of interval webs is 23.72, which does not deviate significantly ($P = 0.31$) from the observed value 22. The expected number of rigid-circuit webs is 25.65, extremely close to the observed number, 26.

Energetically constrained assembly satisfactorily accounts for the observed food web structure in fluctuating environments, but not in constant environments. The reason for this dichotomy is obscure at present, but it amplifies Briand's (1983a) observation that structure is significantly different in the two kinds of environment.

8.2.2.2 Lotka-Volterra Models

The energetic assembly rules described in Section 8.2.2.1 are successful enough to suggest that there may be something in the notion that assembly imposes structure. But those rules depict a very highly idealized version of the assembly process. There are at least two conspicuous faults with this depiction. First, it does not allow for the possibility that new arrivals to the community might serve as prey for some of the species already present. Second, it does not allow for the possibility of what Hastings (1986) calls *unstable invasions:* invasions in which some of the species already present are driven out of the community by a successful invader.

The first of these faults could in principle be remedied within the general conceptual framework of Section 8.2.2.1. The second is a global property of the dynamics and can be addressed only through a global model of some kind (recall the introductory paragraphs to Section 8.2.1).

Post and Pimm (1983) and Drake (1985) have studied community assembly in the context of Lotka-Volterra models (Section 8.2.1). Their procedure is as follows. Start with some particularly simple community—one basal species and one predator (Post and Pimm), say, or two basals and one predator (Drake). Then let a sequence of colonizers attempt to invade, with all parameters b_i, a_{ij} chosen at random from suitable intervals of real numbers. In this way, a community is gradually built up.

These authors always choose **a** such that it is nonsingular. Hence each of their models has a unique equilibrium point. They assume that there are no attractors in the models other than point attractors. With that assumption, three criteria need to be satisfied for a successful invasion.

1. A colonizing species must be able to increase when rare, in the sense discussed in connection with mutual invasibility in Section 5.2.2.
2. When the new species is added to the community, there must be an equilibrium with at least one positive density. Such an equilibrium is called *feasible* (Roberts 1974).
3. That equilibrium must be locally stable.

When a new species invades successfully, it is perfectly possible (though not necessary) for one or more other species to be lost from the community. To take an extremely simple example from a slightly different context, think of a pair of Lotka-Volterra competitors, such that species 1 dominates species 2 (Section 5.3). Suppose species 2 is alone in some habitat. If a small number of species 1 individuals are introduced to the habitat, then

1. They will be able to increase when rare.
2. There will be a feasible equilibrium, namely, the equilibrium with $N_1 = K_1$, $N_2 = 0$.
3. That equilibrium will be locally stable.

In short: species 2 will invade. In doing so, it will eliminate species 1.

Post and Pimm found that in sequences of 200 attempted invasions, two things tended to happen as the community was built up: the return time of the equilibrium increased, and it became more difficult for new species to invade. Drake, following sequences of 2000 attempted invasions, found these same trends, but he also found that after 800 to 1200 colonization attempts (in different randomly generated sequences), no further invasions were possible. *The assembly process terminated, of its own accord, with communities that were totally resistant to invasion.* In particular, every attempted colonization of one of these invasion-resistant communities fails already in step 1 of the above sequence. No colonizer can increase when rare.

What is the biological meaning of this emergent property, invasion resistance? We can easily understand it in terms of the bioenergetic basis for population dynamics sketched in Section 4.1. We deduced there, from bioenergetics, the model

$$dN_i/dt = N_i(-T + AJ) - \text{(losses to mortality)}$$

for the dynamics of a consumer density N_i, where T is specific respiration and AJ is per capita energy intake (specific ingestion).

It is straightforward to interpret Lotka-Volterra models in this way. In a Lotka-Volterra model, the specific respiration T is taken to be a constant, denoted $-b_i$. The losses to mortality are taken as entirely due to predation. Specific ingestion and predation losses will, in general, depend on prey preferences and on functional responses; in the Lotka-Volterra setting (8.3), linear functional responses are assumed, which gives

$$AJ = \sum_{j=\{\text{prey of } i\}} a_{ij}N_j$$

and

$$(\text{Losses to mortality}) = (\text{predation losses}) = - \sum_{j=\{\text{predators of } i\}} a_{ij}N_j$$

Now, what is the condition to increase when rare in a Lotka-Volterra model? It is that the right-hand side of (8.3) is positive when N_i is very small:

$$b_i + \sum_j a_{ij}N_j > 0$$

Writing this as

$$-T + \sum_{\text{prey } j} a_{ij}N_j + \sum_{\text{predators } j} a_{ij}N_j$$

and recalling the last few paragraphs, we see that the condition for increase when rare is an energetic condition: The rate of energy inflow, which is the sum over inflows from all prey in the second term, must be enough to overcome the outflows to respiration (first term) and to predation (last term, which is negative because $a_{ij} < 0$ if j predates i).

So the invasion resistance to which Drake's assembly process leads (and which is due to an inability of colonizers to increase when rare) has a simple biological interpretation: invasion-resistant communities are communities in which there is not enough unutilized energy floating around to support any new colonizers. Assembly based on dynamics leads us back to assembly based on energy.

8.2.2.3 Assembly by Mild Specialists

A major impetus for the lively state of food web research in the past decade came from Cohen's (1978) discovery that observed food webs tend to have the somewhat enigmatic property of intervality. The reason this stimulated so much interest in food webs has two components. First, the property of intervality itself seems very "nontrivial"—it is a rather detailed kind of structure, that one would not expect to pop up at random (and Cohen's statistical tests fortified this intuitive impression). Second, there isn't any immediately obvious reason for food webs to have this property.

Therefore, a number of theorists were intrigued, and began to study food webs.

As we saw in Section 8.2.2.1, energetically constrained community assembly provides an explanation (in the sense of Section 8.1.2) for the observed incidence of intervality, at least in fluctuating environments. And yet, this explanation is not entirely satisfying, for it still leaves one wondering: *Why* should community assembly lead so often to interval food webs?

This element of clarity is provided by the work of Sugihara (1982, 1984), which, moreover, suggests that it is not, after all, intervality that is the significant property, but rigidity.

I mentioned in Section 8.1.1 that a great many observed food webs (36 out of Briand's 40) have the rigid-circuit property. Sugihara noticed this, and looked more closely at rigidity. In the following, I am going to state a number of properties of rigid-circuit graphs without proof. Original sources containing proofs of all these statements are given by Sugihara (1984).

You will remember (Section 8.1.1) that a niche overlap graph is rigid-circuit if every circuit of length greater than 3 has a chord. Plainly, then, rigid-circuit graphs have lots of triangles in them—and another term for a rigid-circuit graph is *triangulated.*

At first glance, one might think this graph

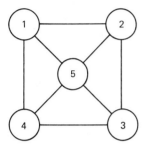

is rigid-circuit, because it does seem full of triangles. But this graph is *not* rigid circuit: the circuit 1-2-3-4-1 has length 4 but no chord. If you remove vertex 5 (and all the edges connected to it), you get a gaping square opening:

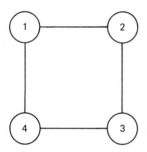

The following somewhat similar graph

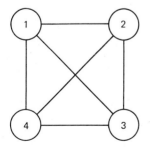

is rigid-circuit. Notice that whenever you remove a vertex from this graph, you never get an "opening" with more sides than a triangle. For instance, removing vertex 1 leaves

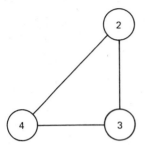

In fact, *every* graph that can be generated from a rigid circuit graph by removing *any* number of vertices has no openings with more sides than a triangle.

From this last statement it follows immediately that every graph generated from a rigid-circuit graph by removing any number of vertices is itself rigid-circuit. To help induce you to keep this in mind, I will call it "important fact number 1" about rigid-circuit graphs. (This is not a standard terminology, however.)

I have already mentioned in Section 8.1.1 that a *clique* is a set of vertices such that every pair of vertices in the set is joined by an edge. (I stated it a little differently there.) An *extreme vertex* has the property that the set of all vertices to which it is connected by edges (that is, all its *neighbors*) forms a clique. For instance, in this graph

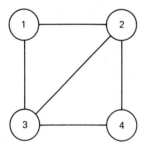

vertex 1 is extreme but vertex 2 is not.

One can show that every rigid-circuit graph possesses at least one extreme vertex—for us this is "important fact number 2" about rigid-circuit graphs.

Now, then: it follows immediately from these two important facts that every rigid-circuit graph has at least one *perfect elimination ordering*. A perfect elimination ordering is an ordering of the vertices such that if we remove the vertices in that sequence, each vertex is extreme in the stage at which it is removed. One can also prove the *converse* of this statement: every graph that has a perfect elimination ordering is rigid-circuit.

For example, the order in which the vertices in the following graph (which is rigid-circuit) are numbered corresponds to a perfect elimination ordering:

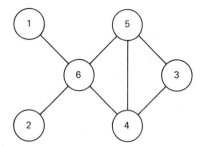

Vertex 1 is extreme because it has only one neighbor (vertex 6), and obviously any one vertex is a clique. In the graph generated by removing vertex 1,

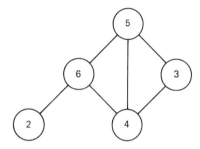

vertex 2 is extreme for the same reason. And so on.

Exercise 8.6. Continue the verification that these vertices are numbered so as to correspond to a perfect elimination ordering.

Obviously, for any graph with a perfect elimination ordering (that is, for any graph that is rigid-circuit, and *only* for a graph that is rigid-circuit) we can reverse the process and think of the graph as built up in a *perfect addition ordering* (Sugihara 1982, 1984): a sequential addition of vertices such that each vertex is added to some existing clique. For instance, this would allow the addition

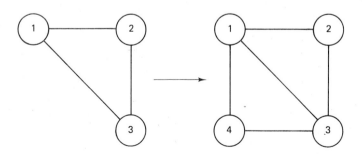

but it would forbid the addition

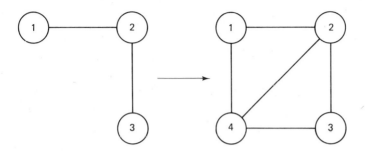

because in the latter case vertex 4 is connected to vertices (1 and 3) that do not belong to the same clique.

Since any graph that has a perfect elimination ordering is rigid circuit, it is also true that any graph that has a perfect addition ordering is rigid-circuit. *If we build up graphs by means of perfect addition orderings, we will get only rigid-circuit graphs.*

What does all this tell us about the structure of niche overlap graphs?

First, what is the significance of a clique in this setting? The members of a clique are all connected to one another by edges, because every pair of them has at least one prey in common. Therefore, the members of a clique will tend to be somewhat similar, while species that belong to different cliques will tend to be quite dissimilar.

Imagine, then, the niche overlap graph that is built up as some community is assembled by a sequence of colonists. Suppose that each new arrival in the community is a "mild specialist," in the sense that it does not prey upon species that belong to different cliques. Then the niche overlap graph will be built up from a perfect addition ordering. Therefore, it will be a rigid-circuit graph.

This argument of Sugihara provides a simple and very plausible biological explanation for the prevalence of rigid-circuit niche overlap graphs in nature: we would expect it to be uncommon for an animal to feed on species that are so dissimilar as to belong to different cliques.

Rigidity seems to be a very robust property of community assembly. Requiring that new colonizers never span different cliques will of course lead to rigid-circuit food webs every time. But as mentioned there, even the assembly process of Section 8.2.2.1, which does not impose this as an a priori requirement, leads to a high proportion of rigid-circuit food webs.

I motivated this section by talking about intervality. But thus far, we have explained rigidity, not intervality. Let us return now to intervality.

We need just a little more terminology. Again, I am going to omit proofs, and again, Sugihara (1984) provides citations of the original sources for all proofs.

A *path* p in an undirected graph is a sequence $V_1, \ldots, V_k$ of distinct vertices such that there is an edge connecting V_{i-1} and V_i, for all $i = 2, \ldots, k$. A set of three vertices V_1, V_2, V_3 in some undirected graph is called an *asteroidal triple* if there exist paths p_{12}, p_{23}, p_{31} such that

1. Each of the three paths p_{ij} joins vertex V_i to vertex V_j.

2. For each path p_{ij}, the third vertex V_k ($k \neq i$, $k \neq j$) is not a neighbor of p_{ij} (that is, V_k is more than one edge away from p_{ij}).

An undirected graph is called *asteroidal* if it contains an asteroidal triple. For example, this graph

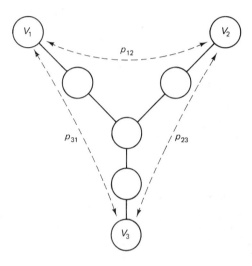

is asteroidal (and I have indicated the asteroidal triple in it), but this one

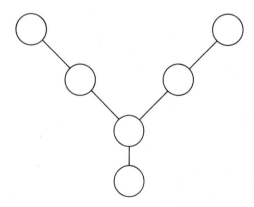

is not.

The asteroidal property is interesting for us because one can show that *a graph is interval if and only if it is a rigid-circuit graph but not an asteroidal graph.*

Exercise 8.7. Prove that both of the two graphs just introduced as examples are rigid-circuit. Show that the second of these is interval but the first is not.

Being asteroidal is a fairly special property of graphs. So among the rigid-circuit graphs, interval graphs happen to be quite common. Therefore, Sugihara suggests, the frequent occurrence of interval food webs in nature is an accidental by-product of the very frequent occurrence of rigid-circuit webs, which is itself an outcome of community assembly.

8.3 BUT . . . WHY ARE FOOD CHAINS SO SHORT?

To summarize: the process of community assembly leads in a natural way to food webs that are very frequently rigid-circuit and frequently interval (Section 8.2.2.3). Eventually this process will, if allowed to go on long enough, terminate with communities in which there is not a great deal of unutilized energy available for new colonizers (Sections 8.2.2.1, 8.2.2.2). On the other hand, as the community is assembled, the return time of its equilibrium increases (Section 8.2.2.2). The assembly process might not ever reach its energetically constrained terminus if at some point this slow return to equilibrium enables environmental fluctuations to disrupt the assembly process (Section 8.2.1).

Thus, both the dynamic stability and the energetic viewpoints are plausible candidates for explaining food web structure. Other factors are involved as well, whose discussion I will defer until the end of this section. For now, let us consider how we can distinguish which of these two factors—energy constraints and return times—might be responsible for terminating the assembly process in nature. We seek specific predictions of the two hypotheses that we can use to test them observationally. In this discussion, I will focus on that classic food web property, food chain lengths.

Consider first the return time hypothesis. On the basis of this hypothesis, we would expect to see two broad trends in the data.

First, systems with larger return times would be less likely to occur where they are exposed to stronger environmental fluctuations. Therefore (Section 8.2.1), we expect to find an inverse correlation between food chain lengths and strength of environmental fluctuations.

Second, one expects a trend having to do with the overall *scaling* of population dynamics (DeAngelis et al. 1978, DeAngelis 1980).

The element A_{ij} of the community matrix (8.2) is the per capita effect of species j on species i's growth *rate*. Therefore, the elements of the community matrix *scale like* those growth rates. That is, if in some fixed units of time the growth rates are faster, then the numbers A_{ij} will be bigger.

For example, in the predator-prey model (4.5), the parameters r, E, and d are all rates [their units involve $(\text{time})^{-1}$], and they all appear linearly in the net growth rates f_R, f_N. Therefore, these parameters will also appear linearly in the derivatives of the growth rates with respect to densities; that is, they will appear linearly in the community matrix.

If, in some fixed units of time, the growth rates are faster, and the A_{ij} are bigger, then also the eigenvalues of $\mathbf{A}$ will be bigger, for the eigenvalues scale like $\mathbf{A}$ [as can be seen from equation (A.33)]. But if the eigenvalues are bigger, the return time T_R is smaller. So faster overall rates in population processes will be associated with shorter return times.

Now, smaller organisms tend to have faster rates of increase, so we would expect, for a given food web topology, communities of smaller organisms to have shorter return times than communities of larger organisms. Therefore, smaller organisms should be able to form longer food chains than larger organisms, given comparable levels of environmental variability.

Consider next the energy hypothesis.

One would think there ought to be some relationship between primary production and food web structure on the energy hypothesis. But it is not at all clear what this relationship should be. One possibility would be longer food chains in more productive environments, on the following reasoning. For a given food web, higher primary production translates into more energy input to the top predators, hence more production by those top predators, which should enable another animal to feed on the (former) top predators.

One problem here is that higher primary production might translate as well into higher *diversity* throughout the web: a larger number of herbivore species, a resultant larger number of other intermediate species, and a resultant larger number of top predators. The top predators as a group would still have more production, but in order to utilize it a presumed new "superpredator" would not only have to subsist on a marginal energy intake, it would have to be a "supergeneralist" too, since the available energy would be spread over a larger number of top predator species.

Omnivory also complicates the picture. The energy hypothesis does not rule out long food chains in habitats of low production, if the animals at the top of such a food chain *also* feed at a lower "trophic level." The argument is complicated further by the influence of ecological efficiency (Section 8.2.2.1). If we could be confident of ecological efficiencies of the order of 0.1, we could look for food web effects associated with differences of an order of magnitude in primary production. But 0.1 is an upper limit on ecological efficiencies (May 1981b); more likely it would require differences of two or three orders of magnitude in primary production to have significant food web effects.

Pimm (1982) has suggested a more subtle and stronger test of the energy hypothesis. It is known (McNeill and Lawton 1970, Humphreys 1979) that invertebrate ectotherms tend to be about an order of magnitude more efficient at energy conversion than endotherms, with vertebrate ectotherms tending to have production efficiencies intermediate between these two extremes. Therefore, if members of the three groups have about the same energy consumption, the invertebrate ectotherms should produce more energy than do the vertebrate ectotherms than do the endotherms, so that the invertebrate ectotherms should support longer food chains than do the vertebrate ectotherms than do the endotherms.

At the time of writing, three types of approach have been undertaken in search of these trends.

Briand and Cohen (1987) looked for environmental correlates of mean food chain length in a sample of 113 food webs. Here mean food chain length of a food web is the average length of all maximal food chains in the web. These authors found that mean food chain length is associated neither with environmental variability (as suggested by the return time hypothesis) nor with primary production (as one conceivably might have expected on the energy hypothesis; but see the above *critique*). Instead, they found a strong association with the *dimensionality* of the environment (Section 8.1.1). This is a fascinating result, raising the possibility that there may be more to all this than any of us have yet suspected. (On the other hand, it could be an artifact of different traditions among researchers working on different habitat types.)

Yodzis (1984c) took up Pimm's suggestion that, given comparable energy consumption, invertebrate ectotherms should support longer food chains than do vertebrate ectotherms than do endotherms. In order to make proper use of this insight we must very carefully decide on criteria for species to be judged to have "comparable energy consumption" and to "support longer food chains."

There are very few systems for which we have both good energetic data and good food web data. So, looking at the food web data, we can do no better than to assume that species that are feeding at the same "trophic level" have, on the average, roughly similar amounts of energy available to them for consumption. But we still need to define "trophic level."

It is easy to do this for a species that is linked to a primary producer through a single food chain: in such a case we can define that species' trophic level as 1 plus the length of the food chain. But most species in any real system will be linked to primary production through several food chains, often with differing lengths. Which one (or ones) are we to use? (Because of ambiguities like this I prefer to speak of "vertical food web structure" rather than "food chain lengths.")

Examining those few food webs that do include energetic flows, one finds, unsurprisingly, that it is generally the case that the shortest food chains are energetically the most important. So from an energetic point of view, the best definition of "trophic level" will involve the shortest food chain linking each species to primary production.

But in measuring food chain lengths we must (again from an energetic point of view) take into account the differing energy transfer efficiencies that were our starting point. In the absence of detailed information on efficiencies, we may adopt the following conventions: a link with a basal species or an invertebrate ectotherm at its lower end will be assigned *length* 1; with a vertebrate ectotherm, length 1.5; and with an endotherm, length 2. In order to avoid the ambiguous term "trophic level," define the *trophic height* of any species to be 1 plus the length in this sense of the shortest food chain linking it to a primary producer. For instance, in Fig. 8.8 I have indicated the length in this sense of each link, and the height in this sense of each species, for the Pamlico River food web (case 16 of Briand 1983a).

At a given trophic height, invertebrate ectotherms should produce, on the average, more energy than do vertebrate ectotherms than do endotherms; so at a given trophic height invertebrate ectotherms should "support longer food chains" than do vertebrate ectotherms than do endotherms. But what does it

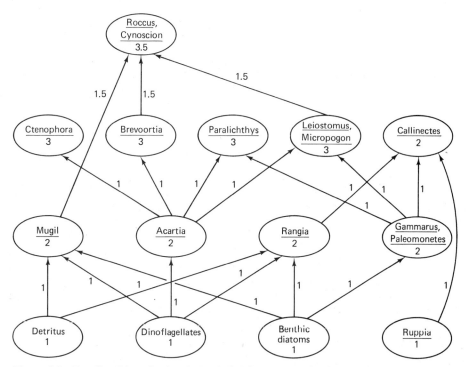

Figure 8.8 Pamlico River food web. Each link is marked with its length in the sense of the text, and each species with its trophic height in the sense of the text. (After Copeland et al. 1974.)

mean for species S, say, to support a "longer food chain" than species T? This is a similar problem to that of defining "trophic level": those species that feed, for example, on species S will in general feed on other species as well, and some of these other species could be at lower trophic heights, hence more energy-rich, than species S. Thus species S may or may not be of energetic importance for its consumers.

We can resolve these ambiguities as follows. Say that a species S *supports a consumer* if species S is fed upon by some other species that, in turn, feeds upon no other species at the same or lower trophic height as S. For example, in the Pamlico River food web just sketched, *Acartia* and *Mugil* are the only animals that support a consumer. Three of the basals also support consumers, but this is not of interest in the present context.

So: on the energy hypothesis we expect that, at a given trophic height, a larger proportion of invertebrate ectotherms than of vertebrate ectotherms than of endotherms will support a consumer. Yodzis (1984c) analyzes from this point of view the 34 Briand food webs that do not include "man" as a trophic category.

Invertebrate ectotherms, vertebrate ectotherms, and endotherms differ as broad categories not only in production efficiency but also in body size: invertebrate ectotherms tend to be smaller than vertebrate ectotherms, which tend to be smaller than endotherms. In order to factor out any possible effect of body size, mean body weights were determined for as many species at height 2 in these food webs as possible. In all, estimates were obtained for 203 of the 277 height 2 consumers in these food webs. There is indeed a clear tendency for the invertebrate ectotherms in these webs (mean body weight 20 g) to be smaller than the vertebrate ectotherms (297 g) to be smaller than the endotherms (8003 g).

The data were broken down into the three metabolic categories, and into size categories to order of magnitude. The proportion of species at height 2 that support a consumer, categorized in this way, is given in Table 8.5.

In the total sample of 203 species, we see a statistically significant overall trend, in the lowermost row of the table, for more invertebrate ectotherms than vertebrate ectotherms than endotherms to support a consumer (chi-squared = 8.08, $P = 0.018$). Moreover, when we look within size categories we see the same trend, except for magnitudes 0 and +3. However, these deviations are not statistically significant. We conclude that the data are consistent with the energy hypothesis. There does not seem to be any coherent effect of body size itself (columns of Table 8.5).

Pimm has begun an ambitious program that aims to determine the factors controlling food chain lengths in certain communities through field experiments. The communities that Pimm is studying are miniature assemblages in the water that collects in tree holes, and in certain plants such as pitcher plants. Early results in this program, reported by Pimm and Kitching (1987), are still largely inconclusive.

What they do show is that it takes time—of the order of the 9 months that the experiments lasted—for these little communities to build up. Moreover, they build up "from the bottom," much as the assembly ideas of Section 8.2.2 would anticipate. That is, first the basal species (in this case, detritus) need to get es-

TABLE 8.5 PROPORTION (SAMPLE SIZE IN PARENTHESES) OF SPECIES AT HEIGHT 2 THAT SUPPORT A CONSUMER, FOR EACH METABOLIC AND SIZE CATEGORY

Magnitude	Invertebrate ectotherms	Vertebrate ectotherms	Endotherms	Total
−6	0.40 (15)	—	—	0.40 (15)
−5	0.0 (3)	—	—	0.0 (3)
−4	0.33 (6)	—	—	0.33 (6)
−3	0.33 (24)	—	—	0.33 (24)
−2	0.06 (17)	—	—	0.06 (17)
−1	0.07 (14)	0.0 (2)	—	0.06 (16)
0	0.04 (24)	0.22 (9)	0.0 (1)	0.09 (34)
+1	0.33 (12)	0.13 (23)	0.0 (8)	0.16 (43)
+2	0.25 (4)	0.07 (15)	0.0 (11)	0.07 (30)
+3	—	0.0 (8)	0.17 (6)	0.08 (14)
+4	—	—	—	—
+5	—	—	1.0 (1)	1.0 (1)
Total	0.20 (119)	0.11 (57)	0.07 (27)	

A species has magnitude N if its body weight in grams can be written $10^N X$, with $1 \leq X \leq 10$.

From Yodzis 1984c. Copyright Springer-Verlag, Berlin.

tablished, then the intermediate species need time to get established, and only then can the top predators invade.

Pimm and Kitching interpret this as support for the return time argument: since it takes time for these communities to build up, it would take time for them to recover from a disturbance. Some might consider that this particular argument stretches the return time concept beyond its proper context.

This study also includes preliminary experiments to test the energy hypothesis for the tree hole communities, by manipulating the rate at which leaf litter falls into the holes. No effect on food chain lengths was seen, but the increase in "primary production" considered—a factor of 4—was surely too small.

Finally, we need to be aware that other factors besides the two that I have been discussing have to be taken into account. For instance, Hutchinson (1959) has pointed out that since predators tend to be larger than their prey, predators will get bigger and bigger as one moves up a food chain, so that eventually a further link in the chain would require an animal that is too large to be practicable. Design constraints of this sort (which are discussed in more detail by Pimm 1982) could prove of crucial importance in some cases.

In answer to the question that heads this section: we do not know why food chains are so short. As we have seen, there is more than one possible explanation, and the empirical evidence at present is inconclusive. Possibly, each of the three explanations I have considered is appropriate under different circumstances—the correct explanation may be a pluralistic one, along the lines sketched in the introductory paragraphs to Chapter 6.

I mentioned in Section 8.2.1.1 that in 1977, every schoolperson knew why food chains are so short! Does this mean that we have regressed in the intervening 10 years? I think not. We have made great progress in our understanding of what the issues are. I think the next 10 years will see equal progress in addressing those issues.

ADDITIONAL EXERCISES

8.8 Use loop analysis to calculate the return times T_R for these two loop diagrams:

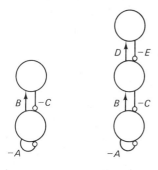

Which has the longer return time? [Hint: use equation (7.6).]

8.9. Use loop analysis to calculate the return times T_R for these two loop diagrams:

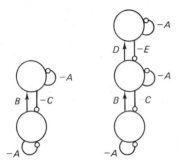

Which has the longer return time?

8.10. Use loop analysis, together with the Routh-Hurwitz conditions, to show that loop-forming omnivore links such as these

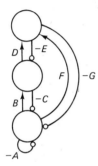

have a detrimental effect on local stability.

8.11. Suppose that all plausible community matrices for the Narragansett Bay food web have major-effect-on graphs like either Fig. 8.5 or Fig. 8.6. (This supposition is false, but let's pretend it's true just for the sake of discussion.) Imagine that you are attempting to conserve (a) bivalves, or (b) Pacific menhaden, or (c) clams, or (d) starfish, or (e) butterfish. What would you recommend in terms of changes in the overall intensity of human exploitation of the system (recall that trophospecies 17 is man) to conserve each of those resources?

8.12. The niche overlap graph of Fig. 8.2 is rigid-circuit. Find a perfect elimination ordering for it. Is the corresponding perfect addition ordering biologically plausible as a scenario for the assembly of this community? If not, can you find a perfect addition ordering that is?

8.13. Computer project (fairly ambitious). The following bounds B_{ij} yield plausible community matrices for the Pamlico River food web of Fig. 8.8:

i	j	B_{ij} (−)	B_{ji} (+)
1	1	1	—
2	2	1	—
3	3	1	—
4	4	1	—

i	j	B_{ij} (−)	B_{ji} (+)
1	6	0.01	0.1
1	8	0.01	0.1
2	5	10	0.1
2	6	10	0.1
2	8	10	0.1
3	6	10	0.1
3	7	10	0.1
3	8	10	0.1
4	12	0.1	10
5	9	10	0.1
5	10	10	0.1
5	11	10	0.1
5	13	1	1
6	12	10	0.1
7	9	10	0.1
7	11	10	0.1
7	12	1	1
8	14	1	1
10	14	1	1
11	14	1	1

All other B_{ij} are zero. The appropriate sign (− or +) of each corresponding community matrix element A_{ij} or A_{ji} is indicated. The trophospecies are numbered as follows: 1 = detritus, 2 = dinoflagellates, 3 = benthic diatoms, 4 = *Ruppia*, 5 = *Acartia*, 6 = *Rangia*, 7 = *Gammarus, Paleomonetes*, 8 = *mugil*, 9 = *Paralichthys*, 10 = *Brevoortia*, 11 = *Leiostomus, Micropogon*, 12 = *Callinectes*, 13 = *Ctenophora*, 14 = *Roccus, Cynoscion*.

Study *species deletion stability* as follows. Generate 100 stable plausible community matrices. For each species in the community, determine how many of these result in a community matrix that is still stable if that species (along with, of course, all its interactions) is removed entirely from the community. Do you see any pattern in your results?

To do this, you will have to be able to test the stability of 14-by-14 matrices. This means you will need access to a ready-made subroutine (for instance, from the IMSL or NAG commercial libraries) that will do this for you.

PART THREE

THE EVOLUTION OF LIFE-HISTORY STRATEGIES

There are, broadly speaking, two ways that theory can develop. One way is to follow through on the consequences of a current set of hypotheses. The other way is to seek to explain the current hypotheses themselves on the basis of some "deeper," "underlying" processes.

Up to now, we have been following mostly the first course. Assuming certain population growth rates and interactions, we have deduced certain phenomena. In this enterprise, the population parameters have been treated as given quantities.

Even so, we have discovered restrictions on the allowable parameter values. For instance, the study of competition led us to the idea of limiting similarity. And this amounts to restrictions on the population parameters, with important observable consequences.

Those restrictions were by-products of our reasoning about the population dynamics itself. In this part, we are going to seek restrictions on the population parameters due to a process distinct from population dynamics, namely, microevolution.

Our treatment will by no means be comprehensive. For one thing, we are going to return to the single-population viewpoint of Part One. While still incomplete, the theory has been worked out extensively enough for single populations to provide us with a substantial illustration of microevolutionary theory.

Furthermore, we are going to study only one particular approach—optimization theory—to these microevolutionary problems. I think it is fair to say that this approach, while embattled, has contributed a great deal to our understanding of how nature is put together, and has the potential to contribute a great deal more.

In this part, we will incorporate age structure into population dynamics but will emphasize density dependence a lot less than in Parts One and Two. The reason for this is not that density dependence has suddenly become less important but that existing theory in our present context is far less well developed for density-dependent population growth.

Chapter 9

Some Basics

9.1 MICROEVOLUTION AND OPTIMIZATION

We have all marveled at the efficacy of natural selection in adapting organisms to function in the world. Indeed the Darwinian motto "survival of the fittest" suggests an evolutionary process which tends to produce the *best* solution to each "evolutionary problem."

In the early days of research in population genetics, this notion seemed to be borne out. It was taken to be The Fundamental Theorem of Natural Selection that fitness (in the precise quantitative form of the Malthusian parameter, or what we will call the intrinsic growth rate) is maximized by natural selection, at a rate proportional to the genetic variance in fitness (Fisher 1930).

The view of natural selection as an optimizing process is extremely appealing, for it opens up vast and important areas of biology to precise theoretical treatment. If we can express the intrinsic growth rate as a function of the ecological parameters (and we can), then we can explicate exactly how natural selection will act to produce the adaptations that we see in nature, simply by maximizing that function with respect to the parameters of interest. There is a large and burgeoning literature that does just this, for all kinds of adaptations ranging from individual life histories (reviewed in the next four chapters) to interactions among species (Futuyma and Slatkin 1983) to social interactions among individual animals (Krebs and Davies 1984).

In this part I will adopt the optimization viewpoint to microevolution, and explore its workings in the context of life history theory. But I want to make it clear at the outset that this viewpoint is seriously flawed and must be applied with certain reservations. First I will sketch what the flaws are; then I will indicate why I am nevertheless devoting a part of this book to optimization (aside from the obvious reason that this methodology has been widely used in theoretical ecology) and what is the spirit in which it makes sense to use optimization arguments.

The difficulties with optimization are as follows (for more details: Oster et al. 1976, Oster and Wilson 1978, Gould and Lewontin 1979, Lewontin 1979, Hunkapiller et al. 1982, Campbell 1982).

1. At the purely phenotypic level, a given characteristic will often have many implications for fitness. For example, an animal's foraging behavior may affect its net intake of energy, but it may also affect its susceptibility to predation. A method of foraging that is good for obtaining energy may be bad for avoiding predators. In applying optimization ideas to evolution, it is hardly avoidable that we will proceed by solving one problem at a time. But an animal has to "solve" many problems simultaneously—and these many problems often overlap and interfere with one another.

2. Still at the phenotypic level, there are constraints on what is possible. For instance, the optimal solution to a foraging problem may require that an animal run faster than it is capable of.

Both of these points, especially point 2, can in principle be incorporated into optimization models, though in practice this will be extremely difficult and require a very great deal of detailed information.

But ultimately, while selection acts through phenotypes, the mechanism of evolution involves genetics, and here we are very far from having enough information to be confident in our predictions. Indeed, a large part of the appeal of the optimization approach is that it neatly sidesteps genetical details, by dealing only with the *results,* the end states, of selection and ignoring the process that yields those results: however the genetics works, the "optimist" assumes that it results in nice phenotypic optima.

3. But there may be no genotype corresponding to the optimal phenotype (or genetic variation in the direction of the optimal phenotype may be too weak for selection to act).

4. Even if there is such a genotype, it may be of the wrong sort. For instance, if the optimal phenotype corresponds to a heterozygote, selection will result at best in a polymorphism rather than a uniform optimization, in the absence of some special genetic mechanism for fixed heterozygosity.

5. Moreover, the past half century of genetical research has shown that the concept of genotype itself is a very complicated one. The simple-minded notion of "a gene for such-and-such characteristic" is seldom very realistic. On the one hand, genes at different loci are often linked; on the other hand, a gene at one locus can have many different phenotypic effects. Thus it is difficult to identify the unit of material at the genetic level on which selection acts; often it must be a "complex" or "cluster" of genes. But through recombination, the identity of these objects can change from one generation to the next.

Advances in molecular genetics in the last decade have complicated the picture still further. Things like split genes, multigene families, and quasi-stable genetic elements could revolutionize evolutionary theory. The genome seems to be a far more dynamic and fluid entity than classical genetics led us to expect; an entity with something of a life of its own.

6. Even within the context of relatively simple genetical models, it sometimes occurs that the dynamics of the evolving genome not only fails to arrive at an optimal end state, it fails to arrive at *any* end state; in such cases the dynamics of population genetics itself is chaotic in the sense of Sections 3.3 and 6.1.

7. Evolutionary biologists are becoming increasingly aware of the importance of epigenetic phenomena in structuring what we observe (for instance, Bonner 1980, Goodwin et al. 1983). The relationship to selection is only beginning to be explicated (Kauffman 1985, 1986).

In the light of these considerations, it would be foolish to insist that microevolution necessarily will result in an optimal final state for each and every "evolutionary problem" that we can contemplate. However, while the objections to optimization theory show that optima need not *necessarily* be attained, there is no proof that optima will never be attained or that they will seldom be attained. And natural selection does have a basic tendency to optimize, despite the preceding catalog of ways in which this tendency can be thwarted. It seems prudent, then, to suspend judgment for the time being while we explore this powerful methodology, see what it predicts, and compare those predictions with what we see in nature. In fact, exactly this activity has been a major theme in recent ecological research.

Optimization methods do not constitute rigorous proofs of what the course of evolution will be, but they do provide reasonable indications of what we might very well expect that course to be. They provide a framework of ideas which can stimulate and lend order to empirical investigations.

9.1.1 Optimization and Evolutionarily Stable Strategies

It is convenient to motivate the optimization method by means of a simplified view of microevolution, in which the process is seen purely as a competitive struggle among phenotypes. This may not be very far from how Darwin himself thought about selection—after all, genes had not yet been discovered in his day. It amounts, in modern terms, to assuming that genetic details are not very important after all, so that one might as well act as if one were dealing with the simplest possible genetic structure: asexual haploid reproduction.

The population is thought of as a set of independently reproducing clones, and each clone is thought of as having adopted a certain evolutionary *strategy*. For instance, if we're talking about life histories, a strategy might correspond to a certain most probable clutch size, or to a certain age at first reproduction, or to some other unambiguous life-history trait, or to some combination of such traits.

Thinking of the population in a very idealized fashion, we may imagine that the whole population has adopted some one strategy. Now imagine further that, by mutation let us say, a small part of the population starts up a new clone that has adopted some other strategy. Then there are four possibilities: (1) the new strategy may spread through the population and replace the old one; it may successfully *invade*, (2) the new strategy may die out after a while, (3) the two strategies may coexist at some fixed proportion (*mixed strategy*), (4) there may be no fixed "end state" at all, but rather a chaotic genetic dynamics, in the sense of Sections 3.3, 6.1.

In case 2 we say that the old strategy is stable against invasion by the new one. A strategy that is stable against invasion by *all* other possible strategies is called an *evolutionarily stable strategy*. Once the population has reached an evolutionarily stable strategy, it will not evolve any further—at least not until the "rules of the game," in the form of environmental constraints, are changed. So populations will tend to evolve toward evolutionarily stable strategies.

This way of thinking about evolution goes back to Fisher (1930), and came to prominence in the work of Hamilton (1967) and Maynard Smith. The name *evolutionarily stable strategy*, often abbreviated *ESS*, seems to have first appeared in print in a paper by Price and Maynard Smith (1973).

In defining ESS, I asked you to think of a population all of whose members had adopted one and the same strategy. Along the way, I mentioned the possibility of mixed strategies. A mixed strategy may also be an ESS, if it is stable against invasion by all other strategies. There are two different interpretations of such a strategy. In one interpretation, each individual adopts different strategies at different times, with certain fixed proportions. In the other interpretation, different individuals in the population adopt different strategies, with certain fixed proportions. The latter interpretation (which requires appropriate genetic mechanisms) can also be called a *polymorphic strategy*.

Now we must address the problem of how to find an ESS. Let us suppose that each clone undergoes density-independent growth, with intrinsic growth rate r^i for clone i. Then if N_t^i is the number (or biomass) per unit area of clone i at time t, we have at time $t + 1$

$$N_{t+1}^i = N_t^i \, e^{r^i} \tag{9.1}$$

as I hope you will recall from your elementary ecology courses. Please bear in mind that the i's here are not powers but (superscripted) labels for clones.

Different clones, having adopted different strategies, will have different intrinsic growth rates r^i. Putting it another way, we can associate the growth rate of each clone with its strategy, and then we can say that each strategy has a different growth rate.

Now I am going to prove that, in the case of density-independent population growth, the evolutionarily stable strategy is that strategy which has the largest value of r.

Let * denote an ESS and let m denote some other ("mutant") strategy that is trying to invade a population that has adopted the ESS *. So there are two kinds of individuals in our population: those with the ESS named * and the mutants with strategy m. As above, let N_t^* be the density of ESS individuals and N_t^m the density of mutants. Then at any time t the proportion of ESS individuals is

$$p_t^* = N_t^* / (N_t^* + N_t^m) \tag{9.2}$$

and the proportion of mutants is

$$p_t^m = N_t^m/(N_t^* + N_t^m)$$ (9.3)

Let r^* be the intrinsic growth rate of strategy $*$ and r^m the intrinsic growth rate of strategy m. Let Δp_t^m be the change in one time unit in the proportion p_t^m of mutants, that is,

$$\Delta p_t^m = p_{t+1}^m - p_t^m$$ (9.4)

Then it is easy to show, using equation (9.1), that

$$\Delta p_t^m = N_t^m N_t^* (1 - e^{r^*-r^m})/(N_t^* + N_t^m)(N_t^* e^{r^*-r^m} + N_t^m)$$ (9.5)

Every factor on the right-hand side of this equation is positive except for the factor $1 - e^{r^*-r^m}$. So the sign of Δp_t^m, for every time t, is the same as the sign of this factor. So the proportion of mutants in the population will steadily decline if and only if $r^m < r^*$, and it will steadily increase if and only if $r^m > r^*$, that is, a mutant strategy m can invade a population all of whose members have adopted strategy $*$ if and only if r^m is larger than r^*. So if $*$ is an ESS, which means that no other strategy can invade, then it must be that r^* is bigger than r^m for *all* other strategies m. And conversely, if r^* is bigger than r^m for all other strategies m, then $*$ is an ESS.

But this is what we wanted to prove: in the case of density-independent population growth, the ESS is the strategy with the largest intrinsic growth rate r. (I have neglected mixed strategies here. They will be discussed later.)

Exercise 9.1. Prove equation (9.5).

Often in this book we will be interested in strategies that need to be labeled with some continuous variable, say s. Then the intrinsic growth rate will be a function of s: $r = r(s)$. If s^* is the value of s that corresponds to an ESS, then s^* must be a point where the function $r(s)$ has a maximum.

Two remarks need to be made about this.

First, the strategic variable s will usually be restricted to some finite range of values, say $[s_{min}, s_{max}]$. For instance, if s is the expected number of eggs produced, this will never be smaller than 0 or larger than permitted by some physiological constraint. If the maximum value of $r(s)$ is at an interior point s^* of the interval $[s_{min}, s_{max}]$,

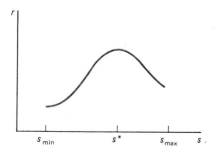

then we must have

$$dr/ds\Big|_{s*} = 0$$

(9.6)

$$d^2r/ds^2\Big|_{s*} < 0$$

from elementary calculus.

However, in case the maximum is at a boundary point

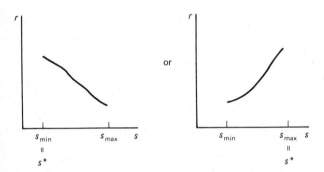

then equation (9.6) does *not* hold. So in searching for maxima, it is not enough just to look for zeros of dr/ds; we have to check any boundary regions separately. This can be done through derivatives; for instance, in the case of a one-dimensional "strategy space" as depicted here, s_{min} is a local maximum if $dr/ds < 0$ at s_{min}, and s_{max} is a local maximum if $dr/ds > 0$ at s_{max}.

The second remark is that we also might have a situation like this:

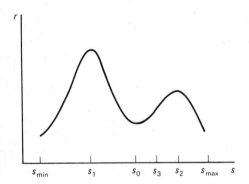

We might have more than one *local* maximum. When this happens, there are two possibilities that need to be considered.

One possibility is that the variation in s that naturally occurs in the population encompasses both maxima. In this case we expect to see selection for the *global* maximum (at s_1 in the above hypothetical example).

The other possibility is that the realized variation in s is quite small relative to the difference between neighboring local maxima. For instance, suppose a population finds itself with $s = s_3 > s_0$ in the preceding picture. Variation in s will tend to be concentrated in a region around $s = s_3$, and if that region is small enough so that values of s less than s_0 are extremely improbable, then selection will tend to push s toward larger values, and eventually to s_2. Such a population will not "see" the other peak at s_1.

It is difficult to know in advance which of these situations we are dealing with in a given population. So in general, all local maxima are to be regarded as ESS's: as possible end states of the evolutionary process.

9.2 AGE-SPECIFIC POPULATION DYNAMICS AND LOTKA'S EQUATION

The life history of a population is summarized in the parameters m_x (age-specific effective fertility) and l_x (age-specific survival). So our first task is to see how these parameters affect the intrinsic growth rate r. This means we will have to take a quick look at age-structured population dynamics. I will develop the discrete time formalism in some detail and will use it in most of what follows.

Let the population density be observed at regularly spaced times, separated by a basic time interval Δt. We can label those discrete observation times with integers, say $t, t + 1, t + 2, \ldots$, where $t + i$ is i basic time intervals later than t. The basic time interval can be anything that happens to be appropriate. For seasonally breeding populations, the length of time between two consecutive breeding seasons is a reasonable choice. For instance, if the basic time interval is 1 year, then t may be 24 April 1986, $t + 1$ would be 24 April 1987, $t + 2$ would be 24 April 1988, and so on. (For short, we would just say t is 1986, $t + 1$ is 1987, $t + 2$ is 1988, and so on.)

Corresponding to the same basic time interval, one can partition the population into *age classes,* the "width" of an age class being equal to the basic time interval. For instance, if the basic time interval is 1 year, then the youngest age class consists of all individuals aged 0 through 1 year, the next age class consists of all individuals aged 1 through 2 years, and so on. It is customary to number the youngest age class 0. There are various standard notations for the oldest age class; I will call it w.

Let $n_{x,t}$ be the expected number (or biomass, whichever is appropriate) density of animals in age class x at time t. Define the *survival rate* P_x to be the expected fraction of individuals in age class x that will survive to age class $x + 1$.

It follows from the definition of P_x that

$$n_{x+1,t+1} = P_x n_{x,t} \qquad x = 0, 1, \ldots, w - 1 \qquad (9.7)$$

Or, if you like, this *is* the definition of P_x, written as a set of w equations (one for each value of x in the stated range).

Next, let m_x be the *effective fertility* of a parent in age class x, meaning the expected number of offspring that are born to a parent in age class x and survive to the upcoming census. (This may be less than the number of offspring actually born.)

The alert reader will have noticed that we're going to get into trouble here if we're not careful about sex. The simplest and most common solution to this difficulty is to consider only females in the whole formalism: $n_{x,t}$ is the density of females, m_x is the effective fertility of females in age class x for female offspring, and so on. This is what we will do in all of the present part. It is quite reasonable if there are plenty of males to go around, which is usually, though not necessarily always, the case.

The expected number of newly born individuals entering the population at time $t + 1$ is

$$n_{0,t+1} = m_0 n_{0,t} + m_1 n_{1,t} + m_2 n_{2,t} + \cdots + m_w n_{w,t} \qquad (9.8)$$

Combining (9.7) and (9.8) we get the $w + 1$ equations

$$\left. \begin{aligned} n_{0,t+1} &= m_0 n_{0,t} + \cdots + m_w n_{w,t} \\ n_{1,t+1} &= P_0 n_{0,t} \\ &\;\;\vdots \\ n_{w,t+1} &= P_{w-1} n_{w-1,t} \end{aligned} \right\} \qquad (9.9)$$

This system of equations fully specifies the dynamics of the population. If we know the m's and the P's and we are given the n's at some initial time, we can use (9.9) to predict the n's at any future time.

In particular, assume that the population in question has attained a *stable age distribution*. This means that all the age classes grow at the same rate, that is to say, there exists a number λ such that

$$n_{x,t+1} = \lambda n_{x,t} \qquad (9.10)$$

for all age classes $x = 0, \ldots, w$ and for all sufficiently large t. Putting this relation into the system (9.9) we find, after substituting the lower equations into the uppermost one,

$$\lambda^{w+1} - m_0 \lambda^w - P_0 m_1 \lambda^{w-1} - P_0 P_1 m_2 \lambda^{w-2} - \cdots - (P_0 P_1 \cdots P_{w-1}) m_w = 0 \qquad (9.11)$$

Exercise 9.2. Prove this.

Let l_x be the *survival* to age x, that is, the probability for a live-born individual to live at least as long as age x. It is easy to see that

$$\left. \begin{aligned} l_0 &= 1 \\ l_1 &= P_0 \\ l_2 &= P_0 P_1 \\ &\;\;\vdots \\ l_w &= P_0 P_1 \cdots P_{w-1} \end{aligned} \right\} \qquad (9.12)$$

If we use equations (9.12) in (9.11), multiply each term in the resulting equation by λ^{-w-1}, and move all the negative terms to the right-hand side, we get

$$1 = \sum_{x=0}^{w} \lambda^{-x-1} l_x m_x \qquad (9.13)$$

Exercise 9.3. Prove (9.13).

Equation (9.13) is called *Lotka's equation* by some people and Euler's equation by others. I will call it Lotka's equation.

Sometimes you will see in the literature this equation written with the summation beginning at 1 instead of at 0, and with the exponent of λ being $-x$ instead of $-x - 1$. Don't worry about this: it just means that the author has numbered his youngest age class 1 instead of 0 as we have done.

Lotka's equation is very important for us as students of life-history theory. To see why, notice that the total density

$$N_t = \sum_x n_{x,t} \qquad (9.14)$$

obeys [from (9.10)]

$$N_{t+1} = \lambda N_t \qquad (9.15)$$

But this is just the well-known equation of exponential growth, with *finite rate of growth* λ.

Using $e^{r \, \Delta t} = \lambda$, where $\Delta t =$ (one basic time interval), we can also write Lotka's equation in terms of the *intrinsic growth rate* r. In a discrete time formalism, it is understood that time is measured in units of basic time intervals, and in those units, $\Delta t = 1$. With the understanding that it is a convenient shorthand, we can then write $e^r = \lambda$. This last equation holds only in the particular units in which $\Delta t = 1$, but, as I just mentioned, we are tied to those units in the discrete time formalism.

So Lotka's equation relates fitness (in the sense of Section 9.1) to the life-history parameters m and P. It's exactly what we need in order to study the evolution of life-history strategies. Of course, maximizing with respect to λ in (9.13) (which I will do throughout the following) is equivalent to maximizing with respect to r.

However, we derived Lotka's equation from the assumption of a stable age distribution. How sensible is this?

If the life-history parameters l_x and m_x depend only on age x, and not, say, on time or on density, there's no problem. In this case, Leslie (1945) has proved, subject to some fairly weak restrictions, that a population growing in accordance with (9.9) will in fact approach a stable age distribution. (I am going to discuss this work in the next subsection.) So with certain exceptions, in the density-independent case the approach to a stable age distribution isn't really an assumption, it's a theorem from population dynamics. And I will show in the next subsection that even in those exceptional cases, Lotka's equation is still the right way to get at fitness.

In the case of density-dependent life-history parameters, given the assumption of stable age distribution, Lotka's equation still holds, with λ a function of the densities. There is in this case no general proof that a stable age distribution will be approached, nor is such a proof likely to be possible without very strong restrictions on the form of the density dependence. But the point here is that the biology of the situation is likely to impose just such restrictions: one expects density dependence to act as a population regulatory factor, so that one is inclined to expect in this case the even stronger relationship ($\lambda = 1$)

$$n_{x,t+1} = n_{x,t} \tag{9.16}$$

that is, *equilibrium*. I will return to the density-dependent case in Section 9.2.2.

In order for the discussion of Section 9.1 to make sense, it is necessary that each life-history strategy uniquely determines a numerical value for r. Does Lotka's equation achieve this? It is certainly to be expected that a life-history strategy uniquely determines numerical values for all the m's and P's. Then Lotka's equation says that r is the logarithm of a root of a polynomial, with real coefficients, of degree $w + 1$. But can't such an equation have as many as $w + 1$ roots? Which one is the right one? Luckily (is it really just luck, or is it the intrinsic sense of our formalism?), one can show (next subsection) that there is one and only one root that is real and positive. It is the one we want.

9.2.1 Density-Independent Population Dynamics

In this subsection I am going to sketch the theory of density-independent, age-specific population dynamics. The essential results that are needed for life-history theory have already been stated in the preceding subsection, so this subsection could be skipped without any loss of continuity. The discussion here will be a little more mathematically sophisticated than the rest of Part Three, but I hope you will decide to stick with me. Rather than take my word for the unproved claims in the previous subsection, you should really, as a student of science, make me prove them to you.

To understand this subsection you will need a basic grasp of complex numbers and matrices. Sections A.1 and A.2, in the Appendix, sketch everything you need to know for present purposes, in case you have not studied these topics or need to review them.

Assume throughout this subsection that P_x and m_x are, for each x, constants. I will use boldface print for column vectors and matrices. If we define a time-dependent column vector $\mathbf{n}_t$ of densities,

$$\mathbf{n}_t = \begin{bmatrix} n_{0,t} \\ n_{1,t} \\ \vdots \\ n_{w,t} \end{bmatrix} \tag{9.17}$$

we can write (9.9) as

$$\mathbf{n}_{t+1} = \mathbf{L}\mathbf{n}_t \tag{9.18}$$

where the matrix

$$\mathbf{L} = \begin{bmatrix} m_0 & m_1 & m_2 & \cdot & \cdot & \cdot & m_w \\ P_0 & 0 & 0 & \cdot & \cdot & \cdot & 0 \\ 0 & P_1 & 0 & \cdot & \cdot & \cdot & 0 \\ 0 & 0 & P_2 & 0 & \cdot & \cdot & 0 \\ & \cdot & \cdot & \cdot & \cdot & \cdot & \cdot \\ 0 & \cdot & \cdot & \cdot & 0 & P_{w-1} & 0 \end{bmatrix} \tag{9.19}$$

is called a *Leslie matrix,* in honor of P. H. Leslie, who (Leslie 1945, 1948), together with Bernadelli (1941) and Lewis (1942), developed the theory surrounding equations (9.18), (9.19).

Among other things, Leslie (1945) proved that any Leslie matrix is diagonalizable. I will use this fact but will not prove it here.

If we rewrite the equation (9.10) for a stable age distribution as

$$\mathbf{n}_{t+1} = \lambda \mathbf{n}_t \tag{9.20}$$

and combine it with (9.18), we obtain

$$\mathbf{L}\mathbf{n}_t = \lambda \mathbf{n}_t \tag{9.21}$$

which is nothing but the eigenvalue equation for $\mathbf{L}$. But in the preceding subsection, we showed that the eigenvalue λ obeys Lotka's equation (9.13). So Lotka's equation, which becomes a real polynomial of degree $w + 1$ in λ if you multiply both sides of it by λ^{w+1} and move everything over to the left-hand side, determines the $w + 1$ eigenvalues of $\mathbf{L}$. Let us begin by studying those eigenvalues. (The following approach is due to Haldane 1927 and Charlesworth 1980.)

Let λ be an eigenvalue. Suppose first that λ is real and positive. Notice that the right-hand side of Lotka's equation (9.13) is a monotonically decreasing function of λ for λ real and positive; that the right-hand side approaches infinity as λ approaches 0; and that the right-hand side approaches 0 as λ approaches infinity. From this it follows immediately that there is one and only one value of λ for which the right-hand side is equal to 1. Hence there exists one and only one real and positive eigenvalue. Denote it λ_1.

In general λ will be complex. Write

$$\lambda = e^{a+ib} = e^a(\cos b + i \sin b) \tag{9.22}$$

Substituting (9.22) into (9.13) and separating the real and imaginary parts, we get

$$\sum_x e^{-a(x+1)} \cos[-b(x + 1)] l_x m_x = 1 \tag{9.23}$$

$$\sum_x e^{-a(x+1)} \sin[-b(x + 1)] l_x m_x = 0 \tag{9.24}$$

I am going to show that no other eigenvalue can possibly be greater than λ_1 in modulus, and that only under certain special circumstances can another eigenvalue even be as great as λ_1 in modulus.

Suppose that λ is greater than λ_1 in modulus. If λ is given by (9.22) and $\lambda_1 = e^{a_1}$, then $a > a_1$, so $e^{-a(x+1)} < e^{-a_1(x+1)}$ for all x. Therefore,

$$\sum_x e^{-a(x+1)} l_x m_x < \sum_x e^{-a_1(x+1)} l_x m_x = 1 \qquad (9.25)$$

But a cosine can never be greater than 1 in value. So this last equation contradicts (9.23). Therefore, no eigenvalue λ can exceed λ_1 in modulus.

Can we have another eigenvalue that is equal to λ_1 in modulus? If $|\lambda| = |\lambda_1|$, then the inequality in (9.25) is an equality, and (9.25) can be consistent with (9.23) only if $\cos[-b(x + 1)] = 1$ for all reproductive ages x, that is to say, for all ages x such that $m_x \neq 0$.

In order to investigate this last condition, we need to draw a distinction. You will recall that any positive integer n can be written as a unique product of prime factors: $n = p_1 p_2 \cdots p_r$, where each factor $p_i \neq 1$ is a prime number, that is, a positive integer that cannot itself be written as a product of two other positive integers $\neq 1$. Two positive integers are said to be *relatively prime* if they have no prime factors in common. Call the effective fertility *honest* if there are at least two ages x_1 and x_2 such that m_{x_1} and m_{x_2} are nonzero, and $(x_1 + 1)$ and $(x_2 + 1)$ are relatively prime. If this condition is not satisfied, call the effective fertility *dishonest*.

I am going to prove that for honest effective fertilities, any eigenvalue that is different from λ_1 has to be smaller than λ_1 in modulus. We already know that no other eigenvalue can be larger than λ_1 in modulus. It is possible to have $|\lambda| = |\lambda_1|$, but only if $\cos[-b(x + 1)] = 1$ for all reproductive ages x.

If the effective fertility is honest, this condition must hold for two ages x_1, x_2 such that $(x_1 + 1)$ and $(x_2 + 1)$ are relatively prime. So we have

$$\cos[-b(x_1 + 1)] = 1 \qquad (9.26)$$

$$\cos[-b(x_2 + 1)] = 1 \qquad (9.27)$$

Now, $\cos z = 1$ if and only if $z = 2n\pi$, where n is an integer. So (9.26) and (9.27) imply

$$-b(x_1 + 1) = 2n_1\pi \qquad (9.28)$$

$$-b(x_2 + 1) = 2n_2\pi \qquad (9.29)$$

where n_1 and n_2 are integers.

From (9.28),

$$b = -2n_1\pi/(x_1 + 1)$$

so (9.29) can be written

$$2n_1(x_2 + 1)\pi/(x_1 + 1) = 2n_2\pi$$

or

$$n_1(x_2 + 1)/(x_1 + 1) = n_2$$

Since n_2 is an integer, the left-hand side of this equation has to be an integer, too. But this can happen only if the $(x_1 + 1)$ in the denominator "cancels out" with some factors in the numerator. But $(x_1 + 1)$ and $(x_2 + 1)$ are relatively prime, so we can only get such a cancellation if $n_1 = n_3(x_1 + 1)$ for some integer n_3. But then (9.28) implies that b is an even multiple of π, whence λ is real and positive, i.e., is λ_1. Therefore, $|\lambda| = |\lambda_1|$ implies $\lambda = \lambda_1$.

To recapitulate: we have proved that *in the case of honest m_x, for every Leslie matrix there exists a unique real, positive eigenvalue λ_1, and every other eigenvalue is smaller than λ_1 in modulus.*

The only dishonest effective fertilities that we can realistically expect to encounter are *periodic* ones: meaning that m_x is nonzero only for ages x such that $x + 1 = ny$, with y a fixed positive integer and n a positive integer which can vary. Let us consider this case next.

There will still be a unique real and positive eigenvalue λ_1. Can there be another eigenvalue whose modulus is equal to that of λ_1? According to the first full paragraph after equation (9.25), for any such eigenvalue we must have $\cos[-b(x + 1)] = 1$ for all reproductive ages x.

This we can achieve by taking $b = 2\pi k/y$, with $k = 1, \ldots, y - 1$. Then for any reproductive age x, with $(x + 1) = ny$, $b(x + 1) = 2\pi kn$ and $\cos[-b(x + 1)] = 1$, even though b is not an even multiple of π, so λ is not real and positive.

Recapitulating, *in the case of periodic, m_x, for every Leslie matrix there exists a unique real, positive eigenvalue λ_1, and $y - 1$ other eigenvalues with the same modulus as λ_1; however, no eigenvalue is larger than λ_1 in modulus.* One can obtain similar results for other dishonest effective fertilities.

The eigenvalues of L determine the asymptotic behavior of solutions to (9.18), much as the eigenvalues of the community matrix determine the asymptotic behavior of multispecies models in a neighborhood of equilibrium (Section 5.1.1).

I have mentioned that every Leslie matrix L is diagonalizable (Leslie 1945). This implies that L has $w + 1$ linearly independent eigenvectors $\mathbf{v}_i$, $i = 0, \ldots, w$, one for each of the $w + 1$ roots of Lotka's equation

$$\mathbf{L}\mathbf{v}_i = \lambda_i \mathbf{v}_i \qquad i = 0, \ldots, w \qquad (9.30)$$

Consider the evolution of some initial density vector $\mathbf{n}_0$ under (9.18):

$$\left.\begin{aligned}
\mathbf{n}_1 &= \mathbf{L}\mathbf{n}_0 \\
\mathbf{n}_2 &= \mathbf{L}\mathbf{n}_1 = \mathbf{L}^2\mathbf{n}_0 \\
&\vdots \\
\mathbf{n}_t &= \mathbf{L}^t\mathbf{n}_0
\end{aligned}\right\} \qquad (9.31)$$

Any vector can be expanded as a linear combination of eigenvectors of L, so there exist constants a_i, $i = 0, \ldots, w$ such that

$$\mathbf{n}_0 = \sum_i a_i \mathbf{v}_i \qquad (9.32)$$

Therefore, using (9.31) and (9.32),

$$\mathbf{n}_t = \sum_i a_i \mathbf{L}^t \mathbf{v}_i \tag{9.33}$$

From (9.30),

$$\mathbf{L}^t \mathbf{v}_i = \lambda_i^t \mathbf{v}_i = \lambda_1^t (\lambda_i / \lambda_1)^t \mathbf{v}_i \tag{9.34}$$

where λ_1 is the unique real positive eigenvector of $\mathbf{L}$.

If $|\lambda_i| < |\lambda_1|$, then $(\lambda_i / \lambda_1)^t$ will approach 0 as t approaches infinity. Therefore, the components of $\mathbf{n}_0$ in the expansion (9.32) corresponding to eigenvectors λ_i whose modulus is less than that of λ_1 will become unimportant as t becomes large. If m_x is honest, any $\mathbf{n}_0$ for which $a_1 \neq 0$ in the expansion (9.32) (i.e., "almost all" initial vectors) will approach a multiple of the eigenvector $\mathbf{v}_1$ as t becomes large, under the mapping (9.31): $\mathbf{n}_t \cong a_1 \lambda_1^t \mathbf{v}_1$. Therefore, for large t, we will have $\mathbf{L}\mathbf{n}_t = \lambda_1 \mathbf{n}_t$—a stable age distribution.

Exercise 9.4. Using the system of equations (9.9), show that the fraction f_x of the population in each age class in the stable age distribution is

$$f_x = \lambda^{-x} l_x \bigg/ \sum_y \lambda^{-y} l_y \tag{9.35}$$

where l_x is the survivorship defined in equation (9.12).

If m_x is periodic or otherwise dishonest, there will be other eigenvalues equal in modulus to λ_1, and so other components in the expansion (9.32) will remain significant at large times. These other components will cause oscillations that do not damp out asymptotically. However, these oscillations will be superimposed upon exponential growth at a rate λ_1, as can be seen from (9.34). Therefore, even in this case, λ_1 is a measure of the overall growth of the population, hence of fitness (as we are using that term). So even in cases involving periodic effective fertilities, we expect λ_1, the unique real positive solution to Lotka's equation, to be maximized by selection.

How do these concepts of honesty and periodicity relate to biological data? Most realistic effective fertilities will be honest. Normally, either for organisms that do not breed seasonally or for seasonal breeders studied (as is natural) with a basic time interval equal to the time between breeding seasons, we expect that the effective fertility will be zero until some age class α, and then nonzero for all age classes equal to and greater than α. This will result, with an exception to be noted below, in at least two sequential ages classes, α and $\alpha + 1$, with nonzero effective fertility. Since $\alpha + 1$ and $\alpha + 2$ are relatively prime for any positive integer α, the effective fertility will be honest.

There seem only two biologically plausible ways in which things could be otherwise. The first is if, for a seasonal breeder, we take the basic time interval between successive measurements of the population to be some fraction of the time between successive breeding seasons. This can result in a periodic effective fertility. A population seen in this way will indeed oscillate, with peaks just after each breeding season.

The second way in which we might encounter dishonest effective fertilities is to look at semelparous organisms—those that breed only once, and then die. For instance, the Leslie matrix

$$
\mathbf{L} = \begin{bmatrix} 0 & 0 & 6 \\ \frac{1}{2} & 0 & 0 \\ 0 & \frac{1}{3} & 0 \end{bmatrix} \tag{9.36}
$$

originally studied by Bernardelli (1941), would describe an organism that needs 2 years to mature, then reproduces and dies. An effective fertility like this, nonzero only for one age class, is periodic in the sense of our definition.

9.2.2 Density-Dependent Selection

In the case of density-independent population growth, we have a rigorous theory which makes it clear how to obtain evolutionarily stable strategies. As we know from Part One, density-dependent population dynamics is a lot more complicated, for in that setting we have new and complicated possibilities such as multiple domains of attraction and chaos—and these complications are certainly not going to be ameliorated by adding age structure. For this reason the theory of density-dependent selection is still incomplete, even at the simple level of ESS's.

We can come up with a *plausible* way of approaching these problems within the restricted domain of equilibrium dynamics, and that is what I am going to do in this subsection.

The demographic parameters will be functions of both density $\mathbf{n}$ and strategy s: $m_x(\mathbf{n}, s)$, $l_x(\mathbf{n}, s)$. For a population containing a mixture of phenotypes, we will assume that the density $\mathbf{n}$ in $m_x(\mathbf{n}, s)$ and $l_x(\mathbf{n}, s)$ is the *total* (age-specific) density, summed over all phenotypes for each age class. In other words, we will allow the effective fertility and survival of a given phenotype to depend on the total number of individuals present, but not on the phenotypes of those individuals. This means that our formalism does not apply to frequency-dependent selection (Ayala and Campbell 1974). Frequency-dependent selection has to be treated on a case-by-case basis, and I am not going to discuss it here.

For each strategy s, we will assume there is an (age-specific) equilibrium, with density vector $\mathbf{n}^s$. Please bear in mind that the s here is a (superscripted) label for a strategy, not a power.

Consider a population all of whose members have adopted some one strategy s. If we could somehow hold all the m_x and l_x fixed at the values corresponding to some density $\mathbf{n}$, then the population would grow at a rate $\lambda(\mathbf{n}, s)$, with $\lambda(\mathbf{n}, s)$ given by Lotka's equation with l_x and m_x evaluated at $(\mathbf{n}, s)$. Assuming equilibrium dynamics, and dropping the notion of artificially holding the demographic parameters at chosen values, the density will tend to approach the equilibrium value $\mathbf{n}^s$. Since the density vector remains constant at this equilibrium value, we will have $\lambda(\mathbf{n}^s, s) = 1$.

Now consider, as in Section 9.1.1, a rare "mutant" strategy m trying to invade a population all of whose members have adopted an ESS * and which is at equilibrium, with density vector $\mathbf{n}^*$. Since the mutants are rare (relative to the ESS individuals), their density vector will be negligible relative to that of the ESS individuals, so the *total* density vector will be, to a good approximation, $\mathbf{n}^*$.

In order for * to be an ESS, it must be that m cannot invade, which will be the case if $\lambda(\mathbf{n}^*, m) < 1$. So * *is an ESS if it is a local maximum with respect to s of the function* $\lambda(\mathbf{n}, s)$ *when* $\mathbf{n}$ *is held fixed at* $\mathbf{n}^*$; that is, a local maximum with respect to s of the function $\lambda(\mathbf{n}^*, s)$.

This is often stated in a somewhat different, but equivalent, way, as follows. The quantity

$$R_0 = \sum_x l_x m_x \tag{9.37}$$

is called the *net reproductive rate* of a population. It is the expected number of female offspring produced by one female over her lifetime.

Exercise 9.5. Prove this last sentence.

For a population in equilibrium, we have $\lambda = 1$, whence $R_0 = 1$ from Lotka's equation. This makes perfect sense: in equilibrium the population precisely replaces itself all the time, so on the average each female will produce one daughter. Similarly, $\lambda > 1$ if and only if $R_0 > 1$, and $\lambda < 1$ if and only if $R_0 < 1$.

Exercise 9.6. Prove this last sentence.

Again imagining a population with density vector held artificially at $\mathbf{n}$, we can compute

$$R_0(\mathbf{n}, s) = \sum_x l_x(\mathbf{n}, s) m_x(\mathbf{n}, s)$$

and for a population at equilibrium we will have $R_0(\mathbf{n}^s, s) = 1$. Because $\lambda(\mathbf{n}, s) < 1$ if and only if $R_0(\mathbf{n}, s) < 1$, we can rephrase the discussion of ESS that we just went through in terms of R_0 instead of λ. Having done that, we will conclude that * *is an ESS if it is a local maximum with respect to s of the function* $R_0(\mathbf{n}, s)$ *when n is held fixed at* $\mathbf{n}^*$; that is, a local maximum with respect to s of the function $R_0(\mathbf{n}^*, s)$.

The quantity λ is really rather foreign to density-dependent population dynamics, so the formulation of ESS in terms of R_0 is the more elegant one in that setting, and the one that is normally stated. However, it is sometimes convenient for calculational purposes to be aware of the equivalent statement in terms of λ, for then one's calculations for the density-independent and density-dependent cases become similar in that one can maximize λ in both cases, with the added constraint that the optimal λ is equal to 1 in the density-dependent case. (However, it would be *wrong* to maximize R_0 in both cases; this quantity is *not* maximized under density independence.)

9.2.3 Continuous Time

A similar formalism can be propounded in continuous time. Let $m(x)$ be age-specific *fertility,* that is, let $m(x)dx$ be the expected number of females born per unit time to females whose ages are in the interval $(x, x + dx)$. Let $l(x)$ be age-specific survival, that is, the probability for a live-born individual to survive at least to age x. Then, assuming that $m(x)$ and $l(x)$ are density-independent and that a stable age distribution has been attained, one can show (Lotka 1913) that

$$dN/dt = rN \qquad (9.38)$$

where N is total density and r is a constant given by

$$1 = \int_0^w dx e^{-rx} l(x) m(x) \qquad (9.39)$$

which is, of course, just the continuous time version of Lotka's equation. (Notice that now we have x rather than $x + 1$ in the exponent.)

ADDITIONAL EXERCISES

9.7. Consider a mutant strategy m invading a population all of whose members have adopted some strategy s, in the context of density-independent population growth, as in Section 9.1.1. Suppose that at first one individual in 10,000 is a mutant. How many basic time intervals will it take until only one individual in 10,000 is a strategy s individual if $r^m - r^s = $ (a) 0.1, (b) 0.01, (c) 0.001, (d) 0.0001, (e) 0.00001?

9.8. (This exercise requires an elementary knowledge of the algebra of complex numbers.) In Exercise 9.4 you worked out the stable age distribution for density-independent population growth. Defining the components of a vector **n** by $n_x = f_x$, where f_x are given by (9.35), results, of course, in an eigenvector belonging to the eigenvalue λ_1 (the unique real and positive eigenvalue) of **L**: $\mathbf{Ln} = \lambda_1 \mathbf{n}$. How would you construct eigenvectors belonging to the other eigenvalues of **L**?

9.9. Starting from the initial density vector

$$\mathbf{n_0} = \begin{bmatrix} 1000 \\ 1000 \\ 1000 \end{bmatrix}$$

examine the development of the density vector for 20 basic time intervals into the future by multiplying with the Leslie matrix (9.36). Do the same for the Leslie matrix

$$\mathbf{L} = \begin{bmatrix} 0 & 1 & 3 \\ \frac{1}{2} & 0 & 0 \\ 0 & \frac{1}{3} & 0 \end{bmatrix}$$

Although you could in principle do these calculations by hand, you will probably want to write a computer program to do them.

Calculate all three eigenvalues for both of these Leslie matrices, using Lotka's equation and the closed-form expressions for the roots of cubics which can be found in most handbooks of mathematical formulae. Verify that in each case there is a unique real and positive eigenvalue λ_1. Verify that for the nonperiodic matrix λ_1 is larger in modulus than each of the other two eigenvalues, but for the periodic matrix all three eigenvalues have the same modulus.

Chapter 10

Cole's Dilemma

The idea of using Lotka's equation to relate the life-history parameters to population ecology and thus to study life-history adaptations mathematically seems to have first appeared in a paper of Lamont Cole (1954), which systematically explored this viewpoint.

Cole immediately hit upon a peculiar dilemma. Like so many interesting discoveries, this one stemmed simply from asking a question that no one had ever thought of asking before. Cole's question was: why do some plants and animals reproduce only once in a lifetime, while others reproduce repeatedly?

Fundamental though this distinction is, there did not even exist general terms to describe the two conditions, so Cole invented the word *semelparity* to describe the condition of multiplying only once in a lifetime (be it by fission, sporulation, or the production of eggs, seeds, or live young), and the word *iteroparity* to describe the contrasting condition.

Semelparity is common among bacteria, plants, and invertebrates but seems to occur only rarely in vertebrates (e.g., lamprey, pacific salmon, freshwater eels). There seems to be no known example of semelparity in birds, and only recently (Braithwaite and Lee 1979) has a mammalian example been published.

Drawing this distinction is not always as straightforward as one might think. For instance, insects as a group are thought of by many life historians as semelparous because, using a basic time interval of one year, they reproduce once per basic time interval. But Fritz, Stamp, and Halverson (1982) point out that many insects should actually be thought of as iteroparous, because when their activities are viewed from the perspective of a more appropriate time scale (say, for instance, a basic time interval of one day) it becomes evident that they actually reproduce several times in their life span. This issue is discussed in a more general context by Kirkendall and Stenseth (1985). Another subtlety, pointed out by Schmidt and Lawlor (1983), is that the seeds of many annual plants (semelparous in the usual scheme of things) remain viable for such long times that these plants become, in effect, iteroparous.

Intuitively, it would seem that iteroparity should confer a considerable gain in intrinsic growth rate, so that one would expect it to be selected for. To get a handle on this, Cole formulated the problem as follows. A semelparous species can increase its growth rate either by producing the same number of young per litter but producing, say, a litter every basic time unit (i.e., by becoming iteroparous), *or* by remaining semelparous but increasing the size of its litter. So one can ask: What is the increase in (semelparous) litter size that is required to produce the same gain in population growth rate that would accrue from switching to iteroparity with no change in fertility?

In order to simplify the discussion, Cole assumed that breeding began in both cases in age class zero. In addition, since he wanted to estimate the *maximum possible* gain from iteroparity, he assumed the ideal case of no mortality whatever, so that his iteroparous population literally (lives and) reproduces forever.

So, we have $l_x = 1$ for all x for both the semelparous strategy and the iteroparous one. For the semelparous strategy, we have $m_0 = b_s$ say, and $m_x = 0$ for all $x > 0$, while the iteroparous strategy corresponds to $m_x = b_i$ for all x. Then for the semelparous strategy Lotka's equation is

$$1 = \lambda_s^{-1} b_s$$

where λ_s is the semelparous growth rate, so

$$\lambda_s = b_s \qquad\qquad (10.1)$$

For the iteroparous strategy, Lotka's question reads

$$1 = \sum_{x=0}^{\infty} \lambda_i^{-(x+1)} b_i$$

where λ_i is the iteroparous growth rate, whence

$$\lambda_i = b_i + 1 \qquad\qquad (10.2)$$

Exercise 10.1. Prove equation (10.2). (Hint: The b_i factors out of Lotka's equation, of course, and we're left with a so-called geometric series. Look up "geometric series" in the old calculus text or in a table of mathematical formulas.)

Equating λ_s and λ_i, we get $b_s = b_i + 1$. But that says the maximum gain possible from switching to iteroparity is equivalent to merely increasing the semelparous litter size by one individual! To quote Cole, "It seems probable that a change in life history which would add one to the litter size would be more likely to occur than a change permitting repeated reproduction."

Cole goes on to make the pithy observation that this conclusion "arouses curiosity as to why iteroparity exists at all."

Murdoch (1966) pointed out that there is often a tradeoff between adult survival and reproductive effort, and in a variable environment an adult that decides not to reproduce may itself have a better chance of surviving to the next breeding season than would the young produced if the adult decided to breed, and Holgate (1967) and Murphy (1968) made similar remarks. Cole's dilemma was later considered within a quite general context of optimal allocation of resources, by Gadgil and Bossert (1970), Schaffer (1974a, 1974b), and Schaffer and Rosenzweig (1977), and we will get into this later on.

But first, we'll look at a much simpler observation, which seems to go at least part of the way to resolving the dilemma.

10.1 THE RATIO OF JUVENILE MORTALITY TO ADULT MORTALITY

Charnov and Schaffer (1973) called attention to what one might call the "eggs in one basket principle": if juvenile mortality is very high, semelparity may be a very risky strategy. They did the same calculation again, but now they assumed a juvenile survival rate C and an adult survival rate P.

The proportion of newborn animals surviving to the first census (effective fertility) is bC, where b is the number of offspring produced. So for the semelparous strategy we have $m_0 = b_s C$ and $m_x = 0$ for all $x > 0$, while for the iteroparous strategy we have $m_x = b_i C$ for all x. And for both strategies we have $l_0 = 1$ and $l_x = P^x$ for all $x > 0$. Putting these into Lotka's equation, we get

$$\lambda_s = b_s C \tag{10.3}$$

$$\lambda_i = b_i C + P \tag{10.4}$$

Exercise 10.2. Prove (10.3) and (10.4).

Equating λ_s and λ_i, we get this time $b_s = b_i + P/C$. Now the gain from switching to iteroparity is equivalent to increasing the average litter size by an amount that is equal to the ratio of adult survival to juvenile survival. So if juvenile mortality is too large relative to adult mortality (of course, mortality = $1 -$ survival), b_s will have to exceed physiological limits and iteroparity will be favored.

Everything we've done so far has been for density-independent population growth. It is instructive to extend the Charnov-Schaffer result to the case of density-dependent growth (Bulmer 1985).

Assume the population is regulated through juvenile mortality. I will work out the condition for the semelparous strategy to be unable to invade an equilibrium population of iteroparous individuals. Since the iteroparous population is at equilibrium, we must have $\lambda_i = 1$, whence, from (10.4),

$$b_i C + P = 1$$

$$C = (1 - P)/b_i \tag{10.5}$$

Therefore, from (10.3)

$$\lambda_s = (1 - P)b_s/b_i \qquad (10.6)$$

and the semelparous strategy will be unable to invade if

$$b_i/(1 - P) > b_s \qquad (10.7)$$

In the same way, one can show that the condition for a mutant iteroparous strategy to be unable to invade a semelparous equilibrium population is exactly the opposite of (10.7).

Exercise 10.3. Prove the previous sentence.

Therefore, iteroparity or semelparity will be selected for, depending upon whether $b_i/(1 - P)$ or b_s is larger.

This condition makes perfect sense if you work out the net reproductive rates (9.37) for the two strategies:

$$R_{0i} = Cb_i/(1 - P)$$

$$R_{0s} = Cb_s$$

Exercise 10.4. Prove these last two equations.

We already know that in the density-dependent case the ESS will have the larger R_0, so it is no surprise that now the winning strategy is simply the one for which each individual leaves more offspring over its whole lifetime.

Of course, the Charnov-Schaffer condition $b_i + P/C > b_s$ for iteroparity still applies in the density-dependent case; in that setting the juvenile survival C is determined by density-dependent processes instead of being a fixed parameter, but still, at the equilibrium densities the Charnov-Schaffer condition has to hold. Although our theory is still very unsophisticated at this point, one is tempted to go through the literature to see whether the Charnov-Schaffer prediction is at all expressed in nature. As it happens, Stearns (1976) has done just this.

The first problem he had to face is that our simple model of constant adult mortality per basic time unit is not very realistic, so we need a definition of "adult mortality" and also one of "juvenile mortality" (since the onset of reproduction may come later than age class 0) that can be applied under these more complicated circumstances. Stearns defines these as weighted averages. Then (with notation as in Section 9.2) his definition for the ratio of average juvenile mortality to average adult mortality is

$$\frac{\sum_{x=0}^{\alpha-1} n_{x,t}(1 - P_x)/\sum_{x=0}^{\alpha-1} n_{x,t}}{\sum_{x=\alpha}^{\infty} n_{x,t}(1 - P_x)/\sum_{x=\alpha}^{\infty} n_{x,t}}$$

where the time t can be chosen arbitrarily, and α is age at first reproduction.

Stearns then takes the number of breeding seasons as a measure of the "degree" of iteroparity. Plotting these two quantities (number of breeding seasons vs. the above ratio) results in Fig. 10.1.

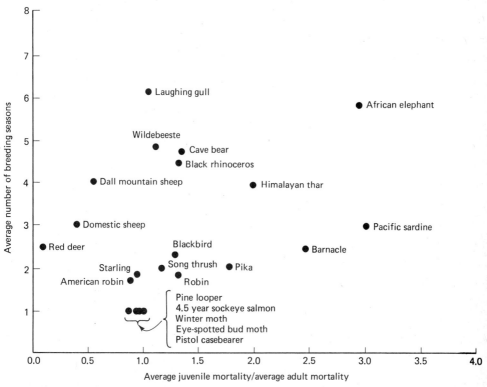

Figure 10.1 "Degree of iteroparity" vs. ratio of juvenile to adult mortality, both as defined in the text. (From Stearns 1976. Used with permission.)

Somewhat surprisingly, given our relative lack of sophistication at this point, there is a correlation here (Kendall's rank-correlation coefficient tau = 0.26, $P = 0.0375$).

10.2 LIFE-HISTORY EVOLUTION FROM THE STANDPOINT OF RESOURCE ALLOCATION

Each animal has certain resources available to it and has to partition these resources among many different needs. If we assume that this allocation is determined at least in part by an animal's genetic makeup, then we expect natural selection to act in such a way as to achieve an optimal allocation.

It is convenient to think of energy as the resource to be allocated. Certainly energy intake is a universal requirement of all animals, and just as certainly this energy is needed for all the basic functions of any animal. So I will speak of energy allocation in what follows, but we should not lose sight of the fact that for some populations (just how many it is exceedingly difficult to say) other resources (perhaps certain nutrients, or space, or time) may be just as, if not more, important.

The energy that an animal has assimilated goes into three broad categories of expenditure: *maintenance, growth,* and *reproduction.* Maintenance includes basal metabolism, and also metabolic expenditures for activity or thermal regulation. In addition, energy is sometimes stored for later use. I will neglect energy storage in what follows.

There is ample evidence of tradeoffs among these three categories (Gadgil and Bossert 1970, Townsend and Calow 1981). Thus animals grow little during their active hours when the demands of maintenance are high; much of their growth takes place while they are resting. Seasonal cycles of growth also reflect the tradeoff between maintenance and growth (Needham 1964). Tradeoffs involving reproduction are so important that I will devote a whole subsection to them.

10.2.1 Reproductive Effort and the Cost of Reproduction

An animal's proportionate investment in reproduction is called its *reproductive effort.* (This concept is due to Fisher 1930.) We can think of it as the proportion of assimilated energy that is expended on reproduction, but sometimes other investments need to be taken into account, too (as indicated three paragraphs ago).

Measuring reproductive effort is as difficult as it is important. Until about the early 1980s, almost all empirical work on reproductive effort was based on the ratio (by weight) of reproductive tissue to somatic tissue. But now there is a growing literature that tries to quantify reproductive effort by determining energy budgets.

In some cases the appropriate life-history strategy is simply for an animal to expend as much energy in reproduction as it possibly can. This would always be the thing to do, were it not for the fact that there are very often costs associated with reproduction. In general, the *cost of reproduction* (sometimes called *reproductive risk*) is any consequence of increased reproductive effort that would, all other things being equal, reduce fitness (again, this concept is due to Fisher 1930). Examples would be an increase in adult or juvenile mortality due to increased exposure to predators (as a result of increased reproductive activity), a decrease in adult growth rate due to increased reproductive effort (especially in fish and many invertebrates), or perhaps malnutrition due to increased reproductive activities.

Indeed, sometimes reproductive activities not only take assimilated energy away from growth and maintenance but actually cause a decrease in gross energy intake, hence in the total assimilated energy available for allocation among the three categories. It's well known that this is often the case for birds, and there is documentary evidence for such a negative energy balance in some marine mammals as well (Lavigne et al. 1982). Whether this is really a *cost* of reproduction is a more subtle question than one might think. One can argue (Norberg 1981), in the case of birds at least, that the associated weight loss, far from harming the parents, actually benefits them by making all that extra flying less costly!

Another complicating aspect of this matter is that the cost of reproduction may not necessarily be immediately apparent. Thus somatic costs are of evolutionary significance primarily insofar as they affect *future* prospects for reproduction. This will emerge very clearly when we get around to discussing semelparity and iteroparity from an energy-allocation point of view, but for now let's just bear in mind that it may be best for an animal to invest less in reproduction now, in order that it may survive until next year to reproduce again.

Additional reading on this topic can be found in Williams (1966, Chap. 6) and Townsend and Calow (1981).

10.2.2 Reproductive Effort and Fertility

Let E_x denote reproductive effort in the age class x. Then if E_x increases, so will the fertility m_x (usually); if we plot m_x as a function of E_x, we will get a curve that starts at the origin (m_x is zero if E_x is zero) and then increases monotonically (usually) up to the maximum value of E_x, which is 1. But what sort of shape will this curve have? Different biological circumstances will give different shapes. This section, which follows Schaffer and Rosenzweig (1977) very closely, will examine how the underlying biology is expressed in the shape of the curve $m_x(E_x)$.

If all offspring are equally expensive, and there is no prereproductive expenditure that must be made by the parent in order to "gear up" for breeding, and juvenile survival is independent of parental expenditure, then we expect a linear relation:

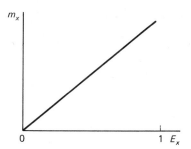

In many species the first young are the most expensive to produce, because of costly behavioral or physiological preludes to reproduction. Examples would be the establishment of a territory and building of a nest, or migration to spawning grounds. In this sort of situation $m_x(E_x)$ will be convex at low values of E_x:

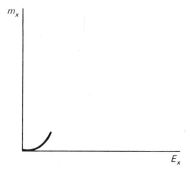

This convexity may continue to higher values of E_x, or it may not. Schaffer and Rosenzweig consider it most likely that m_x will level off at high efforts. This is especially likely if the survival of young declines with increasing (total) parental expenditure (remember that m_x is the number of newborn that survive to the next census). In fact, m_x could even *decline* at high efforts if, for example, the parents weaken or die before the young become independent (Lack 1966). Other factors that would have the same effect are increased predation on large clutches or within-clutch competition among the young. In any of these cases, we get the following sort of curve:

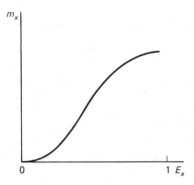

On the other hand, juvenile survival may be independent of, or even in- crease with, litter size. One might expect this in the case of organisms that produce so many offspring that the local predators are swamped. This could be the case for the periodic cicadas (Lloyd and Dybas 1966). The result could be convexity for all E_x:

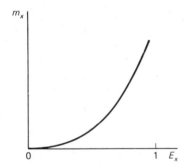

The convex shape of this last curve will be accentuated if the cost of preparing to breed is high.

On the other hand, if this cost is negligible, we may very well have concavity for small E_x's:

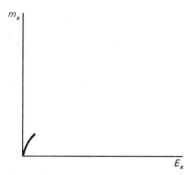

If juvenile survival declines with increasing parental investment, we will probably have concavity also for large E_x:

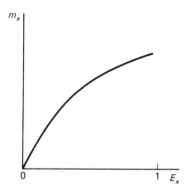

Again, if juvenile survival remains constant or increases with increasing litter size, we may get the following:

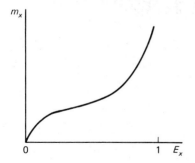

I mentioned at the beginning of this section that m_x will usually be an increasing function of E_x. Certainly the number of offspring produced will always be an increasing function. However, it can occur that juvenile survival decreases dramatically if E_x is too big, so much so that m_x *decreases* for large E_x. Lack's studies on avian clutch size, which I am about to discuss, provide a classic example of this effect.

At first, it might seem as if the very notion that natural selection optimizes must render it impossible to ever *measure* the curves I have been discussing: for the optimal strategy is just a single point on each of these curves, and if it is the optimal strategy that we observe, then we will never see the rest of the curve. However, selection is never quite that monolithic, and a natural population always contains quite a lot of variation. Within that variation, one may be able to discern at least a segment of each curve, and an optimum within that segment.

This is exactly what Lack (1954) and his followers have done with avian clutch size. If increased reproductive effort has no effect on adult survival or on future reproduction, then we have simply l_x = constant for each x, and $m_x = m_x(E_x)$ for each x. Under these circumstances it is easy to see, directly from Lotka's equation, that the optimum strategy is simply to maximize effective fertility m_x for each x.

Exercise 10.5. Prove the statement in the last sentence.

Of course, if m_x is a monotonically increasing function of E_x, such as I have been drawing up to now, then the optimal strategy is to produce as many eggs as is physiologically possible. It is well known that very few birds do this; most lay a definite number of eggs, and in many species if an egg is removed during the laying season it will be replaced (ask any poultry farmer), indicating a physiological capacity for producing more eggs.

You will recall from the definition of m_x in Section 9.2 that it is the number of offspring produced *that survive to the next census*. It contains an element of survival. Taking clutch size C (the number of eggs laid) as reproductive effort (as we are permitted by the discussion at the end of Section 10.2.3), we have then $m_x(C) = CS(C)$, where $S(C)$ is the probability for an egg to produce an individual that survives to the next census. If $S(C)$ declines sufficiently rapidly for large C, m_x can decrease for large C, so m_x will have a peak.

Table 10.1 shows that this is exactly what happens for a certain population of starlings (and this kind of data has been obtained for many other avian populations). If we agree to census 3 months after fledging, then the column of recoveries per 100 ringed is precisely $100S(C)$. It decreases strongly for large broods C—Lack attributes this to malnutrition in the nest. The column of recoveries per 100 broods ringed is $100CS(C)$, that is, $100m_x$. We see that the observed most frequent brood size, 5, is the one that maximizes m_x.

Table 10.1 amounts to a literal measurement of the functional dependence of m_x on reproductive effort. Another approach is to get at these functions (and also at the functional dependence by l_x on reproductive effort) indirectly, by reasoning carefully how changes in the underlying biology would affect the functions, deducing consequences of these changes for life histories, and doing comparative field or lab studies on organisms that differ from one another in just the right way. We will look at such a study (Schaffer and Gadgil 1975, Schaffer and Schaffer 1977) later in this section (not this subsection), when we get back to semelparity and iteroparity.

TABLE 10.1   SURVIVAL OF SWISS STARLINGS (*STURNUS VULGARIS*)
                 AFTER LEAVING NEST

Brood	Young ringed	Recoveries more than 3 months old	
		Per 100 young ringed	Per 100 broods ringed
	Early broods		
1	65		
2	328	1.8	3.7
3	1,278	2.0	6.1
4	3,956	2.1	8.3
5	6,175	2.1	10.4
6	3,156	1.7	10.1
7	651	1.5	
8	120	0.8	10.2
9, 10	28	0.0	
Total	15,757	1.94	
	Late broods		
1	44		
2	192	} 2.3	} 5.8
3	762		
4	1,564	2.2	8.9
5	1,425	1.8	8.8
6	438	1.4	8.2
7	49	0.0	
Total	4,474	1.99	

The young from early broods found dead before they were 2 months old included 0.21 percent of those ringed from broods of 1–4 young, 0.35 percent from broods of 5, and 0.43 percent from broods of 6–10 young. There were too few such recoveries from late broods to tabulate.

For similar data for England and Holland, see Lack (1948).

From Lack (1954).

10.2.3 The Optimization of Reproductive Effort

One can characterize a reproductive strategy by specifying a set of values for the reproductive efforts E_x for all age classes: $E_0, E_1, E_2, E_3, \ldots$. The optimal strategy is that choice for the whole set of E_x's that maximizes the finite rate of growth λ. Viewing life histories from the standpoint of resource allocation places reproductive effort very much in the center of things.

The fertility m_x for age class x depends upon the reproductive effort E_x of individuals in that age class. It also could depend upon the reproductive efforts that these individuals have exerted at earlier ages: $E_0, E_1, \ldots, E_{x-1}$. For example, an excessively large reproductive effort at any earlier age could have an adverse effect on m_x. But, except in the very unusual circumstance of extended parental care (that is, parental care that spans several breeding seasons), reproductive effort at any age later than x has no effect on m_x. So

$$m_x = m_x(E_1, \ldots, E_x) \tag{10.8}$$

Similarly, survival to age class x, l_x, depends on all the reproductive efforts through age class $x - 1$, but not (unless there is extended parental care) on any later efforts:

$$l_x = l_x(E_1, \ldots, E_{x-1}) \tag{10.9}$$

The modifications required when there is extended parental care have been discussed by Schaffer (1979).

Let x be any age class. Then we can write Lotka's equation as

$$1 = \sum_{t=0}^{x-1} \lambda^{-(t+1)} l_t m_t + \sum_{t=x}^{\infty} \lambda^{-(t+1)} l_t m_t \qquad (10.10)$$

Because of (10.8) and (10.9), the first sum in (10.10) depends on F_x only through
λ, while the second sum has a more complicated dependence on E_x. Therefore,
if we give this second sum a name, say u_x, and treat it as one object, we may
expect to arrive at something simple-looking. Actually, for reasons that will soon
become clear, I am going to call the second sum $l_x \lambda^{-x} v_x$ instead. So (10.10) is

$$1 = \sum_{t=0}^{x-1} \lambda^{-(t+1)} l_t m_t + l_x \lambda^{-x} v_x \qquad (10.11)$$

Differentiating (10.11) with respect to E_x, we get

$$0 = \sum_{t=0}^{x-1} -(t+1) \lambda^{-(t+2)} (\partial \lambda / \partial E_x) l_t m_t$$

$$+ l_x [-x \lambda^{-(x+1)} (\partial \lambda / \partial E_x) v_x + \lambda^{-x} (\partial v_x / \partial E_x)]$$

which we can write

$$\partial v_x / \partial E_x = [x \lambda^{-1} v_x + (\lambda^x / l_x) \sum_{t=0}^{x-1} (t+1) \lambda^{-(t+2)} l_t m_t] (\partial \lambda / \partial E_x) \qquad (10.12)$$

Of course, the derivatives here have to be partial derivatives, since we have a
dependence on several different variables E_x, $x = 0, \ldots, w$.

What does (10.12) tell us? The square bracket on the right-hand side of
(10.12) is guaranteed to be positive. So the sign of $\partial v_x / \partial E_x$ is always the same
as the sign of $\partial \lambda / \partial E_x$. Therefore, *for each x, the reproductive effort E_x that locally
maximizes λ also locally maximizes v_x.* (A little thought will make it clear that
this conclusion holds both for maxima that occur at intermediate values of E_x
and for those that occur at the "end points" $E_x = 0$ and $E_x = 1$.)

The quantities v_x were first defined by the prescient Sir Ronald Fisher
(1930), who called v_x the *reproductive value of a female aged x.*

One can understand the biological significance of reproductive value as
follows. First, define the *value* of any organism to be the fraction of the population
which that organism represents. For instance, the value of each organism in a
population of 1000 is $1/1000$. Now define *reproductive value* to be *the total
value of an organism's expected future offspring relative to its own current value.*

Let's calculate the reproductive value of a female just entering age class x
in a population that has achieved a stable age distribution, hence is growing
exponentially. Suppose the population density was N when this female was first
censused. Then the population density is $N\lambda^x$ now. Hence the current value of
our female just entering age class x is $1/N\lambda^x$.

The expected number of offspring produced by this female in age class t

($\geq x$) that survive to be censused for the first time when our female is entering age class $t + 1$, is the probability for a female to survive into age class t if she is a member of age class x, which is l_t/l_x, times the expected fertility in age class t, which is m_t; this product is $(l_t/l_x)m_t$. When these offspring are first censused the population density is $N\lambda^{(t+1)}$, so each of them has value $1/N\lambda^{(t+1)}$. Thus the total value of all offspring produced by our female in age class t is $(l_t/l_x)m_t/N\lambda^{(t+1)}$.

To get the total value of *all* expected offspring, we have to sum this over all future times:

$$\text{Total value of expected offspring} = \sum_{t=x}^{\infty} (l_t/l_x)m_t/N\lambda^{(t+1)}$$

We've already found that the current value of our female is $1/N\lambda^x$, so her reproductive value when she enters age class x, as defined above, is

$$v_x = \left[\sum_{t=x}^{\infty} (l_t/l_x)m_t/N\lambda^{(t+1)} \right] \Big/ (1/N\lambda^x)$$

$$v_x = (\lambda^x/l_x) \sum_{t=x}^{\infty} \lambda^{-(t+1)} l_t m_t \tag{10.13}$$

which is the same as our original definition of v_x, just before equation (10.11).

Fisher (1930), contemplating the question: "To what extent will persons of age x, on the average, contribute to the ancestry of future generations?" came up with reproductive value, and felt intuitively that "the direct action of Natural Selection must be proportional to this contribution." Williams (1966b) gave a hand-waving argument why natural selection should optimize reproductive value, but the first published formal proof of this statement seems to have come only in 1974 (Schaffer 1974a). Schaffer's proof was somewhat more opaque than the one I have given above.

One can give several other formulations for the biological meaning of reproductive value. Fisher (1930) himself called it "the present value of future offspring." Wilson and Bossert (1971) define it as "the number of female offspring produced at this moment by females of age x or over, divided by the number of females which are age x at this moment." MacArthur and Wilson (1967), in their book on biogeography, put it this way: "In biogeographic terms, the reproductive value v_x of an x-year-old may be defined as the expected size of a colony (at some remote future time) founded by a propagule of x-year-olds. We can then divide this number by the size of a simultaneous colony founded by a propagule of newborn individuals to make the definition independent of the exact time interval before the count is made." The definition that I gave originally (italicized phrase on p. 278) is adapted from Roughgarden's (1979) book.

Typically, reproductive value at first increases monotonically with age, reaches a peak (at about the age of first reproduction), and declines thereafter, as can be seen in Fig. 10.2. If you think about the definition of reproductive value, it should become clear why this behavior is typical.

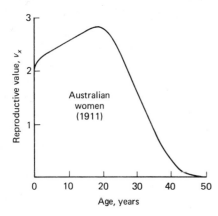

Figure 10.2 Reproductive value plotted against age for Australian women, about 1911. (From Fisher 1958.)

Part of the difference between having a mathematical theorem for the optimization of v_x and having the sort of intuitive approach that Fisher brought to this particular topic (though he also did a lot of mathematical work on other things) is that our theorem tells us in *precisely which sense* v_x is optimized: the optimal value of reproductive effort E_x is that which maximizes v_x. Adjustments in E_x do *not* maximize, say, v_{x+1} (but adjustments in E_{x+1} do).

We begin to see how complicated and interrelated all these adaptive adjustments are: if E_x is adjusted to optimize v_x, this affects v_{x+1}, too, and not necessarily in an optimal way. So E_{x+1} has to be readjusted to optimize v_{x+1}, but this affects v_x, so E_x has to be readjusted again, and so on. . . .

There's another advantage to having a precise mathematical formulation, and that is that since we know precisely what's behind the result, we also know under which circumstances it may cease to be true. Our hypothesis was the dependences (10.8) and (10.9) of m_x and l_x on the parameters $E_0, E_1, \ldots$. If for some reason (10.8) or (10.9) were violated, then reproductive value would no longer be optimized—and *only* if (10.8) or (10.9) is violated will reproductive value not be optimized. I've already mentioned that extended parental care could cause this; it's difficult to think of anything else that might.

One final remark: the parameters E_x were introduced as reproductive efforts, and it's emminently believable that reproductive efforts would have the properties (10.8) and (10.9), at least in the vast majority of animal species. But all we've really used in our proof are the properties (10.8) and (10.9); so the E's could just as well be *any other parameters* that happen to have these properties, and with respect to which we expect λ to be maximized.

This is rather important. It is elegant and convenient to formulate the theory in terms of reproductive effort as defined above, and this entity is certainly a meaningful and important intellectual construct, but it is very difficult to decide precisely how to measure it. On the other hand, it is not hard to find quantities that clearly get at the basic idea of reproductive effort—which are bigger if the organism is investing more in reproduction—and which are easily measured. (The number of offspring produced would be an example in many cases.) These quantities will almost always obey (10.8) and (10.9) if we use them for "E_x," and so the whole theory that we are going to develop could just as well be stated in terms of one of these surrogates for reproductive effort. This makes it far more practicable to relate the theory to observations than it would be if we had to rely upon more specific properties of reproductive effort in order to develop a valid theory.

Caswell (1982a, 1982b) has extended the formalism to apply to organisms with complex life cycles, where some parameter other than age (such as size or developmental stage) might provide the appropriate demographic classification.

10.2.4 Residual Reproductive Value and the Tradeoff Between Present and Future Reproduction

We can rewrite (10.13) as follows:

$$v_x = \lambda^{-1}m_x + \lambda^{-1}v_x^* = \lambda^{-1}(m_x + v_x^*) \qquad (10.14)$$

where

$$v_x^* = (\lambda^{x+1}/l_x) \sum_{t=x+1}^{\infty} \lambda^{-(t+1)}l_t m_t \qquad (10.15)$$

Exercise 10.6. Prove (10.15). Show also that

$$v_x^* = P_x v_{x+1} \qquad (10.16)$$

The quantity v_x^* was called *residual reproductive value* by Williams (1966b), who was the first to point out the utility of the decomposition (10.14). In (10.14), reproductive value is written as a sum of contributions from reproduction now, m_x, and from reproduction in the future, v_x^*. This shows very explicitly the *tradeoff* which is involved in optimizing v_x: for an increase in m_x, which will generally be at the expense of maintenance and/or growth, will generally cause a decrease in v_x^*, and vice versa. We do need to keep in mind, though, that the tradeoff at any one age is affected by adjustments in reproductive efforts at other ages, as mentioned at the end of Section 10.2.3. Pianka (1976) discusses life-history evolution rather extensively in these terms. I will follow here a slightly different approach, due to Schaffer (1974a) and Schaffer and Rosenzweig (1977).

The idea here is to make some assumptions about the functional dependencies of the demographic parameters m_x and l_x that enable us to separate out the effects of reproductive effort at each age, while still retaining a good measure of generality. Schaffer proceeds as follows.

First, he assumes that any cost in terms of adult survival depends only on current reproductive expenditures: $P_x = P_x(E_x)$. This says that we will neglect the possibility that excessive reproduction weakens an organism so much that its chances for survival even in future years are adversely affected.

He assumes that effective fertility in any given age class x amounts to investing some portion $b_x(E_x)$ (dependent only on reproductive effort in age class x) of a "reproductive capital" $G_x(E_0, \ldots, E_{x-1})$, accumulated over all past age classes, hence dependent only on *earlier* reproductive efforts:

$$m_x = b_x(E_x)G_x(E_0, \ldots, E_{x-1})$$

The reproductive capital G_x is an expression of physiological capacity. Previous somatic growth will frequently be an important component of this capacity, hence the notation G.

It is assumed that the rate of accumulation of reproductive capital in each age class depends only on the reproductive effort made in that age class. That is,

$$G_x = g_{x-1}(E_{x-1})G_{x-1}$$

where $g_{x-1}(E_{x-1})$ is monotone nonincreasing. Since there can be no accumulation in a given year if all resources are expended on reproduction, $g_x(1) = 1$. Since this last equation holds for each x, G_x can be written as a product of functions of the individual reproductive efforts:

$$G_x(E_0, \ldots, E_{x-1}) = \prod_{y=0}^{x-1} g_y(E_y)$$

Notice that the proportionate investment b_x is allowed to vary with age, in the sense that, for two different ages x and y, $b_x(E_x)$ can be a different function of E_x than is $b_y(E_y)$ a function of E_y. This is because the number of offspring produced by an x-year-old and surviving to the next census depends not only on the amount of energy allocated to reproduction by the parent but also on other things such as experience, social standing, and health, which vary with age and are at least partly independent of the parent's previous reproductive history.

Putting this all together, we are going to assume

$$\left.\begin{aligned}
P_x &= P_x(E_x) \\[4pt]
m_0(E_0) &= b_0(E_0) \\[4pt]
m_x(E_0, \ldots, E_x) &= G_x(E_0, \ldots, E_{x-1})b_x(E_x) \\[4pt]
&= b_x(E_x)\prod_{y=0}^{x-1} g_y(E_y) \qquad x > 0
\end{aligned}\right\} \qquad (10.17)$$

The assumptions implicit in equations (10.17) and just discussed are only mildly restrictive, and they permit the definition of a modified reproductive value that depends on previous reproductive efforts only through λ. To see this, use the definition (10.17) in equation (10.13):

$$\begin{aligned}
v_x &= (\lambda^x/l_x) \sum_{t=x}^{\infty} \lambda^{-(t+1)}l_t \prod_{y=0}^{t-1} g_y(E_y)b_t(E_t) \\[6pt]
&= \prod_{y=0}^{x-1} g_y(E_y)(\lambda^x/l_x) \sum_{t=x}^{\infty} \lambda^{-(t+1)}l_t \prod_{y=x}^{t-1} g_y(E_y)b_t(E_t)
\end{aligned} \qquad (10.18)$$

If you look back at (10.17) you will recognize the product that I have moved out in front of everything else; it's just $G_x(E_0, \ldots, E_{x-1})$. Notice next that the expression that is multiplied by G_x has the advertised property of depending only on E_z's with $z \geq x$.

Exercise 10.7. Prove that, if $P_x = P_x(E_x)$, then l_t/l_x, $t \geq x$, depends only on the reproductive efforts E_z with $z \geq x$.

So let's try using this quantity as our modified reproductive value; we'll call it w_x:

$$v_x = G_x(E_0, \ldots, E_{x-1})w_x \qquad (10.19)$$

We can deal with equation (10.18) just as we dealt with (10.13) to get (10.14), splitting off the first term in the sum:

$$v_x = (G_x(E_0, \ldots, E_{x-1}) \times [\lambda^{-1}b_x(E_x)$$

$$+ (\lambda^x/l_x) \sum_{t=x+1}^{\infty} \lambda^{-(t+1)}l_t \prod_{y=x+1}^{t-1} g_y(E_y)b_t(E_t)]$$

$$= G_x(E_0, \ldots, E_{x-1})\lambda^{-1}[b_x(E_x) + g_x(E_x)P_x(E_x)w_{x+1}] \qquad (10.20)$$

We can abbreviate this as

$$v_x = G_x(E_0, \ldots, E_{x-1})\lambda^{-1}Q_x \qquad (10.21)$$

or

$$Q_x = \lambda v_x/G_x \qquad (10.22)$$

where

$$Q_x = b_x(E_x) + g_x(E_x)P_x(E_x)w_{x+1} \qquad (10.23)$$

Now, we have already found that the optimal value of E_x is the one that maximizes v_x. Of course, this optimal value of E_x also maximizes λ (that was our starting point!). But if the optimal value of E_x maximizes v_x and λ, one can show that it also maximizes λv_x. Since G_x is independent of E_x, it follows from this together with equation (10.22) that the optimal value of E_x *also* maximizes the quantity Q_x defined by (10.20).

Exercise 10.8. Prove the last two statements "also maximizes" in the preceding paragraph.

The optimization of reproductive value v_x by the action of natural selection on E_x is completely equivalent to optimization of Q_x. Schaffer frames his theory in terms of Q_x because in it the reproductive efforts at different ages are factored out in a somewhat manageable way.

Our whole discussion in Section 10.2.2 of the biological significance of the shape of the curve $m_x(E_x)$ carries over without any modifications to b_x. Now let's think in the same way about how the other part of Q varies with E_x.

Again I will follow Schaffer and Rosenzweig (1977) rather closely. Their analysis is based on a theorem of Taylor et al. (1974) that states that if we hold λ constant at its optimal value, then the optimal E_x still maximizes v_x (hence Q_x) for each x. Since w_{x+1} depends on E_x only through λ, when the optimization is taken in the sense of Taylor et al. w_{x+1} is effectively a constant. So in order to investigate the curves $g_x P_x w_{x+1}$ we need only think about the effects of different biological conditions on the functions $g_x(E_x)$ and $P_x(E_x)$.

First, it is clear that both g_x and P_x are nonincreasing functions of E_x, so that $g_x P_x w_{x+1}$ will also be a nonincreasing function.

Suppose, for instance, that the main effect of increased reproductive effort is to weaken the organism. Then we expect a gradual decrease in P_x and perhaps also g_x, so that we might have something like this:

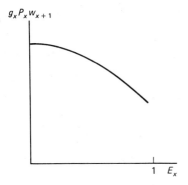

Or it may be that expenditures beyond a certain point E_c render an animal suddenly vulnerable to predators or disease, which might yield a curve like this one:

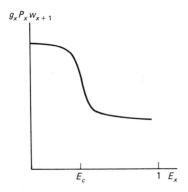

Or breeding might involve an initial risk that is largely independent of reproductive effort, such as increased exposure to predators while building a nest. This would produce an initial drop:

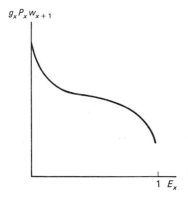

This initial cost might even be so great (perhaps for migratory salmon returning to spawn in their home stream) as to make $g_x P_x w_{x+1}$ entirely convex:

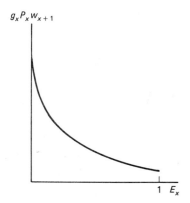

Combining these curves with the ones in Section 10.2.2 (interpreted as being for b_x) gives us a complete picture of how the underlying biology affects the tradeoff between b_x and $g_x P_x w_{x+1}$.

10.2.5 The Tradeoff at One Age

We can draw the curves for b_x and for $g_x P_x W_{x+1}$ on one graph, and see what their sum looks like. Recall from our discussion of Q_x, equation (10.23), that this sum is maximized by selection.

First, suppose (for biological reasons explicated in Sections 10.2.2 and 10.2.4) that both curves are concave:

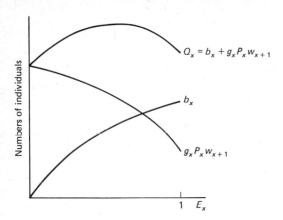

Suppose further that the curve $b_x(E_x)$ has pretty much leveled off by $E_x = 1$, so

$$\left. db_x/dE_x \right|_{E_x=1} < \left. -d(g_x P_x w_{x+1})/dE_x \right|_{E_x=1} \tag{10.24}$$

and that the initial decrease of $g_x P_x w_{x+1}$ at $E_x = 0$ is rather slight, so

$$\left. db_x/dE_x \right|_{E_x=0} > \left. -d(g_x P_x w_{x+1})/dE_x \right|_{E_x=0} \tag{10.25}$$

Then the curves look pretty much as I have drawn them. Under these conditions, the slope of $Q(E_x) = b_x + g_x P_x w_{x+1}$ is positive at $E_x = 0$ [from (10.25)] and negative at $E_x = 1$ [from (10.24)], so the maximum value of Q, hence the optimal E_x, must occur at some intermediate value of E_x (not at $E_x = 0$ or at $E_x = 1$).

Condition (10.24) might not hold if, for instance, reproductive effort E_x at age x had little or no effect on future "reproductive value" $g_x P_x w_{x+1}$. Then Q would have its maximum at $E_x = 1$. Condition (10.25) might not hold if changes in E_x had a much stronger effect on $g_x P_x w_{x+1}$ than on b_x; then the optimal solution would be $E_x = 0$. Either of these cases seem rather extreme, though. The typical case when both curves are concave is for the optimal E_x to lie somewhere *between* 0 and 1. It is impossible for both (10.24) and (10.25) to be violated if both curves are concave.

Iteroparous breeders are those for which the optimal reproductive effort lies at some intermediate point between 0 and 1, at least once they have commenced breeding and with the possible exception of their last breeding (at which point maximal reproductive effort might be called for). So we expect iteroparity to be associated with those biological characteristics that make both of these curves concave, with the exceptions noted in the preceding paragraph.

Similarly, one can argue that the typical behavior when both curves are convex

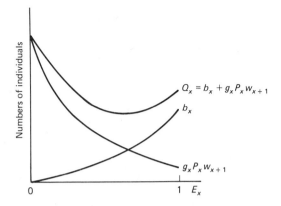

is for the optimal reproductive effort to occur at an end point: either $E_x = 0$ or $E_x = 1$. In fact, this is more than just "typical": one can prove that in this case the optimum must be at one of the end points.

Exercise 10.9. Prove this. (Use the fact that "both curves are convex" means

$$d^2 b_x / dE_x^2 > 0 \quad \text{and} \quad d^2(g_x P_x w_{x+1})/dE_x^2 > 0$$

for all x: $0 \le E_x \le 1$. What condition would the second derivative of Q have to obey at an intermediate optimum?)

So with both curves convex at all ages the optimal strategy will be "all or nothing" at each age. This is how the curves might look for a semelparous breeder.

Even in conjunction with concavity elsewhere in one or both curves, convexity at the upper end of the b_x curve will tend to push that curve high enough at $E_x = 1$ to favor an "all out" optimal strategy $E_x = 1$. Schaffer and Schaffer (1977) (discussed also by Schaffer and Gadgil 1975) have used this to shed some light on a rather subtle difference between the desert plants *Yucca* and *Agave*.

These two genera are quite closely related, similar in basic morphology, and often occurring together in the same habitats. But most species of *Yucca* are iteroparous, while most *Agave* die after a single flowering. Within a population, agaves appear to compete with one another for pollinators (or at least, it appears this way to Schaffer and Schaffer), which prefer the taller flower stalks. Presumably the bees seek out the larger inflorescences in order to minimize the energy expended between visits to successive flowers. Schaffer and Schaffer suggest that pollinator preference for the taller stalks would bow the fertility curve upward for high effort values, favoring semelparity. On the other hand, the moths that pollinate the iteroparous *Yuccas* "do not appear to favor the taller spikes," according to Schaffer and Schaffer.

Table 10.2 substantiates this interpretation by listing a certain measure of competition for pollinators for the semelparous ("big-bang") and iteroparous species. The measure of "competition" is described in the table footnote; it essentially measures to what extent a height above the average (within a species) improves a plant's chance of being fertilized. Notice especially that the "oddball"

TABLE 10.2   INTENSITY OF COMPETITION FOR POLLINATORS
IN POPULATIONS OF YUCCAS AND AGAVES

Species	Big-bang N	Reproductive strategy Competition	Species	Non-big-bang and repeated breeding N	Competition
Agave schottii	95	0.22	*Agave parviflora*	193	−0.01
A. utahensis	86	0.24	*Yucca standleyi*	100	0.00
A. deserti	84	0.15	*Y. utahensis*	162	0.01
A. chrysantha	20	0.18	*Y. glauca*	117	−0.01
A. palmeri	48	0.32	*Y. elata*	84	0.01
Yucca whipplei	23	0.08			
Mean		0.21	Mean		0.00
Standard deviation		0.09	Standard deviation		0.01

Competition was measured as the slope of a regression line of percent flowers fertilized plotted against $(H - \bar{H})/\bar{H}$, where H is stalk height of the plant in question and $\bar{H}$ is mean stalk height in the population. N is the sample size. Note that within populations of big-bang reproducers, competition is significantly more intense ($t = 5.14$; $p(t) < 0.0005$, one-sided) than within populations of repeat breeders.
From Schaffer and Gadgil 1975.

species *Yucca whipplei* and *Agave parviflora* fit into Schaffer and Schaffer's scheme quite nicely.

Another very interesting insight that comes out of this formalism is that the simple dichotomy "semelparous or iteroparous" may be too crude. Consider, for instance, the following situation:

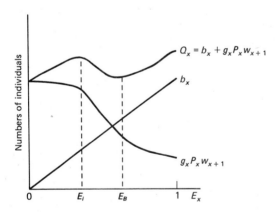

In this case we have two local maxima of Q, hence two evolutionarily stable strategies for the one adaptive system. The direction evolution will take, and the strategy it will end up at, depends upon the starting point, in particular with regard to the "breakpoint" value E_B of reproductive effort. The multiple domains of attraction that we are by now accustomed to in population systems can occur in microevolution as well.

Thus any reproductive effort that is smaller than E_B will tend to evolve to the intermediate (probably iteroparous) optimum E_i, while a reproductive effort that is larger than E_B will evolve toward the "all-out" (perhaps semelparous) optimum at $E_x = 1$.

It would appear that allopatric populations of the same species could evolve profoundly different life histories, but I am not aware of any evidence that this has happened. On the other hand, there are instances of closely related species that have evolved very different life histories. One example of this, cited by Schaffer (1974a), occurs among the Salmonidae, the genus *Salmo* being everywhere iteroparous, whereas *Oncorhynchus* is nearly always semelparous. It could be that alternative ESS's within the same adaptive system played a role in the evolution of this family.

10.2.6 The Joint Optimization of Reproductive Effort at All Ages

The tradeoff at each age, discussed in the previous subsection, is affected—through λ and through w_{x+1}—by the tradeoffs at all other ages, as I have mentioned. The resultant problem in joint optimization has been discussed by Schaffer (1974a) and especially by Schaffer and Rosenzweig (1977). This gets rather complicated mathematically, and up to now has been little applied. Besides, the main thing one needs to understand in order to see how the specific biology of a given situation can influence the life history is the tradeoff at each age. Therefore, I am not going to discuss the joint optimization in any detail.

This does not complete the story of Cole's dilemma, though it does complete this chapter. The rest of the story involves environmental fluctuations. Since optimal strategies depend very much upon survival probabilities, random fluctuations in these probabilities have got to be important for the evolution of itero- or semelparity, and for life-history theory in general. I will, however, defer discussion of this topic until Chapter 13.

ADDITIONAL EXERCISES

10.10. Compute the age-specific reproductive value v_x corresponding to the Leslie matrix (9.36). Do the same for the Leslie matrix introduced in Exercise 9.9.

10.11. Prove the theorem of Taylor et al., used in Section 10.2.4, to the effect that if we hold λ constant at its optimum value, then the optimal E_x still maximizes v_x, for each x. [Hint: Differentiate (10.10) with respect to E_x.]

Chapter 11

The Timing of Reproduction

In this chapter we will be concerned with things like: When in its lifetime should an animal start reproducing? How long should it go on reproducing? When should it reach its peak reproduction? Also: which of these "decisions" is the most important, for instance, will an animal enhance its fitness more by starting reproduction earlier in life or by continuing to reproduce for a longer period of time?

Some of these questions were addressed already by Cole (1954), but the seminal paper in this particular area seems to have been a somewhat later work by Lewontin (1965).

Lewontin worked in a continuous time formalism. Recall (Section 9.2.3) that in this setting Lotka's equation takes the form

$$1 = \int_0^\infty dx e^{-rx} l(x) m(x) \tag{11.1}$$

Because $l(x)$ and $m(x)$ occur in Lotka's equation as the product $l(x)m(x)$, Lewontin thought in terms of this product, which he called the *reproductive function V*:

$$V(x) = l(x)m(x) \tag{11.2}$$

Lewontin assumed an idealized triangular form for $V(x)$, which has the twin virtues of simplifying calculations and of emphasizing the importance of certain basic parameters:

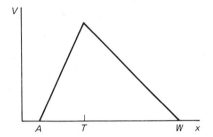

The parameters A (age when first offspring is produced) and W (age when last offspring is produced) require no comment. The turnover point T is a rough measure of how reproductive effort is distributed over the animal's lifetime. If T is relatively close to A, reproduction is concentrated early in life; if it is relatively close to W, reproduction is concentrated late in life; and if it is about midway between A and W, reproduction is spread out more evenly over the animal's lifetime. Of course, the net reproductive rate R_0 (expected total number of offspring produced over a lifetime) is just

$$R_0 = \int_0^\infty V(x)dx \qquad (11.3)$$

As examples of real $V(x)$ functions for which the triangular form is a fairly reasonable approximation, Lewontin gives the data shown in Figs. 11.1 and 11.2, for *Drosophila serrata*. I will discuss these examples a little bit later.

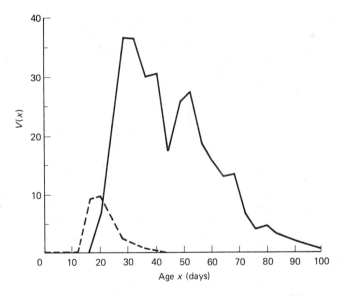

Figure 11.1 Observed $V(x)$ functions for two races of *D. serrata*, one at 20°C (solid line) and one at 25°C (dashed line). Both $V(x)$ functions give the same value of r because of the overriding importance of leftward displacement of the dashed curve. Difference in total offspring is a factor of 10. (From Lewontin 1965.)

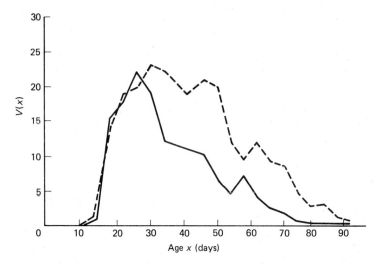

Figure 11.2   Observed $V(x)$ for two races of *D. serrata* at 25°C. Both $V(x)$ functions give the same value of *r* because of lack of contribution of later ages to the rate of increase. (From Lewontin 1965.)

It is easy to write down the analytic form corresponding to the triangular reproductive function $V(x)$. It is

$$V(x) = \begin{cases} 2R_0(x-A)/(T-A)(W-A) & A \le x \le T \\ 2R_0(W-x)/(W-T)(W-A) & T \le x \le W \\ 0 \text{ otherwise} \end{cases} \quad (11.4)$$

Exercise 11.1.   Prove (11.4).

We can substitute $V(x)$, in the explicit form (11.4), into Lotka's equation (11.1) and integrate, which yields

$$(W-A)r^2/2R_0 = (e^{-rA} - e^{-rT})/(T-A) + (e^{-rW} - e^{-rT})/(W-T) \quad (11.5)$$

Exercise 11.2.   Prove (11.5).

I am going to analyze the model using a different procedure from that of Lewontin. Using implicit differentiation, with the total number R_0 of offspring held constant, we obtain from (11.5)

$$\partial r/\partial A = [r^2/2R_0 - re^{-rA}/(T-A) + (e^{-rA} - e^{-rT})/(T-A)^2]/X$$

$$\partial r/\partial W = [-r^2/2R_0 - re^{-rW}/(W-T) - (e^{-rW} - e^{-rT})/(W-T)^2]/X$$

$$\partial r/\partial T = [re^{-rT}(W-A)/(W-T)(T-A) - (e^{-rA} - e^{-rT})/(T-A)^2$$
$$+ (e^{-rW} - e^{-rT})/(W-T)^2]/X \quad (11.6)$$

where

$$X = (W - A)r/R_0 + (Ae^{-rA} - Te^{-rT})/(T - A)$$
$$+ (We^{-rW} - Te^{-rT})/(W - T)$$

Exercise 11.3. Prove this last set of equations.

For any given set of timings A, T, W we can use (11.5) to find the corresponding value of R_0. Then we can use (11.6) to evaluate the relative effects on r of changes in timing.

Our choice of one of the timings A, T, W is arbitrary, reflecting a choice of units (recall Section 2.4.2). So I chose $A = 1$. Then the choice of W, relative to A, depends upon whether maturity comes relatively late or relatively early in life: I chose $W = 2$, 10, or 40. Finally, the choice of T relative to A and W depends upon how reproductive output is distributed over a lifetime: I took $T = A + 0.1 (W - A)$, $T = A + 0.5(W - A)$, or $T = A + 0.9(W - A)$. Figure 11.3 plots each of the derivatives vs. r, for A, T, $W = 1$, 5.5, 10. The qualitative features I will discuss turn out similarly for other choices of A, T, W.

We see that in general earlier reproduction is beneficial. Selection is especially strong on age at maturity, and relatively weak on age at reproductive senescence. The early portion of the reproductive schedule is important; late reproduction is considerably less so. This has been offered as one possible explanation for the phenomenon of aging: whatever may be the cause of that gradual diminution of capacities, there is little selection for any natural mechanism of repair to counter it.

Selection on timing in general is stronger the more rapidly a population is growing. Figure 11.3 can be viewed as a depiction of the "r-K selection" continuum (but see Section 13.5 as to whether there really is such a thing), points more to the right being more strongly "r-selected." "K-selected" populations are near equilibrium, hence have r values near 0; "r-selected" populations flourish

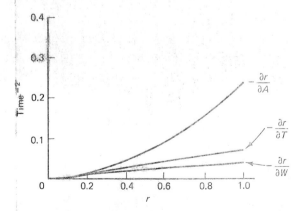

Figure 11.3 Derivatives of the intrinsic rate of increase r with respect to several timing parameters, plotted vs. r.

in nonequilibrium situations such as colonization or high levels of disturbance, which keep densities below equilibrium values, so r values are relatively large.

Some of these features can be seen in the data in Figs. 11.1 and 11.2. In the first pair of observations (Fig. 11.1) we have two races of *Drosophila,* with one race producing many more offspring in its lifetime than the other, but the less fecund race achieving the same r by maturing 4 days earlier.

The other pair of races (Fig. 11.2) have virtually identical reproduction at early ages, but one race is more fecund (or perhaps less subject to mortality) at later ages. But both races have the same r because of the unimportance of late reproduction.

It is interesting to extend these calculations to negative values of r. One finds that for negative r, the derivatives $\partial r/\partial A$, $\partial r/\partial W$, $\partial r/\partial T$ of the timing parameters change sign. So declining populations, if they are around long enough, experience selection for *later* reproduction!

This was first pointed out by Mertz (1971a). It seems unlikely that many populations experience a decline in numbers over a long enough time period for selection to act, but Mertz (1971b) does cite the case of the California condor, whose geographical range may have been decreasing for hundreds or even thousands of years. The bird requires 5 to 7 years to reach sexual maturity.

Unfortunately, this is a classic instance of the old question: Which came first, the condor or the egg? Do condor mature so late because they are declining, or are they declining in part because they mature so late? We can go part of the way toward an answer by looking at the timing of condor reproduction in relation to body size, for it is well known that larger animals tend to mature later, and we might need no more than this (presumably physiological) phenomenon to explain the condor's late reproduction.

If one does a log-log regression of age at maturity on body weight for birds of many different sizes, one finds (Western and Ssemakula 1982) $A = 850B^{0.23}$ days (B in kg). With the California condor's average body weight of 10.1 kg (Koford 1953), this gives just under 4 years to maturity. So even taking its size into consideration, the California condor matures late.

11.1 DELAYED REPRODUCTION

Lewontin's triangular reproductive functions were a tidy way to get at some interesting generalizations, but the approach is somewhat removed from parameters with direct biological significance. In this section we will look in more detail at how ecological factors affect age at first reproduction. We will return to our standard notation α in place of Lewontin's A.

In particular, we will ask what are the selective forces that might lead an organism to begin reproducing at a later age than that permitted by physiological constraints. This is the problem of *delayed reproduction.*

Wiley (1974) thought of a life history as divided into three phases—juvenile, adolescent, and adult—with mortality acting differently in the three phases, and wrote down Lotka's equation accordingly. Here adults are, as always, animals of reproductive age; juveniles are animals in their zeroth year (born but not yet censused); and adolescents are all the rest.

Suppose adults have a constant annual survival rate $P_x = s$, $x \geq \alpha$. Let the average survival rate for juveniles (animals in their zeroth year) be Js, so that

$$m_x = f_x Js \qquad x \geq \alpha \qquad (11.7)$$

where f_x is the fecundity (mean number of offspring) of a female in age class x. Finally, let adolescents (animals in age classes 1 through $\alpha - 1$) have a constant annual survival rate As. Then

$$l_0 = 1$$
$$l_1 = As$$
$$l_2 = (As)^2$$
$$\vdots$$
$$l_\alpha = (As)^\alpha$$
$$l_{\alpha+1} = (As)^\alpha s = A^\alpha s^{\alpha+1}$$
$$\vdots$$
$$l_x = A^\alpha s^x \qquad x \geq \alpha$$

So Lotka's equation is

$$1 = \sum_{x=\alpha}^{\infty} \lambda^{-(x+1)} J A^\alpha s^{x+1} f_x \qquad (11.8)$$

Now suppose reproduction is postponed for d years (or whatever the basic time intervals are), and suppose that associated with this postponement are new fecundities f'_x, new survival factors J', A', and a new finite rate of growth λ'.

Such a delay may well have effects on the demographic parameters, reflecting various tradeoffs. Wiley explores two such effects. He supposes that the entire age-specific schedule of fecundity is displaced by d years and multiplied by a factor M:

$$f'_{x+d} = M f_x \qquad (11.9)$$

In addition, he allows for the possibility that juvenile and adolescent survival are increased by a common factor E,

$$J' = EJ$$
$$A' = EA \qquad (11.10)$$

where $1 \leq E <$ smaller of $[(Js)^{-1}, (As)^{-1}]$.

With (11.9) and (11.10) Lotka's equation for the new growth rate λ' reads

$$1 = \sum_{x=\alpha+d}^{\infty} (\lambda')^{-(x+1)} E^{\alpha+d+1} J A^{\alpha+d} s^{x+1} M f_{x-d} \qquad (11.11)$$

We want to compare this with (11.8). The most conspicuous differences between these two equations are that the summation in (11.11) starts at $\alpha + d$ instead of at α and that the fecundities f_{x-d} occur in (11.11) instead of f_x. Both of these differences can be made to vanish if we define a new summation variable in (11.11): $y = x - d$. Then (11.11) reads

$$1 = \sum_{y=\alpha}^{\infty} (\lambda')^{-(y+1+d)} E^{\alpha+d+1} JA^{\alpha+d} s^{y+1+d} M f_y$$

$$= (\lambda')^{-d} E^{\alpha+d+1} A^d s^d M \sum_{x=\alpha}^{\infty} (\lambda')^{-(x+1)} JA^\alpha s^{x+1} f_x$$

$$= (L/\lambda')^d \sum_{x=\alpha}^{\infty} (\lambda')^{-(x+1)} JA^\alpha s^{x+1} f_x \qquad (11.12)$$

where

$$L = As(ME^{\alpha+d+1})^{1/d} \qquad (11.13)$$

Notice that the sum that occurs in the last line of (11.12) is precisely the same as the sum in (11.8), except that λ in (11.8) is replaced by λ' in (11.12). Now, it must be true either that $\lambda' = \lambda$ or that $\lambda' > \lambda$ or that $\lambda' < \lambda$. If $\lambda' = \lambda$, then the sum in the last line of (11.12) is equal to 1 [this is just equation (11.8)], whence $\lambda' = L$. If $\lambda' > \lambda$, then it follows from (11.8) that the sum in the last line of (11.12) is smaller than 1, whence $L > \lambda'$; then $L > \lambda' > \lambda$. If $\lambda' < \lambda$, then by a similar reasoning we have $L < \lambda' < \lambda$. The converses of these three statements can easily be shown to hold.

We can restate these conclusions in the following somewhat more suggestive way:

$$L \begin{Bmatrix} > \\ = \\ < \end{Bmatrix} \lambda \leftrightarrow \lambda' \begin{Bmatrix} > \\ = \\ < \end{Bmatrix} \lambda \qquad (11.14)$$

(The double arrow means "if and only if.")

The condition for the delayed strategy [which includes, of course, (11.9) and (11.10)] to be selected for is $\lambda' > \lambda$, which is, from (11.14), equivalent to $L > \lambda$. The smaller λ is, the more likely the condition is to be satisfied; so we recover Mertz' result that there will be a tendency toward delayed reproduction in declining populations, if there is enough time for selection to act. But in addition, we see that under certain circumstances delayed reproduction can evolve in populations for which $\lambda \geq 1$.

If both M and E are equal to 1, then $L = As < 1$. So, unsurprisingly, delayed reproduction can evolve in a stable or growing population only if there is some "payoff" for it. The two payoffs considered by Wiley are an increase in fecundity as in (11.9), and in preadult survival as in (11.10). It is easy to show that either of these factors operating alone can suffice to make delayed reproduction advantageous [if, of course, the increase is "big enough," where the precise meaning of "big enough" is given by the inequality (11.14)].

Exercise 11.4. Show that if the increase in survival associated with delayed reproduction applies only to ages between α and $\alpha + d$, then $L = AsEM^{1/d}$.

If the increase in survival associated with delayed reproduction applies only to the years of delay (those between α and $\alpha + d$), then $L = AsEM^{1/d}$. If this increase in survival is the only effect of delayed reproduction ($M = 1$), then $L = AsE$, which must be less than 1 since, as noted just after equation (11.10), $E < (As)^{-1}$. So if this is the only effect of delayed reproduction, then the delay will not evolve in stable or increasing populations.

This model shows that there is more to the timing of first reproduction than a simple physiological race to breed as early as possible. It shows that ecological factors can render it advantageous to breed at a later time than is physiologically possible, and it begins to elucidate those ecological factors. So delayed reproduction is a nontrivial topic for study. Having established that much, we must establish contact with observations.

11.1.1 Salamanders and Lizards

Stearns and Crandall (1981) have fitted a similar model to Wiley's to data from several salamander and lizard populations. Where α is age at first reproduction, they allow fertility and survival to be functions of α as well as age: $m(\alpha, x)$, $l(\alpha, x)$. These authors work in continuous time. Then Lotka's equation (11.1) reads

$$1 = \int_{\alpha}^{\infty} dx e^{-rx} l(\alpha, x) m(\alpha, x) \tag{11.15}$$

Let $q(\alpha, x)$ be the instantaneous mortality rate for an x-year-old: that is, let $q(\alpha, x)dx$ be the probability for an x-year-old to die before it reaches age $x + dx$. Then the probability to survive from age x to age $x + dx$ is $1 - q(\alpha, x)dx$. Thus the probability to survive from birth to age $x + dx$ [which is $l(\alpha, x + dx)$] is the probability to survive to age x [which is $l(\alpha, x)$] times the probability to survive from age x to age $x + dx$ [which is $1 - q(\alpha, x)dx$]:

$$l(\alpha, x + dx) = l(\alpha, x)[1 - q(\alpha, x)dx]$$

Writing this as

$$[l(\alpha, x + dx) - l(\alpha, x)]/dx = -q(\alpha, x)l(\alpha, x)$$

and taking the limit $dx \to 0$, we obtain

$$\partial l(\alpha, x)/\partial x = -q(\alpha, x)l(\alpha, x)$$

Integrating this equation yields

$$l(\alpha, x) = \exp\left[-\int_0^x q(\alpha, y)dy\right] \tag{11.16}$$

Exercise 11.5. Prove (11.16).

Stearns and Crandall express the effect of delayed reproduction on adolescent mortality through the instantaneous rate of mortality q. Specifically, they assume that q has one value, $h(\alpha)$, before maturity, and another value, d, after maturity:

$$q(\alpha, x) = \begin{cases} h(\alpha) & x \leq \alpha \\ d & x > \alpha \end{cases} \qquad (11.17)$$

Note that while the adolescent mortality rate $h(\alpha)$ is independent of age x, it does depend on when the animal matures. This dependence is thought of as inherited (along with a tendency to mature at a certain age) from the parents, who can produce stronger offspring if they reproduce later. Stearns and Crandall write

$$h(\alpha) = d + M(\alpha) \qquad (11.18)$$

thus M is the excess of adolescent mortality over adult mortality.

Finally, these authors assume

$$m(\alpha, x) = F\alpha + H \qquad (11.19)$$

where F and H are constants. This says that fertility increases linearly as maturity is delayed but remains constant thereafter.

Putting (11.17) to (11.19) into Lotka's equation (11.15), we obtain an expression that can immediately be integrated, yielding

$$1 = \{(F\alpha + H)e^{-r\alpha}e^{-\alpha[d + M(\alpha)]}\}/(r + d) \qquad (11.20)$$

TABLE 11.1 PREDICTED AGES AT MATURITY

Popu-lation[‖]	Empirically estimated constants					Ob-served α in yr	Predicted optimal age at maturity						Refer-ence§
							LFM		QYM		SAM		
	F	H	λ	d	H^*		α	r	α	r	α	r	
a	1.32	10.6	0.54	0.08	11.7	0.83	‡	‡	0.56	1.63	0.59	1.61	1
b	29.1	21.0	0.13	0.80	45.2	0.83	‡	‡	0.14	6.05	0.18	4.30	2
c	28.8	−13.8	0.28	0.50	5.0	0.83	0.98	1.51	0.44	0.92	1.10	1.34	3
d	54.0	−15.0	0.07	0.83	14.3	0.75	0.62	2.13	0.12	3.77	0.65	2.01	3
e	12.0	−3.0	0.86	0.67	11.8	1.75	0.84	1.03	0.80	0.69	1.43	0.60	3
f	6.5	3.6	0.26	0.73	7.9	1.80	‡	‡	0.37	1.19	0.56	1.00	3
g	3.75	−2.9	0.28	0.60	4.6	1.61†	1.95	0.25	0.46	0.75	2.12	0.20	4
h	1.42	−1.46	4.25	0.26	5.6	5.0	2.86	0.29	3.23	0.15	5.40	0.11	5
i	1.78	−2.49	1.44	0.37	4.6	4.0	3.22	0.18	1.48	0.29	3.98	0.11	5

† Author reported a range of 1.0–2.0; we used the weighted arithmetic mean.

‡ Indicates that equation (11.22) has no solution with α, $r > 0$.

‖ a: Side-blotched lizard, *Uta stansburiana*, Texas; b: Rusty lizard, *Sceloporus olivaceus*, Texas; c, d, e, f: Eastern Fence lizard, *S. undulatus*, South Carolina, Texas, Ohio, Colorado; g: Striped Plateau lizard, *S. virgatus*, Arizona; h, i: Appalachian Dusky salamander, *Desmognathus ochrophaeus*, North Carolina, Whiteside and Dry Falls, respectively.

§ (1) Tinkle (1967); (2) Blair (1960); (3) Tinkle and Ballinger (1972); (4) Vinegar (1975); (5) Tilley (unpublished). From Stearns and Crandall (1981).

Differentiating (11.20) with respect to α and setting $dr/d\alpha = 0$, we obtain

$$r = -M(\alpha) - \alpha \, dM(\alpha)/d\alpha + (\alpha + H/F)^{-1} - d \qquad (11.21)$$

Substituting (11.21) for r into (11.20), we get finally

$$1 = [F(\alpha + H/F)^2 \, e^{-\alpha/(\alpha+H/F)} \, e^{\alpha^2 dM/d\alpha}]/$$

$$[1 + (\alpha + H/F)(-M - \alpha \, dM/d\alpha)] \qquad (11.22)$$

Exercise 11.6. Prove (11.20), (11.21), and (11.22).

If α is optimized at some intermediate value with respect to the tradeoffs expressed by (11.17) to (11.19), then the parameters must be related as in (11.22).

To fit data from salamanders and lizards, Stearns and Crandall (1981) assumed $M(\alpha) = k/\alpha^2$, k = constant. They tried three versions of the model for each of nine populations, using data from the published literature. Their three models are (1) the linear fecundity model (LFM), defined by $k = 0$, in which age at maturity has no effect on adolescent survival; (2) the quality of young model (QYM), defined by $F = 0$, in which age at maturity has no effect on fertility; and (3) the salamander model (SAM), in which both effects are present.

For each population, one needs to estimate F (if it is not assumed to be zero), H, and k (if it is not assumed to be zero). Please consult the original paper for details of how this was done. Then one can use (11.22) to calculate the optimal α. The results are summarized in Table 11.1.

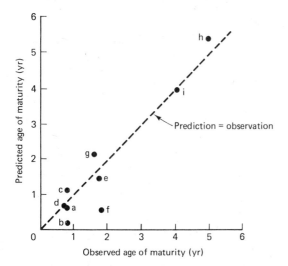

Figure 11.4 Relations between observed and predicted ages at maturity for nine populations of lizards and salamanders. Note the poor fit for observed ages at maturity less than 2.0 a, b, c, d, e, f, g, h, i indicate the populations similarly labeled in Table 11.1. Predications made with the Salamander model. (From Stearns and Crandall 1981).

The salamander model is the most successful of the three. For it, the product-moment correlation of predicted with observed ages at maturity is $r = 0.956$ ($P < 0.01$). From a plot of observed and predicted ages at maturity (Fig. 11.4), we see that this good correlation depends very strongly on the two populations (h and i) that mature relatively late; the model is less successful with the populations that mature early. Still, even for those populations the predicted age at maturity is, except in one case, correct to within 1 year. Basically, it seems fair to see here a tendency for timing to be optimized.

ADDITIONAL EXERCISES

11.7 Another factor that might select for delayed reproduction would be an increase in adult survival rate due to the delay. Formulate this precisely, and use Wiley's methods (Section 11.1) to derive quantitative conditions for such a delay.

11.8. In the model of Stearns and Crandall, Section 11.1.1, (11.21) is the condition for an extremum $dr/d\alpha = 0$. Find the condition that has to be satisfied in order for this extremum to be a maximum. Is this condition automatically satisfied for all plausible choices for the parameters?

11.9. In the LFM, Stearns and Crandall sometimes found no solution to (11.22) with α and $r > 0$ (Table 11.1). What does this mean?

Clutch Size

In this chapter we investigate the question: how many young should be produced? Historically, this issue has been studied most thoroughly, at least from an evolutionary perspective, for birds, owing largely to the influence of David Lack. Most of what we do in this chapter will be meant to apply to altricial birds.

12.1 AVIAN CLUTCH SIZE: AN OVERVIEW

The simplest explanation for avian (or any other) clutch size would be that the maximum physiologically possible number of offspring are produced. There are no doubt organisms for which this is the correct view, but few, if any, birds are among them. Most bird species lay a definite number of eggs, and in many species if an egg is removed during the laying season it will be replaced. Several experiments have been done in which the eggs laid by wild bird species were methodically removed; in this way a yellow-shafted flicker, *Colaptes auratus,* was induced to lay 71 eggs in 73 days (Phillips 1887, cited in Bent 1939), and the same phenomenon has been observed for the willow ptarmigan, *Lagopus lagopus,* and the ostrich, *Struthio camelus* (Welty 1962). So we must look beyond mere physiological capacity for an explanation.

Another quite simple possibility has been suggested by some people, namely, that the size of a clutch is limited by the number of eggs that a sitting bird can cover. While there must be such a limit (just as there must be a limit imposed by physiological capacity), it does not correspond to the normal clutch. For instance, the commonest clutch of the partridge in England is 15 eggs, and of the wood duck in Iowa 11 to 14 eggs, but in both species the percentage of eggs that hatch successfully is similar for clutches up to 20 eggs and more (Lack 1954).

A third view is that clutch size has been adjusted by natural selection to adjust to the mortality of the species (Wynne-Edwards 1962, Skutch 1967). The problem with this, as with so many other group selectionist arguments, is the difficulty of articulating a mechanism that could possibly make it work—especially considering that ordinary "selfish" selection, for which we *do* have a mechanism, would seem to favor "cheaters" who would not participate in the restraint of the rest of the group.

The history of what might be called the modern theory of clutch size begins with a paper of David Lack (1947). Lack's point of view, which was further elaborated in several books, particularly those published in 1954 (which thoroughly sets forth his ideas) and 1966 (which consists largely of replies to his critics), stimulated a great deal of controversy in its day. In order to understand this controversy, it is important to understand that Lack's viewpoint consists basically of *two* claims. I will call them Lack's first claim and Lack's second claim.

Lack's first claim is that birds produce, on the average, the most productive clutch size, where "most productive" means the clutch size that results in the most young surviving to maturity. Lack defined "production" of a clutch as *CS*, where *C*, clutch size, is the number of eggs laid and *S* is the probability of an egg's resulting in an individual that survives for 3 months after fledging. I discussed the maximization of this product in Section 10.2.2, including Lack's observational test of his first claim (Table 10.1).

This sort of data has been very thoroughly studied by Lack and others; Klomp (1970) summarizes the results as follows:

1. The most productive brood size is, or is near to, the most frequent brood size in the great tit, blue tit, starling, bullfinch, swift, Alpine swift, Laysan albatross, Manx shearwater, Leach's petrel, and the redfooted booby. When small discrepancies are present, as in the starling and the swift, the most productive size tends to be larger than the size of the commonest brood.
2. The most productive brood size is larger than the most frequent family in the pied and collared flycatchers, redwing, song thrush, blackbird, boat-tailed grackle, kestrel, gannet, kittiwake, glaucous-winged gull, and lesser black-backed gull.
3. The most productive brood seems to be smaller than the commonest family size in the common heron only.

Lack's first claim makes evolutionary sense, and it has a fair bit of observational support. But it doesn't make complete evolutionary sense, and neither is it completely supported by the data. The problem is that Lack didn't think in terms of reproductive risk, of the tradeoff between reproduction now and the potential for reproduction in the future, a point which seems to have first been raised by Williams (1966b) in this context.

If there is a real risk in terms of adult mortality involved in reproduction, and if that risk increases with clutch size, then the kind if thinking that we discussed in Section 10.2.5 implies that clutch size may be adjusted somewhat *below* the most productive in order to avoid this risk, as proved by Charnov and Krebs (1974).

Exercise 12.1. Prove this, using graphs like those in Section 10.2.5.

It's easy to think of possible elements of reproductive risk for birds (increased exposure to predation, perhaps parental malnutrition, . . .), and if you look at Klomp's summary of the data again, you will see that there is only one known case in which the commonest clutch size is larger than the most productive.

I've gone into this matter in some detail because I think the data on avian clutch size provide about the most thorough and direct observational support for the whole notion of optimal life histories. That notion, though appealing, is, as explained in Section 9.1, fraught with peril. The data on avian clutch size seem to me an impressive vindication, at least in one area of application, of the idea of optimal life history.

End of chapter, right? Hardly.

While we seem to be on the right track, there are at least two issues that still have to be clarified before we can feel that we understand avian clutch size. The first issue is: Just how important is reproductive risk in determining clutch size?

Klomp's summary, cited above, suggests that reproductive risk is not very important for birds. And yet, there seems to be a rather strong correlation between avian fertility and survival, as shown in Table 12.1. In this table, M is the annual mortality rate, estimated from recoveries of banded birds, and B is fertility, estimated as the number of young fledged per parental pair, divided by 2. There is a significant linear regression of log B on log M ($r = 0.91$, $P < 0.01$), with a slope of 1.14 ± 0.15 *se* (Ricklefs 1977a).

TABLE 12.1   DEMOGRAPHIC PARAMETERS M AND B FOR
REPRESENTATIVE SPECIES OF BIRDS

Species	Locality	M	B
Wandering albatross	S. Georgia Is.	0.043	0.17
Gannet	England	0.061	0.40
Black-and-white manakin	Trinidad	0.11	0.50
Kittiwake	England	0.12	0.75
Yellow-eyed penguin	New Zealand	0.16	0.81
Shag	England	0.20	1.00
Brown pelican	Southeastern U.S.	0.20	0.43
Scrub jay	Florida	0.20	0.57
Great blue heron	Eastern U.S.	0.22	1.00
Red-shouldered hawk	Eastern U.S.	0.31	0.94
Barn swallow	Eastern U.S.	0.43	2.99
Black-capped chickadee	Eastern U.S.	0.50	3.00
Robin	Eastern U.S.	0.50	2.59
Tree sparrow	Poland	0.55	6.60

From Ricklefs (1977a).

Such a tradeoff would seem to suggest that reproductive risk does play an important role in determining clutch size: one would think that if reproductive risk is significant, then a phenotype that has good prospects for survival should moderate reproduction each year in order to allow for future reproductive success, while poor prospects for survival imply a higher reproductive effort "now," which would yield data something like Table 12.1. This seeming paradox is addressed in Section 12.2.

The second issue we need to clarify is: Just what are the ecological factors that determine the most productive clutch size?

This second issue brings us around to Lack's second claim, which is that the most productive clutch is determined by the ability of the parents to feed their young, with the most productive clutch size corresponding to the maximum number of young that the parents can nourish.

Much of the controversy surrounding Lack's ideas has involved criticism of his second claim, and it is important to realize that even if the second claim is false, this does not, as pointed out by Lack, in any way refute the first claim; the two claims are logically independent.

Some of the strongest opposition to Lack's second claim came from Skutch (1949), who suggested in his "predation hypothesis" that the main factor determining the most productive clutch is increased predation on nestlings in larger clutches, due to the need for more feeding trips (giving away the location of the nest) and more noise from the nest. I will return to Skutch's hypothesis in Section 12.3.

Another interesting aspect of avian clutch size, which any theory of clutch size must explain, is a quite clear latitudinal gradient in clutch size for the same or related species. Thus, for example, typical passerine clutch sizes are four to six at temperate latitudes, but only two in the tropics. One can even see a latitudinal gradient within Europe, as shown in Fig. 12.1.

12.2 REPRODUCTIVE RISK AND OPTIMAL AVIAN CLUTCH SIZE

Ricklefs (1977a) has considered the optimization of avian clutch size with respect to reproductive risk. In birds, adult fecundity and mortality are approximately constant after the onset of reproduction. So it is a quite good approximation to take $P_x = 1 - M$, $x \geq \alpha$, with M independent of age. Then survivorship takes the form

$$l_x = l_\alpha (1 - M)^{x-\alpha} \qquad x \geq \alpha \qquad (12.1)$$

Furthermore,

$$m_x = \begin{cases} 0 & x < \alpha \\ B = \text{constant} & x \geq \alpha \end{cases} \qquad (12.2)$$

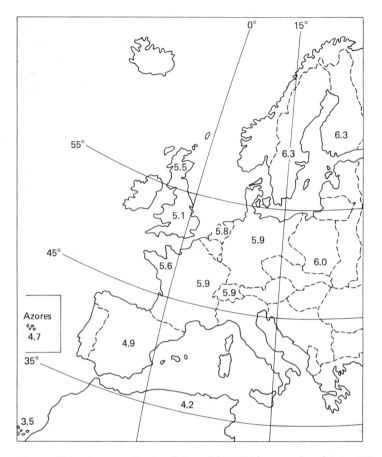

Figure 12.1 Average clutch of the robin (*Erithacus rubecula*) in different countries. (From Lack 1954.)

These bird populations show strong density-dependent regulation; so we will optimize the net reproductive rate

$$R_0 = \sum_{x=\alpha}^{\infty} l_\alpha (1 - M)^{x-\alpha} B \qquad (12.3)$$

We can sum this using, once again, the geometric series, to obtain

$$R_0 = l_\alpha B / M \qquad (12.4)$$

Before we proceed we must analyze the mortality rate M more closely, distinguishing between mortality associated with reproductive activities and with other sources of mortality. It is only mortality factors associated with reproductive activities, in particular those which increase with increasing reproductive effort, that are involved in the optimization of reproductive effort.

Let m be the annual risk of death resulting from reproductive activities that influence fertility, and let K be the risk that is not influenced by fertility.

Thus K includes any risks due to behavior preparatory to breeding, such as courtship or nest building, which do not affect the number of eggs produced but are necessary for any level of reproduction.

Ricklefs takes K constant. The reproductive risk m should be a monotonically increasing function of fertility B, and it should be zero when B is zero. A rather general family of functions with this behavior can be written

$$m = (B/f)^Z \qquad\qquad (12.5)$$

where f and Z are constants.

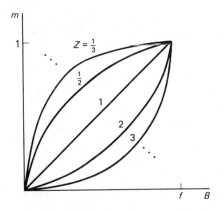

Notice that m approaches 1 as B approaches f. So f is an absolute upper limit on fecundity; it expresses the influence of such factors as food availability and nesting season length. The parameter Z is a "shape parameter" for the curve $m = m(B)$.

There are two different ways that one can combine the reproductive and nonreproductive components m and K of mortality to get the annual survivorship $1 - M$, corresponding to two biologically different setups. On the one hand, it could be that an individual experiences reproductive and nonreproductive risk at the same time. If so, these risks combine additively:

$$(1 - M) = (1 - m - K) \qquad \text{(model I)} \qquad\qquad (12.6)$$

Ricklefs refers to this as model I. On the other hand, it could be that exposure to the two kinds of risk comes at different times. Then the risks are independent and

$$(1 - M) = (1 - m)(1 - K) \qquad \text{(model II)} \qquad\qquad (12.7)$$

Ricklefs calls this model II.

In reality, exposure to nonreproductive risk occurs both during and outside the period of reproductive activity, so that each real population will lie somewhere between model I and model II. These two models represent two idealized extremes. But since these two extremes bracket the real populations, we can cover all the real cases if we do these two extremes and find comparable results for those things that interest us.

Now we are ready to apply our optimization principle. Consider first model I. Putting (12.5) and (12.6) into (12.4), we get

$$R_0 = l_\alpha B / [(B/f)^Z + K] \qquad (12.8)$$

Differentiating with respect to B, we get

$$dR_0/dB = l_\alpha / [(B/f)^Z + K] - \{l_\alpha B / [(B/f)^Z + K]^2\} Z (B/f)^{Z-1} f^{-1}$$

We are assuming that density-dependent regulatory factors are maintaining the population in equilibrium, so $R_0 = 1$. Using (12.8) with $R_0 = 1$ we can simplify this last equation to

$$dR_0/dB = [1 - Z(B/f)^Z / l_\alpha B] / B \qquad (12.9)$$

The optimal value B^* of B occurs when $dR_0/dB = 0$. From (12.9), this is

$$B^* = (l_\alpha f^Z / Z)^{1/(Z-1)} \qquad \text{(model I)} \qquad (12.10)$$

Exercise 12.2. Prove that $d^2 R_0/dB^2 < 0$ at the extremum (12.10), whence this extremum is a maximum.

For model II, equation (12.7), we proceed in exactly the same way, obtaining the optimal fertility

$$B^* = [l_\alpha f^Z / (1 - K)Z]^{1/(Z-1)} \qquad \text{(model II)} \qquad (12.11)$$

Exercise 12.3. Prove that (12.11) gives the optimal fertility for model II.

The optima (12.10) and (12.11) for our two extreme models I and II differ only by a factor $[1/(1 - K)]^{1/(Z-1)}$. This factor is close to 1 for large Z and small K, though it can be very large for large K, especially as Z approaches 1. In most of the field situations to which we will apply the model, this factor will differ from 1 by less than 0.2; so the difference between our two extremes is not very great.

We now have to draw another distinction. We are assuming that our population is regulated by some density-dependent factors, but the biological situation is different, and we will get different answers, depending on just what those factors are.

Ricklefs (1977a) considers two possibilities. The first, which I will call *f-regulation,* is that population density is regulated primarily through factors that influence the upper limit f on fecundity. Availability of food or length of nesting season would be such factors.

The other possibility, which I will call *l-regulation,* is that population density is regulated primarily by factors that influence the probability l_α of survival to reproductive maturity or, in other words, factors that influence juvenile mortality.

Consider first *f*-regulation. In this case f in equations (12.10) and (12.11) is a function of population density. This makes things rather messy, so we will try to eliminate f from our equations before going any further.

For model I we have, from (12.4) with $R_0 = 1$, (12.5), and (12.6)

$$l_\alpha B = (B/f)^Z + K \qquad (12.12)$$

whence

$$f^Z = B^Z/(l_\alpha B - K)$$

Putting this into (12.10),

$$B^* = [l_\alpha B^{*Z}/Z(l_\alpha B^* - K)]^{1/(Z-1)}$$

Now we want to solve this equation for B^*. To do this, first raise both sides to the power $Z - 1$:

$$B^{*Z-1} = l_\alpha B^{*Z}/Z(l_\alpha B^* - K)$$

Next divide both sides by B^{*Z-1}:

$$1 = l_\alpha B^*/Z(l_\alpha B^* - K)$$

From this we easily find

$$B^* = KZ/l_\alpha(Z - 1) \qquad (12.13)$$

Exercise 12.4. Do the corresponding calculation for model II [using (12.7) instead of (12.6) and (12.11) instead of (12.10)]. Verify that the final result is identical with (12.13): this equation holds for both models in the case of f-regulation.

Because $R_0 = 1$ (the condition for equilibrium) implies, with (12.4), that $Bl_\alpha = M$, we can rewrite (12.13) as

$$M^* = KZ/(Z - 1)$$

where M^* is the optimal adult mortality, and we can combine this with (12.6) to obtain for model I

$$m^* = K/(Z - 1) \qquad \text{(model I)} \qquad (12.14)$$

for the optimal reproductive risk m^*. If we use (12.7) instead, we find in model II

$$m^* = K/(Z - 1)(1 - K) \qquad \text{(model II)} \qquad (12.15)$$

Now let us treat the case of l-regulation. In this case we want to eliminate l_α from our equations.

For model I, we can put

$$l_\alpha = B^{Z-1}/f^Z + K/B$$

obtained from (12.12), into (12.10) to get

$$B^* = [(B^{*Z-1}/f^Z + K/B^*)f^Z/Z]^{1/(Z-1)}$$

whence

$$B^* = [Kf^Z/(Z-1)]^{1/Z} \qquad \text{(model I)} \qquad (12.16)$$

Exercise 12.5. Show that the corresponding result for model II is

$$B^* = [Kf^Z/(Z-1)(1-K)]^{1/Z} \qquad \text{(model II)} \qquad (12.17)$$

Since equations (12.14) and (12.15) do not involve either f or l_α, they will obviously hold both for f-regulation and for l-regulation.

We now have solutions for optimal clutch size and reproductive risk under four different biological assumptions (reproductive and nonreproductive risk occurring concurrently or not; f-regulation or l-regulation).

I mentioned in Section 12.1 that B and M seem to be strongly correlated in avian populations, with a linear regression of log B on log M showing a slope around 1. (discussion of Table 12.1). Let us see how this relationship looks in our model. For the case of f-regulation, we have from (12.13)

$$\log B^* = \log K + \log[Z/(Z-1)] - \log l_\alpha$$

But from the equation before (12.14),

$$\log M^* = \log K + \log[Z/(Z-1)] \qquad (12.18)$$

So

$$\log B^* = \log M^* - \log l_\alpha \qquad (12.19)$$

On the hypothesis of f-regulation, l_α is simply a density-independent parameter. So we can differentiate (12.19) thus:

$$\partial \log B^*/\partial \log M^* = 1 \qquad (12.20)$$

Consider now the case of l-regulation. For model I we have, from (12.16),

$$\log B^* = [\log K + Z \log f - \log(Z-1)]/Z$$

$$= (\log M^* - \log Z + \log f)/Z$$

from (12.18) (which, it will be recalled, applies equally well for f- and l-regulation). On the hypothesis of l-regulation, f is a constant and Z is considered to be an intrinsic property of a species. So

$$\partial \log B^*/\partial \log M^* = 1/Z \qquad (l\text{-regulation}) \qquad (12.21)$$

Because of the factor $(1-K)$ in equation (12.17), (12.21) will not hold exactly for model II. But since K is generally small compared with 1, the factor $(1-K)$ will not vary much. Therefore, (12.21) can be considered a reasonable approximation also for model II.

In order to compare (12.20) and (12.21) with the empirical slope from Table 12.1, we just have to know Z. So estimating this quantity is our next task.

From equation (12.14) and the equation just preceding it,

$$Z = M^*/m^* \qquad \text{(model I)} \qquad (12.22)$$

and from (12.15) and the equation just before (12.14)

$$Z = M^*/m^*(1 - K) \quad \text{(model II)} \quad (12.23)$$

These equations hold for both f- and l-regulation. Ricklefs estimates Z as M^*/m^*; we see from (12.23) that this underestimates Z for model II, but this is just as well since he anyway finds rather high values of Z.

There are a good many field studies reported in the literature in which the annual adult mortality M is measured, either from studies of survivorship in marked populations or from the recovery of dead individuals that were banded as nestlings. But the reproductive component m is much more difficult to measure.

For species for which survivorship or recovery data are available on a monthly basis, Ricklefs has used two methods to estimate m. In the first method ("total"), all deaths that occurred during the breeding season were included in m. In the second method ("excess") m was estimated as the excess of deaths during the breeding season over the average number of deaths for months immediately preceding and immediately following the breeding season.

For a few other species m can be estimated from differences in annual mortality rates of males and females, when the relative reproductive effort of each sex can be "guessed with confidence." For instance, the male cowbird (*Molothrus ater*) does not participate in reproduction beyond mating, so Ricklefs took m to be the difference between female and male mortality rates in this case.

The resultant estimates of Z can be seen in Table 12.2. Most Z-values lie between 4 and 10, with an average of 6.2 ± 2.5 se, when m is calculated from excess mortality. This way of estimating m has the effect of including in m mortality due to breeding activities that do not affect fertility. These risks were supposed to have been included in K rather than m; hence we have overestimated m, which means that we have underestimated Z. This is all for model I [equation (12.22)]. For model II [equation (12.23)], the overestimate is still higher.

It seems safe to conclude that Z will rarely be less than 4 and will usually be considerably larger.

With these Z-values, the measured slope of 1.14 ± 0.15 se (Table 12.1) is inconsistent with equation (12.21) for l-regulation. On the other hand, it accords with equation (12.20) for f-regulation.

We may conclude that f-regulation predominates in these bird populations: they are regulated primarily by the direct response of fertility B to "potential fertility" f in the relation (12.5), which we can rewrite as $B = fm^{1/Z}$. But then the dependence of B on reproductive risk m (which goes like $m^{1/Z}$, with $Z > 4$) is, by comparison, very weak. Thus, reproductive risk plays a relatively minor role in determining the optimal clutch size, as suggested by the data on most productive clutches (Section 12.1) and, we now see, by the data in Table 12.1. The kind of intuitive argument that I gave when I first discussed Table 12.1 is good as a starting point for our thinking, but it needs to be checked against rigorous theory.

TABLE 12.2 ESTIMATED VALUES FOR Z

Species	Basis for calculation	Values for Z calculated from m estimated as	
		Total	Excess
Sparrow hawk	Recoveries	2.4	5.4
California quail	Sex ratio		6.0
Great blue heron:			
Owen	Recoveries	3.5	12.0
Henny	Recoveries	4.2	10.5
Black-crowned night heron	Recoveries	2.3	4.1
Silver gull	Recoveries	5.6	
Southern black-backed gull	Recoveries	6.7	
Herring gull	Recoveries	2.2	3.8
Black-headed gull	Recoveries	5.5	
Glaucous-winged gull	Recoveries	5.6	
Barn owl	Recoveries	3.2	7.4
Little owl	Recoveries	3.4	4.6
Tawny owl	Recoveries	1.6	4.3
Robin:			
2+ year	Recoveries	2.6	9.6
1st year	Recoveries	2.2	4.9
English blackbird			
2nd calendar year	Recoveries	1.8	6.7
Later years	Recoveries	1.8	4.6
Starling	Sexual differences in mortality		7.0
House sparrow:			
1	Recoveries	1.9	2.9
2	Returns	1.8	3.9
Cowbird	Sexual differences in mortality		7.4
Song sparrow	Returns	3.5	7.0

From Ricklefs (1977a).

12.3 THE MOST PRODUCTIVE CLUTCH

Ricklefs (1977b) went on to produce a simple model for the most productive clutch, which attempts to analyze the importance of various ecological factors. Again, he tried to establish contact with a fairly large body of observational data.

Let C be clutch size, S the probability of survival until the relevant census. Then "production" in Lack's sense (effective fertility in our sense) is given by

$$P = CS \qquad (12.24)$$

Ricklefs (1977b) breaks the survival probability S down into four components, each of which is influenced differently by clutch size and duration of nesting period:

S_1 = independent of both clutch size and duration of nesting period. Hatching success, to the extent that it is determined by infertility of eggs, falls into this category.

S_2 = influenced by duration but not by clutch size. This would include, for example, most forms of predation, and also death from adverse weather conditions.

S_3 = dependent on clutch size only. This would include things like hatching failure due to difficulties in incubating large clutches, and starvation of young due to chronic unavailability of food. Starvation caused by brief food shortages brought on, say, by bad weather, would fall into the second category if entire broods died, and in the last category if some young were unaffected.

S_4 = dependent on both clutch size and duration. This would include predation that is influenced by the number of eggs or young in the nest.

Putting all this together, we can write for (12.24)

$$P = CS_1S_2S_3S_4 \tag{12.25}$$

The next step is to write down plausible forms for the dependencies of S_1 on the appropriate quantities.

The survival S_1 is, of course, simply a constant.

For the purely duration-dependent factors embodied in S_2, assume a constant risk m_2 acting over the whole nesting period. That is, assume that the rate of loss dN/dt of (average number of) nestlings N is a constant proportion m_2 of the remaining nestlings:

$$dN/dt = -m_2 N$$

Then

$$N(t) = N(0)\, e^{-m_2 t}$$

so

$$S_2 = N(t)/N(0) = e^{-m_2 t} \tag{12.26}$$

where t is the nesting period.

The probability S_3 is more difficult to explicate. The relation of, say, starvation to brood size is not well known for any species and may very well be quite different for different species. So a fairly general and flexible expression is needed here. The function should equal 1 when clutch size is zero, remain near 1 until a clutch size is reached that corresponds to the largest number of young that can be nourished, and decrease rapidly as clutch size increases beyond this point. The function

$$S_3 = e^{-aC^X} \tag{12.27}$$

where a and X are constants, satisfies these requirements and is fairly flexible within these restrictions.

For S_4, we can write a similar form to S_2:

$$S_4 = e^{-m_4 t} \qquad (12.28)$$

but while m_2 was a constant, m_4 will depend on clutch size C. Again, Ricklefs assumes the rather general form

$$m_4 = bC^Y \qquad (12.29)$$

with b and Y constants. Then

$$S_4 = e^{-tbC^Y} \qquad (12.30)$$

If we assume that the optimal clutch is the most productive one (i.e., that reproductive risk is negligible), then our optimization principle is to maximize P, equation (12.25), with respect to C. Using (12.26), (12.27), and (12.30), we have

$$P = CS_1 \, e^{-m_2 t - aC^X - tbC^Y} \qquad (12.31)$$

So

$$dP/dC = [S_1 + CS_1(-aXC^{X-1} - tbYC^{Y-1})] \, e^{-m_2 t - aC^X - tbC^Y}$$

The optimal clutch size C^* corresponds to $dP/dC = 0$, or

$$1 = XaC^{*X} + YtbC^{*Y} \qquad (12.32)$$

Exercise 12.6. Show that $d^2 P/dC^2 < 0$ at the optimum, hence that C^* corresponds to the largest productivity, not the smallest.

It should be no surprise that S_1 and m_2, which are independent of clutch size, do not appear in the criterion (12.32) for the most productive clutch size.

12.3.1 Skutch's Predation Hypothesis

I've mentioned earlier Skutch's suggestion that the most productive clutch size is determined not as in Lack's second claim but through clutch-size-dependent predation. As pointed out by Skutch, this would yield a smaller clutch size than Lack's maximum number of young the parents can nourish. Snow (1970) has invoked Skutch's hypothesis to explain the small clutches of some tropical bird species that are known to suffer great nest mortality. Ricklefs (1977b) uses the formalism just set out to try to evaluate Skutch's proposal.

If we assume that predation is the major factor determining optimal clutch size, we can set X in equation (12.32) equal to zero:

$$1 = YtbC^{*Y} \qquad (12.33)$$

This we can easily solve for the optimal clutch size C^*:

$$C^* = (1/Ytb)^{1/Y} \qquad (12.34)$$

The relationship between C^* and Y, for several different b-values, and with $t = 15$ days, can be seen in the top set of curves in Fig. 12.2. It will be seen that by playing with the two free parameters at our disposal—Y and b—we can get just about any optimal clutch size we choose. This is not very informative: it just reflects the flexibility we wanted to build into the model to start with.

We can, however, get some nontrivial information out of the model by putting our optimal clutch size (12.34) into equation (12.29) for the corresponding daily mortality rate m_4:

$$m_4^* = 1/Yt \qquad\qquad (12.35)$$

This relationship is plotted in the lower curve in Fig. 12.2, again for $t = 15$ days.

Let's take a close look at this curve. We may well imagine that the risk of predation would increase linearly with clutch size: n hatchlings would make about n times as much noise as 1 hatchling and would require perhaps n times as many feeding trips by the parents. This would suggest a Y-value of 1. The corresponding daily mortality m_4 is then 0.067—almost 7 percent a day!

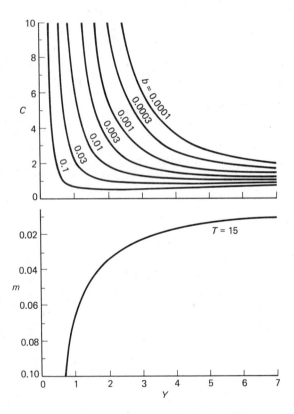

Figure 12.2 Above: optimum clutch size (C^*) as a function of Y and b when clutch-size-dependent mortality determines C^* (see text). Below: daily mortality (m) resulting from clutch-size-dependent predation as a function of Y; m is independent of optimum clutch size. Nestling period (t) is 15 days. (From Ricklefs 1977b.)

We may imagine that the risk of predation increases faster than linearly. For instance, perhaps fledglings in larger broods are more hungry and have to compete with their sibs more actively for food, so they cry disproportionately louder than fledglings in smaller broods. But even if $Y = 3$ (a quite strong nonlinearity), we still get a rather large daily mortality m_4 of 2.2 percent.

These results are difficult to assess on the basis of currently available data. Ricklefs (1969) has estimated daily total mortality rates for whole clutches and broods using Skutch's data for tropical lowland birds, finding an average of about 4 percent per day. Most of this mortality is indeed caused by predators, but there is surely a non-clutch-size-dependent component to it, which belongs in m_2 rather than in m_4; so it is very hard to say just what m_4 is, except that it is certainly less than 4 percent per day.

Ricklefs (1977b) discusses some other rough determinations of m_4 from existing data and concludes that on the whole m_4 seems to be too small for clutch-size-dependent predation to be a major factor in the evolution of clutch size. I think it is fair to say that the case for Skutch's hypothesis seems rather implausible at the moment, but it would be interesting to see field studies that are *designed* to test Skutch's hypothesis, by measuring precisely m_4.

12.3.2 Food Resources and Optimum Clutch Size

If we assume clutch-size-dependent predation to be negligible, then $Y = 0$ in equation (12.32) and

$$C^* = (1/aX)^{1/X} \qquad (12.36)$$

For each value of C^*, this implies a relationship between a and X, which is plotted in Fig. 12.3.

Figure 12.4 shows the effect of the parameter X on the survival curve $S_3(X)$ and on the production curve $P(X)$, with optimal clutch size held constant at 5.

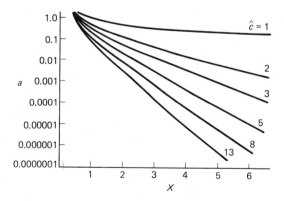

Figure 12.3 Relationship between a and x for optimum clutch size of 1, 2, 3, 5, 8, and 13, when clutch-size-dependent starvation determines optimum clutch size (see text). (From Ricklefs 1977b.)

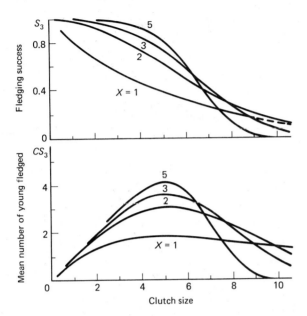

Figure 12.4 Relationship between survival and clutch size for different values of *X* when the optimum clutch size is 5. Lower portion of graph shows number of young produced (survival × clutch size). (From Ricklefs 1977b.)

A higher value of *X* corresponds to a sharper falloff of survival with increasing clutch size, and to a more sharply defined peak in the production curve.

Taking the logarithm of both sides of equation (12.27) twice converts it into an equation involving a linear function of log *C*, with log(*a*) and *X* as coefficients:

$$\log(-\log S_3) = \log(a) + X \log C \qquad (12.37)$$

So if one has data for survival as a function of clutch size and if one is willing to assume that S_3 predominates, one can get the parameters *a* and *X* from a linear regression of log(−log S_3) on log *C*. This yields a fit of a curve of the form of equation (12.27) to the data for survival as a function of clutch size.

Having obtained the parameters *X* and *a* for each species, one can compute the optimal clutch size from equation (12.36) and compare it with the observed most common (modal) clutch size. Ricklefs has done this for quite a few species (using mostly data from the published literature). The results are summarized in Table 12.3.

A good many of the "calculated" optimal clutch sizes agree fairly well with the corresponding modal clutch sizes, with most deviations putting the optimal clutch size higher than the modal. This is hardly a surprise: we already know from the work of Lack and his followers that modal clutch sizes tend to be most productive. In a way, this is little more than an exercise in fitting data to a family of curves. And yet, there is (or ought to be) more information here than that.

For one thing, recall that for a given optimal clutch size, larger *X* values

TABLE 12.3 THE CONSTANTS X AND a OF THE EQUATION $S_3 = \exp(-aC^X)$ FITTED TO THE RELATIONSHIP BETWEEN SURVIVAL AND CLUTCH OR BROOD SIZE. THE CORRELATION COEFFICIENT OF THE REGRESSION (r) AND THE OPTIMUM CLUTCH SIZE (C^*) PREDICTED BY X AND a [EQUATION (12.36)] ARE ALSO TABULATED

Species	Period	Clutch or brood size					
		Mode	Range*	r	a	X	C^*
Black-footed albatross† *Diomedea nigripes*	Nestling	1	1–2	1.00	0.400	2.62	1.0
Manx shearwater† *Puffinus puffinus*	Nestling	1	1–2	1.00	0.0513	5.21	1.3
Heron *Ardea cinerea*	Nestling		2–5	0.98	0.000698	4.20	4.0
	Fledging to September 1		2–4	0.93	0.000757	5.24	2.9
Buzzard *Buteo buteo*	Nestling	3	3–4	1.00	0.0135	1.69	4.7
Kestrel *Falco tinnunculus*	Nestling	6	5–7	0.99	0.000864	2.99	7.3
Western gull† *Larus occidentalis*	Nestling, 1971 1972	3 3	1–6 1–6	0.96 0.96	0.0132 0.0144	1.72 1.89	9.0 6.8
Forsters tern *Sterna forsteri*	Nestling	2	1–3	0.97	0.148	1.82	2.1
Arctic tern *Sterna paradisea*	Nestling	2	2–3	1.00	0.0812	2.00	2.5
Woodpigeon† *Columba palumbus*	Nestling Fledging to 1 month	2 2	2–3 2–3	1.00 1.00	0.000507 0.000741	5.32 8.51	3.0 2.4
Swift *Apus apus*	Nestling	2	2–4	0.99	0.00145	4.49	3.1
Pied flycatcher *Fidecula hypoleuea*	Fledging to breeding	7	6–9	0.99	0.000294	3.43	7.5
Great tit *Parus major*	Nestling Fledging to 3 months‡	10	3–12 9–13	0.99 0.96	0.00692 2.17×10^{-14}	1.47 12.81	22.8 9.6
Blue tit *Parus caeruleus*	Fledging to 3 months	11	3–14	0.95	0.000390	3.22	8.0
Blackbird *Turdus merula*	Nestling§	4	2–5	0.85	0.0156	1.58	18.6
Starling *Sturnus vulgaris*	Nestling† Fledging to 3 months	5 5	3–7 4–8	0.88 0.98	0.00148 0.000410	2.68 3.76	7.9 5.6
Common grackle *Quiscalus quiscula*	Nestling	5	4–6	0.92	5.33×10^{-7}	8.55	4.2
Boat-tailed grackle *Cassidix mexicanus*	Nestling	3	3–5	0.99	0.000565	5.21	4.8

* Range of brood sizes used to calculate constants a and X.

† Larger than normal clutches were made by the investigators.

‡ Broods of 1949–1950, 1952–1955 only; no clutch size-dependence in 1947–1948.

§ Botanic Garden only, no clutch-size dependence in Wytham Wood.

From Ricklefs (1977b).

correspond to a sharper peak in the production curve. This means that for a given optimal clutch size, species with smaller values of X in their survival curves should display more *variation* in clutch size than species with larger values of X. Ricklefs does not seem to have looked particularly at this aspect, although he does give in the above table a range of clutch sizes for each species. For given modal clutch sizes, these ranges seem quite unrelated to X. But presumably these ranges refer simply to the data base used, and not to natural variations (for instance, in many of these studies clutch sizes are manipulated by adding or taking away eggs). It would be very interesting to compare data for variances of naturally occurring clutch sizes with fitted values for X.

To further assess the meaning of X, Ricklefs (1977b) has developed a simple model for fledgling survival. He calls it the maximum rearable clutch size model.

In this model, it is assumed that a particular species can rear no more young than some maximum number C_{max} determined by resource availability. It is assumed that all young hatching from clutches that are smaller than C_{max} fledge successfully, and that larger clutches produce exactly C_{max} successful off-spring. For instance, if $C_{max} = 3$, then clutches of 1, 2, or 3 would be successful; clutches of 4 would be 75 percent successful (3/4); clutches of 5 would be 60 percent successful (3/5); and so on. This gives the curves for $S_3(C)$ shown in Fig. 12.5, with C_{max} set at 1, 2, 3, 5, or 8.

Ricklefs gets the best fits to these curves with functions of the form (12.27) by the same procedure used to fit real data to get Table 12.3. The results are given in Table 12.4. We see that for a considerable variation in C_{max} (from 1 through 8), X varies only from 3.756 to 4.590. So one can use the maximum rearable clutch size model as a sort of conceptual base, and ask why the "mea-sured" values of X in Table 12.3 deviate from it in the interesting way that they do.

We can see just how interesting those deviations are in Fig. 12.6, which plots in the X-a parameter space the parameter values summarized in Table 12.3 (open numbered circles), along with the expected values for X and a on

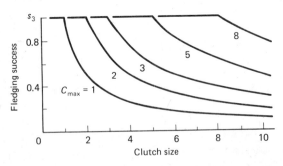

Figure 12.5 Relationship between survival and clutch size in accordance with the max-imum rearable clutch model for maximum rearable clutches (C_{max}) of 1, 2, 3, 5, and 8. (From Ricklefs 1977b.)

TABLE 12.4 CONSTANTS X AND a IN THE EQUATION $S_3 = \exp(-aC^X)$ FITTED TO VALUES OF SURVIVAL CALCULATED IN ACCORDANCE WITH THE MAXIMUM REARABLE CLUTCH SIZE MODEL. SURVIVAL OF YOUNG IN CLUTCHES OF THE MAXIMUM REARABLE SIZE WAS ARBITRARILY SET AT 0.95

Clutch of maximum rearable size	Range of clutch size*	r	a	X	C^*
1	1–2	1.000	0.0513	3.756	1.55
2	2–4	0.974	0.00414	3.844	2.94
3	3–6	0.963	0.00108	3.747	4.35
5	5–9	0.967	0.0000965	4.071	6.86
8	8–13	0.977	0.00000458	4.590	10.45

* Range used to calculate a and X.
From Ricklefs (1977b).

the basis of the maximum rearable clutch size model (solid circles and solid curve).

There are five species that seem to lie fairly near the region of parameter space that corresponds to the maximum rearable clutch size model. These are the swift, heron, kestrel, starling, and pied flycatcher. Ricklefs indicates in his text that the predicted optimal clutch size is not very close to the model clutch size for the heron, although he gives no value for the model size in Table 12.3. The remaining four species have one trait in common: they are all hole nesters (I thank John Hickey for pointing this out to me). There is another hole nester in Ricklefs' sample which, however, lies far away from the maximum rear-

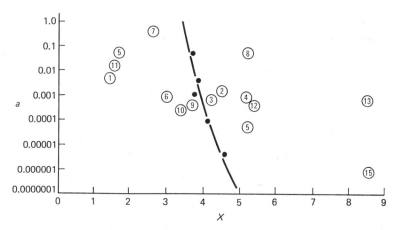

Figure 12.6 Relationship between a and X calculated from field observations on several species of birds compared with the relationship expected from the maximum rearable clutch model (solid line). 1, Great tit; 2, swift; 3, heron (nestling); 4, heron (fledgling); 5, boat-tailed grackle; 6, kestrel; 7, black-footed albatross; 8, manx shearwater; 9, starling; 10, pied flycatcher; 11, blackbird; 12, woodpigeon (nestling; 13, woodpigeon (fledgling); 15, common grackle. (From Ricklefs 1977b.)

able clutch size model, and that is the great tit (which has the smallest X-value of all).

Now, hole nesters should be relatively free from predation. Thus one possibility is that the deviations from the maximum rearable clutch size model are due at least in part to clutch-size-dependent predation. This issue could be clarified by careful measurements of m_4.

Ricklefs (1977b) considers two other effects that can yield such deviations.

First, he looks at the effect of environmental uncertainty. Suppose the predicted optimal clutch size varies about some mean, either from one year to another or from one territory or breeding site to another. How does this affect the optimal clutch size and the value of X? Ricklefs has calculated the survival curve for the maximum rearable clutch size model with environmental variation as follows.

For a given mean and standard deviation of the maximum rearable clutch size, he calculates the proportion of years with each maximum rearable clutch size from a normal distribution. Then he calculates survival for any clutch size as the weighted mean of survival values for that clutch size for the various maximum rearable clutch sizes. The resultant values of C^* and X can be seen in Table 12.5, for a mean maximum rearable clutch size of 5 and a selection of values for the standard deviation of variations about this mean. We see that as environmental variation increases, C^* increases and X decreases.

Second, Ricklefs considers deviations from the maximum rearable clutch size model itself. For instance, suppose there is an extra penalty imposed on large clutch sizes, as follows: multiply survival by a factor reducing survival by one-tenth for each egg laid over the maximum rearable. For instance, if C_{max} is 5, the survival of young raised from clutches of 8 would be multiplied by 0.7. The effect on $S_3(C)$ and on $P(C)$ can be seen in Fig. 12.7, in which the solid curves correspond to the maximum rearable clutch size model as originally formulated and the dashed curves correspond to the model, which adds an extra penalty on large clutches as just described. Table 12.6 shows the effect on X: imposition of a penalty on large clutches causes X to increase. Similarly, placing a premium on large clutches will cause X to decrease.

TABLE 12.5   CONSTANTS X AND a IN THE EQUATION $S_3 = \exp(-aC^X)$
FITTED TO VALUES OF SURVIVAL CALCULATED IN
ACCORDANCE WITH THE MAXIMUM REARABLE CLUTCH
SIZE MODEL FOR A MEAN MAXIMUM REARABLE CLUTCH
SIZE OF 5 AND STANDARD DEVIATIONS
BETWEEN 0 AND 4

Standard deviation of maximum rearable clutch size	r	a	X	C^*
0	0.967	0.0000965	4.071	6.86
1	0.985	0.00243	2.621	6.88
2	0.997	0.0137	1.792	7.92
4	0.999	0.0756	1.005	12.99

From Ricklefs (1977b).

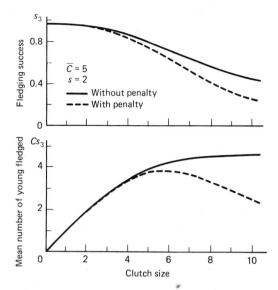

Figure 12.7 Relationship between survival and clutch size (above) for an average maximum rearable clutch size of 5 ± 2 (S.D.). Dashed line represents the addition of a penalty reducing survival by a factor of 0.1 for each egg in excess of the maximum rearable clutch size (see text). Lower portion of graph shows the relationship between productivity and clutch size with and without having a penalty applied. (From Ricklefs 1977b.)

Returning to Fig. 12.6, Ricklefs suggests that the species lying to the left of the solid curve (having X-values that are too small for the maximum rearable clutch size model) could be experiencing more environmental variation than the other species, or they could have for some reason a premium on large clutch sizes. As for the species that show anomalously large values of X, Ricklefs proposes that we are seeing a penalty on large clutches here.

As another possible explanation for the anomalously small X-values, we may note that for all these species, the observed model clutch size is smaller than the predicted optimum, so these species might be experiencing significant reproductive risk.

TABLE 12.6 CONSTANTS X AND a IN THE EQUATION $S_3 = \exp(-aC^X)$ FITTED TO VALUES OF SURVIVAL CALCULATED IN ACCORDANCE WITH THE MAXIMUM REARABLE CLUTCH HYPOTHESIS WHEN A PENALTY IS APPLIED TO THE SURVIVAL OF CLUTCHES LARGER THAN THE MAXIMUM REARABLE CLUTCH SIZE OF 5

Standard deviation of maximum rearable clutch size	Penalty applied*	r	a	X	C^*
0	No	0.967	0.0000965	4.071	6.86
0	Yes	0.957	0.0000232	5.035	6.04
2	No	0.997	0.0137	1.792	7.92
2	Yes	0.999	0.00772	2.280	5.87

* Penalty reduces survival by a factor of 0.1 for each egg in excess of the maximum rearable clutch size.
From Ricklefs (1977b).

On the whole, this study raises more questions than it answers, but they are interesting questions and they are questions that suggest sharper hypotheses to test observationally.

12.4 CLUTCH SIZE AND LATITUDE

I have already mentioned the tendency for the same or related bird species to rear smaller clutches at lower latitudes. This is a very widespread trend, with few exceptions. In this section I will briefly sketch some of the ideas that have been put forward to explain it; we are still pretty far away from a definitive solution.

Lack (1947) proposed a simple explanation for the latitudinal gradient, which follows directly from his first and second claims. Since the vast majority of bird species rear their young after the vernal equinox, when days are shorter at lower latitudes, birds living at lower latitudes have (so Lack reasoned) less time to gather food for their young, hence can feed fewer young, hence should have smaller clutches.

The crossbill and the raven, which breed before the vernal equinox in Europe, would seem to be the exceptions that prove the rule, for the latitudinal gradient is also reversed in these species. (On the other hand, it has been pointed out that the crossbill, though laying its eggs before the equinox, feeds its young *after* the equinox.) But there are tropical species that show the usual gradient, although they breed before the equinox. Besides, nocturnal species like owls, which (on Lack's hypothesis) ought to reverse the direction of the gradient, do not display such a reversal.

Owen (1977) has put forward a refinement of Lack's theory. He accepts Lack's view that availability of food is the main factor but suggests that (somewhat paradoxically one might think) food availability is lower in the tropics. Or rather, effective food availability is lower, because searching for food is more difficult.

His reason for this claim is that where the diversity of food types is greater, birds will have a harder time finding food items that fit their search image. It should be possible to check this by observing the food value gathered per unit time by the same or related species at different latitudes.

Skutch (1949) based his predation hypothesis largely on the latitudinal gradient in clutch size. It is widely accepted that there tends to be more predation in the tropics than in temperate zones in general, and on birds in particular. Possibly Lack's explanation for clutch size is correct in temperate zones, and Skutch's in the tropics. It does, though, seem very unlikely that Skutch's hypothesis could explain the latitudinal gradient completely: for instance, one wonders whether it could explain the European trend depicted in Fig. 12.1.

Cody (1966) tried to explain clutch sizes in general, and the latitudinal gradient in particular, on the basis of a different tradeoff than the one between fecundity and reproductive risk. He thought in terms of a three-way tradeoff among clutch size, predator avoidance, and intraspecific competition.

Partly this incorporates Skutch's ideas, and partly it is tied up with the notions of r- and K-selection. Cody suggested (as have many others before and since) that the tropics are in some sense a more stable habitat, which makes for more K-selection there, whence (in the conventional picture) a premium on competitive ability. This need to compete, together with the need to expend more time and energy avoiding predators, leaves less energy over for reproduction, resulting in smaller tropical clutch sizes.

This is plausible, especially since some other regions that might be thought of as "stable" (such as coastal regions) also see smaller clutches. But such claims are notoriously hard to check: how do you measure the "stability" of a habitat?

ADDITIONAL EXERCISES

12.7. Work out the numerical values corresponding to the graph in Fig. 12.5, for C_{max} = 1 and for $C_{max} = 5$.

12.8. (Computer project) Work out Table 12.5.

12.9. Work out the numbers corresponding to the upper graph in Fig. 12.7.

Chapter 13

Optimal Adaptation to a Variable Environment

Environmental variation, both spatial and temporal, is commonplace in nature. Clearly, this will influence the attempt to optimize with respect to the kinds of tradeoffs discussed in Section 10.2. Indeed, environmental variability plays a significant role in the folklore of life-history theory.

I am going to discuss in this chapter some of the basic concepts having to do with environmental variability and its influence on optimal life histories. As we will see, the influence of a variable environment is more complex than some of the well-known generalizations in this field lead one to believe.

13.1 ENVIRONMENTAL GRAIN

We can conceive of environmental variation, either spatial or temporal, in terms of *patchiness*. In doing so, there are two extreme kinds of patchiness (and a continuum of intermediate types in between them) which we must distinguish (MacArthur and Levins 1964).

Think first of an organism that lives in a habitat that is a mosaic of distinct spatial patches, with two or more different environmental types represented among the patches. If the patches are very small compared with the extent of the normal day-to-day movements of the organism, that organism experiences the different patch types in pretty much the same proportion in which they occur in the habitat. In this case we say that the organism is experiencing "fine-grained" patchiness. On the other hand, if the patches are so large that an organism may spend its whole life in one patch although the population to which the organism belongs straddles several different patch types, then we say that the patchiness is "coarse-grained" for that population.

Similarly, we can idealize temporal variation as a sequence of constant "patches":

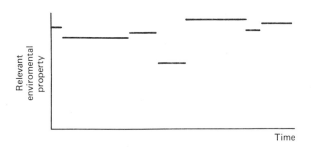

If the duration of the constant "patches" is very short compared with the lifetime of an organism, that organism is experiencing fine-grained temporal variation; if this duration is very long compared with the lifetime of an organism, the population to which that organism belongs is experiencing coarse-grained temporal variation.

The concept of environmental grain depends upon both organism and environment: different species may experience the same environmental property as having quite different grain (thus orangutans experience tropical fruits as fine-grained, but *Drosophila* larvae experience them as coarse-grained), and a species may experience different environmental properties of one habitat as having different grain (fruits are coarse-grained for *Drosophila* larvae, but ambient temperature is fine-grained).

Indeed, we can extend the concept of grain beyond spatial or temporal patches to just about any environmental property. For instance, since most animals eat many times in a lifetime, food differences are generally fine-grained; alternative hosts, when several are available for a parasite, are coarse-grained differences.

In greatest generality: an environmental property is *fine-grained* for a population when each individual in the population experiences variation in that property in the proportion in which it occurs in the habitat; it is *coarse-grained* if each individual can spend its entire lifetime experiencing a single "type" of the property (but the population as a whole experiences variation in the property). I remind you once again that fine and coarse grain are extreme types in a continuum of possibilities.

13.2 THE FITNESS SET

We will pursue the theory of optimal adaptation to a patchy environment along lines adapted by Levins (1968 and earlier works) from the theory of nonlinear programming.

We want to find the fittest phenotype in a patchy environment, and in order to do so it will be convenient first to have an appropriate way to represent the set of all possible phenotypes. One way to do this is by means of a fitness set.

Consider an organism that experiences two patch types (or "environments" in Levins' language) with respect to some property. For the sake of concreteness, we may imagine a predator that has two (and only two) prey types available to it. Suppose the organism has some adaptive (with respect to the "types" of the patches) feature, which can be quantified by labeling it with a real number. For instance, for our imaginary predator, such an adaptive feature may be body size (if we suppose that one prey type is considerably smaller than the other). We can think of the adaptive feature as a label for the phenotype.

In each patch type, the fitness of a phenotype will vary in some way as the adaptive feature varies. For instance, thinking again of our imaginary predator, smaller individuals may feed more efficiently on smaller prey types. So we can make a graph of fitness as a function of phenotype for each patch type (meaning in a habitat that consists of that patch type only):

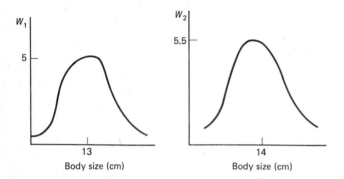

Here W_1 denotes fitness in a habitat of pure patch type 1, and W_2 fitness in a habitat of pure patch type 2.

Thus, if our imaginary predator feeds exclusively on prey type 1 ("experiences only patch type 1"), the corresponding fitness W_1 may vary with the predator's body size (= phenotype) as shown in the left-hand graph. The optimal body size is 13 cm. If our predator feeds exclusively on the rather larger prey type 2, its fitness W_2 may vary as shown in the right-hand graph; now the optimal predator body size is 14 cm.

The two graphs above are one way to portray the set of all possible phenotypes. Another way is to combine these two graphs into one:

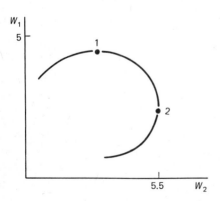

Each point on the curve plotted in this graph represents a possible phenotype; its coordinates give the fitness W_1 in a pure patch type 1 habitat and the fitness W_2 in a pure patch type 2 habitat.

For instance, for our imaginary predator, the point marked 1 is the phenotype with body size 13 cm; it has fitness 5 (optimal) in a habitat containing only prey type 1, and fitness 3 in a habitat containing only prey type 2. These values for the fitnesses can be read off of the above two graphs for W_1 and W_2 as functions of body size. Similarly, the point marked 2 is the phenotype with body size 14 cm. Each point on the curve corresponds to a body size.

This kind of representation of the set of all possible phenotypes is called a *fitness set* (Levins 1968 and earlier works). Specifically, the fitness set consists of the curve in the above graph.

Each point of the fitness set represents a phenotype. Now consider a population that is a mixture of two phenotypes, say of our two optimal phenotypes 1 and 2 in the proportion $p:(1 - p)$. Such a population has a mean fitness $pW_{11} + (1 - p)W_{12}$ in a pure patch type 1 habitat (where W_{ij} is the fitness in patch type i of phenotype j), and $pW_{21} + (1 - p)W_{22}$ in a pure patch type 2 habitat. If we draw a straight line joining points 1 and 2 on the boundary of the fitness set, then the point on that line (let us call it point 3) that has distances from points 1 and 2 in the radio $(1 - p):p$ has as its coordinates on the W_1 and W_2 axes precisely these mean fitnesses. So that point can appropriately be taken as a representation of just such a mixed population.

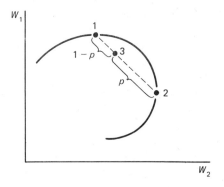

Similarly, for any mixture of phenotypes there is a point in the graph whose coordinates on the W_1 and W_2 axes are the fitnesses of that mixture in the two kinds of pure habitat.

For any set S of points in a plane, the *convex hull* of S is the set of all points that lie on straight lines joining pairs of points in S. So we can also interpret the fitness set in the following way: the convex hull of the fitness set is a representation of the mean fitnesses in the two pure habitat types of pure or mixed populations. The pure populations are, once again, represented by points of the fitness set itself.

If the fitness set is convex (as in our example of the imaginary predator), then all the points that represent mixed populations will lie inside the boundary of the fitness set (that is just the definition of a convex set). But a fitness set can also be concave, and then some of the points representing mixed populations will lie outside the fitness set, as here:

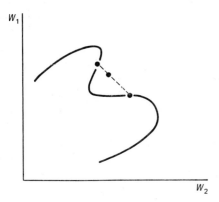

It is not difficult to see that if the two optimal phenotypes in the two "pure" habitats are very similar, then the fitness set will be convex, while the farther apart those two phenotypes are, the more likely is the fitness set to be concave.

Relating this back to our earlier development of ESS, Levins' use of the word "phenotype" in the present context is in the same spirit as our use of the word "strategy" in Section 9.1.1, and I will sometimes use the word strategy instead of phenotype. When a "mixed strategy" in the sense of Section 9.1.1 corresponds to the adoption of different strategies by different individuals in a population, we have a "mixed population" in the present sense.

13.3 THE ADAPTIVE FUNCTION

Now we are ready to get on with our original problem, which was to maximize fitness in a patchy environment. In order to proceed, we must next answer the following question: supposing that a population has fitness W_1 in a pure type 1 habitat and fitness W_2 in a pure type 2 habitat, what is its fitness in a habitat that is a mixture of patches of types 1 and 2.

The calculation of fitness in a variable environment will be different in fine-grained and in coarse-grained environments (which is why we drew this distinction in Section 13.1), so we will consider these two cases separately.

In a fine-grained environment, where each individual experiences the different patch types in given proportions, the fitness of a phenotype will be the mean taken over all patch types. That is: if each individual member of a phenotype experiences the two patch types 1 and 2 in the proportion $P:(1 - P)$, then the fitness of that phenotype will be

$$W = PW_1 + (1 - P)W_2 \qquad (13.1)$$

In a fine-grained environment with patches of types 1 and 2 occurring in the proportion $P:(1 - P)$, we will call the function

$$A(W_1, W_2) = PW_1 + (1 - P)W_2 \qquad (13.2)$$

the *adaptive function,* following Levins (1968 and earlier works). It gives the fitness in the specified fine-grained environment of a population whose fitness in an environment of pure type 1 is W_1 and whose fitness in an environment of pure type 2 is W_2. If we plot the contours $A(W_1, W_2) =$ constant, we get the following (for the particular case $P = 0.1$):

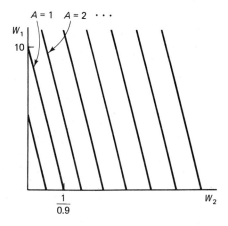

For $P = 0.5$ we get

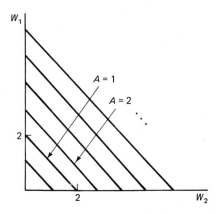

and for $P = 0.9$ we get

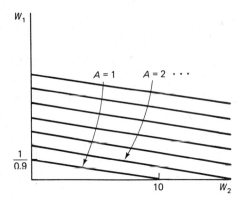

Now, each population corresponds to a point in this same plane, as we saw in the preceding subsection. Our optimization hypothesis is that selection acts to maximize A, subject to appropriate constraints. The appropriate constraint is that only those populations are possible that lie in the convex hull of the fitness set. So putting together the fitness set and the adaptive function in one picture gives a graphical solution for the optimal phenotype or mixture of phenotypes: it corresponds to the point in the convex hull of the fitness set that lies on the contour with the largest value of $A(W_1, W_2)$.

For instance, let's look again at our imaginary predator from Section 13.2, and find the optimal body size for this predator in an environment in which the two food types occur, in a fine-grained way, equally often ($P = 0.5$). We found the fitness set in Section 13.2; now we'll superimpose the adaptive function contours on it:

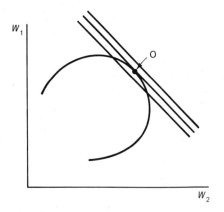

The optimal population is at the point marked "O"; it is a pure population, consisting of a single phenotype, because it occurs on the border of the fitness set. We could find out the corresponding body size by going back to our first two graphs in Section 13.2.

The above "derivation" of the adaptive function (13.2) is, admittedly, a hand-waving argument. I think it is quite plausible, but it bothers me that I do not know of a more rigorous argument. The coarse-grained case has been studied a lot more and is, I think, better understood.

Suppose, then, that the patch types occur in the proportion $P:(1 - P)$, but in a coarse-grained way. This means that each individual spends its whole life in one patch type, but each of its ancestors occupied either patch type 1 or patch type 2, in the ratio $P:(1 - P)$. Fitness W is the ratio of individuals in one generation to individuals in the next, so the ratio of individuals in the nth generation to individuals in the first is W^n. But of these n generations, Pn experience patch type 1 (and have fitness W_1), while $(1 - P)n$ experience patch type 2 (and have fitness W_2). So

$$W^n = W_1^{Pn} W_2^{(1-P)n}$$

or

$$W = W_1^P W_2^{(1-P)}$$

Therefore, the adaptive function in a coarse-grained environment is

$$A(W_1, W_2) = W_1^P W_2^{(1-P)} \tag{13.3}$$

To recapitulate: this is the fitness in an environment in which patch types 1 and 2 occur in a coarse-grained way in the ratio $P:(1 - P)$, for a population whose mean fitness in an environment that is pure type 1 (resp. 2) is W_1 (resp. W_2).

Actually, we have already discussed population growth (without age structure) in a coarse-grained environment, in Section 3.6. That discussion can shed some light on the adaptive function (13.3).

You will recall that in Section 3.6 we looked at the behavior of the expected population density, and of the extinction probability. The former depended on the arithmetic mean over all patches (in our present language) of the growth rate. But the adaptive function (13.3) is a *geometric* mean.

The extinction probability was found in Section 3.6 to depend on the arithmetic mean $\overline{[\ln(\lambda)]}$ of the logarithms of the growth rates over all patches. Taken over n generations (with the index i labeling generations), this is

$$\overline{[\ln(\lambda)]} = \left(\sum_i \ln \lambda_i \right) \Big/ n = \left(\ln \prod_i \lambda_i \right) \Big/ n$$

$$= \left\{ \ln \left[\left(\prod_i \lambda_i \right)^{1/n} \right]^n \right\} \Big/ n = \ln \left(\prod_i \lambda_i \right)^{1/n}$$

which is just the logarithm of the adaptive function (13.3)—again arguing, as in obtaining (13.3), that the product contains Pn factors of W_1 and $(1 - P)n$ factors of W_2.

Therefore, at least in the absence of age structure, maximization of the adaptive function (13.3) is equivalent to minimization of the extinction probability for phenotypes. The phenotype with the smallest extinction probability is the one that is most likely to predominate in the long run (Haldane and Jayakar 1963, Bulmer 1985).

For populations with age structure, the mathematics is much more complicated. The reason is that, as you will recall from Section 9.2, with age structure the finite rate of increase λ is a meaningful measure of population growth only asymptotically, as we approach a stable age distribution. In a random environment, with the Leslie matrix changing from one iteration to the next, the concept of stable age distribution becomes problematical. So the argument used above to obtain (13.3), and the considerations in Section 3.6, do not generalize in a straightforward way to age-structured populations.

These problems have been dealt with by Tuljapurkar and Orzack (1980) and Tuljapurkar (1982a, 1982b). I am not going to go into them here. Instead, when it comes to applying the formalism to life-history theory in Section 13.5, I will assume constant fertility and survival, so that in effect there is no age structure and the above arguments apply.

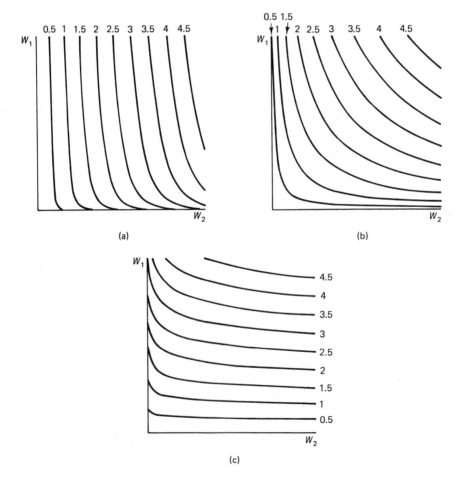

Figure 13.1 The contours $A(W_1, W_2)$ = constant, for (a) $P = 0.1$, (b) $P = 0.5$, (c) $P = 0.9$. Each contour is labeled with its A-value.

The contours $A(W_1, W_2)$ = constant for the adaptive function (13.3) are "hyperbolic" in form (that is, asymptotic to both axes). Defining W_1 as the vertical axis, the smaller P in equation (13.3) is, the steeper are the slopes of these contours. Figure 13.1 shows the forms of the contours A = const., for $P = 0.1$, $P = 0.5$, and $P = 0.9$. Just as before, the optimal population in the patchy environment is given by that point of the convex hull of the fitness set that has the highest value of A associated with it. Using again our imaginary predator as an example (with $P = 0.5$):

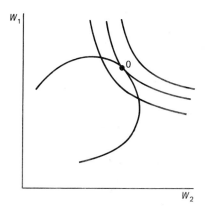

13.4 FURTHER REMARKS

The adaptive contours $A(W_1, W_2)$ = constant are straight lines for extremely fine-grained environments and hyperbolas for extremely coarse-grained environments. For intermediate environments, the adaptive contours will be curves lying somewhere between straight lines and hyperbolas.

If the fitness set is convex, the optimal strategy will always be a pure one (lying on the boundary of the fitness set). The same is true if the fitness set is not convex and the patchiness is fine-grained. But for a concave fitness set and a coarse-grained environment, the optimal strategy may be a mixed population (lying outside the fitness set but within its convex hull:

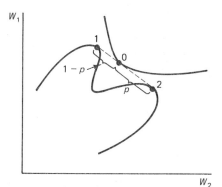

In the case depicted above, the optimum O is a mixture of phenotypes 1 and 2 in the proportions $p:(1 - p)$.

The formalism characterizes the optimal population but, in the spirit of ESS theory, it does not provide a mechanism for attaining or for maintaining the mixture. For instance, if the two "horns" of a nonconvex fitness set represented simply alternative alleles, one could easily be lost through a run of encounters of one patch type. It would seem that one genotype has to produce both morphs. This is a deep problem in ESS theory.

In some cases the mixed strategies simply will not be attainable owing to genetic constraints. In such a case, points outside the fitness set itself (corresponding to mixed populations) are not realistic possibilities for end states of evolution, so we must no longer use the convex hull in the optimization. The result, when the fitness set is not convex, will be multiple *local* optima:

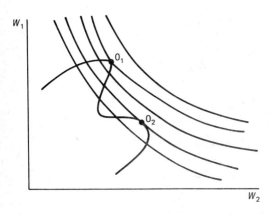

Here the (pure) strategies O_1 and O_2 are both maxima (of the adaptive function) with respect to local variations of phenotype. As well, O_1 is the global maximum, the one phenotype that has the highest fitness of all. If the variation within a population could realistically encompass both O_1 and O_2, we expect to observe the global maximum O_1. If this kind of variation is improbable, we might also observe O_2 in some isolated population.

One mechanism that might make mixed strategies attainable is to invoke epigenetic factors. In this view, the outcome of development would not be completely fixed genetically, though (if we are to invoke selection and hence optimization) certain proclivities (i.e., probabilities for different outcomes of development, possibly in response to environmental cues) would be. An optimality approach to epigenesis has been formulated along very similar lines to what we are doing here (Cooper 1981, Cooper and Kaplan 1982) and applied to newt egg sizes (Kaplan and Cooper 1984).

To my knowledge, the most striking examples of seeming multiple strategies within a species involve animal behavior (Gross 1984). It is interesting to note that the possibilities for epigenetic influences are particularly numerous in the realm of animal behavior (Jamieson 1986).

To summarize, there are three different ways to analyze a nonconvex fitness set, each of which makes sense in a different biological context: (1) If mixed strategies are feasible, there is a unique optimum on the convex hull of the fitness set. (2) If only pure strategies are feasible and there is enough variation, there is a unique (global) optimum on the fitness set. (3) If only pure strategies are feasible and realized variation is small relative to the extent of the fitness set, different (local) optima on the fitness set may be observed in different populations.

When there are more than two patch types the same formalism can be developed in higher-dimensional fitness spaces with axes $W_1, W_2, \ldots, W_n$. This is harder to visualize and work with than the two-dimensional case we have discussed so far, and most work on fitness sets has been with only two patch types. Notable exceptions are Cody's work on clutch size (1966) and on the organization of grassland bird communities (1974).

13.5 OPTIMAL REPRODUCTIVE EFFORT IN FLUCTUATING ENVIRONMENTS

Schaffer (1974b) has extended his formalism to the case of coarse-grained environmental fluctuations, for the special case in which reproductive effort and survival rates do not change with age and fertility is either constant or grows geometrically with age. This means, first, that $E_0 = E_1 = E_2 = \cdots = E_w = E$ (reproductive effort the same for all ages). Further, in terms of the quantities b_x and g_x introduced in Section 10.2.4, it means

$$b_x(E_x) = b(E) \qquad \text{for all } x$$

$$g_x(E_x) = g(E) \qquad \text{for all } x$$

so that

$$m_x = b(E)g(E)^x \qquad (13.4)$$

Finally, for the survival rate P_x we have

$$P_x = P(E) \qquad \text{for all } x \qquad (13.5)$$

Exercise 13.1. Use (13.4), (13.5), and Lotka's equation to show that in this case

$$\lambda(E) = b(E) + P(E)g(E)$$

We can save ourselves some writing by assuming fertility (13.4) to be constant, $g(E) = 1$, so let us hereby adopt this restriction. The results generalize immediately to geometrically increasing fertility $[g(E) > 1]$, simply by using the name $P(E)$ for the term $P(E)g(E)$ in the preceding equation. So we will take

$$\lambda(E) = b(E) + P(E) \qquad (13.6)$$

Now suppose that environmental conditions fluctuate on a rather long time scale (annually may be long enough), with only two states for the sake of simplicity: good years and bad years (denoted by subscripts g and b), randomly distributed and with equal probability. Then we have from the equation before (13.3), with $P = 0.5$,

$$W^2 = W_g W_b \qquad (13.7)$$

for fitness in the fluctuating environment.

The answers that we get are going to depend on exactly how the environmental fluctuations affect population processes. There are two kinds of distinction that we need to draw here. The first thing we have to distinguish is whether environmental variations affect b or P or both. The second class of distinctions involves the way in which fluctuations affect the quantities that they do. I am going to start by discussing the form assumed by Schaffer for the environmental effects, and then I will come back to this issue of the second class of distinctions, in Section 13.5.2.

If reproductive success is the only parameter affected by the environmental variation, Schaffer assumes [recall (13.6)]

$$W_g = \lambda_g = b(1 + s) + P$$
$$W_b = \lambda_b = b(1 - s) + P \qquad (13.8)$$

where s measures the departure of good and bad years from the arithmetic mean. If adult survival is the only parameter affected by environmental change, he assumes a similar form

$$W_g = b + P(1 + s)$$
$$W_b = b + P(1 - s) \qquad (13.9)$$

13.5.1 Semelparity and Iteroparity in a Fluctuating Environment

Let us now inquire how environmental fluctuations affect the reproductive strategies of species that are semelparous or iteroparous in the absence of fluctuations, under the assumptions (13.8) and (13.9). We can investigate this question using the method of fitness sets developed in the preceding section.

The two "patch types" with which we are concerned are good years and bad years. So we will construct a fitness set with axes W_g (fitness in an environment with only good years) and W_b (fitness in an environment with only bad years), with W_g and W_b given by either (13.8) or (13.9).

Each possible phenotype corresponds to a choice of reproductive effort E, so we can think of the curve that gives the boundary of the fitness set as being parametrized by E. So if we label our axes with W_g on the vertical axis:

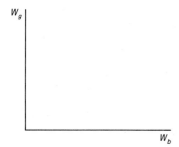

the slope of this curve will be given by

$$dW_g/dW_b = (dW_g/dE)/(dW_b/dE) \qquad (13.10)$$

Similarly, the second derivative is

$$d^2W_g/dW_b^2 = [d(dW_g/dW_b)/dE]/(dW_b/dE) = [(dW_b/dE)(d^2W_g/dE^2)$$
$$- (dW_g/dE)(d^2W_b/dE^2)]/(dW_b/dE)^3 \qquad (13.11)$$

Exercise 13.2. Prove (13.11).

Consider first a species for which both curves $b(E)$ and $P(E)$ are concave (recall Section 10.2.5):

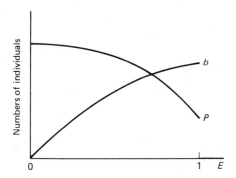

This is (Section 10.2.5) our canonical form for an iteroparous breeder. "Both curves concave" means

$$d^2b/dE^2 < 0 \quad \text{and} \quad d^2P/dE^2 < 0 \qquad \text{for all } E: 0 \le E \le 1 \qquad (13.12)$$

Assume also for the moment that the fluctuations affect primarily fertility, so that equations (13.8) give the fitnesses.

Because of (13.6), the optimal reproductive effort E^* in the arithmetic mean environment is the one for which $db/dE = -dP/dE$:

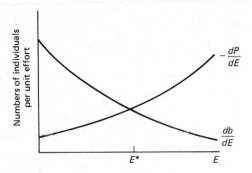

In a "purely good" environment, the optimal reproductive effort E_g^* is given by $(1 + s)db/dE = -dP/dE$:

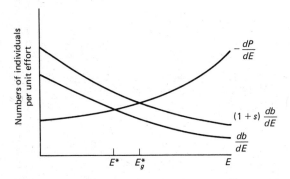

and in a "purely bad" environment the optimal reproductive effort E_b^* is given by $(1 - s)db/dE = -dP/dE$:

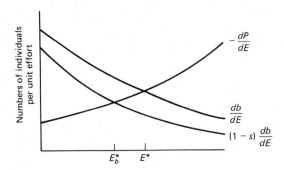

Notice that

$$E_b^* < E^* < E_g^* \qquad (13.13)$$

How do the first derivatives dW_g/dE and dW_b/dE behave? Since E_g^* and E_b^* are the unique maxima of W_g and W_b for $0 \le E \le 1$, it must be that

$$dW_g/dE \begin{cases} >0 & 0 \le E < E_g^* \\ =0 & E = E_g^* \\ <0 & E_g^* < E \le 1 \end{cases} \qquad (13.14)$$

and

$$dW_b/dE \begin{cases} >0 & 0 \le E < E_b^* \\ =0 & E = E_b^* \\ <0 & E_b^* < E \le 1 \end{cases} \qquad (13.15)$$

Now we are ready to construct the fitness set.

First, when $E = 0$ we have $W_g = W_b = P(0)$ [using (13.8) and $b(0) = 0$]:

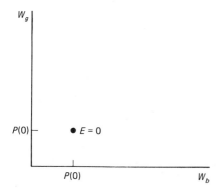

For values of E that are near zero, the slope of our phenotype curve is positive [from (13.10), (13.14), and (13.15)]. What about the second derivative? Substituting equations (13.8) into (13.11), we get

$$d^2W_g/dW_b^2 = -2s[(db/dE)(d^2P/dE^2)$$
$$- (dP/dE)(d^2b/dE^2)]/(dW_b/dE)^3 \qquad (13.16)$$

From (13.12), (13.15), and the fact that $db/dE > 0$ and $dP/dE < 0$ for all E, we see that the second derivative as given by (13.16) is positive for all $E < E_b$. This means that our curve, which has positive slope, is getting steeper as we approach E_b:

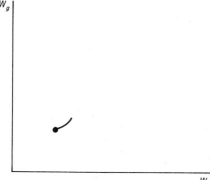

When $F = E_b^*$ the slope is infinite because $dW_b/dE = 0$ [remember (13.10)].

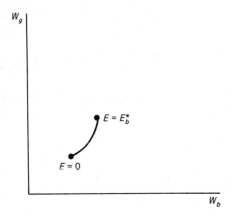

As E increases from E_b^* to E_g^*, we have negative slope [from (13.10), (13.14), and (13.15)] and negative second derivative [from (13.12), (13.15), (13.16), and $db/dE > 0$ and $dP/dE < 0$)]. The slope is zero at E_g^* [from (13.10) and (13.14)]. So we have

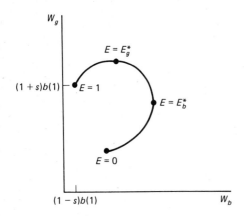

Notice that I have continued the curve past $E = E_g^*$ and filled in the segment to $E = 1$. You can verify for yourself that it has the form I have shown (positive first derivative, negative second derivative for $E_g^* < E \leq 1$).

We now have the complete fitness set for the case of an iteroparous species with environmental fluctuations acting on fecundity. It is convex, and the optimal reproductive effort in a fluctuating environment is something intermediate between E_b^* and E_g^*. In the same way, we can obtain the same result for the case where environmental changes affect adult survival [equation (13.9)]. We will look more closely at this optimum in the next subsection.

But first, let us consider our canonical example of a semelparous species, with both $b(E)$ and $P(E)$ convex (Section 10.2.5):

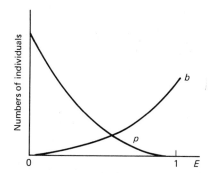

Reasoning in the same way that we just did for the iteroparous case, one can show that now the fitness set is no longer convex.

Exercise 13.3. Assuming that the fluctuations mainly affect fertility [equation (13.8)] and $P(1) = 0$, prove that (a) if $P(0) < (1 - s)b(1)$, the fitness set looks like this:

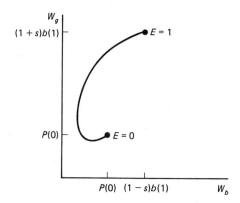

(b) if $P(0) > (1 + s)b(1)$ the fitness set looks like this:

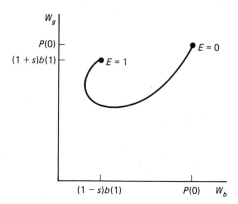

(c) if $(1 - s)b(1) < P(0) < (1 + s)b(1)$, the fitness set looks like this:

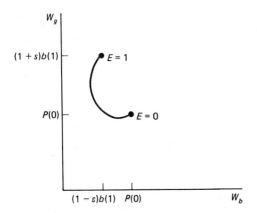

This raises the possibility of a polymorphic strategy. To see what are the conditions for a polymorphic strategy, recall that a mixed strategy is optimal if some contour of the adaptive function is tangent to the boundary of the convex hull of the fitness set (which is simply the straight line joining the extreme points $E = 0$ and $E = 1$):

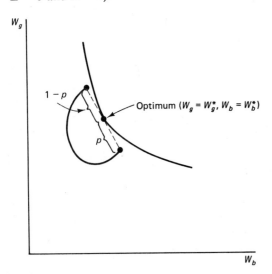

Let us obtain the conditions for such a point of tangency.

First, the straight line joining the phenotypes $E = 0$ and $E = 1$ has a linear equation of the form

$$W_g = AW_b + B \tag{13.17}$$

for some constants A and B. It must pass through the two points $(W_g, W_b) = (P, P)$ and $[(1 + s)b, (1 - s)b]$, where I have set $P = P(0)$ and $b = b(1)$, which gives us the two equations

$$P = AP + B$$

$$(1 + s)b = A(1 - s)b + B$$

Solving these equations for A and B, we find that (13.17) is

$$W_g = [(1 + s)b - P]W_b/[(1 - s)b - P] - 2sbP/[(1 - s)b - P] \qquad (13.18)$$

Exercise 13.4. Prove (13.18).

We are talking about a coarse-grained environment with $P = 0.5$. So the adaptive function is, from (13.3),

$$A(W_g, W_b) = W_g^{1/2}W_b^{1/2} \qquad (13.19)$$

At any point of tangency, the slope of a contour $A(W_g, W_b)$ = constant must be the same as the slope of the straight line (13.18). The slope of such a contour is given by

$$0 = dA = [(1/2)W_g^{-1/2}dW_g]W_b^{1/2} + W_g^{1/2}[(1/2)W_b^{-1/2}dW_b]$$

since A is by definition constant along the contour, so

$$dW_g/dW_b = -W_g/W_b \qquad (13.20)$$

This slope is always negative. So it can be the same as the slope of the straight line (13.18) only if we have the last case in Exercise 13.3. So we need $(1 - s)b < P < (1 + s)b$, and we also need [from (13.18) and (13.20)]

$$-W_g/W_b = [(1 + s)b - P]/[(1 - s)b - P] \qquad (13.21)$$

Equations (13.18) and (13.21) are two equations that must hold simultaneously at the point of tangency. These two equations can be solved for the two quantities W_g and W_b at the point of tangency. It suffices to find just one of these, for instance,

$$W_b^* = sP/[(1 + s) - P/b] \qquad (13.22)$$

Exercise 13.5. Prove (13.22).

Now, there are three possibilities:

1. If $W_b^* \leq (1 - s)b$, the optimum strategy is the pure strategy $E = 1$.
2. If $W_b^* \geq P$, the optimum strategy is the pure strategy $E = 0$.
3. If $(1 - s)b < W_b^* < P$, the optimum strategy is a mixture of individuals with $E = 1$ and individuals with $E = 0$ in the ratio $p{:}(1 - p)$, where $p = (P - W_b^*)/[P - (1 - s)b]$.

It is not hard to show, using (13.22), that the condition on W_b^* that yields case 1 is equivalent to $P/b \leq (1 - s^2)$, and the condition for case 2 is equivalent to $P/b \geq 1$. Nor is it difficult to calculate, using (13.22), the proportion p in the mixed case 3. Summarizing, one obtains, where p is the proportion of individuals with $E = 1$:

$$\left. \begin{array}{ll} p = 0 & \text{if } P/b \geq 1 \\ p = (P/b)(1 - P/b)/[s^2 - (1 - P/b)^2] & \text{if } (1 - s^2) < P/b < 1 \\ p = 1 & \text{if } P/b \leq (1 - s^2) \end{array} \right\} \quad (13.23)$$

Exercise 13.6. Prove (13.23). Our reasoning has applied to the case $(1 - s)b < P < (1 + s)b$ [recall the remark just after equation (13.20)]. Prove that (13.23) is still valid if this restriction is dropped.

Let us recall what the mixed strategy means in the present context: it means that in any given year some individuals (a proportion p of the population) make an all-out reproductive effort, and others (a proportion $1 - p$ of the population) make no reproductive effort at all. It almost sounds like group selection when we put it that way, but we can also put it another way: each individual has a probability p of reproducing in any given year. This has the same end effect.

I think plants are the place to look for this kind of behavior. Notice that the theory makes a testable prediction: increasing either the strength s of environmental fluctuations or the ratio P/b will select for reducing the fraction of individuals breeding yearly. I am not aware of any data bearing on this prediction!

At first, the solutions with $p = 0$ seem preposterous: these are populations in which *no* individuals ever reproduce. A population like this has to die out: how can that possibly be optimal? The answer is, these populations are doomed to die out eventually anyway, owing to their extremely low effective fertility [$b < P < 1$ from (13.23)]. With such a low fertility [and a rather high cost of reproduction since $P(1) = 0$], the population will die out *more slowly* if it doesn't reproduce at all. Viewed in this way, not only result (13.23) but also, maybe, the seemingly contradictory strategy of the California condor (end of the introductory section to Chapter 11) begins to make sense.

13.5.2 Optimal Reproductive Effort for an Iteroparous Species

Within the framework that we have now developed, we can easily consider the effect of environmental fluctuations on reproductive effort for an iteroparous species. Specifically: do increased fluctuations cause optimal reproductive effort to increase or to decrease?

Suppose first that the fluctuations influence mainly effective fertility. Recalling equation (13.7) and using equation (13.8),

$$W^2 = (b + P)^2 - s^2b^2 \qquad (13.24)$$

So the optimal reproductive effort with fluctuation strength s, E_s^*, is given by $dW^2/dE = 0$, or

$$[1 - s^2b/(b + P)](db/dE) = -dP/dE \qquad (13.25)$$

Going back to the top graph on page 338, we get

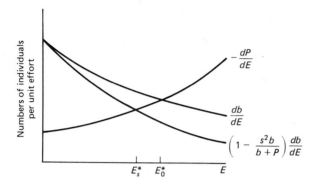

So increased fluctuations cause decreased reproductive effort.

Now suppose the fluctuations mainly influence adult survival. Then the optimal reproductive effort is given, from (13.9), by

$$db/dE = -[1 - s^2P/(b + P)](dP/dE) \qquad (13.26)$$

Exercise 13.7. Prove (13.26).

Now we get

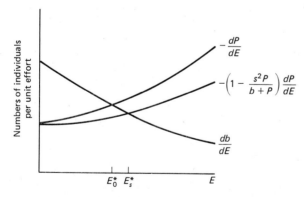

So under these circumstances increased fluctuations select for *increased* reproductive effort.

We see once again the danger of generalizations that seem plausible but are not based on rigorous theory. In the $r - K$ selection scheme of things, increased environmental fluctuations are associated with larger reproductive effort. The calculation we have just done supports this view when the fluctuations act on adult survival, but when the fluctuations act on effective fertility (either through the number of offspring produced or through juvenile survival), we get the *opposite* answer: environmental fluctuations are associated with *smaller* reproductive effort. This view has been dubbed "bet hedging" by Stearns (1976).

Bet hedging refines $r - K$ selection by drawing finer distinctions in the pluralistic fashion of Chapter 6. (In case you have not already done so, you should now read the introductory paragraphs to Chapter 6.) But those distinctions still are not fine enough. You will recall that when I was setting up the present formalism, just after equation (13.7), I mentioned that we need to distinguish not only which parameters are affected by fluctuations but also *how* they are affected. So far, we have assumed the forms (13.8) and (13.9) for environmental effects. But one can certainly contemplate other possibilities. For example, Hastings and Caswell (1979) have explored the forms

$$\left. \begin{aligned} W_g &= b(1 + s) + P \\ W_b &= b/(1 + s) + P \end{aligned} \right\} \tag{13.27}$$

$$\left. \begin{aligned} W_g &= b + P(1 + s) \\ W_b &= b + P/(1 + s) \end{aligned} \right\} \tag{13.28}$$

for environmental effects on effective fertility or on adult survival. With this form, we find, proceeding as earlier in this section, that the optimum effort E_s^* is given by

$$db/dE = -\frac{1 + s^2 b/[2(1 + s)(b + P)]}{1 + s^2 P/[2(1 + s)(b + P)]} \, dP/dE \tag{13.29}$$

on the basis of *either* (13.27) *or* (13.28).

Exercise 13.8. Prove that both (13.27) and (13.28) yield (13.29).

Fluctuations now have the same effect whether they act on b or on P. The direction of that effect now depends on the relative magnitudes of b and P at the optimal value of reproductive effort, rather than depending upon the affected parameter, as earlier in this section. If $b > P$ at the optimal effort, increased fluctuations cause decreased effort; if $P > b$, increased fluctuations cause increased effort.

Exercise 13.9. Prove the last sentence.

I think it would be rash to suggest that either of the forms (13.8), (13.9) or (13.27), (13.28) is "wrong" or "right" or even "typical." [My own prejudice is that if any particular form stands a chance of being typical, it is neither of these (see Exercise 13.14).] The point is that there is biological content in these functional forms, having to do with the specific ways that environmental fluctuations affect specific populations.

Both the $r - K$ and bet hedging schemes appear to be too crude in their present forms, and you will not be surprised to learn that attempts to apply them have met with highly mixed results (for instance, Stearns 1977, Aldridge 1983, Barclay and Gregory 1982, Millar and Zammuto 1983). I think it is realistic to hope that we will eventually sort all this out and arrive at a set of distinctions that is sufficiently refined to be of real use, but at present we are still far from having done so.

13.5.3 Cole's Dilemma in a Fluctuating Environment

We have considered organisms that are semelparous and organisms that are iteroparous in a fluctuating environment, but we have not yet discussed the evolution of semel- vs. iteroparity in a fluctuating environment. Within the context of the resource allocation view of life-history evolution that we have been developing in Sections 10.2 and 13.5, there are two ways that such evolution might take place.

One way is for the shapes of the functions b_x, g_x, P_x, and so on to change. Our entire treatment has been based on inquiring how selection acts on the reproductive efforts E_x within a context fixed, through the overall biological situation, by these functions of reproductive effort. But that biological situation (and hence, the shapes of the functions b_x, P_x, and so on) is defined in part by an organism's behavior, morphology, and physiology, and these things can change in the course of evolution. In general one would expect that in the processes underlying such changes there will be tradeoffs that link changes in different functions. This could lead to quite a fascinating theory, but it is a theory that has yet to be created, at least to my knowledge.

The second way that semel- and iteroparity might both be contained in one adaptive complex is for *given* functions b_x and so on to result in multiple domains of attraction, as mentioned in Section 10.2.5, and I will investigate this possibility here.

Consider, for example, the following situation:

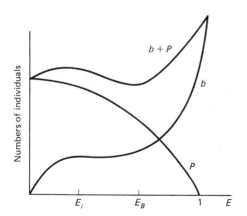

The effort E_i is the iteroparous local optimum, and the effort E_B is the breakpoint (in the terminology of Section 2.2) between the domain of attraction of E_i and the domain of attraction of the semelparous local optimum at $E = 1$. Of course, the effort E_B corresponds to a local *minimum* of λ.

Consider the case in which environmental fluctuations act additively on effective fertility, as in equation (13.8). In a purely bad environment, we have

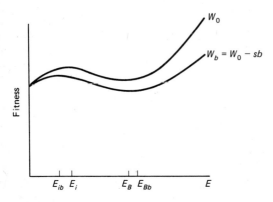

where $W_0 = b + P$ is the growth rate in the arithmetic mean environment. In a purely good environment, we have

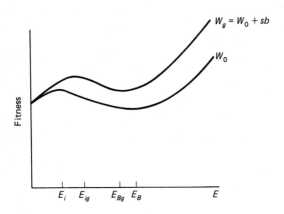

so long as the good years are not so good that we lose the iteroparous optimum and the breakpoint in good years.

Thus we have $E_{ib} < E_{ig} < E_{Bg} < E_{Bb}$, and

$$
dW_b/dE \begin{cases} >0 & 0 \le E < E_{ib} \\ =0 & E = E_{ib} \\ <0 & E_{ib} < E < E_{Bb} \\ =0 & E = E_{Bb} \\ >0 & E_{Bb} < E \le 1 \end{cases} \qquad (13.30)
$$

$$dW_g/dE \begin{cases} >0 & 0 \leq E < E_{ig} \\ =0 & E = E_{ig} \\ <0 & E_{ig} < E < E_{Bg} \\ =0 & E = E_{Bg} \\ >0 & E_{Bg} < E \leq 1 \end{cases} \qquad (13.31)$$

We can sketch the fitness set just as we did in Section 13.5.1:

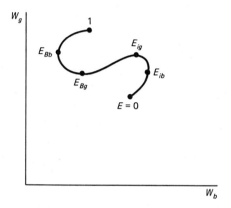

Exercise 13.10. Verify that the fitness set looks like this.

The fitness set is not convex, so there will always be two local optima, one at $E = 1$ (semelparity) and another at some value of E, which I will call E^*, between E_{ib} and E_{ig} (iteroparity). I will analyze this adaptive system on the assumption that polymorphic strategies are ruled out by genetic constraints, and both optima are accessible within the realized variation.

The square of the expected fitness is still given by (13.24), which reads

$$W_i^2 = [b(E^*) + P(E^*)]^2 - s^2 b(E^*)^2 \qquad (13.32)$$

at the iteroparous optimum and

$$W_s^2 = (1 - s^2)b(1)^2 \qquad (13.33)$$

at the semelparous optimum. In the limit of vanishing fluctuations, $s = 0$, we recover the result of Section 10.1 (remembering that what we are calling b here is called bC in Section 10.1): the semelparous strategy is selected for if the number of offspring produced in that strategy exceeds the number produced in the iteroparous strategy by more than the ratio of adult to juvenile survival. How is this result modulated by environmental variation?

From (13.32) and (13.33), the semelparous strategy will be favored if

$$b(1)^2 > b(E^*)^2 + [2b(E^*)P(E^*) + P(E^*)]/(1 - s^2) \qquad (13.34)$$

Suppose first that E^* remains constant as s varies. Then an increase in s will cause an increase in the right-hand side of this inequality; this raises the minimum effective fertility required for the semelparous strategy to be the fitter. So environmental fluctuations select for iteroparity in this case (Schaffer and Gadgil 1975).

However, arguing exactly as in Section 13.5.2, we can show that as s increases, E^* will decrease. This means that $b(E^*)$ and $P(E^*)$ are not independent of s. As s increases, $b(E^*)$ decreases and $P(E^*)$ increases. Unfortunately, this affects the inequality (13.34) in a very complicated way, and while the basic tendency is still selection for iteroparity, one cannot rule out the possibility, depending on the exact shapes of the functions $b(E)$ and $P(E)$, for fluctuations to select for semelparity.

Exercise 13.11. Show that if fluctuations affect primarily adult survival, as in (13.9), this tends to select for semelparity.

This is all based on the additive model (13.8), (13.9) for the effect of environmental variation. With the multiplicative form (13.27), (13.28), we find that the basic tendency (ignoring effects of fluctuations on E^*) is always for environmental fluctuations to favor iteroparity, independently of whether the action of those fluctuations is on b or on P (Hastings and Caswell 1979).

Exercise 13.12. Prove the last sentence.

Clearly, a reliable theory for the influence of environmental fluctuations on life histories is going to have to be highly pluralistic (introductory paragraphs to Chapter 6). I would like at this point to show you a nice table like the one in Section 6.4, summarizing the required distinctions and giving the influence of environmental fluctuations in each case. Unfortunately, a lot more research needs to be done before we can attempt such a synthesis. What I do hope to have accomplished in this chapter is to have given you an appreciation for what the issues are, how we might approach them, and why we need to be very careful in doing so.

ADDITIONAL EXERCISES

13.13. Work out the case of a semelparous species in a fluctuating environment, with environmental change influencing adult survival [equation (13.9)]. That is, obtain the relations that correspond to (13.23) in this case.

13.14. The "additive" and "multiplicative" models for the action of fluctuations [equations (13.8) and (13.9), (13.27) and (13.28), respectively] are not the only possibilities. One might imagine instead that bad years are all pretty much the same, but the "goodness" of good years can vary in magnitude:

$$\lambda_g = b(1 + s) + P$$

$$\lambda_b = b + P$$

Similarly, we might have, for example,

$$\lambda_g = b + P$$

$$\lambda_b = b + (1 + s)P$$

Work out the effects of these two kinds of environmental variability on optimal reproductive effort for an iteroparous species and on Cole's dilemma.

13.15. Holding the strength s of fluctuations constant, consider the effect on Cole's dilemma of different values for the probability P of a good year. If good years are rare, will this tend to select for semelparity or iteroparity? (Don't forget what you learned in Section 13.3!) Which distinctions do you need to draw in order to answer this question?

Chapter 14

Epilogue

The role of theory in scientific endeavor has been pithily summarized by Robert MacArthur (cited in Hutchinson 1975) as follows:

> Scientists are perennially aware that it is best not to trust theory until it is confirmed by evidence. It is equally true, as Eddington pointed out, that it is best not to put too much faith in facts until they have been confirmed by theory. This is why scientists are reluctant to believe in ESP in spite of indisputable facts. This is also why group selection is in such dispute among selectionists. Only when a reasonable theory can account for these facts will scientists believe them.

This appendix briefly sketches a few areas of mathematics that may not be covered in a first-year course in calculus.

A.1 COMPLEX NUMBERS

Many applications of mathematics in ecology require that we solve for the roots of real polynomials, that is, the values of x such that

$$a_n x^n + a_{n-1} x^{n-1} + a_{n-2} x^{n-2} + \cdots + a_1 x + a_0 = 0 \qquad \text{(A.1)}$$

where the coefficients a_i, $i = 0, \ldots, n$, are real numbers, $a_n \neq 0$, and the left-hand side of this equation is called a *polynomial* of *degree n*. If we consider only real values of x, then in general there can be as many as n or as few as 0 solutions to (A1). For instance, the polynomial

$$x^2 - 3x + 2 \qquad \text{(A.2)}$$

has the two roots $x = 1$, $x = 2$; the polynomial

$$x^2 - 2x + 1 \qquad \text{(A.3)}$$

has the one real root $x = 1$; while the polynomial

$$x^2 + 1 \qquad \text{(A.4)}$$

has no real roots.

However, if we extend the real number system to a new system of numbers, the so-called complex numbers (which include real numbers as a special case), then every real polynomial of degree n has exactly n roots. Moreover, in many applications (including some in this book), the new, nonreal roots have a definite observable meaning and are necessary for a full understanding of the problem.

353

The complex numbers are obtained by adding one new object to the set of real numbers. This object is symbolized by the letter i and has the property that $i^2 = -1$. A *complex number* is any object of the form

$$z = a + ib \tag{A.5}$$

where a and b are real numbers. One calls a the *real part* of z and b the *imaginary part* of z.

Algebraic operations with complex numbers are done using the usual rules for real numbers, but remembering that $i^2 = -1$. Thus the sum, difference, product, and quotient of two complex numbers are calculated as follows:

$$(a_1 + ib_1) + (a_2 + ib_2) = (a_1 + a_2) + i(b_1 + b_2) \tag{A.6}$$

$$(a_1 + ib_1) - (a_2 + ib_2) = (a_1 - a_2) + i(b_1 - b_2) \tag{A.7}$$

$$(a_1 + ib_1)(a_2 + ib_2) = a_1 a_2 + ia_1 b_2 + ib_1 a_2 - b_1 b_2$$

$$= (a_1 a_2 - b_1 b_2) + i(a_1 b_2 + b_1 a_2) \tag{A.8}$$

$$(a_1 + ib_1)/(a_2 + ib_2) = [(a_1 + ib_1)(a_2 - ib_2)]/[(a_2 + ib_2)(a_2 - ib_2)]$$

$$= [(a_1 a_2 + b_1 b_2)/(a_2^2 + b_2^2)]$$

$$+ i[(b_1 a_2 - a_1 b_2)/(a_2^2 + b_2^2)] \tag{A.9}$$

In each case the result of the operation is another complex number.

There is a unique complex number 0 [$a = 0$ and $b = 0$ in (A.5)] with the property that $0 + z = z$ and $0 \cdot z = 0$ for any z; and there is a unique complex number 1 ($a = 1$ and $b = 0$) with the property that $1 \cdot z = z$ for any z.

For real functions that can be expressed by power series, the same series are used to define the corresponding complex functions. For example,

$$\sin z = z - z^3/3! + z^5/5! - \cdots \tag{A.10}$$

$$\cos z = 1 - z^2/2! + z^4/4! - \cdots \tag{A.11}$$

$$e^z = 1 + z + z^2/2! + \cdots \tag{A.12}$$

From these three series it follows immediately that for any real x

$$e^{ix} = \cos x + i \sin x \tag{A.13}$$

Exercise A.1. Prove (A.13).

This important result is known as *de Moivre's theorem.*

For any pair of real numbers x, y, we can always find a unique pair of real numbers r, θ such that

$$x = r \cos \theta \qquad y = r \sin \theta \tag{A.14}$$

namely

$$r = (x^2 + y^2)^{1/2} \qquad \theta = \arctan(y/x) \tag{A.15}$$

Therefore, we can write any complex number as

$$z = x + iy = r(\cos \theta + i \sin \theta) = re^{i\theta} \tag{A.16}$$

from de Moivre's theorem. This *polar representation* of complex numbers (so called because if we view x, y as cartesian coordinates in a plane, then r, θ are the corresponding polar coordinates)

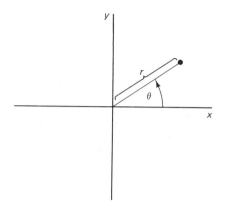

is convenient for a number of purposes. For instance, it is easy to multiply and divide complex numbers in this representation:

$$r_1 \, e^{i\theta_1} \cdot r_2 \, e^{i\theta_2} = r_1 r_2 \, e^{i(\theta_1 + \theta_2)} \tag{A.17}$$

$$[r_1 \, e^{i\theta_1}]/[r_2 \, e^{i\theta_2}] = (r_1/r_2) \, e^{i(\theta_1 - \theta_2)} \tag{A.18}$$

The polar representation also calls attention to the important possibility of assigning "magnitudes" to complex numbers. The "radius" r in polar representation is called the *modulus* of a complex number and is written $|z|$; equivalently, if $z = re^{i\theta} = a + ib$, then

$$|z| = r = (a^2 + b^2)^{1/2} \tag{A.19}$$

Notice that $|z| = 0$ if and only if $z = 0$.

A.2 MATRICES AND EIGENVALUES

Often in ecology it is natural to regard *vectors* of real numbers, rather than individual real numbers, as the basic entities with which one is working. For instance, in multispecies population dynamics, say with s species, it is convenient to think of the whole set of s densities as one mathematical object.

You are probably aware that in working with individual real numbers, functions— mappings of real numbers into real numbers—are tremendously useful. Just so, when working with vectors, one wants to have things that map vectors into vectors. An important class of such mappings (namely, linear ones) can be represented as *matrices*.

An n-dimensional real *column vector* $\mathbf{v}$ is a set of n real numbers $v_1, \ldots, v_n$ arranged in a vertical column:

$$\mathbf{v} = \begin{bmatrix} v_1 \\ v_2 \\ \vdots \\ v_n \end{bmatrix}$$

When I want to represent a whole column vector by one symbol, I will use boldface, as above. (When writing, you can distinguish these objects by underlining.) The individual numbers v_i are called the *components* of **v**; the order in which they are arranged in the column is meaningful: the first component at the top, the others in order toward the bottom.

Strictly speaking, a vector is an abstract object and a column vector is a representation of a vector, but I will use the word *vector* also to refer to a representation as a column vector, to save writing.

One can add and subtract vectors by adding and subtracting their components. Thus if **u** and **v** are vectors,

$$\mathbf{u} = \begin{bmatrix} u_1 \\ u_2 \\ \vdots \\ u_n \end{bmatrix}$$

$$\mathbf{v} = \begin{bmatrix} v_1 \\ v_2 \\ \vdots \\ v_n \end{bmatrix}$$

we can define

$$\mathbf{u} + \mathbf{v} = \begin{bmatrix} u_1 + v_1 \\ u_2 + v_2 \\ \vdots \\ u_n + v_n \end{bmatrix} \tag{A.20}$$

and

$$\mathbf{u} - \mathbf{v} = \begin{bmatrix} u_1 - v_1 \\ u_2 - v_2 \\ \vdots \\ u_n - v_n \end{bmatrix} \tag{A.21}$$

There is a unique vector **0** with the property that $\mathbf{v} + \mathbf{0} = \mathbf{v}$ for any vector **v**; all n components of the *zero vector* **0** are equal to (the real number) 0.

One can also multiply real numbers times vectors. If a is a real number, then

$$a\mathbf{v} = \begin{bmatrix} av_1 \\ av_2 \\ \vdots \\ av_n \end{bmatrix} \tag{A.22}$$

In applications involving vectors, we often run into mappings of one vector into another in which the components of the second vector are linear combinations of the components of the first vector, for instance,

$$u_i = \sum_j M_{ij} v_j \qquad i = 1, \ldots, n \tag{A.23}$$

where u_i are the components of a vector **u** and v_i are the components of a vector **v**.

Again, it is useful to think of the n^2 numbers M_{ij} as the elements of one mathematical object, which we can denote **M**. When one wants to conceive of **M** as being comprised of the individual elements M_{ij}, it is handy to think of the elements as arranged in a square array, or *matrix*, thus:

$$\mathbf{M} = \begin{bmatrix} M_{11} & M_{12} & M_{13} & \cdots & M_{1n} \\ M_{21} & M_{22} & M_{23} & \cdots & M_{2n} \\ & & \vdots & & \\ M_{n1} & M_{n2} & M_{n3} & \cdots & M_{nn} \end{bmatrix} \tag{A.24}$$

Then we can write (A.21) as

$$\mathbf{u} = \mathbf{Mv} \tag{A.25}$$

if the multiplication on the right-hand side of (A.23) is properly defined. But that's no problem: we simply define the components of $\mathbf{Mv}$ to be precisely what is written on the right-hand side of (A.23).

Having mapped $\mathbf{v}$ into $\mathbf{u}$ as in (A.25), we might want to map $\mathbf{u}$ into a new vector by multiplying it with some matrix $\mathbf{P}$. If so, we would like to think it would make sense to write

$$\mathbf{Pu} = \mathbf{PMv} \tag{A.26}$$

which requires that we assign some meaning to the product $\mathbf{PM}$ of two matrices. The demand that $(\mathbf{PM})\mathbf{v} = \mathbf{P}(\mathbf{Mv})$ for any vector $\mathbf{v}$ uniquely determines $\mathbf{PM}$. In terms of components, in order to satisfy this demand we have to define the product by

$$(\mathbf{PM})_{ij} = \sum_k P_{ik} M_{kj} \tag{A.27}$$

Exercise A.2. Prove that (A.27) is the correct definition, by expanding (A.26) in components using (A.23).

Multiplication of real numbers is commutative: if a and b are real numbers, then $ab = ba$. This is not in general true of matrices: for two matrices $\mathbf{P}$, $\mathbf{M}$ we may very well have $\mathbf{PM} \neq \mathbf{MP}$.

There is a unique n-by-n matrix I, called the *unit matrix*, with the property that $\mathbf{IM} = \mathbf{M}$ and $\mathbf{MI} = \mathbf{M}$ for any matrix $\mathbf{M}$. You can easily see from (A.27) that I has the components: $I_{ij} = 1$ if $i = j$, $I_{ij} = 0$ if $i \neq j$.

For any real number $a \neq 0$ there exists a real number a^{-1} such that $aa^{-1} = 1$. This property also does not necessarily carry over to matrices. A matrix $\mathbf{M}$ is called *nonsingular* in case there exists a matrix $\mathbf{M}^{-1}$ with the property that $\mathbf{MM}^{-1} = \mathbf{I}$. (Then it is also true that $\mathbf{M}^{-1}\mathbf{M} = \mathbf{I}$.) A matrix that is not nonsingular is called *singular*. When $\mathbf{M}^{-1}$ exists, it is called the *inverse* of $\mathbf{M}$.

A matrix $\mathbf{D}$ is *diagonal* if $D_{ij} = 0$ for all i, j such that $i \neq j$. That is, a diagonal matrix $\mathbf{D}$ has the form

$$\mathbf{D} = \begin{bmatrix} D_{11} & 0 & 0 & \cdots & 0 \\ 0 & D_{22} & 0 & \cdots & 0 \\ & & \vdots & & \\ 0 & 0 & 0 & \cdot 0 & D_{nn} \end{bmatrix} \tag{A.28}$$

A lot of matrices have the very nice property of being diagonalizable. A matrix M is *diagonalizable* if there exists a nonsingular matrix S such that $\mathbf{S}^{-1}\mathbf{MS}$ is a diagonal matrix. If a matrix is diagonalizable, there is more than one S that will diagonalize it. However, no matter which of these S's one uses, one will get the same n numbers for the diagonal elements D_{ii} of a diagonalized version $\mathbf{D} = \mathbf{S}^{-1}\mathbf{MS}$ of M, though they might not necessarily occur in the same order along the diagonal. These n numbers are called the *eigenvalues* of **M**.

Just as some roots of real polynomials are complex numbers (Section A.1), some eigenvalues of real matrices are complex numbers. In fact, one can show that the n eigenvalues of a matrix are the roots of an nth-degree real polynomial. This means that the matrices **S** that achieve the diagonalization will sometimes have complex numbers for some of their elements, but that's no problem: everything we've done for vectors and matrices with real elements can be done just as well for vectors and matrices with complex elements.

Let some matrix **M** be transformable to the diagonal form $\mathbf{D} = \mathbf{S}^{-1}\mathbf{MS}$. Let $\mathbf{e}_i$ be the vector whose ith component is equal to 1, and all of whose other components are equal to zero:

$$(\mathbf{e}_i)_j = \begin{cases} 1 & \text{if } j = i \\ 0 & \text{if } j \neq i \end{cases} \tag{A.29}$$

Then clearly

$$\mathbf{De}_i = \lambda_i \mathbf{e}_i \qquad i = 1, \ldots, n \tag{A.30}$$

where I have set $\lambda_i = D_{ii}$.

Exercise A.3. Prove (A.30).

Now let

$$\mathbf{v}_i = \mathbf{Se}_i \qquad i = 1, \ldots, n \tag{A.31}$$

Then for each $i = 1, \ldots, n$,

$$\mathbf{Mv}_i = (\mathbf{SDS}^{-1})(\mathbf{Se}_i) = \mathbf{SD}(\mathbf{S}^{-1}\mathbf{S})\mathbf{e}_i = \mathbf{SDe}_i = \mathbf{S}\lambda_i \mathbf{e}_i = \lambda_i \mathbf{Se}_i = \lambda_i \mathbf{v}_i \tag{A.32}$$

The n vectors $\mathbf{v}_i$ are clearly *linearly independent,* that is, no one of them can be expressed as a linear combination of the others. We have shown that if a matrix **M** is diagonalizable, there exist n (possibly complex) linearly independent vectors $\mathbf{v}_i$, $i = 1, \ldots, n$, such that for each i

$$\mathbf{Mv}_i = \lambda_i \mathbf{v}_i \tag{A.33}$$

A vector $\mathbf{v}_i$ satisfying (A.33) is called an *eigenvector* of **M** belonging to the eigenvalue λ_i.

Let **u** be any vector. Then there certainly exists a vector **a** such that $\mathbf{u} = \mathbf{Sa}$, namely, $\mathbf{a} = \mathbf{S}^{-1}\mathbf{u}$. If a_i are the components of **a**, then clearly

$$\mathbf{a} = \sum_i a_i \mathbf{e}_i \tag{A.34}$$

where $\mathbf{e}_i$ are defined in (A.29). Therefore

$$\mathbf{u} = \mathbf{Sa} = \mathbf{S}\sum_i a_i \mathbf{e}_i = \sum_i a_i \mathbf{Se}_i = \sum_i a_i \mathbf{v}_i \tag{A.35}$$

We have shown that *any vector can be written as a linear combination of n linearly independent eigenvectors of a diagonalizable matrix.*

A.3 BLOCK MATRICES

It is sometimes convenient (an example occurs in Section 7.3.2) to break matrices down into *blocks*, for instance, with $n + m = s$, we can express the s-by-s matrix $\mathbf{A}$ as

$$\mathbf{A} = \begin{bmatrix} A(11)_{11} & \cdots & A(11)_{1n} & A(12)_{11} & \cdots & A(12)_{1m} \\ & \cdot & & & \cdot & \\ & \cdot & & & & \\ A(11)_{n1} & \cdots & A(11)_{nn} & A(12)_{n1} & \cdots & A(12)_{nm} \\ A(21)_{11} & \cdots & A(21)_{1n} & A(22)_{11} & \cdots & A(22)_{1m} \\ & \cdot & & & \cdot & \\ & \cdot & & & & \\ A(21)_{m1} & \cdots & A(21)_{mn} & A(22)_{m1} & \cdots & A(22)_{mm} \end{bmatrix}$$

That is, we set

$$A(11)_{ij} = A_{ij} \qquad i = 1, \ldots, n \qquad j = 1, \ldots, n$$

$$A(12)_{ij} = A_{i\,n+j} \qquad i = 1, \ldots, n \qquad j = 1, \ldots, m$$

$$A(21)_{ij} = A_{n+i\,j} \qquad i = 1, \ldots, m \qquad j = 1, \ldots, n$$

$$A(22)_{ij} = A_{n+i\,n+j} \qquad i = 1, \ldots, m \qquad j = 1, \ldots, m$$

Each of the four blocks $\mathbf{A(KL)}$, $K, L = 1, 2$, is itself a matrix: $\mathbf{A(11)}$ is an n-by-n matrix, $\mathbf{A(12)}$ is an n-by-m (rectangular) matrix, $\mathbf{A(21)}$ is an m-by-n (rectangular) matrix, and $\mathbf{A(22)}$ is an m-by-m matrix. So we can write $\mathbf{A}$ as

$$\mathbf{A} = \begin{bmatrix} \mathbf{A(11)} & \mathbf{A(12)} \\ \mathbf{A(21)} & \mathbf{A(22)} \end{bmatrix}$$

for short.

In multiplying block matrices, the same rule (A.27) applies, except that now the blocks are treated as "elements." Thus if $\mathbf{C} = \mathbf{AB}$, with $\mathbf{A}, \mathbf{B},$ and $\mathbf{C}$ all divided into blocks as above (with the same n and m), we have

$$\mathbf{C(I, J)} = \sum_K \mathbf{A(I, K)B(K, J)} \qquad I, J = 1, 2$$

That is,

$$\begin{bmatrix} \mathbf{A(11)} & \mathbf{A(12)} \\ \mathbf{A(21)} & \mathbf{A(22)} \end{bmatrix} \begin{bmatrix} \mathbf{B(11)} & \mathbf{B(12)} \\ \mathbf{B(21)} & \mathbf{B(22)} \end{bmatrix}$$

$$= \begin{bmatrix} \mathbf{A(11)B(11)} + \mathbf{A(12)B(21)} & \mathbf{A(11)B(12)} + \mathbf{A(12)B(22)} \\ \mathbf{A(21)B(11)} + \mathbf{A(22)B(21)} & \mathbf{A(21)B(12)} + \mathbf{A(22)B(22)} \end{bmatrix}$$

You can easily convince yourself of this by experimentation with the case $n = 2, m = 2$.

These ideas extend straightforwardly to subdivisions into more blocks than four, but we will only need divisions into four blocks for our purposes.

A.4 A LITTLE SPECTRAL THEORY

The material in this section is needed only for Section 7.2.2 of the text, and is a little more abstract than the rest of this appendix; so you might want to omit this section on first reading.

In Section A.2 I reminded you that mappings often turn out to be tremendously useful, and motivated matrices as linear mappings of vectors into vectors. Now I am going to suggest that it might be just as useful to think about linear mappings of vectors into numbers.

Such a map has the form

$$a = \sum_i \bar{u}_i v_i \qquad\qquad\qquad (A.36)$$

where a is a number, v_i are the components of a vector $\mathbf{v}$, and $\bar{u}_i$ are the numerical coefficients in the linear mapping. Once again, it will be useful to think of the *collection* of numbers $\{\bar{u}_i, i = 1, \ldots, n\}$ as *one* mathematical object, which I will denote by a boldface character with a bar over it: $\bar{\mathbf{u}}$ and will call a *dual vector*. Then we can abbreviate (A.36) as

$$a = \bar{\mathbf{u}}(\mathbf{v}) \qquad\qquad\qquad (A.37)$$

or even as

$$a = \bar{\mathbf{u}}\mathbf{v} \qquad\qquad\qquad (A.38)$$

Matrices can act on dual vectors in a natural way. Thus if $\mathbf{M}$ is a matrix and $\mathbf{v}$ is a vector, we would like to be able to write

$$\bar{\mathbf{u}}(\mathbf{M}\mathbf{v}) = (\bar{\mathbf{u}}\mathbf{M})\mathbf{v}$$

This we can certainly do, if we just define the dual vector $\bar{\mathbf{u}}\mathbf{M}$ as the row vector with components

$$(\bar{\mathbf{u}}\mathbf{M})_j = \sum_i \bar{u}_i M_{ij} \qquad j = 1, \ldots, n \qquad\qquad (A.39)$$

Exercise A.4. Verify that (A.39) follows from (A.36) and (A.23).

Notice that *matrices multiply to the right on vectors, as in (A.25), and to the left on dual vectors, as in (A.39)*.

If $\mathbf{v}$ is a vector and $\bar{\mathbf{u}}$ is a dual vector, what sort of meaning can we assign to the symbol $\mathbf{v}\bar{\mathbf{u}}$? We might be tempted to view it as identical to (A.38), but a more elegant view is to notice that if we multiply $\mathbf{v}\bar{\mathbf{u}}$ to the right times a vector in the following "natural" way

$$(\mathbf{v}\bar{\mathbf{u}})\mathbf{w} = \mathbf{v}(\bar{\mathbf{u}}\mathbf{w})$$

we get a vector, for $(\bar{\mathbf{u}}\mathbf{w})$ is a number. If we similarly multiply $\mathbf{v}\bar{\mathbf{u}}$ to the *left* times a dual vector $\bar{\mathbf{w}}$, we get a dual vector,

$$\bar{\mathbf{w}}(\mathbf{v}\bar{\mathbf{u}}) = (\bar{\mathbf{w}}\mathbf{v})\bar{\mathbf{u}}$$

since $(\bar{\mathbf{w}}\mathbf{v})$ is a number.

In short: $\mathbf{v}\bar{\mathbf{u}}$ acts exactly like a matrix—therefore, it *is* a matrix. The elements of this matrix are

$$(\mathbf{v}\bar{\mathbf{u}})_{ij} = v_i \bar{u}_j \tag{A.40}$$

If $\{\mathbf{v}_i, i = 1, \ldots, n\}$ is a set of n linearly independent vectors, one can show that there exists a set of n linearly independent dual vectors $\{\bar{\mathbf{v}}_i, i = 1, \ldots, n\}$ such that

$$\bar{\mathbf{v}}_i \mathbf{v}_j = \delta_{ij} \tag{A.41}$$

where δ_{ij} is the *Kronecker delta*

$$\delta_{ij} = \begin{cases} 1 & i = j \\ 0 & i \neq j \end{cases} \tag{A.42}$$

Then the matrix

$$\mathbf{P}_i = \mathbf{v}_i \bar{\mathbf{v}}_i \tag{A.43}$$

is a *projection matrix,* in the following sense. If $\mathbf{w}$ is a linear combination of the set $\{\mathbf{v}_i\}$ of vectors:

$$\mathbf{w} = \sum_i a_i \mathbf{v}_i \tag{A.44}$$

where each a_i is a number, then

$$\mathbf{P}_i \mathbf{w} = a_i \mathbf{v}_i \tag{A.45}$$

The projection $\mathbf{P}_i$ picks out the component of $\mathbf{w}$ "in the direction of" $\mathbf{v}_i$. In particular,

$$\mathbf{P}_i \mathbf{v}_j = \delta_{ij} \mathbf{v}_j \qquad i, j = 1, \ldots, n \tag{A.46}$$

Exercise A.5. Prove (A.45).

Summing over the projections in all "directions," we get the unit matrix:

$$\sum_i \mathbf{P}_i = \mathbf{I} \tag{A.47}$$

for summing both sides of (A.45) over i, we get

$$\left(\sum_i \mathbf{P}_i\right)\mathbf{w} = \sum_i a_i \mathbf{v}_i = \mathbf{w}$$

which is exactly what the unit matrix does.

If $\{\mathbf{v}_i, i = 1, \ldots, n\}$ is a set of linearly independent eigenvectors of some diagonalizable matrix $\mathbf{A}$, as in equation (A.33), then of course (A.41) to (A.47) still apply. We can, however, in this case do some other interesting things with the projections $\mathbf{P}_i$. Consider, for instance, the sum

$$\sum_i \lambda_i \mathbf{P}_i$$

where λ_i is the eigenvalue corresponding to $\mathbf{v}_i$.

We showed at the end of Section A.2 that any vector can be written as a linear combination of the eigenvectors of $\mathbf{A}$, as in (A.44). Let's see what the previous quantity does to such a linear combination:

$$\sum_i \lambda_i \mathbf{P}_i \mathbf{w} = \sum_i \lambda_i \mathbf{P}_i \sum_j a_j \mathbf{v}_j = \sum_i \sum_j \lambda_i a_j \delta_{ij} \mathbf{v}_j = \sum_i \lambda_i a_i \mathbf{v}_i$$

But

$$\mathbf{A}\mathbf{w} = \mathbf{A} \sum_i a_i \mathbf{v}_i = \sum_i a_i \lambda_i \mathbf{v}_i$$

which is the same as our previous answer. This is true for *any* vector $\mathbf{w}$. Therefore

$$\sum_i \lambda_i \mathbf{P}_i = \mathbf{A} \tag{A.48}$$

Equation (A.48) is called the *spectral resolution* of $\mathbf{A}$.
        Similarly, one can show that

$$\sum_i \lambda_i^2 \mathbf{P}_i = \mathbf{A}^2 \tag{A.49}$$

and reasoning further in the same way, one readily sees that

$$\sum_i \lambda_i^m \mathbf{P}_i = \mathbf{A}^m \tag{A.50}$$

for any nonnegative integer m.

Exercise A.6. Prove (A.49). [It will then be obvious to you how to prove (A.50) as well.]

Bibliography

Abraham, R. H., and C. D. Shaw. 1983. *Dynamics—The geometry of behavior. Part 2: Chaotic behavior.* Aerial Press, Inc., Santa Cruz, Calif.

Abrams, P. 1977. Density-independent mortality and interspecific competition: A test of Pianka's niche overlap hypothesis. *Am. Nat.* 111:539–552.

Abrams, P. 1980. Consumer functional response and competition in consumer-resource systems. *Theoret. Pop. Biol.* 17:80–102.

Abrams, P. 1982. Functional response of optimal foragers. *Am. Nat.* 120:382–390.

Abrams, P. 1984. Variability in resource consumption rates and the coexistence of competing species. *Theoret. Pop. Biol.* 25:106–124.

Addicott, J. F. 1974. Predation and prey community structure: An experimental study of the effect of mosquito larvae on the protozoan communities of pitcher plants. *Ecology* 55:475–492.

Aldridge, D. W. 1982. Reproductive tactics in relation to life-cycle bioenergetics in three natural populations of the freshwater snail, *Leptoxis carinata. Ecology* 63:196–208.

Allee, W. C. 1931. *Animal aggregations: A study in general sociology.* University of Chicago Press, Chicago.

Allen, J. A. 1959. On the biology of *Pandalus borealis* Kroyer with reference to a population off the Northumberland coast. *J. Mar. Biol. Assoc. UK* 38:189–220.

Anderson, R. M. 1981. Population ecology of infectious disease agents. *In* May, R. M. (ed.). *Theoretical ecology.* second edition. Blackwell Scientific Publishers, Oxford.

Anderson, R. M., and R. M. May. 1985. Helminth infections of humans: Mathematical models, population dynamics, and control. pp. 1–102 *in* Baker, J. R., and R. Muller (eds.). *Advances in parasitology,* vol. 24. Academic Press, London.

Andrewartha, H. G., and L. C. Birch. 1954. *The distribution and abundance of animals.* University of Chicago Press, Chicago.

Armstrong, R. A., and R. McGehee. 1976. Coexistence of species competing for shared resources. *Theoret. Pop. Biol.* 9:317–328.

Armstrong, R. A., and R. McGehee. 1980. Competitive exclusion. *Am. Nat.* 115:151–170.

Arneodo, A., P. Coullet, J. Peyraud, and C. Tresser. 1982. Strange attractors in Volterra equations for species in competition. *J. Math. Biol.* 14:153–157.

Askenmo, C. 1979. Reproductive effort and return rate of male pied flycatchers. *Am. Nat.* 114:748–752.

Ayala, F. S., and C. A. Campbell. 1974. Frequency dependent selection. *Ann. Rev. Ecol. Syst.* 5:115–139.

Ayling, A. M. 1981. The role of biological disturbance in temperate subtidal encrusting communities. *Ecology* 62:830–847.

Bak, R. P. M., and B. E. Luckhurst. 1980. Constancy and change on coral reef habitats along depth gradients at Curacao. *Oecologia* 47:145–155.

Barclay, H. J., and P. Y. Gregory. 1982. An experimental test of life history evolution using *Drosophila melanogaster* and *Hyla regilla*. *Am. Nat.* 120:26–40.

Barnes, H. 1962. So-called anecdysis in *Balanus balanoides* and the effect of breeding upon the growth of the calcareous shell of some common barnacles. *Limnol. Oceanogr.* 7:462–473.

Batschelet, E. 1971. *Introduction to mathematics for life scientists.* Springer-Verlag, Berlin.

Bender, E. A., T. J. Case, and M. E. Gilpin. 1984. Perturbation experiments in community ecology: Theory and practice. *Ecology* 65:1–13.

Bent, A. F. 1939. Life histories of North American woodpeckers. *U.S. Nat. Mus. Bull.* 174.

Berger, M. E. 1972. Population structure of olive baboons (*Papio anubis*) (J. P. Fisher) in the Laikipia district of Kenya. *E. Afr. Wildl. J.* 10:159–164.

Bernadelli, H. 1941. Population waves. *J. Burma Res. Soc.* 31:1–18.

Beverton, R. J. H., and S. J. Holt. 1957. *On the dynamics of exploited fish populations.* H. M. Stationery Off., London, Fish. Invest., ser. 2, vol. 19.

Birch, L. C. 1948. The intrinsic rate of natural increase of an insect population. *J. Anim. Ecol.* 16:15–26.

Blair, W. F. 1960. *The rusty lizard.* Texas University Press, Austin.

Bonner, J. T., ed. 1980. *Evolution and development.* Springer-Verlag, Berlin.

Botkin, D. B., J. F. Janak, and J. R. Wallis. 1972. Some ecological consequences of a computer model of forest growth. *J. Ecol.* 60:849–872.

Bradley, D. J., and R. M. May. 1978. Consequences of helminth aggregation for the dynamics of schistosomiasis. *Trans. Roy. Soc. Trop. Med. Hyg.* 72:262–273.

Braithwaite, R. W., and A. K. Lee. 1979. A mammalian example of semelparity. *Am. Nat.* 113:151–155.

Briand, F. 1983a. Environmental control of food web structure. *Ecology* 64:253–263.

Briand, F. 1983b. Biogeographic patterns in food web organization. *In* DeAngelis, D. L., W. M. Post, and G. Sugihara (eds.). *Current trends in food web theory,* Oak Ridge National Laboratory Technical Report ORNL-5983.

Briand, F. 1985. Structural singularities of freshwater food webs. *Verh. Internat. Verein. Limnol.* 22:3356–3364.

Briand, F., and J. E. Cohen. 1984. Community food webs have scale-invariant structure. *Nature* 307:264–266.

Briand, F., and J. E. Cohen. 1987. Environmental correlates of chain length in community food webs. MS.

Brody, S. 1945. *Bioenergetics of growth.* Reinhold, New York.

Brown, J. H., D. W. Davidson, J. C. Munger, and R. S. Inouye. 1986. Experimental community ecology: the desert granivore system. *In* Diamond, J. M., and T. J. Case (eds.). *Community ecology.* Harper & Row, New York.

Brown, J. H., D. W. Davidson, and O. J. Reichman. 1979. An experimental study of competition between seed-eating desert rodents and ants. *Am. Zool.* 19:1129–1142.

Brown, W. L., and E. O. Wilson. 1956. Character displacement. *Syst. Zool.* 5:49–64.

Browne, R. A. 1982. The costs of reproduction in brine shrimp. *Ecology* 63:43–47.

Bulmer, M. G. 1985. Selection for iteroparity in a variable environment. *Am. Nat.* 126: 63–71.

Buss, L. W. 1986. Aspects of competition on hard surfaces in the sea. *In* Diamond, J. M., and T. J. Case (eds.). *Community ecology.* Harper & Row, New York.

Calder, W. A. III. 1984. *Size, function, and life history.* Harvard University Press, Cambridge, Mass.

Campbell, J. H. 1982. Autonomy in evolution. *In* Milkman, R. (ed.). *Perspectives on evolution.* Sinauer Associates, Sunderland, Mass.

Case, T. J., and M. E. Gilpin. 1974. Interference competition and niche theory. *Proc. Nat. Acad. Sci. USA* 71:3073–3077.

Caswell, H. 1978. Predator mediated coexistence: A non-equilibrium model. *Am. Nat.* 112:127–154.

Caswell, H. 1982a. Optimal life histories and the maximization of reproductive value: A general theorem for complex life cycles. *Ecology* 63:1218–1222.

Caswell, H. 1982b. Stable population structure and reproductive value for populations with complex life cycles. *Ecology* 63:1223–1231.

Caughley, G. 1976. Plant-herbivore systems. *In* May, R. M. (ed.). *Theoretical ecology.* Blackwell Scientific Publishers, Oxford.

Caughley, G. 1979. What is this thing called carrying capacity? *In* Boyle, M. S., and L. D. Hayden-Wing (eds.). *North American elk: Ecology, behavior, and management.* University of Wyoming Press.

Champeney, D. C. 1973. *Fourier transforms and their physical applications.* Academic Press, London.

Charlesworth, B. 1980. Evolution in age-structured populations. Cambridge University Press, Cambridge.

Charnov, E. L., and J. R. Krebs. 1974. On clutch-size in birds. A review. *Ardea* 58:1–124.

Charnov, E. L., and W. M. Schaffer. 1973. Life history consequences of natural selection: Cole's result revisited. *Am. Nat.* 107:791–793.

Chay, T. R. 1986. Oscillations and chaos in the pancreatic beta-cell. *In* Othmer, H. G. (ed.). *Nonlinear oscillations in biology and chemistry.* Springer-Verlag, Berlin.

Chesson, P. L. 1983. Coexistence of competitors in a stochastic environment: The storage effect. *In* Freedman, H. I., and C. Strobeck (eds.). *Population biology.* Springer-Verlag, Berlin.

Chesson, P. L. 1986. Variation and species interactions. *In* Diamond, J. M., and T. J. Case (eds.). *Community ecology.* Harper & Row, New York.

Chesson, P. L., and R. R. Warner. 1981. Environmental variability promotes coexistence in lottery competitive systems. *Am. Nat.* 117:923–943.

Childress, J. R. 1972. Behavioral ecology and fitness theory in a tropical hermit crab. *Ecology* 53:960–964.

Chodorowski, A. 1959. Ecological differentiation of turbellarians in Harsz Lake. *Polskie Archwm. Hydrobiol.* 6:33–73.

Clark, C. W. 1976. *Mathematical bioeconomics.* Wiley, New York.

Clarke, K. U., and J. B. Sardesai. 1959. An analysis of the effects of temperature upon growth and reproduction of *Dysducus fasciatus* Sign. (hemiptera, Pyrrhocoridae). *Bull. Entomol. Res.* 50:387–405.

Clough, G. C. 1965. Viability in wild meadow voles under various conditions of population density, season, and reproductive activity. *Ecology* 46:119–134.

Cody, M. L. 1966. A general theory of clutch size. *Evolution* 20:174–184.

Cody, M. L. 1974. *Competition and the structure of bird communities.* Princeton University Press, Princeton, N.J.

Cohen, J. E. 1976. Schistosomiasis: A human host-parasite system. *In* May, R. M. (ed.). *Theoretical ecology.* Blackwell Scientific Publishers, Oxford.

Cohen, J. E. 1977a. Mathematical models of schistosomiasis. *Ann. Rev. Ecol. Syst.* 8: 209–233.

Cohen, J. E. 1977b. Ratio of prey to predators in community food webs. *Nature* 270: 165–167.

Cohen, J. E. 1978. *Food webs and niche space.* Princeton University Press, Princeton, N.J.

Cohen, J. E., and F. Briand. 1984. Trophic links of community food webs. *Proc. Nat. Acad. Sci. USA* 81:4105–4109.

Cole, L. C. 1954. The population consequences of life history phenomena. *Q. Rev. Biol.* 29:103–137.

Connell, J. H. 1970. A predator-prey system in the marine intertidal region. I. *Balanus glandula* and several predatory species of *Thais. Ecol. Monogr.* 40:49–78.

Connell, J. H. 1983. On the prevalence and relative importance of interspecific competition: Evidence from field experiments. *Am. Nat.* 122:661–696.

Connor, E. F., and D. Simberloff. 1984. Neutral models of species' co-occurrence patterns. *In* Strong, D. R., D. Simberloff, L. G. Abele, and A. B. Thistle (eds.). *Ecological communities: Conceptual issues and the evidence,* Princeton University Press, Princeton, N.J.

Cooper, W. S. 1981. Natural decision theory: A general formalism for the analysis of evolved characteristics. *J. Theoret. Biol.* 92:401–415.

Cooper, W. S., and R. H. Kaplan. 1982. Adaptive "coin-flipping": A decision-theoretic examination of natural selection for random individual variation. *J. Theoret. Biol.* 94: 135–151.

Copeland, B. J., K. R. Tenore, and D. B. Horton. 1974. Oligohaline regime. *In* Odum, H. T., B. J. Copeland, and E. A. McMahan (eds.). *Coastal ecological systems of the United States, Volume 2,* The Conservation Foundation, Washington, D.C.

Copson, E. T. 1935. *An introduction to the theory of functions of a complex variable.* Oxford University Press, Oxford.

Cramer, N. F., and R. M. May. 1972. Interspecific competition, predation and species diversity: A comment. *J. Theoret. Biol.* 34:289–293.

Crisp, D. J., and B. S. Patel. 1961. The interaction between breeding and growth rate in the barnacle *Elminius modestus* Darwin. *Limnol. Oceanogr.* 6:105–115.

Cushing, D. H. 1971. The dependence of recruitment on parent stock in different groups of fishes. *J. Cons. Intern. Explor. Mer* 33:340–362.

Cushing, D. H., and J. G. K. Harris. 1973. Stock and recruitment and the problem of density dependence. *Rapp. Procès-Verb. Cons. Intern. Explor. Mer* 164:142–155.

Darwin, C. R. 1859. *On the origin of species by natural selection.* John Murray, London.

Davidson, D. W., R. S. Inouye, and J. H. Brown. 1984. Granivory in a desert ecosystem: Experimental evidence for indirect facilitation of ants by rodents. *Ecology* 65:1780–1786.

Day, R. J. 1972. Stand structure, succession, and the use of southern Alberta's Rocky Mountain forest. *Ecology* 53:472–478.

Dayton, P. K. 1971. Competition, disturbance, and community organization: The provision and subsequent utilization of space in a rocky intertidal community. *Ecol. Monogr.* 41:351–389.

Dayton, P. K. 1973a. Two cases of resource partitioning in an intertidal community: Making the right prediction for the wrong reason. *Am. Nat.* 107:662–670.

Dayton, P. K. 1973b. Dispersion, dispersal, and persistence of the annual intertidal alga, *Postelsia palmaeformis* ruprecht. *Ecology* 54:433–438.

DeAngelis, D. L. 1975. Stability and connectance in food web models. *Ecology* 56:238–243.

DeAngelis, D. L. 1980. Energy flow, nutrient cycling, and ecosystem resilience. *Ecology* 61:764–771.

DeAngelis, D. L., R. H. Gardner, J. B. Mankin, W. M. Post, and J. H. Carney. 1978. Energy flow and the number of trophic levels in ecological communities. *Nature* 273: 406–407.

Dickman, M. D., and M. B. Gochnauer. 1978. Impact of sodium chloride on the microbiota of a small stream. *Environ. Pollut.* 17:109–126.

Drake, J. A. 1985. *Some theoretical and empirical explorations of structure in food webs.* Ph.D. thesis, Purdue University.

Ducklow, H. W., D. A. Purdie, P. J. LeB. Williams, and J. M. Daviues. 1986. Bacterioplankton: A sink for carbon in a coastal marine plankton community. *Science* 232: 865–867.

Farlow, J. O. 1976. A consideration of the trophic dynamics of a late cretaceous large dinosaur community (Oldman Formation). *Ecology* 57:841–857.

Feller, W. 1968. *An introduction to probability theory and its applications.* Vol. I. Third edition. Wiley, New York.

Fenchel, T. 1975. Character displacement and coexistence in mud snails (Hydrobiidae). *Oecologia* 20:19–32.

Fisher, R. A. 1930. *The genetical theory of natural selection.* Oxford University Press, Oxford.

Forsythe, G. E., M. A. Malcolm, and C. B. Moler. 1977. *Computer methods for mathematical computations.* Prentice-Hall, Englewood Cliffs, N.J.

Fotheringham, N. 1971. Life history patterns of the littoral gastropods *Shaskyus festivus* (Hinds) and *Ocenebra poulsoni* (Carpenter) (Prosobranchia: Muricidae). *Ecology* 52: 742–757.

Frazer, R. A., W. J. Duncan, and A. R. Collar. 1960. *Elementary matrices*. Cambridge University Press, Cambridge.

Fritz, R. S., N. E. Stamp, and T. G. Halverson. 1982. Iteroparity and semelparity in insects. *Am. Nat.* 120:264–268.

Fujii, K. 1977. Complexity-stability relationship of two-prey-one-predator species system model: Local and global stability. *J. Theoret. Biol.* 69:613–623.

Futuyma, D. J., and M. Slatkin. 1983. *Coevolution*. Sinauer Associates, Sunderland, Mass.

Gadgil, M., and W. Bossert. 1970. Life history consequences of natural selection. *Am. Nat.* 104:1–24.

Gardner, M. R., and W. R. Ashby. 1970. Connectance of large dynamical (cybernetic) systems: Critical values for stability. *Nature* 288:784.

Geist, V. 1971. *Mountain sheep: A study in behavior and evolution*. University of Chicago Press, Chicago.

Gilpin, M. E. 1975a. Limit cycles in competition communities. *Am. Nat.* 109:51–60.

Gilpin, M. E. 1975b. Stability of feasible predator-prey systems. *Nature* 254:137–139.

Gilpin, M. E. 1979. Spiral chaos in a predator-prey model. *Am. Nat.* 113:306–308.

Gilpin, M. E., and T. J. Case. 1976. Multiple domains of attraction in competition communities. *Nature* 261:40–42.

Gilpin, M. E., and J. M. Diamond. 1984. Are species co-occurrences on islands non-random, and are null hypotheses useful in community ecology? *In* Strong, D. R., D. Simberloff, L. G. Abele, and A. B. Thistle (eds.). *Ecological communities: Conceptual issues and the evidence*. Princeton University Press, Princeton, N.J.

Glynn, P. W. 1976. Some physical and biological determinants of coral community structure in the eastern Pacific. *Ecol. Monogr.* 46:431–456.

Goodwin, B. C., N. Holder, and C. C. Wylie (eds.). 1983. *Development and evolution*. Cambridge University Press, Cambridge.

Gould, S. J., and R. Lewontin. 1979. The spandrels of San Marco and the Panglossian paradigm: A critique of the adaptationist programme. *Proc. Roy. Soc. Lond., B. Biol. Sci.* 205:581–598.

Grant, P. R. 1986. Interspecific competition in fluctuating environments. *In* Diamond, J. M., and T. J. Case (eds.). *Community ecology*. Harper & Row, New York.

Gross, M. R. 1984. Sunfish, salmon, and the evolution of alternative reproductive strategies and tactics in fish. *In* Potts, G. W., and R. J. Wootton (eds.). *Fish reproduction: Strategies and tactics*. Academic Press, London.

Grubb, P. J. 1986. Roles for sparsity and patchiness in the maintenance of species richness in plant communities. *In* Diamond, J. M., and T. J. Case (eds.). *Community ecology*. Harper & Row, New York.

Grubb, P. J. 1977. The maintenance of species richness in plant communities: the importance of the regeneration niche. *Biol. Rev.* 52:107–145.

Guckenheimer, J. 1979. The bifurcation of quadratic functions. *Ann. N.Y. Acad. Sci.* 316:78–85.

Guckenheimer, J., G. Oster, and A. Ipaktchi. 1977. The dynamics of density dependent population models. *J. Math. Biol.* 4:101–147.

Haigh, J., and J. Maynard Smith. 1972. Can there be more predators than prey? *Theoret. Pop. Biol.* 3:290–299.

Haldane, J. B. S. 1927. A mathematical theory of natural and artificial selection. Part IV. *Proc. Camb. Phil. Soc.* 23:607–615.

Haldane, J. B. S., and S. D. Jayakar. 1963. Polymorphism due to selection of varying direction. *J. Genet.* 58:237–242.

Hall, C. A. S., and J. W. Day, Jr. (eds.). 1977. *Ecosystem modelling in theory and practice.* Wiley, New York.

Hamilton, W. D. 1967. Extraordinary sex ratios. *Science* 156:477–488.

Hammond, J. 1958. Fertility. *In* Parkes, A. S. (ed.). *Marshall's physiology of reproduction,* Vol. 2, pp. 648–740. Longmans, Green, London.

Hanski, I. 1981. Coexistence of competitors in patchy environment with and without predation. *Oikos* 37:306–312.

Hardin, G. 1968. The tragedy of the commons. *Science* 162:1243–1246.

Harper, J. L. 1969. The role of predation in vegetational diversity. *Brookhaven Symposium in Biology No. 22, Diversity and Stability in Ecological Systems,* 48–62.

Hassell, M. P., J. H. Lawton, and R. M. May. 1976. Patterns of dynamical behaviour in single species populations. *J. Anim. Ecol.* 45:471–486.

Hastings, A. 1980. Disturbance, coexistence, history, and competition for space. *Theoret. Pop. Biol.* 18:363–373.

Hastings, A. 1986. The invasion question. *J. Theoret. Biol.* 121:211–220.

Hastings, A., and H. Caswell. 1979. Role of environmental variability in the evolution of life history strategies. *Proc. Nat. Acad. Sci. USA* 76:4700–4703.

Hayssen, V., and R. C. Lacy. 1985. Basal metabolic rates in mammals: Taxonomic differences in the allometry of BMR and body mass. *Comp. Biochem. Physiol.* 81A:741–754.

Heinselman, M. L. 1973. Fire in the virgin forests of the boundary waters canoe area, Minnesota. *Quart. Res.* 3:329–382.

Heusner, A. A. 1985. Body size and energy metabolism. *Ann. Rev. Nutr.* 5:267–293.

Holgate, P. 1967. Population survival and life history phenomena. *J. Theoret. Biol.* 14:1–10.

Holling, C. S. 1959. The components of predation as revealed by a study of small-mammal predation of the European pine sawfly. *Canad. Entomol.* 91:293–320.

Holling, C. S. 1966. The strategy of building models of complex ecological systems. *In* Watt, K. E. F. (ed.). *Systems analysis in ecology.* Academic Press, New York.

Holling, C. S. 1973. Resilience and stability of ecological systems. *Ann. Rev. Ecol. Syst.* 4:1–23.

Holt, R. D. 1977. Predation, apparent competition, and the structure of prey communities. *Theoret. Pop. Biol.* 12:197–229.

Holt, R. D. 1983. Optimal foraging and the form of the predator isocline. *Am. Nat.* 122:521–541.

Holt, R. D. 1984. Spatial heterogeneity, indirect interactions, and the coexistence of prey species. *Am. Nat.* 124:377–406.

Holt, R. D. 1985. Density-independent mortality, non-linear competitive interactions, and species coexistence. *J. Theoret. Biol.* 116:479–493.

Horwood, J. W. 1981. *Dynamics of large mammal populations.* Wiley, New York.

Hsu, S. B., and S. P. Hubbell. 1979. Two predators competing for two prey species: An analysis of MacArthur's model. *Math. Biosci.* 47:143–171.

Hubbell, S. P. 1986. Biology, chance and history and the structure of tropical rainforest tree communities. *In* Diamond, J. M., and T. J. Case (eds.). *Community ecology.* Harper & Row, New York.

Humphreys, W. F. 1979. Production and respiration in animal populations. *J. anim. ecol.* 48:427–454.

Hunkapiller, T., H. Huang, L. Hood, and J. H. Campbell. 1982. The impact of modern genetics on evolutionary theory. *In* Milkman, R. (ed.). *Perspectives on evolution.* Sinauer Associates, Sunderland, Mass.

Hunter, R. D. 1980. Effects of grazing on the quantity and quality of freshwater aufwuchs. *Hydrobiologia* 69:251–259.

Hunter, R. D., and W. D. Russell-Hunter. 1983. Bioenergetic and community changes in intertidal aufwuchs grazed by *Littorina littorea. Ecology* 64:761–769.

Hutchinson, G. E. 1959. Homage to Santa Rosalia, or why are there so many kinds of animals? *Am. Nat.* 93:145–159.

Hutchinson, G. E. 1961. The paradox of the plankton. *Am. Nat.* 95:137–145.

Hutchinson, G. E. 1967. *A treatise on limnology. Volume II. Introduction to lake biology and the limnoplankton.* Wiley, New York.

Hutchinson, G. E. 1975. Variations on a theme by Robert MacArthur. *In* Cody, M. L., and J. M. Diamond (eds.). *Ecology and evolution of communities.* Harvard University Press, Cambridge, Mass.

Hutchinson, G. E. 1978. *An introduction to population ecology.* Yale University Press, New Haven.

Hutchinson, G. E., and R. H. MacArthur. 1959. A theoretical ecological model of size distributions among species of animals. *Am. Nat.* 93:117–125.

Iooss, G., and D. D. Joseph. 1980. *Elementary stability and bifurcation theory.* Springer-Verlag, Berlin.

Isaacs, J. D. 1972. Unstructured marine food webs and "pollutant analogues." *Fish. Bull.* 70:1053–1059.

Jackson, J. C. B., and L. Buss. 1975. Allelopathy and spatial competition among coral reef invertebrates. *Proc. Nat. Acad. Sci. USA* 72:5160–5163.

Jamieson, I. G. 1986. The functional approach to behavior: Is it useful? *Am. Nat.* 127:195–208.

Jordan, P., and G. Webbe. 1969. *Human schistosomiasis.* C. C. Thomas, Springfield.

Kaplan, R. H., and W. S. Cooper. 1984. The evolution of developmental plasticity in reproductive characterstics: An application of the "adaptive coin-flipping" principle. *Am. Nat.* 123:393–410.

Karlson, R. H. 1981. A simulation study of growth inhibition and predator resistance in *Hydractinia echinata. Ecol. Modelling* 13:29–47.

Karlson, R. H., and L. W. Buss. 1984. Competition, disturbance and local diversity patterns of substratum-bound clonal organisms: A simulation. *Ecol. Modelling* 23:243–255.

Karlson, R. H., and J. C. B. Jackson. 1981. Competitive networks and community structure: A simulation study. *Ecology* 62:670–678.

Kauffman, S. A. 1985. Self-organization, selective adaptation, and its limits. *In* Depew, D. J., and B. H. Weber (eds.). *Evolution at a crossroads,* MIT Press, Cambridge, Mass.

Kauffman, S. A. 1986. Selective Adaptation and its Limits in Automata and Evolution. *In* Bienenstock, E., F. Fogelman-Soulie, and G. Weisbuch (eds.). *Disordered systems and biological organization,* NATO ASI Series in Computer and Systems Sciences, Springer-Verlag, Berlin.

Kerr, S. R. 1974. Theory of size distribution in ecological communities. *J. Fish. Res. Bd. Can.* 31:1859–1862.

Kirkendall, L. R., and N. Chr. Stenseth. 1985. On defining "breeding once." *Am. Nat.* 125:189–204.

Klomp, H. 1970. The determination of clutch-size in birds. A review. *Ardea* 58:1–124.

Koch, A. L. 1974. Competitive coexistence of two predators utilizing the same prey under constant environmental conditions. *J. Theoret. Biol.* 44:387–395.

Koford, C. B. 1953. The California condor. *Nat. Audubon Soc. Res. Report* 4.

Kolata, G. 1986. What does it mean to be random? *Science* 231:1068–1070.

Kolmogorov, A. N. 1936. Sulla teoria di Volterra della lotta per l'esisttenza. *Giorn. Instituto Ital. Attuari* 7:74–80.

Krebs, C. J. 1989. *Ecological methodology.* Harper & Row, New York.

Krebs, J. R., and N. B. Davies. 1984. *Behavioural ecology: An evolutionary approach.* Sinauer Associates, Sunderland, Mass.

Kremer, J. N., and S. W. Nixon. 1978. *A coastal marine ecosystem.* Springer-Verlag, Berlin.

Kurnick, A. A., H. B. Hinds, M. W. Pasvogel, and B. L. Reid. 1961. Dietary energy levels for laying hens as related to age and environmental temperatures. *Poul. Sci.* 40:1483–1491.

Lack, D. 1947. The significance of clutch-size. *Ibis* 89:302–352.

Lack, D. 1948. Natural selection and family size in the Starling. *Evolution* 2:95–110.

Lack, D. 1954. The natural regulation of animal numbers. Oxford University Press, Oxford.

Lack, D. 1966. Population studies of birds. Oxford University Press, Oxford.

Lamming, G. E. 1969. Nutrition and reproduction. *In* Cuthbertson, D. (ed.). *Nutrition of animals of nutritional importance,* Vol. 1, pp. 411–453. Pergamon, Elmsford, N.J.

Lavigne, D. M. 1982. Similarity of energy budgets in animal populations. *J. anim. ecol.* 51:195–206.

Lavigne, D. M., W. W. Barchard, S. Innes, and N. A. Øritsland. 1982. Pinniped bioenergetics. *FAO Fisheries Series* 5(4):191–235.

Lawlor, L. R. 1978. A comment on randomly constructed ecosystem models. *Am. Nat.* 112:445–447.

Lawton, J. H., and S. L. Pimm. 1978. Population dynamics and the length of food chains. *Nature* 272:189–190.

Leslie, P. H. 1945. On the use of matrices in certain population mathematics. *Biometrika* 33:183–212.

Leslie, P. H. 1948. Some further notes on the use of matrices in population mathematics. *Biometrika* 35:213–245.

Levin, S. A. 1974. Dispersion and population interactions. *Am. Nat.* 108:207–228.

Levine, S. 1976. Competitive interactions in ecosystems. *Am. Nat.* 110:903–910.

Levins, R. 1968. *Evolution in changing environments.* Princeton University Press, Princeton.

Levins, R. 1974. The qualitative analysis of partially specified systems. *Ann. N.Y. Acad. Sci.* 231:123–138.

Levins, R. 1975. Evolution in communities near equilibrium. *In* Cody, M. L., and J. Diamond (eds.). *Ecology and evolution of communities.* Harvard University Press, Cambridge, Mass.

Levins, R. 1979. Coexistence in a variable environment. *Am. Nat.* 114:765–783.

Lewis, E. G. 1942. On the generation and growth of a population. *Sankhya* 6:93–96.

Lewontin, R. C. 1965. Selection for colonizing ability. pp. 79–94 *in* Baker, H. G., and G. L. Stebbins (eds.). *The genetics of colonizing species.* Academic Press, New York.

Lewontin, R. C. 1979. Fitness, survival, and optimality. *in* Horn, D. J., G. R. Stairs, and R. D. Mitchell (eds.). *Analysis of ecological systems.* Ohio State University Press, Columbus, pp. 3–21.

Lewontin, R. C., and D. Cohen. 1969. On population growth in a randomly varying environment. *Proc. Nat. Acad. Sci. USA* 62:1056–1060.

Lloyd, M., and H. S. Dybas. 1966. The periodical cicada problem. II. Evolution. *Evolution* 20:466–505.

Loeb, L. 1917. The concrescence of follicles in the hypotypical ovary. *Biol. Bull.* 32:187–193.

Lorenz, E. N. 1963. Deterministic nonperiodic flow. *J. Atmos. Sci.* 20:130–141.

Lotka, A. J. 1913. A natural population norm. II. *J. Wash. Acad. Sci.* 3:289–293.

Loucks, O. L. 1970. Evolution of diversity, efficiency, and community stability. *Amer. Zool.* 10:17–25.

Lubchenco, J. 1978. Plant species diversity in a marine intertidal community: Importance of herbivore food preference and algal competitive abilities. *Am. Nat.* 112:23–39.

Ludwig, D. 1974. *Stochastic population theories.* Springer-Verlag, Berlin.

Ludwig, D., D. D. Jones, and C. S. Holling. 1978. Qualitative analysis of insect outbreak systems: The spruce budworm and forest. *J. Anim. Ecol.* 47:315–332.

MacArthur, R. H. 1972. *Geographical ecology.* Harper & Row, New York.

MacArthur, R. H., and R. Levins. 1964. Competition, habitat selection, and character displacement in a patchy environment. *Proc. Nat. Acad. Sci. USA* 51:1207–1210.

MacArthur, R. H., and R. Levins. 1967. The limiting similarity, convergence and divergence of coexisting species. *Am. Nat.* 101:377–385.

MacArthur, R. H., and E. O. Wilson. 1967. *The theory of island biogeography.* Princeton University Press, Princeton.

MacDonald, G. 1965. The dynamics of helminth infections, with special reference to schistosomes. *Trans. Roy. Soc. Trop. Med. Hyg.* 59:489–506.

Mackey, M., M. Santavy, and P. Selepova. 1986. A mitotic oscillator with a strange attractor and distributions of cell cycle times. *In* Othmer, H. G. (ed.). *Nonlinear oscillations in biology and chemistry.* Springer-Verlag, Berlin.

Maguire, L. A., and J. W. Porter. 1977. A spatial model of growth and competition strategies in coral communities. *Ecol. Modelling* 3:249–271.

Markus, H. C. 1934. Life history of the black-headed minnow, *Pimephales promelas. Copeia* 70:116–122.

May, R. M. 1972a. Limit cycles in predator-prey communities. *Science* 177:900–902.

May, R. M. 1972b. Will a large complex system be stable? *Nature* 238:413–414.

May, R. M. 1973. Stability in randomly fluctuating versus deterministic environments. *Am. Nat.* 107:621–650.

May, R. M. 1974a. *Stability and complexity in model ecosystems.* Princeton University Press, Princeton, N.J.

May, R. M. 1974b. On the theory of niche overlap. *Theoret. Pop. Biol.* 5:297–332.

May, R. M. 1975. Biological populations obeying difference equations: Stable points, stable cycles, and chaos. *J. Theoret. Biol.* 51:511–524.

May, R. M. 1976. Simple mathematical models with very complicated dynamics. *Nature* 261:459–467.

May, R. M. 1977a. Thresholds and breakpoints in ecosystems with a multiplicity of stable states. *Nature* 269:471–477.

May, R. M. 1977b. Togetherness among schistosomes: Its effect on the dynamics of the infection. *Math. Biosci.* 35:301–343.

May, R. M. 1978. The dynamics and diversity of insect faunas. *In* Mound, L. A., and N. Waloff (eds.). *Diversity of insect faunas.* Blackwell, Oxford.

May, R. M. 1981a. Models for single populations. *In* May, R. M. (ed.). *Theoretical ecology.* second edition. Blackwell Scientific Publishers, Oxford.

May, R. M. 1981b. Patterns in multi-species communities. *In* May, R. M. (ed.). *Theoretical ecology.* second edition. Blackwell Scientific Publishers, Oxford.

May, R. M. 1981c. *Theoretical ecology.* second edition. Blackwell Scientific Publishers, Oxford.

May, R. M., and W. J. Leonard. 1975. Nonlinear aspects of competition between three species. *SIAM J. Appl. Math.* 29:243–253.

May, R. M., and R. H. MacArthur. 1972. Niche overlap as a function of environmental variability. *Proc. Nat. Acad. Sci. USA* 69:1109–1113.

May, R. M., and G. F. Oster. 1976. Bifurcations and dynamic complexity in simple ecological models. *Am. Nat.* 110:573–599.

McGehee, R., and R. A. Armstrong. 1977. Some mathematical problems concerning the ecological principle of competitive exclusion. *J. Differ. Equations* 23:30–52.

McKendrick, H. G. 1914. Studies on the theory of continuous probabilities, with special reference to its bearing on natural phenomena of a progressive nature. *Proc. Lond. Math. Soc.,* Ser. II, 13:401–416.

McNaughton, S. J. 1970. Fitness sets for *Typha. Am. Nat.* 104:337–341.

McNeill, S. 1973. The dynamics of a population of *Leptoterna dolabrata* (Heteroptera: Miridae) in relation to its food resources. *J. Anim. Ecol.* 42:495–507.

McNeill, S., and J. H. Lawton. 1970. Annual production and respiration in animal populations. *Nature* 225:472–474.

McQueen, D. J., J. R. Post, and E. L. Mills. 1985. Trophic relationships in freshwater pelagic ecosystems. MS.

Menge, B. A. 1976. Organization of the New England rocky intertidal community: Role of predation, competition, and environmental heterogeneity. *Ecol. Monogr.* 46:355–393.

Mertz, D. B. 1971a. Life history phenomena in increasing and decreasing populations. pp. 361–399 *in* Patil, G. P., E. C. Pielou, and W. E. Waters (eds.). *Statistical ecology,* Vol. 2. Pennsylvania State University Press, University Park.

Mertz, D. B. 1971b. The mathematical demography of the California condor population. *Am. Nat.* 105:437–454.

Millar, J. S., and R. M. Zammuto. 1983. Life histories of mammals: An analysis of life tables. *Ecology* 64:631–635.

Minchella, D. J., and P. T. Loverde. 1981. A cost of increased early reproductive effort in the snail *Biomphalaria glabrata. Am. Nat.* 118:876–881.

Morley, F. H. W. 1966. Stability and productivity of pastures. *Proc. N. Z. Soc. Anim. Prod.* 26:8–21.

Moser, J. W. 1972. Dynamics of an uneven-aged forest stand. *Forest Sci.* 18:184–191.

Murdoch, W. W. 1966. Population stability and life history phenomena. *Am. Nat.* 100: 45–51.

Murphy, G. I. 1968. Pattern in life history and the environment. *Am. Nat.* 102:390–404.

Nasell, I., and W. M. Hirsch. 1973. The transmission dynamics of schistosomiasis. *Comm. Pure & Appl. Math.* 26:395–453.

Needham, E. 1964. *The growth process in animals.* Van Nostrand, Princeton.

Neill, W. E. 1972. Effects of size-selective predation on community structure in laboratory aquatic microcosms. Ph.D. dissertation, University of Texas, Austin. 177 pp.

Nisbet, R. M., and W. S. C. Gurney. 1982. *Modelling fluctuating populations.* Wiley, Chichester.

Norberg, R. 1981. Temporary weight loss in breeding birds may result in more fledged young. *Am. Nat.* 118:838–850.

Odum, H. T. 1983. *Systems ecology: An introduction.* Wiley, New York.

Osman, R. W. 1977. The establishment and development of a marine epifaunal community. *Ecol. Monogr.* 47:37–63.

Oster, G., A. Ipaktchi, and S. Rocklin. 1976. Phenotypic structure and bifurcation behavior of population models. *Theoret. Pop. Biol.* 10:365–382.

Oster, G. F., and E. O. Wilson. 1978. *Caste and ecology in the social insects.* Princeton University Press, Princeton, N.J.

Owen, D. F. 1977. Latitudinal gradients in clutch size: An extension of David Lack's theory. *in* Stonehouse, B., and C. Perrins (eds.). *Evolutionary ecology,* University Park Press, Baltimore, pp. 171–180.

Packard, N. H., J. P. Crutchfield, J. D. Farmer, and R. S. Shaw. 1980. Geometry from a time series. *Phys. Rev. Lett.* 45:712–716.

Paine, R. T. 1966. Food web complexity and species diversity. *Am. Nat.* 100:65–75.

Paine, R. T. 1971. A short-term experimental investigation of resource partitioning in a New Zealand rocky intertidal habitat. *Ecology* 52:1096–1106.

Paine, R. T. 1974. Intertidal community structure. Experimental studies on the relationship between a dominant competitor and its principal predator. *Oecologia* 15:93–120.

Paine, R. T. 1984. Ecological determinism in the competition for space. *Ecology* 65: 1339–1348.

Paris, O. A., and F. H. Pitelka. 1962. Population characteristics of the terrestrial isopod *Armidillidium vulgare* in California grassland. *Ecology* 43:229–248.

Park, T. 1954. Experimental studies of interspecies competition. II. Temperature, humidity, and competition in two species of *Tribolium. Physiol. Zool.* 27:177–238.

Parrish, J. D., and S. B. Saila. 1970. Interspecific competition, predation and species diversity. *J. Theoret. Biol.* 27:207–220.

Patten, B. C. 1971. *Systems analysis and simulation in ecology.* 4 vols. Academic Press, New York.

Peters, R. H. 1983. *The ecological implications of body size.* Cambridge University Press, Cambridge.

Peterson, C. F., E. A. Sauter, D. H. Conrad, and C. F. Lampman. 1960. Effect of energy level and laying house temperature on the performance of white leghorn pullets. *Poul. Sci.* 39:1010–1017.

Pianka, E. R. 1975. Niche relations of desert lizards. *In* Cody, M. L., and J. M. Diamond (eds.). *Ecology and evolution of communities.* Harvard University Press, Cambridge, Mass.

Pianka, E. R. 1976. Natural selection of optimal reproductive tactics. *Amer. Zool.* 16: 775–784.

Pimm, S. L. 1980. Properties of food webs. *Ecology* 61:219–225.

Pimm, S. L. 1982. *Food webs.* Chapman & Hall, London.

Pimm, S. L., and J. H. Lawton. 1977. The number of trophic levels in ecological communities. *Nature* 268:329–331.

Pimm, S. L., and J. H. Lawton. 1978. On feeding on more than one trophic level. *Nature* 275:542–544.

Pimm, S. L., and R. L. Kitching. 1987. The determinants of food chain lengths. *Oikos* 50:302–307.

Platt, T., and K. Denman. 1977. Organization in the pelagic ecosystem. *Helgol. Wiss. Meeresunters.* 30:575–581.

Platt, T., and K. Denman. 1978. The structure of pelagic marine ecosystems. *Rapp. P.-V. Reun. Cons. Int. Explor. Mer* 173:60–65.

Porter, J. W. 1972. Predation by *Acanthaster* and its effect on coral species diversity. *Am. Nat.* 106:487–492.

Porter, J. W. 1974. Community structure of coral reefs on opposite sides of the Isthmus of Panama. *Science* 186:543–545.

Post, W. M., and S. L. Pimm. 1983. Community assembly and food web stability. *Math. Biosci.* 64:169–192.

Price, G., and J. Maynard Smith. 1973. The logic of animal conflict. *Nature* 246:15–18.

Pulliam, H. R. 1975. Coexistence of sparrows: a test of community theory. *Science* 184: 474–476.

Pulliam, H. R. 1983. Ecological community theory and the coexistence of sparrows. *Ecology* 64:45–52.

Quinn, J. F. 1982. Competitive hierarchies in marine benthic communities. *Oecologia* 54:129–135.

Rapp, P. E., I. D. Zimmerman, A. M. Albano, G. C. deGuzman, N. N. Greenbaum, and T. R. Bashore. 1986. Experimental studies of chaotic neural behavior: Cellular activity and electroencephalographic signals. *In* Othmer, H. G., ed., *Nonlinear oscilations in biology and chemistry.* Springer-Verlag, Berlin.

Rappoldt, C., and P. Hogeweg. 1980. Niche packing and number of species. *Am. Nat.* 116:480–492.

Rejmánek, M., and P. Starý. 1979. Connectance in real biotic communities and critical values for stability of model ecosystems. *Nature* 280:311–313.

Rescigno, A., and I. W. Richardson. 1967. The struggle for life. I. Two species. *Bull. Math. Biophys.* 29:377–388.

Ricker, W. E. 1954. Stock and recruitment. *J. Fish. Res. Bd. Canada* 11:559–623.

Ricker, W. E. 1958. Handbook of computations for biological statistics of fish populations. *J. Fish. Res. Bd. Canada* 119.

Ricklefs, R. E. 1969. An analysis of nesting mortality in birds. *Smithson. Contrib. Zool.* 9:1–48.

Ricklefs, R. E. 1977a. On the evolution of reproductive strategies in birds: Reproductive effort. *Am. Nat.* 111:453–478.

Ricklefs, R. E. 1977b. A note on the evolution of clutch size in altricial birds. *in* Stonehouse, B., and C. Perrins (eds.). *Evolutionary ecology,* University Park Press, Baltimore, pp. 193–214.

Risch, S. J., and C. R. Carroll. 1982. Effect of a keystone predaceous ant, *Solenopsis geminata,* on arthropods in a tropical agroecosystem. *Ecology* 63:1979–1983.

Roberts, A. 1974. The stability of a feasible random ecosystem. *Nature* 251:607–608.

Root, R. B. 1967. The niche exploitation pattern of the blue-gray gnatcatcher. *Ecol. Monogr.* 37:317–350.

Rössler, O. E. 1976. Different types of chaos in two simple differential equations. *Z. Naturforsch. B* 31:1664–1670.

Rössler, O. E. 1979. Chaos. *In* Guttinger, W., and H. Eikemeier (eds.). *Structural stability in physics.* Springer-Verlag, Berlin.

Roughgarden, J. 1974. Species packing and the competition function with illustration from coral reef fish. *Theoret. Pop. Biol.* 5:163–186.

Roughgarden, J. 1977. Coevolution in ecological systems. Results from loop analysis for purely density-dependent coevolution. *In* Christiansen, F. B., and T. Fenchel (eds.). *Measuring selection in natural populations.* Springer-Verlag, Berlin.

Roughgarden, J. 1979. *Theory of population genetics and evolutionary ecology: An introduction.* Macmillan, New York.

Roughgarden, J., and M. Feldman. 1975. Species packing and predation pressure. *Ecology* 56:489–492.

Royama, T. 1984. Population dynamics of the spruce budworm *Choristneura fumiferana. Ecol. Monogr.* 54:429–462.

Sammarco, P. W. 1982. Effects of grazing by *Diadema antillarum* Philippi (Echinodermata: echinoidae) on algal diversity and community structure. *J. Exp. Mar. Biol. Ecol.* 65: 83–105.

Sansone, G., and R. Conti. 1964. *Non-linear differential equations.* Pergamon Press, London.

Saunders, P. T. 1978. Population dynamics and the length of food chains. *Nature* 272: 189.

Schaffer, W. M. 1974a. Selection for optimal life histories: The effects of age structure. *Ecology* 55:291–303.

Schaffer, W. M. 1974b. Optimal reproductive effort in fluctuating environments. *Am. Nat.* 108:783–790.

Schaffer, W. M. 1979. Equivalence of maximizing reproductive value and fitness in the case of reproductive strategies. *Proc. Nat. Acad. Sci. USA* 76:3567–3569.

Schaffer, W. M. 1981. Ecological abstraction: The consequences of reduced dimensionality in ecological models. *Ecol. Monogr.* 51:383–401.

Schaffer, W. M. 1984. Stretching and folding in lynx fur returns: Evidence for a strange attractor in nature? *Am. Nat.* 124:798–820.

Schaffer, W. M. 1985. Order and chaos in ecological systems. *Ecology* 66:93–106.

Schaffer, W. M. 1986. *In* Boyce, M. (ed.). *Evolution of life histories: Theory and patterns from mammals.* Yale University Press, New Haven.

Schaffer, W. M., and M. D. Gadgil. 1975. Selection for optimal life histories in plants. *in* Cody and Diamond (eds.). *Ecology and evolution of communities.* Harvard University Press, Cambridge, Mass.

Schaffer, W. M, and M. Kot. 1985a. Differential systems in ecology and epidemiology. *in* Holden, A. V. (ed.). *Chaos.* Manchester University Press, Manchester.

Schaffer, W. M., and M. Kot. 1985b. Nearly one dimensional dynamics in an epidemic. *J. Theoret. Biol.* 112:403–427.

Schaffer, W. M., and M. Kot. 1985c. Do strange attractors govern ecological systems? *BioScience* 35:342–350.

Schaffer, W. M., and M. L. Rosenzweig. 1977. Selection for optimal life histories. II. Multiple equilibria and the evolution of alternative reproductive strategies. *Ecology* 58:60–72.

Schaffer, W. M., and M. V. Schaffer. 1977. The adaptive significance of variations in reproductive habit in Agavaceae. *in* Stonehouse, B., and C. Perrins (eds.). *Evolutionary ecology.* University Park Press, Baltimore.

Schmidt, K. P., and L. R. Lawlor. 1983. Growth rate projection and life history sensitivity for annual plants with a seed bank. *Am. Nat.* 121:525–539.

Schoener, T. W. 1976. Alternatives to Lotka-Volterra competition: Models of intermediate complexity. *Theoret. Pop. Biol.* 10:309–333.

Schoener, T. W. 1978. Effects of density-restricted food encounter on some single-level competition models. *Theoret. Pop. Biol.* 13:365–381.

Schoener, T. W. 1983. Field experiments on interspecific competition. *Am. Nat.* 122: 240–285.

Schoener, T. W. 1986. Patterns in terrestrial vertebrate versus arthropod communities: do systematic differences in regularity exist? *In* Diamond, J. M., and T. J. Case (eds.). *Community ecology.* Harper & Row, New York.

Schoener, A., and T. W. Schoener. 1981. The dynamics of the species-area relation in marine fouling systems. 1. Biological correlates of changes in the species-area slope. *Am. Nat.* 118:339–360.

Scott, D. P. 1962. Effects of food quantity on fecundity of rainbow trout, *Salmo gairdneri. J. Fish. Res. Bd. Can.* 19:715–731.

Scudo, F. M. 1971. Vito Volterra and theoretical ecology. *Theoret. Pop. Biol.* 2:1–23.

Shaw, R. 1985. *The dripping faucet as a model chaotic system.* Aerial Press, Inc., Santa Cruz, Calif.

Shugart, H. H., Jr., T. R. Crow, and J. M. Hett. 1973. Forest succession models: A rationale and methodology for modelling forest succession over large regions. *Forest Sci.* 19:203–212.

Sih, A. 1984. Optimal behavior and density-dependent predation. *Am. Nat.* 123:314–326.

Silvert, W., and T. Platt. 1978. Energy flux in the pelagic ecosystem: A time-dependent equation. *Limnol. Oceanogr.* 23:813–816.

Silvert, W., and T. Platt. 1980. Dynamic energy-flow model of the particle size distribution in pelagic ecosystems. *In* Kerfoot, W. C. (ed.). *Evolution and ecology of zooplankton communities.,* University Press of New England, Hanover, N.H.

Skutch, A. F. 1949. Do tropical birds rear as many young as they can nourish? *Ibis* 91: 430–455.

Skutch, A. F. 1967. Adaptive limitation of the reproductive rate of birds. *Ibis* 109:579–599.

Slatkin, M. 1974. Competition and regional coexistence. *Ecology* 55:128–134.

Slobodkin, L. B. 1960. Ecological energy relationships at the population level. *Am. Nat.* 95:213–236.

Sklobodkin, L. B. 1964. Experimental populations of Hydrida. *J. Anim. Ecol.* (suppl.) 33:131–148.

Smale, S. 1976. On the differential equations of species in competition. *J. Math. Biol.* 3: 5–7.

Snell, T. W., and C. E. King. 1977. Lifespan and fecundity patterns in rotifers: The cost of reproduction. *Evolution* 31:882–890.

Snow, B. K. 1970. A field study of the Bearded Bellbird in Trinidad. *Ibis* 112:299–329.

Sokal, R. R., and F. J. Rohlf. 1981. *Biometry.* Second edition. Freeman, San Francisco.

Stearns, S. C. 1976. Life-history tactics: A review of the ideas. *Quart. Rev. Biol.* 51:3–47.

Stearns, S. C. 1977. The evolution of life history traits: A critique of the theory and a review of the data. *Ann. Rev. Ecol. Syst.* 8:145–171.

Stearns, S. C., and R. E. Crandall. 1981. Quantitative predictions of delayed maturity. *Evolution* 35:455–463.

Steele, J. H. 1985. A comparison of terrestrial and marine ecological systems. *Nature* 313:355–358.

Steele, J. H., and E. W. Henderson. 1984. Modeling long-term fluctuations in fish stocks. *Science* 224:985–987.

Stewart, F. M., and B. R. Levin. 1973. Partitioning of resources and the outcome of interspecific competition: A model and some general considerations. *Am. Nat.* 107: 171–198.

Strong, D. R., Jr. 1983. Density vague ecology and liberal population regulation in insects. *In* Price, P. W., C. N. Slobodchikoff, and W. S. Gaud (eds.). *A new ecology: Novel approaches to interactive systems.* Wiley, New York.

Strong, D. R., J. H. Lawton, and R. Southwood. 1984. *Insects on plants.* Harvard University Press, Cambridge, Mass.

Strong, D. R. 1985. Pink noise, density vagueness, and liberal regulation: Appreciating variance in demography of real populations. *In* Diamond, J. M., and T. J. Case (eds.). *Community ecology.* Harper & Row, New York.

Sugihara, G. 1982. *Niche hierarchy: Structure, organization and assembly in natural communities.* Ph.D. thesis, Princeton University.

Sugihara, G. 1984. Graph theory, homology and food webs. *Proc. Sym. Appl. Math.* 30: 83–101.

Summers-Smith, D. 1956. Mortality of the house sparrow. *Bird Study* 3:265–270.

Sutherland, J. P. 1974. Multiple stable points in natural communities. *Am. Nat.* 108: 859–873.

Sutherland, J. P., and R. H. Karlson. 1977. Development and stability of the fouling community at Beaufort, North Carolina. *Ecol. Monogr.* 47:425–446.

Takens, F. 1981. Detecting strange attractors in turbulence. *In* Rand, D. A., and L.-S.

Young (eds.). *Dynamical systems and turbulence, Warwick 1980.* Lecture notes in mathematics, Vol. 898, Springer-Verlag, Berlin.

Takeuchi, Y., and N. Adachi. 1983. Existence and bifurcation of stable equilibrium in two-prey, one-predator communities. *Bull. Math. Biol.* 45:877–900.

Taylor, D. L. 1973. Some ecological implications of forest fire control in Yellowstone National Park, Wyoming. *Ecology* 54:1394–1396.

Taylor, H. M., R. S. Gourley, C. E. Lawrence, and R. S. Kaplan. 1974. Natural selection of life history attributes: an analytical approach. *Theoret. Pop. Biol.* 5:104–122.

Thomas, W. R., M. J. Pomerantz, and M. E. Gilpin. 1980. Chaos, asymmetric growth, and group selection for dynamical stability. *Ecology* 61:1312–1320.

Tilman, D. 1982. *Resource competition and community structure.* Princeton University Press, Princeton, N.J.

Tinkle, D. W. 1967. The life history and demography of the side-blotched lizard, *Uta stansburiana. Misc. Publ. Mus. Zool. Univ. Mich.* 132:1–182.

Tinkle, D. W., and R. E. Ballinger. 1972. *Sceloporous undulatus:* A study of the intraspecific comparative demography of a lizard. *Ecology* 53:570–584.

Toft, C. A. 1986. Communities of species with parasitic life-styles. *In* Diamond, J. M., and T. J. Case (eds.). *Community ecology.* Harper & Row, New York.

Tomkins, D. J., and W. F. Grant. 1977. Effects of herbicides on species diversity of two plant communities. *Ecology* 58:398–406.

Townsend, C. R., and P. Calow. 1981. *Physiological ecology: An evolutionary approach to resource use.* Sinauer Associates, Sunderland, Mass.

Tuljapurkar, S. D. 1982a. Population dynamics in variable environments. II. Correlated environments, sensitivity analysis, and dynamics. *Theoret. Pop. Biol.* 21:114–140.

Tuljapurkar, S. D. 1982b. Population dynamics in variable environments. III. Evolutionary dynamics of r-selection. *Theoret. Pop. Biol.* 21:141–165.

Tuljapurkar, S. D., and S. H. Orzack. 1980. Population dynamics in varying environments. I. Long-run growth rates and extinction. *Theoret. Pop. Biol.* 18:314–342.

Turelli, M. 1978a. A reexamination of stability in randomly varying versus deterministic environments with comments on the stochastic theory of limiting similarity. *Theoret. Pop. Biol.* 13:244–267.

Turelli, M. 1978b. Does environmental variability limit niche overlap? *Proc. Nat. Acad. Sci. USA* 75:5085–5089.

Turner, F. B., G. A. Hoddenbach, P. A. Medica, and J. R. Lannom. 1970. The demography of the lizard *Uta stansburiana* (Baird and Girard), in southern Nevada. *J. Anim. Ecol.* 39:505–519.

Vance, R. R. 1978. Predation and resource partitioning in one predator–two prey model communities. *Am. Nat.* 112:797–813.

Vance, R. R. 1984. Interference competition and the coexistence of two competitors on a single limiting resource. *Ecology* 65:1349–1357.

Vinegar, M. B. 1975. Demography of the striped plateau lizard, *Sceloporous virgatus. Ecology* 56:172–182.

Waser, N. M., and M. V. Price. 1981. Effects of grazing on diversity of annual plants in the Sonoran Desert. *Oecologia* 50:407–411.

Watt, K. E. F. 1968. *Ecology and resource management.* McGraw-Hill, New York.

Welty, J. C. 1962. *The life of birds.* Saunders, Philadelphia.

Western, D., and J. Ssemakula. 1982. Life history patterns in birds and mammals and their evolutionary interpretation. *Oecologia* 54:281–290.

Wiley, R. H. 1974. Effects of delayed reproduction on survival, fecundity, and the rate of population increase. *Am. Nat.* 108:705–709.

Williams, G. C. 1966a. Adaptation and natural selection. Princeton University Press, Princeton, N.J.

Williams, G. C. 1966b. Natural selection, the costs of reproduction, and a refinement of Lack's principle. *Am. Nat.* 100:687–690.

Wilson, E. O., and W. H. Bossert. 1971. *A primer of population biology.* Sinauer, Sunderland, Mass.

Wynne-Edwards, V. C. 1962. Animal dispersion in relation to social behaviour. Oliver and Boyd, Edinburgh.

Yodzis, P. 1976. The effects of harvesting on competitive systems. *Bull. Math. Biol.* 38:97–109.

Yodzis, P. 1977a. Limit cycles in space-limited communities. *Math. Biosci.* 37:19–22.

Yodzis, P. 1977b. Harvesting and limiting similarity. *Am. Nat.* 111:833–843.

Yodzis, P. 1978. *Competition for space and the structure of ecological communities.* Springer-Verlag, Berlin.

Yodzis, P. 1980. The connectance of real ecosystems. *Nature* 284:544–545.

Yodzis, P. 1981a. The stability of real ecosystems. *Nature* 289:674–676.

Yodzis, P. 1981b. The structure of assembled communities. *J. Theoret. Biol.* 92:103–117.

Yodzis, P. 1982. The compartmentation of real and assembled ecosystems. *Am. Nat.* 120:551–570.

Yodzis, P. 1984a. How rare is omnivory. *Ecology* 65:321–323.

Yodzis, P. 1984b. The structure of assembled communities. II. *J. Theoret. Biol.* 107:115–126.

Yodzis, P. 1984c. Energy flow and the vertical structure of real ecosystems. *Oecologia* 65:86–88.

Yodzis, P. 1986. Competition, mortality, and community structure. *In* Diamond, J. M., and T. J. Case (eds.). *Community ecology.* Harper & Row, New York.

Yodzis, P. 1988a. The indeterminacy of ecological interactions. *Ecology* 69:508–515.

Yodzis, P. 1988b. The dynamics of highly aggregated models of whole communities. *In* Hastings, A. (ed.). *Scale in theoretical community ecology.* Springer-Verlag, Berlin.

Yoshiyama, R., and J. Roughgarden. 1977. Species packing on two dimensions. *Am. Nat.* 111:107–121.

Yule, G. U. 1924. A mathematical theory of evolution based upon the conclusions of Dr. J. C. Willis, F. R. S. *Phil. Trans. Roy. Soc. Lond.,* Ser. B, 213:21–87.

Zicarelli, J. 1975. Mathematical analysis of a population model with several predators on a single prey. Ph.D. thesis, University of Minnesota.

Zweifel, R. G., and C. H. Lowe. 1966. The ecology of a population of *Xantusia vigilis,* the desert night lizard. *Amer. mus. novitates* 2247:1–57.

Index

ISBN 0-06-047369-X